The Lands of Hawaii

The Lands of Hawaii

THEIR USE AND MISUSE

Thomas H. Creighton

THE UNIVERSITY PRESS OF HAWAII ⨝
Honolulu

333.7
C91L

Am

Library of Congress Cataloging in Publication Data

Creighton, Thomas Hawk.
 The lands of Hawaii.

 Bibliography: p.
 Includes index.
 1. Land use—Hawaii—History. I. Title.
HD211.H3C73   333.7'09969   77–16124
ISBN 0–8248–0482–1

For GWEN

Contents

Preface

Mahalo

A grant-in-aid from the State Foundation on Culture and the Arts made possible the research and much of the writing for this book, particularly regarding urban design and environmental planning in Hawaii. The writer is most grateful for this assistance. Any study of Hawaii's recent past depends largely on material which is available in the several excellent libraries and depositories in Honolulu and the informed assistance of their librarians and staffs. This writer is especially thankful for information gained in the Archives of Hawaii, the Hawaiian Mission Children's Society and the Hawaiian Historical Society libraries (now housed in the same mission building), and the Hawaiian and Pacific Collections in Sinclair Library of the University of Hawaii.

Great thanks are due historian-writer Gavan Daws for reading the manuscript and suggesting many improvements. Alfred Preis, director of the State Foundation on Culture and the Arts, was most helpful with advice, particularly on urban design and land planning. Notwithstanding this counsel, interpretation of events and opinions on their significance are, of course, the writer's own responsibility, as are any faults in fact, disregard of salient data, and slips in style.

Hawaiian Words

Hawaii's native Polynesian language is all but lost to common usage. Some older, proud Hawaiians, fewer in number each year, know their forebears' mellifluent tongue, but for most of the population of the islands individual words are all that remain of the Hawaiian language. Many of these words have become substitutes which the English-speaking newcomers have adopted to use along with the *haole kama'āina*s and the locals. No one who has lived for any time in Hawaii speaks of having difficulty; the trouble is *pilikia*.[1] One no longer refers to a hole in something; the cavity is a *puka*. Assistance is *kokua;* gratitude for it is expressed as *mahalo*. Few of these words have the precise meanings that their translations into English imply; when the missionaries tried to express the poetic, allusive Hawaiian language in more familiar terms and reduce it to a written medium they faced a difficult task. The Hawaiiana scholar Martha Beckwith recognized "the fondness for indirect speech in the everyday language of the people" and found half a dozen possible translations of the preface to a chant.

Yet to understand the early Hawaiians' concern for and use of their land, one must try to learn the meanings, or the implications, of the terms they used. Some words are direct and descriptive: the *ahupua'a,* a major land division that usually extended from the uplands to the ocean, was so named, apparently, because its boundaries were marked by a heap *(ahu)* of stones and tax for its use was paid by a pig *(puaa)* laid upon an altar. Others, more figurative, have inferential shifts in meaning. *Kuleana,* word for the small piece of land on which the Hawaiian commoner lived and farmed, also meant any right or title, jurisdiction or authority, function or responsibility. "That's not my kuleana," have disclaimed many developers when they were asked to preserve

the environment. Following is a brief glossary of words used
in this book whose primary, generally understood meanings
must be known to appreciate certain passages in the history
of land in Hawaii. To indicate their pronunciation the
accepted phonetic clues are given: hyphens (-) separating
word/syllables; macrons (ā) showing where stress occurs
and vowels are long; and glottal stops ('), almost consonants
in themselves, with a sound like that between the *oh*'s in
oh-oh. (Remember too that most vowels are pronounced
individually—in their unstressed state with *a* as in *above, e* as
in *bet, i* as in *city, o* as in *sole*, and *u* like *oo* in *moon*.)

'a'ā	brittle, rough lava
ahupua'a	basic land division
ali'i	chief
aloha	love, kindness, greeting, farewell
haole	white person
hapa	half, part, as in *hapa-haole*
heiau	temple
hui	association, partnership
hula	a dance
'ili	land division within *ahupua'a*
kahuna	priest, sorcerer, expert
kama'āina	native-born
kanaka	human being, subject
kāne	man, husband
kapu	taboo, prohibition
konohiki	headman, landlord, agent
kuhina	premier, regent
kuleana	small land division commonly for individual livelihood
lau hala	pandanus leaf
māhele	division, share
maka'āinana	commoner
makai	toward the ocean
malihini	stranger, newcomer
mauka	inland, toward the mountain
mele	song, chant
moku	major land district

mo'o	land division within *ahupua'a*
mu'umu'u	long, loose gown
nui	great, important
pāhoehoe	smooth, hard lava
pili	a grass used for thatching
pilikia	trouble
'ulu maika	game with small stone
wahine	woman, wife

Place Names

Hawaiian place names are meaningful, and very often an understanding of the meaning adds tremendously to appreciation of the place.[2] Knowing the proper phonation of a place name is essential to understanding its meaning, but even kamaainas in Hawaii today, even those with native backgrounds, are inclined to be careless about the way they pronounce them and heedless of their meanings. The most blatant instance must be the distortion of *Kamehameha* when the word is used to identify a territory. Hawaii's first islands-wide ruler was called Ka-mehameha, The Lonely One, with the article *ka* ("the") followed by the adjective *mehameha,* meaning lonely or solitary. The Kamehameha Highway, however, is generally known as Kam Highway—with the *a* flat as in *fat.*

This writer had hoped at one time to write all Hawaiian words used in this book, including place names, with their phonetic signals. That is really the only way to distinguish, for instance, between the first letters in the written word Ka-imu-ki (a neighborhood mauka of Diamond Head), which means the (that *ka* sound again) underground cooking oven, or *imu,* and Kai-mu (a village on the island of Hawaii), where *kai* means sea and *mu* is a gathering together, so that Kai-mu was a place where people gathered to watch surfing. The result of such conscientiousness, however, would have been a clumsy-looking page to the reader of English, interfering with the intended course of the writing. Following is a listing of names of some of the places mentioned most often in the book, simply to indicate the richness of this resource. Again phonetic clues to their spelling and pronunciation are given, as well as indications of their literal meanings.

Hanalei	village on Kaua'i (crescent bay)
Honolulu	city on O'ahu, capital of state (protected bay)
Ho'okena	village on Hawai'i (to satisfy thirst)
Ka-'ena	point of land on O'ahu (the heat)
Ka-hului	town on Maui (the winning)
Kai-lua	town on O'ahu, also Hawai'i, also Maui (two sea currents)
Kāne-'ohe	town on O'ahu (bamboo-sharp—cruel—husband)
Ke-ala-ke-kua	village, and bay on Hawai'i (pathway of the god)
Kona	leeward districts on most islands (leeward)
Lahaina	town on Maui (cruel sun)
Līhu'e	city on Kaua'i (cold chill)
Mākaha	village, valley, bay on O'ahu (fierce)
Po'ipu	town, beach, on Kaua'i (crashing, as waves)
Wahi-a-wā	town on O'ahu (place of noise)
Wai-kīkī	beach, tourist area, on O'ahu (spouting water)
Wai-luku	city, on Maui (destructive water)

Prologue: Hawaii's Green Heritage

ON the leeward coast of the island of Oahu there lies a
stretch of land at the entrance to a beautiful valley that the
Hawaiians called Makaha. The ocean shore at Makaha arcs
to form a fine sandy beach, and a close-in reef breaks the
waves high, ideal for surfing. *Mauka,* inland from the
sea, the land rises slowly at first to enter a wide, lush valley
between rugged ridges, steepening as it leads upward toward
the peak of the Waianae mountain range.

Several hundred years ago there was a quiet Hawaiian
village in Makaha Valley, and a rough boulder trail came
down toward it from the highlands above, dotted with houses
along the way. One branch of the path led to a *heiau,* a temple, in the foothills; another went past the cluster of homes
in the valley mouth and the lands on which the people grew
taro and yam, later joining the coastal trail that circled the
island. There, on the shore, a fleet of outrigger fishing
canoes berthed on the sandy circle. The traveler could go on:
east toward Puuloa (long hill), where the body of water that
would later be Pearl Harbor fingered in from the coast, or
west toward the end point called Kaena, after a brother of
fire-goddess Pele, and then around to Oahu's north shore.

A native historian who was twenty years old when the first
missionaries arrived in Hawaii described the beauties and the

hazards of the area.[1] When he was young, the upper valley
was always cool; along the coast the mornings were comfortable but the afternoons became warm enough to tempt a
walker to stop, to rest, or to try for the bright-colored fish
that could be caught on the reef. But in a cave near Makaha
(which means fierce or ferocious) there lurked a band of rob-
bers who profited from lone travelers, although they wisely
let larger companies pass untroubled.

On a lazy Sunday in the early 1970s a haole (Caucasian)
resident of Hawaii and his wife relaxed beside the swimming
pool in a complex of comfortable cottagelike buildings that
formed a hotel in the center of Makaha Valley. They were
there for a needed local vacation away from the urban
excitements of Honolulu. They had driven out past Pearl
Harbor on an absurdly six-laned mainland-type freeway that
covered the old trail and, for the time being, led nowhere but
to a narrow road on the Waianae coast and the quiet towns,
including Makaha, that lay along it.

At one side of the hotel pool was a separate building
intended as a conference hall but until now unused on the
Sunday afternoon. Then there came an incongruous intrusion
on the vacation atmosphere: across the pool terrace and up
the broad steps leading to the meeting room walked a
number of portly, dignified Hawaiian women, dressed in the
tasteful long muumuus that missionaries had taught their
great-grandmothers to wear, their hair coiled neatly beneath
handwoven straw hats banded with woven flower leis. Others
followed, and a magnificent procession of dark-skinned,
pleasant-faced, strong-featured women, large, proud,
straight, walked slowly to the building where they were
obviously gathering in some numbers. When the haoles asked
a pool attendant, a local part-Hawaiian, what the group
was, they were told with pride that it was a branch of the
Hawaiian Civic Club, an organization defensively formed by
Hawaiian Prince Kuhio in the early years of this century
after the Hawaiian monarchy had been overthrown.

It was a remarkable sight, these stately people holding to

their history, coming to meet in foreign quarters on the land
where their ancestors' village had stood. One could not help
being moved, but with what emotions? Admiration that they
maintained their pride and what was left of their traditions?
Sadness that they had lost their own powers and their true
culture, so that they were willing to meet among Makaha's
tourist guests in quarters where a mainland salesmen's conference would convene tomorrow? Anger at the forces that
were moving Makaha's people and their beach and their
valley ever further from their natural ways, their natural
setting, their natural beauty?

The story of Makaha's lands and others like them is the
subject of this book. The changes in their quality and their
use began immediately when new groups of people came to
Hawaii after explorers found the islands in the late eighteenth century. As time went on, scattered towns replaced the
Hawaiian villages along the Waianae coast, as they did in
other parts of the islands—built by imported techniques for
strange uses by new inhabitants. Makaha, for one, became a
community of new inhabitants with mixed origins—Japan,
China, Samoa, the Philippine Islands, Portugal, Puerto
Rico—together with a goodly proportion of descendants of
the original Hawaiians who remained. Since that stretch of
coast is quite far removed from the plantations that had
brought most of the immigrants to Hawaii, those who lived
there raised hogs and some chickens, grew vegetables, and
found other ways to make the land support them, as the early Hawaiians had.[2] But Makaha and its sister towns along
the coast never became affluent; Farrington "Highway" is
still a narrow road skirting the shore, and the homes along it
shelter people who value their rural, tropical environment
but, by mainland haole standards, are poor and under-
privileged.

Many others who came to Hawaii did prosper, however,
and no method of gaining wealth—and power along with
it—surpassed that of finding profitable uses for the land.
Makaha Valley was too tempting a stretch of real estate to be

ignored; one of Hawaii's most ambitious local entrepreneurs, Chinn Ho (born in Waikiki in 1902), acquired most of the buildable land between the ridges and, in the late 1960s, began developing it. A cluster of high-rise apartment houses rose to flank the west valley wall, a low quite pleasant hotel surrounded by golf courses appeared in the center of the slope, and a master plan was prepared that would gradually add dwelling and resort places of various kinds and shapes across the valley floor. The heiau in the lower hills was kept in the plan, of course, as a sightseeing attraction.

Chinn Ho's architect made sure that in the beginning his incursion into the valley was not too destructive.[3] The shore-line was less fortunate. An obtrusive wall of condominium apartments was permitted along the coast by Honolulu's city council and its mayor, who made an unequal swap: for the city, some waterfront land for a small park; for the developer, a change in zoning to permit a large stretch to be developed.

What the next chapter in the history of Makaha may be is anyone's guess. Chinn Ho has sold most of the already-built-upon valley property to interests in Japan. The freeway that goes nowhere, built with federal "interstate" highway funds, is obviously intended to serve a highly developed Waianae coast and bring many more tourists and golf players to Makaha—although that will require additional land-use zoning changes.

To the haole couple who had watched the Civic Club ladies with mixed emotions, a part-Hawaiian waiter recruited local-ly said: "We like the hotel—it brings work to us out here—but we don't like what happens to our land." The Hawaiians have had "their" land taken away from them in gradual stages—not slowly, because the process has been rapid, but in increments almost imperceptible at each step. Now they live along the Waianae coast and watch its changing uses and adapt to them, as Hawaiians do throughout the islands. Some of them have benefited from homestead laws to feel again, to some extent, that they are at home on their own land, and increasingly aggressive groups of them are moving to get more of that land back in Hawaiian hands. In the meantime they and their mixed-heritage neighbors and relatives work in the hotel as porters and maids. Those with the most pride in their Hawaiian background form into societies and clubs to plan ways to preserve what remains of their culture and their political entity—and go back up to Chinn Ho's development to hold their meetings among the tourists.

Such contrasts are common in Hawaii. The change has been violently rapid from sensitive, respectful living on the land to exploitative development of the land, from a love of the land itself to a love of what monetary gain the land might bring. If that speedy shift in values does not seem unique—there are, after all, other places in other parts of the world that have also suffered the trauma of sudden entry into modern society (certainly in Australia and New Zealand the contrasts are still sharp, and in Africa and many parts of Asia the transformation is still in process)—then it must be considered that Hawaii, having made a violent leap from the past, is about to vault into a future where expansion on its land will be so intense as to make mainland America seem underdeveloped. Hawaii, a kingdom ruled by brown-skinned monarchs eighty years ago, now an odd mix of verdant mountains and valleys, fertile plains and sandy beaches along with sprawling tracts and haphazard high rises, faces the likelihood of overextended and overloaded urbanism and depletion of its natural resources—including its lands—before most of the rest of the world meets such blunt threats so directly. From primitivism to futurism—from stone age to postindustrial age—in two hundred years.

In historical perspective it may still seem that the only difference between Hawaii's present plight and that of other rapidly developing areas is that the changes have happened and are still happening so fast. But there is another aspect of Hawaii's position, uniquely touching and especially tragic, that moves those who are concerned about people, respect land, and are sensitive to people-land relationships. A par-

ticular poignancy results from the intense love the early
Hawaiian people had for the land of their islands, the land
that now grew their food, now threatened to spew lava across
their villages, was always the obvious generator, the recognized source of life. In losing their land they lost the very
foundation of their being. The transformation, then, has not
only been hasty. It has also been harrowing.

While the people of Hawaii were fierce in many ways, in
the time before Captain James Cook chanced on the islands
in 1778 and used them as resting place on his way to further
exploration, they were gentle and sensitive in other ways.
Their wars were vicious, their games were violent, and, as
Cook discovered when he overstayed his welcome, their reactions could be direct and elemental. But their greeting was
generous, their devotion deep, and their affection genuine
(that is what *aloha* meant before it became a tourist greeting). And in no way was that compassion more clear than in
their love of the land.

The Polynesian Hawaiians, like all primitive people, were
innate ecologists. They took full advantage of the natural
systems that formed the life of the islands: for food (picking
the growing things, pounding the root of the taro to produce
the nutritious staple they called *poi*), for shelter (weaving and
thatching plant strands around wooden poles became a
skilled building art), and even for recreation (riding above a
wave on a shaped board and sliding down a steep hill on
carefully chosen ti leaves were games as close to nature as a
sportsman could get). And along with enjoyment and respect,
a deep devotion to nature had developed.

Their dances were eloquent, their songs and chants lyric,
their unwritten tales and legends creative, their theology
imaginative. And in all these expressions there was ever
evident a sensitive feeling for the qualities of the physical
environment—the sea that surrounded them, the sky suspended above them, and, primarily, the land on which they lived.

They had a perceptive appreciation of the individual
characters of the separate islands—a difference that is still

apparent even though the developments on them now may be distressingly similar. The difference in ages is apparent on the islands' surfaces: Kauai and Niihau the oldest; Hawaii, still being formed by the lava of active volcanoes, the youngest.[4] The windward coasts are wet, lined with steep sea cliffs cut by the northeast trade winds. The leeward sides of the islands show coastal plains, watered by runoffs from the volcanic mountains. The soils vary: where liquid *pahoehoe* lava ran down, where the flow broke into cindery *'a'a*, where earth slowly covered the porous slopes. The Hawaiians respected these differences, enjoyed each for its particular quality, sang to their beauties, and knew how to make use of their virtues.

"Beautiful is Kauai beyond compare . . . for none other do I yearn; she is all that is good," began a *mele kua*, a song of praise. And on the land of each island special places were eulogized for their particular natural qualities. "Hanalei . . . like a green fern, spangled with dew . . . the land where the clouds hover" is indeed a beautiful coast on Kauai's north shore, even today.[5] So tempting has it been to so many later admirers that successive groups of newcomers used it early as a settlement, then for a sugarcane plantation, later as site for a luxurious hotel built around the plantation manager's mansion. Now a tour club for affluent travelers enjoys the shore as a Japanese investment; and nearby is under way a massive second-home-vacation-retreat condominium project financed with mainland American capital. The people of Polynesian Hawaiian ancestry who have stayed in Hanalei have watched the spangling of their beloved land with much more than dew.

Changes of that magnitude in a comparatively short time have inevitably taken their toll both from the land itself and from the people who so lately occupied it. The world has recently become concerned with the future. Some scholars predict what may come, others plan what would be best, and most agree that inevitable change will bring serious social and psychological trauma. In that regard the Hawaiian peo-

ple of Polynesian ancestry can be looked on as the prototypical sufferers from future shock.

In actual numbers, Cook found a population of about
250,000 people in Hawaii in 1778. Forty years later there
were less than 150,000 people on the islands; in another forty
years, by 1860, the number of native Hawaiians had dropped
to 70,000. Early in the twentieth century, about 1920, there
were only 24,000 pure-blooded Hawaiians in Hawaii, although marriages with other groups were bringing up the size
of the part-Hawaiian population. Today the number of those
with some Hawaiian blood has again approached 150,000
(which is now only 17 percent of the population of the state),
while pure-blooded Hawaiians compose only 1 percent of the
residents of "their" islands.[6]

The disintegration of the Hawaiian people lay in more
than numbers, however. In the first eighty years after "discovery," the death by waves of thousands came not only
from obvious physical causes, such as imported illnesses for
which they had neither immunity nor cure and overindul-
gence in tempting foods and liquors to which they were not
accustomed. There was an unwillingness to face the modern
world that had been thrust upon them, a reluctance to make
the sudden leap from primitive simplicity to strange moral
and material complexity. Their early confusion soon became
a hopelessness that was close to loss of the will to live. And
adding to their social demoralization, it was noted, was a
deep sadness from seeing the land they loved transformed in
nature and quality by the novel new ways it was being used:
from buildings being put upon it and unfamiliar animals
brought to graze it to trees and vegetation stripped from it.

They had to learn that, according to the new values the
visitors were introducing, their pleasures in pursuit of an un-
fettered life were shiftless, unambitious laziness; their happy
freedom in social, marital, sexual relations was shocking im-
morality; their preservation of land's natural qualities for the
common good was inefficient use of a valuable commodity.

Changes in land values and land uses illustrate both the

rapidity and the scope of the social shifts that the Hawaiian people suffered. At the time of Cook's visits the Hawaiian islands were not the lush landscapes that later imported plantings made them. In many more areas than now, recent lava flows lay bare, not yet covered with even the beginnings of new vegetation; forests, more dense than those of today, opened to dry, barren stretches and to other large areas used for growing foodstuffs.[7] The early explorers noted that all the arable land appeared planted; it seemed hardly possible for the country to be cultivated to greater advantage for the purpose of the inhabitants. They tilled, plowed, and even irrigated carefully their principal crops: taro, sweet potato, yam. Many of the first visitors commented on the neat villages and well-constructed homes.[8]

Villages were formed from kinship or fellowship and for closeness to fishing and farming places, not from the necessities of commerce or government, yet they grew to considerable size. Cook's men found several hundred houses clustered together at their first landing place on the shores of Kauai—and even more on the two flat areas either side of the cliffs rising from Kealakekua Bay on the island of Hawaii when they anchored there the following year.[9]

Some of these gatherings of homes grew up around the chiefs' houses and those of their relatives and retainers—not only could these personages command work allegiance from the common people but, most important, they controlled the land and its uses. Land and politics were interwoven then as they always have been everywhere, to a large extent, and probably will continue to be no matter how much the nature of political controls may change.

In Polynesian Hawaii all land belonged to the principal chief *(ali'i nui)* of an island, and he distributed it to those other chiefs who supported him—in a political sense to secure their continued allegiance, in a practical sense to be sure the land was used well. These alii in turn divided their holdings into slices, called *ahupua'a,* devised in the most intelligent way possible. These holdings ran usually from the mountain to the sea, and thus each contained grazing land above, agricultural land below, and land bordering the sea at the foot, with plenty of building sites of various kinds at any level. An ahupuaa might be in the charge of a *konohiki,* landlord or manager for the chief. There might be smaller divisions: *'ili,* sometimes separately "owned"; *mo'o, pauka,* and *koele,* parcels for cultivation (farmlands in a sense); and the sites occupied by the tenant farmers, or commoners, called *kuleanas.*[10]

The low man in this hierarchy of land tenure and land use was the commoner. Apparently in most cases he could move if he wanted to for any reason—whim, weather, malcontent, or mistreatment (much of the land was held by absentee alii, and their konohiki could be cruel caretakers)—and in this respect the old Hawaiian land ownership pattern differed from European feudalism, to which it is often compared. (In various ways the Hawaiian land system was different, also, from that of other Polynesian island groups.)[11] Nevertheless, there seems to have been a sense of responsibility as well as fondness in the common man's regard for his own patch of land, his kuleana.

The key to land tenure was central ownership by the alii nui: allocations were revocable, and land returned for redistribution when an alii died or was replaced. This acceptance of central ownership of land, as a principle, and the understanding that nature should be altered only as sustenance required it, as a corollary, have seemed naive and wasteful to immigrants to the islands from Cook's visits through last week's sale of development rights to prime agricultural land. And to a major extent they have been replaced with different values.

Consider the rapidity of that change. A period of some eighty years (from Cook's arrival in 1778 to the death of Kamehameha III in 1854) saw a radical shift in values from a Polynesian stone-age sense of what was worthy to an industrial-age commercial ranking of what was desirable and Puritan missionary standards of what was good and bad. By

1860 the change had been quite fully effected: in the precepts that had been taught to the Hawaiian people and in the laws they had been persuaded to adopt.

By then the Hawaiian principles of commonality, sharing, and aloha had been replaced by canons of privacy, personal ownership, and aggrandizement. The land that had been held in fief and used for common sustenance and respected for its natural qualities was largely held in fee-simple allodial ownership (much of it by non-Hawaiians)—free to be bought, sold, and used for private purposes, held in respect mostly for its monetary value.

Then consider another eighty-year change, this one at our end of the time spectrum. As the first eighty years of Hawaii's modern life marked abrupt change in the social value structure, the last eighty years have seen an equally sharp change in governmental structure. Between 1900 and now the people of Hawaii have had to adjust to the transformation from life under a Polynesian monarchy to membership in a modern democratic government. Granted that the monarchy was unique—colorful, fanciful, headed by a king (or a queen it was, at the end) who wore when it seemed appropriate a cloak and a helmet woven of small bright bird feathers—and that it was shaky and unsure, bolstered by all sorts of imported constitutional provisions, dependent on a legislature whose upper house was composed of the noble alii, chiefs still jealous of their hereditary rights. Nonetheless it was a monarchy. In fact, one has to grant equally that the present governmental structure is also a peculiar one, based as it is on the identification of eight islands and numerous islets in the center of the Pacific Ocean as a constituent state owing allegiance to a continental nation three thousand miles away with which it quite obviously has neither physical nor historical ties. But odd as the situations at the beginning and end of that eighty-year span seem, the more remarkable thing is that *that* great change also took place so quickly.

Rapidity of change, then, is not the only notable aspect of the metamorphosis of a Polynesian culture into a modern urban community; the degree of change is also a key part of the story. Singling out one other place on Oahu for a quick comparison of old and new uses may reinforce the Makaha story. In the Ewa district, also west of Honolulu but not so far out as the Waianae coast, there is a land area that the Hawaiians named Halawa (curve, bend), where the trail coming down from the hills at that point turned toward the coast.[12] It was considered good land, and Kamehameha the Great gave portions of it to two of his earliest and most valued haole advisers early in the white man's visitations. Later a town grew there, again by no means an affluent one, but a place where a number of people with Hawaiian ancestry lived. Still later, in the 1960s, when the need for a major league, mainland-type athletic stadium for complicated reasons became a pressing political issue, Halawa was chosen as the proper place for it. The federally sponsored freeway complex spawned one of its typical spaghettilike tangles of interchanges and on-and-off ramps at that point, spewing automobiles toward Pearl Harbor. By modern transportation criteria, that made the location accessible from many directions.

There was one difficulty, however, which the stadium planners ignored: the community of local people at Halawa would be displaced by the stadium. It was not a new problem by mainland standards, certainly; the need to relocate the poor, because highway and public works construction normally points toward them, has become an accepted part of American redevelopment activity. But in Hawaii the results were unique. The Halawa residents resisted moving. When the rector of history-laden Kawaiahao Church, a contemporary Christian counterpart of the *kahuna,* or priest, was called on to bless the land before construction began, as he typically is for any major event in Honolulu, a local part-Hawaiian woman rose in anger and denounced the ceremony —put a curse on the land, as some termed it. Abashed, the Reverend Abraham Akaka contented himself and the officials present by spilling sacred water on the site from the calabash he uses for such occasions, but he refrained from the blessing that had been requested.[13]

When the stadium construction was quite far along, two workers fell from scaffolding and were killed. Under the circumstances these mishaps were not looked on as typical big-building casualties but as a direct result of the *kupua*'s (witch's) curse. The construction workers refused to go on with the job until the problem was met and the land made safe to work on. In time, the Reverend Akaka was prevailed on to complete the blessing ceremony, the angry *wahine,* by then rehoused, was persuaded to remain silent, and the stadium went on toward completion. Hawaiian traditions had fused with Christian customs to allow development to proceed. Hawaiian trails had been covered with concrete freeway tangles; Hawaiian lands had passed from monarch to friendly haoles to professional sports promoters; Hawaiian people had been pushed from there to elsewhere with no land of their own any longer. That, surely, is abstracted land use history.

PART 1

The Story of Hawaii's Lands

THE story of the Hawaiian islands is a story of land: land
rising from the sea, land supporting life, land discovered by
people from other places, land valued variously by those living on it, land changing its own qualities as it was treated in
different ways. The many parts of that story of land need to
be brought together and told here as a tale with a beginning,
a middle, and at least a speculative end. Otherwise it would
be presumptuous even to review Hawaii's history, because it
has been written so many times. There is no lack of well-told
narrative about the tremendously interesting people of the
islands and the fascinating events they took part in, from
remembered legends to recent scholarly research. Some are
about dark-skinned people, some about light; some telling of
warriors, some of businessmen; some concerned with religion, some with government, some with industry, some with
sports. What holds all these accounts together is land—the
lands of Hawaii. Those small volcanic islands in the middle
of the Pacific Ocean have supported many dissimilar peoples
and have been the scene of many divergent activities. The
story that the first part of this book wants to tell briefly is
what really happened to those lands during those times.

chapter 1

The Loss of the Past

THE Pacific island group called Hawaii has for some years now been an unlikely partner with the otherwise continental areas joined in the United States of America. There are many chapters in the sad story of the destruction of the Polynesian society that enjoyed those volcanic isles until they were found by English explorers, occupied by aliens from many lands, and finally absorbed by America. None, surely, is more distressing than the capsule chronicle it offers of how people can first love, then ignore, and finally ravage the land they live on.

History can be written largely as a record of the ways we have successively treated the land surface on which we are destined to spend our lives. People have found existence on this crust of the planet sustainable and even enjoyable, so long as they have respected it and the community of other living things it supports.[1] That, of course, is what ecology is all about.

On the other hand, people find life unpleasant, sometimes almost unbearable, when they ignore their relationship with the earth on which they and other organisms depend.[2] Then famines come, and pestilence, and floods and avalanches and

other instances of nature's angry response. It is this result
that the environmentalists try to warn about.

Now we are learning that life may actually become impossible if we carry contempt for the land further, cover over
its nourishing green, poison its soils, and use it as dump for
our wastes.[3] Pollution is the word we have given to that stage
—as though the threat to life on the earth's surface is just a
kind of dirtiness.

This tale of the worsening relationship between people and
land began as soon as homo rose erectus, grew sapiens, and
began to scratch the earth to cultivate plants for food and
fix poles for shelter. Its development can be traced in many
lands in all parts of the world, but there are few places other
than Hawaii where the whole history is shown so clearly in
so small a spot, ready to be read by anyone standing on it or
tramping across it. Land unspoiled since stone-age aborigines
used it lovingly and sang of its charm lies but a few miles
from land stripped of all its tropic quality, land built upon
so badly that its only future can be some manner of physical
renewal. And these two extremes are no distance at all from
land that has neither been preserved nor developed but simply shuffled and bartered as speculative merchandise until its
high cost has made it useless.

The histories and fictions of the lands of Hawaii commonly start with awed speculation on the volcanic actions at the
ocean floor that finally, perhaps fifteen million years later,
began pushing the tips of rocky masses above the surface of
the sea.[4] It is indeed a remarkable movement to ponder: that
roiling upward thrust through aeons of time, producing the
Hawaiian archipelago of volcanic islands, shoals, and subsided volcanoes, stretching 1,600 miles along the center of the
Pacific Ocean. It was this great upheaval that formed the
land found by Polynesian peoples from islands farther south
when they sailed forth in search of a new homeland.

That search, the Polynesian exploration across the Pacific,
is also a remarkable story, going back as it does at least a
thousand years before Christ to the time when migrants from

the east, whose origins historians and anthropologists still debate, moved out into the South Pacific island groupings. The daring and the skill of further travels, first short trips to visible landmarks, then voyages to distant, imagined destinations, are alluring legend well documented as fact.[5]

Those who settled Hawaii seem to have come first from the Marquesas, then from Tahiti and other Society Islands. By A.D. 1000 they had occupied all of Hawaii. Those Polynesian pioneers took with them some small animals—pigs, dogs, chickens—and some seeds and plants, probably including the fruits and vegetables that became staple foods in the islands: yams, sweet potatoes, taro, sugarcane, coconuts. These importations had radical impact on indigenous species and produced Hawaii's first great ecological alteration.

The history of the Polynesian Hawaiians is known only from anthropological and other deductive studies and from word-of-mouth accounts passed down through the generations. With "discovery" of the islands by Captain James Cook in 1778, recorded history begins, and that modern documented period from Cook's arrival until today divides itself conveniently into segments of approximately forty-year lengths. It was during the first two of these divisions that the mores and customs of the Hawaiian people suffered their sharpest change. Of that stretch of time, the first forty years, from about 1780 to about 1820, is marked by the ascendancy and rule of Hawaii's first islands-wide monarch, Kamehameha I, known as The Great, and is terminated by two almost simultaneous events: Kamehameha's death and the arrival of the first shipload of New England missionaries. The following forty years, from 1820 to just before 1860, comprise the reigns of the two next members of the Kamehameha dynasty, ending at the time of the death of Kamehameha III.[6]

Described in a different way, the first period was a time of *introduction* of the values of the foreigners who were arriving; it was the time when Polynesian Hawaii began to disintegrate in the face of strange new ways, even as the

consolidated monarchy was being founded. The second
period was the time of *establishment* of the new values; alien
control over the government increased, and foreign, primarily American, concepts of property, including land tenure
and land use privileges, were established by law.

The third period in Hawaii's modern history—approximately from 1860 to 1900—was the time of *consolidation* of
the imported value systems and the influences won by their
importers. Jockeying for control by outsiders weakened the
reigns of the last five monarchs (Kamehameha IV, Kamehameha V, Lunalilo, Kalakaua, and Liliuokalani) to a point of
final dissolution of the monarchy and then annexation by the
United States of America.

The course of the fourth period, from annexation until the
beginning of World War II, more or less from 1900 to 1940,
can be described as *exploitation* of the powers that had now
been well established by white foreigners. Those who had
legalized their own ways on the islands were now the absolute colonial rulers, masters of the way *their* land was used
(primarily for raising sugarcane and pineapple) and masters
of the way *their* workers (Hawaiians, part-Hawaiians, and
successive waves of immigrants recruited from other places)
should live on that land. The attack on Pearl Harbor ended
that sovereignty.

The most recent period in Hawaii's history, from the
beginning of World War II until the present, has been a time
of intense, rapid *Americanization* of the islands and their
inhabitants.[7] Not only the haole power elite but also the
descendants of the earlier Hawaiians and the many other
groups with varied ethnic backgrounds who comprised the
plantation laborers have learned American democratic
principles and American political methods—along with the
collateral American compulsion to grow, to expand, to
continue increasing everything from activity to possessions
to affluence. Particularly they have learned how to make
more profitable use of their lands, just as the American
mainland was doing.

Introduction, establishment, consolidation, exploitation of American societal and commercial tenets—and then outright imitation of the continental society and economy these values had produced. Five forty-year time intervals forming Hawaii's history since its modern discovery. Five stages of change, from disintegration of the old to absorption of the new. For the lands of the islands, five steps in the transition from respected resource to coveted commodity.

The First Step: Land Grants

That transition began, then, when the Polynesian Hawaiians were still singing of the land's variable gentleness and violence, and one of them grew ambitious, as he matured, to rule all of that land. Kamehameha ("the lonely one") was the strong figure who succeeded in bringing together in one monarchy the governments and the lands of the scattered islands that had been ruled, during his youth, by four separate kings and numerous chiefs under them.

There are a number of noteworthy things about Kamehameha's rise in power and his successful consolidation of command. The most significant is the fact that his rule coincided with the coming of the white man. His military and political successes began just at the time the haoles first found the islands; his reign stretched over the period when the early influx of newcomers, often transients, began arriving in numbers; and his death occurred the year before the first of the next wave of arrivals, the New England missionaries, came to impose their strong permanent influence.

The importance of this historical coincidence to the story of Hawaii's lands cannot be exaggerated: a radical local governmental change was taking place at the same time as the western powers discovered exploitable new territories in the mid Pacific. While the two events occurred simultaneously, neither bringing about the other, subsequent relationships came quickly: the new government needed help and advice, and the haoles could furnish ships and firearms to assist

Kamehameha in his moves toward consolidation, as well as counsel in the more sophisticated social and political situations that were developing; the king on his part, controlling all of the islands' lands, could provide a reasonably stable government, much easier to deal with than a divided, warring group of separated kingdoms and chiefdoms would have been, as commerce and industry expanded.

Kamehameha, great-nephew to a local king on the Big Island of Hawaii, was about twenty years old when Captain James Cook's ships the *Resolution* and the *Discovery* first appeared as strange, brief visitors off the Waimea coast of the island of Kauai. And when they returned a year later, to anchor at Kealakekua Bay on the leeward, Kona coast of the Big Island (less than a hundred miles from Kamehameha's birthplace), the young man was there.

Cook's expedition remained for several months that second time, and it became clear toward the end of the visit that they had overstayed their welcome. They set sail from Kealakekua Bay in February 1779 with much aloha, however, and it was a nasty trick of fate that a mast broke before they were far out, forcing their return. During that uncomfortable berth for repairs tempers frayed, and the disastrous upshot was the killing of Captain Cook.[8]

Very shortly after that tragedy Kamehameha made his first military moves, in his home territory, and in 1782 won an important victory just south of Kealakekua Bay to clinch it. He went on to increase his power in other parts of the Big Island, then moved to occupy Maui, Lanai, Molokai, and then, a few years later, Oahu. Only the island of Kauai, to the west of Oahu, remained under the rule of a local king for some time.[9]

Kamehameha's successes were followed by twenty-four years of quite stable rule. Yet it was during that rule that the Hawaiian society lost its strength under alien incursions. By the time the missionaries arrived to convert the heathen savages, as they were inevitably called by their new mentors, those native people were no longer the naive, unspoiled bar-

barians that Cook had found and Kamehameha had brought together into one kingdom. The strength of their old religion had been broken as the *kapus*—sacred privileges, rights, prohibitions, directions—had lost their meaning and force in new situations. They were no longer described by visiting writers as vigorous and strong; now they were called apathetic, lazy, and sick: they had acquired western diseases, from measles to syphilis. While they might still sing of the natural things around them, they were now selling off their precious sandalwood, as fast as it could be leveled, to gain a new kind of valuation called profit.

As newcomers arrived in Hawaii following Cook's visits, they were generally welcomed. Soon they were arriving in numbers. For some time the fur trade, based on America's northwest coast, brought visitors, and at first Hawaii was simply a stopping-off place on the way to China, the sales point. Two English ships and two French vessels came in 1786, and then many others followed. Involvement in Kamehameha's wars of consolidation was inevitable—the explorer George Vancouver helped the king build a ship, for instance, and others gave aid from time to time either to him or to his adversaries.[10] The nature of native wars was completely changed as the foreigners introduced cannon and other firearms on both sides.

Soon more permanent newcomers began to arrive and the desirability of Hawaii as a place to stay, not just a jumping-off place or a layover point for commercial activities further on, dawned on individual explorers and entrepreneurs and also, in time, on their home governments. The number of foreigners in permanent residence on the islands increased steadily. From a dozen or so aliens who were with Kamehameha during his battles, the number grew to perhaps several hundred at the turn of the century and continued to swell. Among other results, inevitably, was intermarriage. A new ethnic category appeared: the part-Hawaiian or, to put the mixture in reverse, the half-white or *hapa-haole*.[11]

Hawaii's land underwent its first change in character as the social adjustments took place. While ownership of all land remained in the king's name, some of the haoles who achieved respected advisory posts in the island government were "given" or "granted" tracts of land to use as they wished during their tenure. One early visitor noted that the king "rewards liberally with grants of land" those in his employ as artisans,[12] and for the more respected who had been drawn into advisory positions even larger properties were turned over. A rugged English seaman named John Young (who went ashore sightseeing and was persuaded by Kamehameha to remain) became a valued adviser to the king and was rewarded with many bounties, including a good deal of land. A sister ship of the one Young had deserted was attacked by a vindictive Hawaiian chief, and its boatswain, Isaac Davis, survived to become also a friend and adviser to Kamehameha. (These two were granted, among other holdings, tracts of land at Halawa on Oahu, where the stadium was built much later.)[13] A Spaniard, Francisco de Paula Marin, made himself useful to the king in numerous ways and was repaid with land in several locations, including a piece near the new town of Honolulu, just off the main traffic artery in what is now the heart of the city. John Parker, an American who aided the king with help and advice, was given a large area on the Big Island which formed the basis of what became the Parker Ranch, now one of the largest cattle ranches in the world.[14]

In addition to these sizable grants to newcomers who became prominent personages in the islands, there were many other lesser ones for sometimes minor services. As one instance, a ship's tailor named Robert Kilday was persuaded to leave his vessel, where he was seen by a curious Hawaiian making a jacket for the chief mate, to become personal tailor to Kamehameha's son Kauikeaouli. The king was pleased with Kilday's job of making "coats and pantaloons" for the prince and clothing for the native soldiers, so pleased that he rewarded him with land.[15]

These early acquisitions of land by aliens could not be considered grasping or selfish. For some decades the property thus gained was used for essential, functional purposes, primarily as homesites or small farms. The harm, if it was that in the early stages of transformation, lay in the disturbing nature of change itself. Marin's interests, for instance, were mainly in new kinds of agricultural production. Other newcomers were anxious to add to the islands' flora and fauna specimens that would improve the local diet or would in time have commercial potential. Captain Cook had introduced goats to Hawaii on his last trip, and Vancouver brought cattle and plants, which the haoles who had land were anxious to propagate. This was the second great ecological change in the islands, made without recognition that the importations would upset the natural balance and result, ultimately, in loss of thousands of the endemic species that had developed over many centuries to give Hawaii its unique character.[16]

If new things were put into the ground and strange creatures allowed to graze its surface, unfamiliar structures were also built upon it. Thatched and laced buildings supported by poles were too primitive to suit the new residents, and tools and materials for more familiar construction began to arrive, along with furniture and household utensils, as additional ships came. Around the various homes that the ruler had built for himself—in Waikiki, in the growing town of Honolulu, in Kailua on the Big Island, and elsewhere—the foreigners who were in some way useful to the court were allowed land on which to build along with the native alii.[17]

Not only were new buildings built. In keeping with their new uses—selling and storing of merchandise as well as "civilized" residential needs—their groupings also had to be changed. The scattered, casual Hawaiian villages gave way in key places on the larger islands (primarily where ships could berth) to tighter towns more conveniently arranged for the new activities. Waikiki, a pleasant place with a fine surfing beach, where Kamehameha at first followed the custom of Oahu's earlier alii nui and built a royal village, soon was

replaced as the center of activity by Honolulu, where a
usable protected harbor made possible access by ships from
abroad. An English ship captain named William Brown
discovered the harbor's possibilities in the 1790s,[18] and at
first just a few shacks and shanties were put up there, frontier waterfront fashion. Soon, however, some simple stores
were built back of the shore and before long a bustling harbor town appeared. In 1810 Kamehameha moved the court to
Honolulu and built a residence group for himself there. By
1812 there were perhaps a hundred houses in the town, with
Kamehameha's cluster of buildings dominant. Back of the
waterfront, where both native and foreign ships berthed,
were homes for the chiefs and for several of the king's haole
advisers. Davis and Marin had rather prominent places. Adjacent to a gun-drilling field, where Kamehameha's soldiers
learned to use the new weapons, an area was set aside for the
Hawaiian martial exercise of spear throwing. Behind the
town lay an extensive yam field, and as in all native villages
a good deal of space was reserved for sports, including a
foot-racing field and courts for *ulu maika,* a bowling game
with several variations. John Papa Ii watched all this with
fascination as a small boy, and he described later how
"crowds of chiefs and commoners gathered on all sides and
Kamehameha joined them."[19]

All this activity—a new kind of "urbanism" for the
islands—was certain to affect the attitudes of both newcomers and natives toward the land. When haoles were
granted land parcels, there was always the proviso that these
would return in time to the king.[20] The chiefs were accustomed to the revocability of land grants, but the new residents were not. Within a very short time dissatisfaction with
the tenure system appeared. The chiefs began to worry, too.
Now that government seemed more stabilized than it once
had been, questions of inheritance arose, and the privilege of
passing one's land on to heirs seemed a reasonable right to
ask. To Kamehameha and the son who succeeded him to the
throne this privilege began to seem sensible too, and they

were inclined to allow lands to pass on in a chief's family by hereditary succession. The Act of 1825, adopted by the Council of Chiefs when twelve-year-old Kamehameha III ascended the throne, gave the process of land inheritance a kind of legal basis.

These changes in tenure and use of land in the first forty-year period of recent Hawaiian history epitomized what was happening to almost every aspect of the older Polynesian life on the islands. Convictions and customs that had evolved over the centuries quickly dissolved in the excitement of new ideas and new activities. The society which the old conventions and dictates had bound together then began to disintegrate, and the Hawaiian people and their land were ready for transformation into something different.

The next group of arrivals set out at once to achieve that metamorphosis.

The Next Step: A Wish to Own

Twelve companies of missionaries arrived at Honolulu between 1820 and 1848, sent by the American Board of Commissioners for Foreign Missions of the Congregationalist Church. Largely, the arrivals on the mission ships were ordained ministers of the gospel and, often, their wives, but the band included physicians and teachers, secular agents, printers, a bookbinder, and a farmer. Their functions were not only preaching and teaching Christian tenets but included such activities as translating the Hawaiian language into a written, printable form, giving secular as well as religious advice to the local people, assisting in the formation of a stable government, and ultimately activity by some in professional, commercial, and agricultural development.[21]

The two rulers following Kamehameha I were his sons: Liholiho, crowned as Kamehameha II; then Kauikeaouli, who became Kamehameha III. However, during much of this time an able, powerful woman—Kaahumanu, Kamehameha I's most respected wife—shared the rule with her stepsons as

kuhina nui, a title which originally meant something like
prime minister but which Kaahumanu made into a position
more like that of regent.

During this period the monarchy was increasingly dependent on haole advice—strongly tinged with missionary influence but tending also to favor foreign business interests.
(There were differences in principles between the two
groups, but the alien entrepreneurs were after all Christian
and the missionaries became increasingly involved in entre-
preneurism.) The Reverend William Richards, an ordained
minister, resigned from the mission in 1838 and became officially an adviser to Kamehameha III. In 1842 Dr. Gerrit P.
Judd, a medical missionary, made a similar decision and, for
a decade, was the most powerful individual in the government. It was under their influence that a basic set of laws
was developed to replace the old kapus (Kamehameha II had
dramatically abolished the kapu system soon after his accession, recognizing that it had lost its meaning), a constitutional form of government was adopted, and new concepts of
land ownership were formulated.

The kings tried to resist pressure for too rapid change that
came from within Hawaii, as the growing business community pushed for more freedom to act—and more land to act
on—and also from sovereign powers abroad. England,
France, and the United States, particularly, jockeyed for control of the islands just short of takeover. On one occasion
officials from England and on another a French naval officer
did indeed move, without authority, for physical possession.
The French incident was more annoying than frightening: a
troublesome consul commissioner named Guillaume Patrice
Dillon, pressing a number of trumped-up claims, was backed
by a French admiral whose flagship called at Honolulu at
just that time, and for several weeks in 1849 French sailors
occupied the fort in Honolulu and vandalized the city. The
French government disavowed the acts of its officers and
later sacked Dillon.

The earlier British incident was much more serious in implication and in fact. It was rooted in the problem of land ownership, which, during the reign of Kamehameha III, became the most troublesome of the conflicts between haoles and natives. A British consul general, Richard Charlton, had acquired parcels of land in a number of places in the islands and now laid claim to one in particular which he said had been granted to him fifteen years before, a claim which the king disputed. Nursing this grievance, among others, Charlton sailed for England in September 1842 to argue against a treaty which was being negotiated and, incidentally, to try to get the English government to back him in his personal dispute. While he was away, his surrogate, one Alexander Simpson, pursued Charlton's land claim and, as in the case of the later Dillon trouble, was able to call on the support of a warship which arrived at a crucial point in the controversy. Lord George Paulet, commander of the frigate *Carysfort,* backed Simpson to such an extent that he forced cession of Hawaii to England under threat of naval attack upon the town of Honolulu.

When the true facts of the seizure became known in England, the British government repudiated the acquisition of the islands, but Kamehameha III and his subjects had a very unhappy five months. The white residents of Honolulu suffered an uneasy time too, but in a sense they were still guests, not home folks. At the cession ceremony the king spoke in moving terms only to the Hawaiians. "I am in perplexity," he said. "I have given away the life of our land. . . . But my rule over you, my people, and your privileges, will continue, for I have hope that the life of our land will be restored." And indeed it was, for another fifty years: British Rear Admiral Richard Thomas arrived in Honolulu in July 1843 and returned the islands to their native government. An impressive ceremony was held as the Hawaiian flag was again raised, on a plain in Honolulu later dedicated gratefully as Thomas Square.[22]

So confused was land ownership by that time, however, that Charlton's claim continued to be a controversial matter

through 1847, an issue discussed endlessly in meetings of the
Privy Council as well as in sessions of a land commission
that was appointed in 1846.[23] Despite insistence of the king
and the chiefs that Charlton's supposed proof of ownership
was a fake, the British government insisted that the claim be
respected. The Hawaiian government finally gave in.

The Charlton-Paulet case was the most angry ado over
land ownership during that time, but there were many others.
By then the question of the chiefs' ownership of their lands
seemed to be fairly well settled; the Act of 1825 had established even their hereditary rights, they believed. But confusion was increasing about the claims of foreigners to the
lands they had acquired through gift or grant or lease or
some kind of transfer of rights that they called a "sale." The
practice of Kamehameha I to grant land in return for services
rendered was continued by his sons, by Kaahumanu, and
even by the governors of the individual islands. The story of
the tailor Kilday was repeated many times. One Charles
Cockett was given a parcel on Maui by the governor of that
island after four years of faithful work at various tasks.
When the chief died, his daughter wanted Cockett to continue working for her; and when he demurred, she moved to
take the land away from him.[24] Was she right? Did the old
precepts of reversion of land ownership to the king or to the
chiefs, on death or disloyalty, still prevail? Or were new policies in order now?

By that time the wish to own property was not entirely
artless; land was clearly becoming a valuable commodity.
Kaahumanu, in acknowledging a claim of one George Pelly
to a parcel in Nuuanu, admonished him about his greediness.
"I give to you this land," she wrote him, "but of your idea
to take to yourself land in this place and that without my being informed, this is not right."[25] Yet there was reason for
honest indecision about the question of ownership among the
Hawaiian rulers and understandable confusion among the
foreigners. Kamehameha III issued a proclamation in 1841
allowing fifty-year leases but advising that "all those who are

in possession of building lots or farms would do well to go to the governors . . . and obtain a written title."[26] The foreigners resented this order, and the king was further disturbed by their reaction, which seemed to him unreasonable. He complained that "we did indeed wish to give foreigners lands the same as natives and so they were granted, but to the natives they are revertible and the foreigners would insist that they had them forever."[27]

The government itself admitted its ambiguous attitude toward ownership—by deeds if not by words. An American named Stephen Reynolds proposed to sell his rather extensive properties back to the government, in early 1846, for $40,000. The ministers and the king were upset, but they agreed to Reynolds' proposition "without admitting the full validity of his title."[28] The chiefs were as uncertain about questions of ownership as any other members of the community. By an act of 1841 the alii were permitted to lease out their land, and many haoles took advantage of this opportunity to negotiate leases for set terms. After they had paid taxes on the land for some years, as though they owned it, they felt a sense of actual possession.

Land changed hands by bills of sale, and land was passed on to the original owners' heirs—always, of course, with the caveat that such transfers were subject to any claims the government might impose. Thus it soon became possible to make money by selling land, even with the tacit understanding that title was "revertible" to the kingdom. Later, when the early land grants were legally recognized, many "sales" of the right to use land, live on it, farm it, or pasture it were produced to substantiate claims.[29] One James Robinson had been early granted property for a home in Honolulu "on the street leading to the sugar mill," which in 1830 he sold to Richard Ridley, carpenter, who in turn sold it in 1835 to the acquisitive George Pelly. Each made a profit. Harriet Blanchard claimed a plot "on the street leading to the printing office" by inheritance, after it had changed hands several times.[30]

Among the foreigners holding land—and sometimes selling it—there were a number of missionaries. Contrary to the generally held belief, however, they were no more grasping than any other newcomers and were just as confused about the ownership rights to their individual holdings—even to the mission properties—as any other haoles. In many cases, if not most, the land they held was reward for long and arduous service to the rulers, the chiefs, and their families: as teachers, accountants, attorneys, doctors, personal counselors. Records of landholdings and land transfers by the original mission bands show no speculative dealings; at the most there were small margins of profit as some properties were traded about.[31] It was the more secular-minded among the mission group, a number of whom left the church and joined the business community, who in time became land manipulators. And it was the second- and third-generation "mission boys," a number of whom became influential members of the plantation-centered economic elite, who acquired large land blocks.

If house lots and small farms had remained the only items of contention, the ambiguous land-ownership situation might not have been so troublesome, but it was not long before some newcomers became more ambitious. Most aspiring of the venturers in the early decades of the century were three partners who formed an enterprise called Ladd & Co. William Ladd, Peter Brinsmade, and William Hooper arrived from Boston in 1833 and, after establishing a successful mercantile venture in Honolulu, leased from the government a thousand acres of land on Kauai (for $300 a year). There, at Koloa, they began the first large-scale venture into plantation agriculture on the islands, so successfully in the beginning that they soon began to dicker for more land. Even though the partners overextended themselves at Koloa and ran into financial difficulties, they remained ambitious and optimistic—and were able to wangle a further contract with Kamehameha III which gave them the right to farm "any now unoccupied and unimproved localities on the several islands of the Sandwich Islands."

After vain attempts to form a corporation with foreign capital, Ladd & Co. tried to recoup its fortunes by suing the Kingdom of Hawaii for $378,000, claiming that their troubles were caused by the government's noncooperation and even interference. As a settlement, they proposed setting up a joint stock company with the Hawaiian government, the government to subscribe four hundred shares of stock for $200,000, with this sum paid in cash to the partners of Ladd & Co. The king and chiefs were merely amused at that point; it is a proposal, said Land Commissioner John Ii, "that might deceive a drunken man but would not deceive any man in his sober senses."[32]

Eventually, however, the sober-minded advisers of King Kamehameha III saw that the whole disorder would have to be straightened out. Two pressures finally forced legislation intended to reform land tenure: one came from the foreigners, who wanted full rights to what they held; the other came from the Hawaiian people, who wanted full rights to the kuleanas they were occupying and using.

Pressure was strongest from the haoles—the beginnings of commercial agriculture in the islands provided a strong impetus to the movement. The difficulties of Ladd & Co. did not deter other potential plantation entrepreneurs, and sugar mills began to appear in various places on several of the islands, some operated by missionaries to bolster the finances of the church. Coffee, cotton, and other products were grown with some success, but it quickly became clear that production of sugar would be the most profitable enterprise.[33] The English missionary William Ellis wrote in 1822 that "large tracts of fertile land lie waste in the islands," and he foresaw the day "when the natives become more industrious and civilized."[34] It was not native industry that ended "waste" of the land, however; it was Yankee business acumen. Land was necessary for the growing areas and milling operations, and in one way or another land was acquired. One observer noted that in the mid-1840s Americans alone held over a million dollars worth of real property, much of it under cultivation.[35]

The Hawaiian government was more moved by the plight of the commoners, and its haole advisers were sympathetic also. Judd fought ownership of land by foreigners to the end, and the king gave way unhappily;[36] the principle of the people's right to their land was not openly disputed, although some of the older alii agreed reluctantly. The indecisive policy of the government resulted in a petition, sent to Kamehameha III in 1845, signed by over 1,600 natives—they objected, first, to foreigners being accepted as Hawaiian subjects and, second, to the sale of land to foreigners. The king's council replied in troubled tones that foreigners settling permanently had a right to "a proper sovereign," and although "it is by no means proper to sell land to aliens," when foreigners became citizens they were entitled to have land "that they may have a home."

Some natives were not satisfied (among them, David Malo) and nineteen of them responded in writing: "Foreigners come on shore with cash, ready to purchase land, but we have not the means to purchase lands . . . we have been subject to the ancient laws, till within these few years." They argued that without a change in the situation, they could foresee "the land with the life of the land passing into possession of foreigners." Everyone seemed to agree, then, that a change, a reform in the policy of land tenure, was necessary, even though there was no unanimity on the nature of that change.[37]

End of the Ancient System

During the 1840s and 1850s decisions were made by king, council, and legislature that marked the end of Hawaii's ancient land ownership and land use system. The first move would seem an obvious statement of fact to a landowner today, but it was a radical admission in 1839: a simple statement that real property, with other possessions, actually belonged to a person to whom it had been granted, sold, or otherwise put in his possession. A bill of rights adopted that year, sometimes referred to as Hawaii's Magna Charta,

stated: "Protection is hereby secured to the persons of all the
people, together with their lands, their building lots and all
their property, and nothing whatsoever shall be taken from
any individual except by express provisions of the law."[38]
Not a chief, not even a king, but the law. The act also said
that a "landlord cannot causelessly dispossess his tenants."
Modern *rights* of ownership were thus established, replacing
custom and taboo. In 1840 the monarchy adopted its first
constitution, which established a bicameral legislature (allowing election of commoners to the house), set up a supreme
court, and otherwise provided a constitutional base for the
kingdom. The constitution attempted to explain the old
Hawaiian land tenure system in modern terms by recalling
that although Kamehameha I had owned "all the land from
one end of the islands to the other," it had not been his
private property but really belonged "to the chiefs and people in common, of whom Kamehameha I was the head, and
had the management of the landed property."[39] This still left
rights of tenure rather vague. Then, with pressure increasing
for further clarification of rights and titles, on 10 December
1845 a body with the descriptive title "Board of Commissioners to Quiet Land Titles" was appointed.

The task of the Land Commission, as it became known,
was at first intended to be "investigation and final ascertain-
ment or rejection of all claims of private individuals, whether
natives or foreigners, to any landed property acquired an-
terior to the passage" of the act.[40] The work the commission
did went much further, however, and it remained active for
ten years. In the set of principles the commission adopted,
the problem and its background were well stated: during
Kamehameha I's time each person had rights in the land
to some degree—"not very clearly defined, but nevertheless
universally acknowledged." Now, however, what had been
simple had become legally tangled—some "may have acquired allodial ownership of landed property" while many
others retain "a freehold less than allodial." It was not an
easy tangle to unsnarl.

After considering the overall question for some time, the

Land Commission decided that the basic problem was a clear division of property rights between king and chiefs. This division, or *mahele,* was accomplished with the help of a special committee appointed by the legislature. All the agreements that the king reached with some 240 chiefs and their konohikis were recorded in the *Mahele Book,* the king's lands described on one page and the chief's on the facing page.[41] Descriptions were sometimes vague, and a huge task of surveying and clarifying borders followed (with much of the work done by missionaries).

The next step in the "quieting" of titles was a distinction made by the king, immediately after the last mahele had been signed, between lands that he retained as his own and lands that he turned over to the kingdom as its property (government lands, so called). Chiefs were required to pay a "commutation" before their titles were secured; most supplied them in kind, turning back portions of their awarded properties, which were then added to the government lands the king had established.

The work of the Land Commission in investigating personal claims by foreigners and natives continued for some years. There were recorded fifty handwritten volumes of testimony before the commission, with its supporting documentation, and ten volumes describing awards the commission made.[42] Its work assumed greater importance as two additional pieces of legislation were passed. The first act was passage of a law on 10 July 1850 that allowed alien residents in Hawaii to acquire and hold land in fee-simple title, as citizen residents could, and to dispose of it as they wished to anyone living in Hawaii, subject or alien.[43] The foreigners had finally won their way. As a leader in the haole community wrote in a paper for the Hawaiian Historical Society later in the century: "A brief ten years had been sufficient for the Hawaiian nation to break down the hoary traditions and venerable customs of the past, and to climb the difficult path from a selfish *[sic]* feudalism to equal rights."[44] The second was an act, adopted by the legislature on 6 August 1850,

known as the Kuleana Grant.[45] The mahele between king and
alii had promised protection of tenants' rights, but did not
allow for fee-simple land ownership by commoners. The new
law did, for anyone who was occupying and cultivating his
own kuleana on government, king's, or chiefs' lands.

At the end of the Land Commission's work about a
million acres had been set aside for the king, nearly a million
and a half acres declared to be government land, and another
million and a half awarded to the chiefs as their personal
property. Although less than thirty thousand acres had been
granted to the commoners as kuleanas, this move was a
remarkable gesture toward common land ownership, far in
advance of its time. As we shall see, during the next period
in Hawaii's modern history these figures changed quite
radically; the new ability of the haole population to acquire
lands legally, in fee simple as well as by lease, was utilized to
the full.

Although a number of plantations and fairly large farms
were put in operation toward the middle of the century and
land was desirable primarily for agricultural purposes, urban
land ownership was also growing in importance, and in
value, through the activities of the trader-settlers who were
arriving in greater numbers. The missions established by the
successive bands of churchly arrivals—at Kailua and Waimea
on the Big Island, at Lahaina on Maui, in several places on
Kauai, and principally in Honolulu—contributed to the
townlike character these places were assuming.

The change in Honolulu between 1820 and the 1840s and
1850s was the most remarkable of these developments. When
the first groups of missionaries came, the town was still a
rather scrabbly stretch of flatland behind the harbor inlet.
Streets connecting the nondescript buildings were "narrow,
irregular, and dirty," not much more than paths, as one
disappointed arrival noted. Busy as the town was becoming,
the several hundred buildings in which the activity took place
were mostly adobe-covered thatched huts. The missionary
William Ellis noted the appearance of several wood and

stone structures, however, and within a short time both the
physical quality of buildings and the orderliness and self-
respect of the foreign community using them had improved.[46]

By the 1840s perhaps eight thousand people lived in Honolulu, about six hundred of them Caucasians, according to an
estimate made by *Polynesian,* a haole-oriented newspaper
that was started that year by an ambitious young man named
James Jackson Jarves.[47] There were twenty families from the
United States, the editor counted, amounting to seventy-six
individuals, and five from England totaling seventeen persons. Bragging of growth and progress, the paper inventoried
twenty retail shops and four wholesale stores. (Ladd & Co.
in their advertisements indicated the variety of products
available: everything from sugar and molasses to paint and
cordage, glassware for the table, comestibles for the kitchen,
prints for dressmaking, and coral, lava, and limestone for
construction.) Although the partners of Ladd & Co. became
involved in other enterprises, a number of mercantile ventures which were building themselves working space in the
1840s remained to become part of the later commercial
establishment headed by the sugar production factors known
as the Big Five. C. Brewer & Co., for instance, were beginning their ship chandling offices; two missionaries left the
fold to found the firm of Castle & Cooke.

There were two hotels in Honolulu by 1840. There were,
moreover, twelve hostels described by Jarves as "sailors'
boarding houses, alias grog shops," at least three churches,
four schools, and two hospitals. These were inclined to be
makeshift buildings, but the Rev. Hiram Bingham, who had
been one of the earliest missionaries to arrive, was building a
new church for the Kawaiahao parish: "an imposing structure of one hundred and ten feet in length and seventy in
breadth, with columns in front," constructed of timber
brought from the American northwest and coral stone from
the islands. John Dominis, a beached merchant seaman from
New York, was constructing for himself an ambitious house.
It was to be finished later by his widow, occupied for a time

by Hawaii's last monarch, Queen Liliuokalani, and ultimately remain, extensively remodeled, as the official home of the
State of Hawaii's governors.

The town was already beginning to spread beyond the immediate harbor area. A Mr. Skinner was finishing a rather
"elegant structure" for himself a bit outside the town center,
and a large home was being completed in Nuuanu Valley,
mauka of the downtown area, where Kamehameha I had
fought his decisive battle for Oahu. Shortly, Jarves predicted, "we shall see the surface [of the valley] dotted with
neat cottages." And he added, editorially: "This is as it
should be." *Polynesian* essayed other bits of critical appraisal: Skinner's ambitious house was "an ornament to the
town"; Kawaiahao Church was in a style "somewhat antiquated for our day, but [with] the merit of convenience"; a
new retail store downtown, built for Sam & Mow, Bakers,
"looks much like a retired post office for some flourishing
village in the United States."

By then the character of the town was totally different
from what it had been in the time of the first Kamehameha.
The drilling fields, playing fields, and even the heiaus had
fallen into disrepair and been abandoned or torn down to
make way for new "changes and improvements." True
streets were replacing the trails and byways. Properties, now
secured, were being surveyed and carefully defined. There
was a crowded neighborhood of native thatched huts along
the water, pushed aside by the new commercial and residential construction and the beginnings of a public works program (at first modest: a bridge across the Nuuanu stream,
leading toward the plantation lands at Ewa, cost $1,200 in
the 1840s).[48] There was sufficient road construction outside
of Honolulu (even on the other islands) so that a law was
enacted in 1840 "respecting the making of roads and recompense for land taken."[49] Government business, domestic and
foreign, required the construction of a "government house"
and three consulates.

Crudities persisted in the new life in the towns. "Thieves

and vandals are becoming as plentiful as swine in the
streets," *Polynesian* noted toward the end of 1840.[50] There
were the beginnings of a mannered social life for the haoles
that extended to the royalty and some of the chiefdom; but
the ordinary Hawaiians, attracted to the towns by the advantages that were apparently offered, were outsiders in
their own country, unable to find work once they left their
kuleanas.[51] The king and his advisers recognized the problem:
they saw that the commoners who had left the land could not
even pay the commutation fees for the kuleanas that had
been granted them. The Privy Council proposed in 1847 that
"in order to encourage the people who live in towns to
return to the country to farm," their kuleana commutation
costs be forgiven. This was the first of many homesteading
efforts designed to return native Hawaiians to the land. It
was no more successful than any have proved to be.

After the 1840s "the outlines of a town committed to western property laws became visible," writes historian Gavan
Daws. In 1850 Honolulu was declared by the king to be a
city; the new metropolis had a population of about fourteen
thousand. During the 1850s regular mail service was instituted. A board of health was appointed. A school tax of $2 a
year was levied. In 1859 the tax load was increased by imposition of real and personal property taxes, and by then an
elementary water system and some other basic utilities were
undertaken. In fact, capital public improvements amounted
to more than a million dollars spent between the mid-1850s
and the mid-1870s. Observers noted that the streets were still
poor, however, and the town grew haphazardly. Despite the
"improvements," there was no plan and no structure of true
architectural merit.

Yet by 1860 Honolulu must have been a very colorful
place. It was, after all, capital of a Polynesian island kingdom. Its resident population enjoyed band concerts on the
palace lawn, did business in sturdy (if not handsome) structures, and found professional services ranging from legal
advice to dentistry. Many lived in sprouting suburban neigh-

borhoods where, as Mark Twain and others described them, neat white cottages sat surrounded by green grass and bright flowers brought from home. Amenities and luxuries were not lacking. A merchant, in his journal, noted that he filled a request from a good customer for "a pen for a young lady, either gold or ebony with gold bands—not more than $5.00."[52]

The leap from the past had been made. Hawaiian culture had been replaced by a new society. The Polynesian way of life, indigenous to Hawaii, had been supplanted by a nostalgia for other manners—by a mid-Pacific enactment of a European-cum-New England living style, on the part of the haoles, and by a willing wish to emulate what they saw performed, on the part of the Hawaiian royalty and alii. The Hawaiian commoners were confused. As they had explained to their king: "We have lived under the chiefs, thinking to do whatever they desired, but not according as we thought; hence we are not prepared to compete with foreigners."[53] That their trouble was real, not imagined, is attested by their biological vulnerability to the new life. By 1860 the population that Cook had found had already dwindled to some 70,000.

chapter **2**

Paths to the Present

HAWAII'S roots in a Polynesian past withered quickly under
the impact of exotic importations, social and physical, but it
took longer for the islands to implant themselves in the present. From the middle of the nineteenth century on, the original Hawaiians had even less control over their land. More
and more residents of Hawaii were Hawaiians by location
only: their origins reached from east to far west.

To the new Hawaiians the past meant anything from a
stiff New England town to a simple oriental village, and their
pictures of a desirable present were as varied. What sort of
modern world should Hawaii join? In what seemed a wide
set of alternatives, in what could have been a time of utter
confusion, Hawaii's development pointed in a fairly straight
direction for one impelling reason: the social, political, and
economic controls soon were concentrated in the hands of a
single group, the predominantly American white businessmen.[1] There were periodic attempts by the missionaries to
interfere, but the Hawaiians had less and less to say about
life on their islands, and the other, growing groups, at first
primarily Chinese and then increasingly Japanese, remained
powerless for a long while.

The period from about 1860 to 1900, or more accurately from Kamehameha III's death in 1854 to annexation of Hawaii by the United States in 1898, saw a gradual weakening of the monarchy as the non-Hawaiians consolidated the rights they had won and pressed harder for the end of Hawaii's sovereign independence.

The last five monarchs were Alexander Liholiho, a grandson of Kamehameha the Great, crowned as Kamehameha IV in 1854; his brother Lot, who became the fifth and last of the Kamehameha dynasty in 1863; William Charles Lunalilo, who was elected king by the legislative assembly in 1873 and died of pulmonary tuberculosis thirteen months later; David Kalakaua, elected by the legislature to the royal position in 1874; and finally Kalakaua's sister Lydia Kamakaeha Paki (Mrs. John O. Dominis), who was elected to the throne as Queen Liliuokalani.

Each of these last five Hawaiian monarchs ruled briefly—Kalakaua's reign for seventeen years was the longest; Lunalilo and Liliuokalani had two-year or less royal tenancies. Their health, generally, was not hearty; most of them drank much;[2] the tensions produced by pressures on the kingdom simply weighed too heavily on these handsome alii nuis with such recent primal antecedents.

The haole business community in the islands (along with those non-Hawaiians in government and the remaining band of missionaries) moved efficiently to consolidate the controls that had been legalized during Kamehameha III's reign.[3] Politically, they pressed for additional constitutional reform, while the royalty, through most of the period, leaned toward absolutism in government. The question was further complicated by the Hawaiians' desire for the right to vote and the haoles' fear of the results of universal suffrage. The foreigners made strong invasions into the government itself: Kamehameha IV appointed three non-Hawaiian cabinet members; the proportion increased until, under Kalakaua, the entire cabinet was at times Caucasian.

With more land available for the growing of sugarcane,

the next needs of the planters were for a profitable market and a satisfactory work force. Two political activities resulted from the wish to assure advantageous sales: lobbying in Washington for a reciprocity treaty that would eliminate tariffs on sugar shipped to mainland America, and working both in Hawaii and in the United States toward annexation of the island kingdom to that nation.

The fight for reciprocity was won through a treaty signed in 1875 and renewed in 1887 (one clause giving the United States rights to Pearl Harbor). The push toward annexation was more complicated and took longer to succeed. Most American residents wanted the islands to be annexed, believing that their interests would be better served under American control. Others feared annexation, preferring to maintain the holds they had achieved over local politics, economics, and land tenure, by means that American democracy might frown on.[4]

The end of the kingdom came when the polarity between royalists (most Hawaiians and some whites who wanted above all to maintain a monarchy strong enough to assure independence) and annexationists (most haoles, who wanted an American takeover to end what remained of native Hawaiian sovereignty) reached an impossible point of tension.[5] An outright revolution was engineered by a band of haole business and professional men in January 1893, and a revolutionary government was formed.[6] It was followed by a self-proclaimed republic headed by a moderate named Sanford Ballard Dole, son of a missionary family and a unique character with odd and unexpected principles—altogether an unlikely person to be a revolutionary, as indeed were other dignified, frock-coated conservative gentlemen among those who took part.

The life of the republic was a shaky one, and the United States felt that it had no choice, ultimately, but to solve the sorry mess by annexation, which was ordained by a majority but by no means unanimous vote of Congress in 1898.

The other need of the plantation owners—for labor of a

sufficient quantity, at low enough wages, and with satisfactorily docile dispositions—was resolved during the last half of the nineteenth century and for some time afterward by wholesale importation of contracted laborers from other lands.[7] The Hawaiians had proved to have no taste for such work, and in any event they retained too much independence to become compliant field hands (though a number of them were trained for supervisory jobs).[8] Three hundred Chinese coolies were brought to Hawaii in 1851—the planters having taken immediate advantage of an act passed by the legislature which permitted contract labor—and then, as the imported Chinese workers showed signs of restiveness under the miserable plantation conditions and extremely low pay, increasingly large groups were brought from Japan.[9] In the years just before annexation some forty thousand Japanese arrived, and toward the end of the century more than half the population of the islands was Japanese, other Orientals constituting another fifth. By that time workers from other countries were being brought in—the Portugese in quite large numbers.

The fate of Hawaii's lands during this period of consolidation of foreign control was closely related to agricultural and other commercial developments. Land acquisition by aliens continued on a large scale: by the end of the century close to 70 percent of Hawaii's surface was owned by non-Hawaiians. As an instance of the search for land, Claus Spreckels, San Francisco's insatiable sugar magnate, came to Hawaii determined to dominate the industry in the islands.[10] From a Hawaiian princess, Ruth Keelikolani, he "bought" for $10,000 the crown lands of Hawaii—which she did not own and could not sell—and later actually did gain extensive acreage on Maui by influencing legislation.

The use of land for producing commodities other than sugar continued, but not to an impressive extent, during this period.[11] Rice and a few other agricultural staples and even a usable fiber formed from the fern tree were grown and, for a time, found markets. Some products did catch on permanently and are profitable items even today: bananas, guava (especially as a jelly), and coffee (which seemed always to suffer from one production difficulty or another). The most important of these successes was, of course, pineapple, grown in some quantity during the last decades of the century, improved in quality through importation of new varieties, but held back as exportable merchandise because of transportation problems and the price penalties of heavy American tariffs.

Several societies were formed to foster local agricultural and botanical businesses, and both of the last two Kamehamehas supported these movements enthusiastically. Once more, however, little thought was given to protection of indigenous species. As growers found that they had to fight pests, insectivorous birds were introduced, such as the obtrusive myna bird, and became destructive nuisances in their own turn.

Raising cattle and, to a lesser extent, goats and sheep became successful enterprises and in some places even began to compete with the sugar interests in the need for land. In the 1860s and 1870s a number of large ranches were established, some of them remaining as viable enterprises.

Mercantile activity was increasing in the towns, and the urban locations themselves were thus expanding and requiring more land on which to continue growing. At first the outlying built-up locations were satisfied with a kind of frontier construction (like Carson City in the 1850s or Helena, Montana, in the 1870s, as one architectural historian has put it). But soon, especially in Honolulu, there came a more ostentatious importation of mannerisms from Europe and America, and toward the end of the century there was a strong dominance of styles brought directly from America in its Victorian period.[12] This bosomy, corseted, double-breasted architecture seemed quite appropriate to the dress that the haole gentlemen and their fair ladies wore, emulated as they were by the nobles of the Hawaiian court. A new Iolani

Palace, built in 1882, combined in an engaging architectural fantasy many of these imported tastes.

The urbanized areas began to spread, and as they grew they demanded more urban amenities. Honolulu developed eastward, as far as was reasonable along the coast, and westward as well, reaching toward the plantation lands. Hilo on the island of Hawaii, Lahaina and Wailuku on Maui, and Lihue on Kauai, all early settlements, grew to be the urban centers of those islands.

Transportation rapidly became a problem.[13] Horse and buggy traffic was soon so dense in downtown Honolulu that residents and businessmen complained. Horse-drawn hacks provided public transport for some time, and in the 1880s mule-powered carriages, moving on rails laid along the developing urban corridor, were introduced. Railroads appeared to many to be a necessary adjunct to public transportation, and several small stretches of track were laid on Oahu and on Maui before the largest and most successful, reaching from Honolulu to the plantations of Ewa, was opened in 1890. Further railroad construction followed, some of remarkable engineering skill. A triple-spurred road reaching out from Hilo on Hawaii spanned the Laupahoehoe Gulch on a 568-foot-high trestle, and Benjamin F. Dillingham's Oahu Railway and Land Company extended its tracks past Ewa, around the rocky point of Kaena, to Kahuku on the northeast corner of the island. The economics of railroading did not, in the end, work out in Hawaii, but before the lines were discontinued they provided weekend travel experiences for the residents as well as cartage for the plantations.

The utility services essential to a modern community were begun in this period before annexation: artesian water supply was found feasible, and pipes were laid to reservoirs in several of the upper valleys; electric light was at first an exciting display in a few places, but by 1891 the Hawaiian Electric Company was providing lighting for those who wanted it and could afford it; the telephone went through a similar stage of

display and ostentation, but as early as 1880 the furnishing
of telephone service had become a competitive business.[14]

The Land Changes Hands

The land which was being acquired by western venturers in
ever greater quantities, either in full ownership or through
leases, came from several sources. Some was sold or leased
by the aliis, or by the king, from the lands that had been set
aside for them at the time of the Great Mahele. A primary
source was the stock of government land that had been
formed. And in a lesser but still important quantity the acquisition came from the kuleanas which the Hawaiian commoners had received.

The shrinking of the kuleanas is a sad story.[15] While the
total of thirty thousand acres distributed was small, it represented in principle an important move toward a democratic,
freeholding society. There were 11,300 individual grants, and
one historian has noted that the Hawaiian native population
at that time was only 80,000 persons, which probably
represented not more than some 16,000 families. Thus the
kuleana grants must have been awarded to almost two out of
three Hawaiian families—a record of fee-simple ownership
among natives unique in the early nineteenth century.

There were mixed emotions among the haoles about this
gain for the local people. An editorial writer in *The Maile
Quarterly* in the 1860s saw the natives "with a taro patch, a
garden plot, a good suit of clothes and four horses" becoming "independent, lazy and vicious." An angry response
from one of his readers argued that the Hawaiians were industrious people, who valued and used their kuleanas and
"with almost religious zeal . . . hoard their title deeds and
landmarks."[16] Neither comment was really correct. While
some Hawaiians hung onto their home-farm plots, many let
them go. Most of the kuleanas were good growing land, but
some were not; many of them were inaccessible, a number

had tangled, fractionated ownership claims, and some were sketchily surveyed (so that remembered "landmarks" were important and sometimes arguable). Often their owners were tempted away by plantation work or drawn by the attractions of the towns. For whatever reason, large numbers of the kuleanas were abandoned, to be absorbed by neighboring plantations and never recovered. Others were mortgaged, leased, or sold. By one calculation, on the island of Kauai only about a third of the kuleana grants remained in their owners' hands soon after the end of the century.[17]

The alii were not always good farmers or land managers either, and many of them lost their lands, often through accumulated debts or unsustainable mortgages.[18] At times cooperative ventures were tried: chiefs and commoners would pool their lands to make a try at larger-scale farming. These efforts were seldom successful, although at times they worried the large plantation owners. A *hui* (business association) of this sort at Makalupu, near the Koloa plantation on Kauai, bolstered by land deeded to its members by the ubiquitous Princess Ruth Keelikolani, became sufficiently bothersome that the Koloa Sugar Company gradually bought up the shares of individual members.[19]

The greatest sources of plantation acreage, however, were lands held by the monarch and government lands. Rights to the use of the king's personal properties, the crown lands, and the government lands became confused as time went on, despite attempts to clarify the legal distinctions. But by one means or another new haole owners dipped into all three resources.

Fundamentally, the Great Mahele had first separated the king's lands and the chiefs' lands, and then from each source the government's lands were formed. This seemed clear enough. One difficulty developed, however: some of the king's holdings remained his personal property, which he handled as he wished (the Kamehameha lands, in time, became a tremendous estate), and some became his property

only as ruler, as wearer of the crown.[20] Status of these
"crown" lands and the king's right to dispose of them
became a difficult issue during the later nineteenth century,
even though a commission was set up in 1865 to govern their
use.[21]

By the time Kamehameha V ascended to the throne, so
much of this crown property had been sold or tied up with
long leases or mortgages that the legislature recognized a
crisis. In 1864 the Hawaiian Supreme Court ruled that crown
meant crown, not king, and that the crown lands were "inalienable"—that is, they could not be taken away from the
crown to be broken up or disposed of. This seemed to the
legislature a sensible ruling, and on 3 January 1865 a law
was passed that said "Crown Lands shall remain henceforth
inalienable and shall descend to the heirs and successors of
the Hawaiian throne forever."

Again legal words would seem to have settled the problem,
but they did not. The government managed to pay off most
of the mortgages and terminate many of the leases, but the
manipulation by Claus Spreckels in 1880 indicated that rights
and titles were still confused. Later monarchs continued to
gain considerable income from leasing crown lands, and one
of the blows to Queen Liliuokalani when the throne was
taken from her was loss of that income.[22] In the end, of
course, the crown lands along with the government lands
were assumed by the provisional government, then by the republic, and finally, at the time of annexation, by the United
States government.[23]

The government lands, the true public domain, were both
sold and leased during the later years of the monarchy. Between the end of the Great Mahele activities and the overthrow of the monarchy, over 600,000 acres of government
land, including the best agricultural acreage in the islands,
were sold.[24] Much more was leased. Most of the sales took
place in the twenty-year period from 1846 to 1865; prices
averaged $1.11 an acre and in one instance went as low as
four cents.[25]

The Whites Take Charge

In the roughly four decades between annexation of Hawaii by the United States and the bombing of Pearl Harbor, that American property in the Hawaiian Islands, the resident Caucasian businessmen and professionals made full capital of the controls they had already established. The Americans especially found themselves no longer "foreigners"; they were now the most powerful native group in this territory of the United States. It was about this time that the word *kama'āina,* which meant to the Hawaiians "familiar," "accustomed," and hence "native-born," came to be applied by the second and third generation of white natives only to themselves—using the term *kanaka* (person) for the Hawaiian descendants—so that today the select kamaaina group in the islands is composed of scions of the early white settlers, like the Dillinghams and the Alexanders and the Cookes, in some instances with a touch of Hawaiian blood but in more cases pure haole.

Hawaiian royal titles became a badge of local prestige without power. The Hawaiian people struggled vainly to establish a new potency for themselves within the democratic framework that now enclosed them, but they failed just as miserably as wards of the United States as they had as subjects of their monarchy. The visitors who had come from abroad, seen great resources to exploit, and stayed on to become kamaainas were too ruthless and too clever for a decimated population of simple and friendly islanders to cope with. In competition with the Orientals who were being brought in, the Hawaiians did not do too well either. Some natives retired to pockets of village life, often in isolated valleys. Others tried, without much success, to find their way in the towns.[26]

During Hawaii's term as a territory it was governed under the Organic Act, adopted by the U.S. Congress, with a governor appointed by the president of the United States, a voteless delegate to Congress in Washington, a bicameral local

legislature, and, for the first time, universal suffrage for all
who had held citizen status under the republic.[27] Since the
Hawaiian and part-Hawaiian population constituted a majority of the electorate (Orientals, making up more than half the
resident population, were not regarded as citizens and for
some time could not vote), it seemed as though they were in
a position to control the legislature and have one of their
own become delegate to Congress, the most important elec-
tive post.

The allegiance of the white community was almost completely to the Republican party. From time to time a local
Democratic party made attempts to surface but, although it
attracted some colorful and competent figures, it remained
deep in the minority until after World War II. Only three of
the eight territorial governors were Democrats, appointed
without much attention to island affairs by Woodrow Wilson
in 1913 and 1918 and by Franklin Roosevelt in 1934, and
even they were of conservative cast. To the dismay of the
white business community, the first election for delegate to
Congress was indeed won by Robert W. Wilcox, a part-
Hawaiian who had joined in an abortive counterrevolution
attempting to reseat Queen Liliuokalani. From then on,
however, through ten elections until 1922, the delegate was
Prince Jonah Kuhio Kalanianaole, a Hawaiian of royal descent who chose to lead his people into an unhappy coalition
with the white Republicans. The haole political strategy was
to split the Hawaiian vote and gain most of it for the Republican policies; the Hawaiian hope was to win advantages, by
bartering and as a kind of gratuity, within the ranks of the
party that obviously had prestige and leverage in Washington. The move worked to disadvantage the Hawaiians as
effectively as compromise had failed for them in the last
years of the monarchy.

The territorial legislature was at first, by preponderance
of their votes, controlled by Hawaiians. As Wilcox's election
had frightened the haoles, so did that of native legislators,
who began conducting their sessions in the Hawaiian lan-

guage. But haole strategy succeeded in this sphere too. Soon the legislature was predominantly Republican, elected by a coalition of Caucasians (mostly Americans, bolstered by the Portuguese) and Hawaiians who deserted their own Home Rule party.

Sugar was dominant in every way in the first part of the twentieth century in Hawaii. Annexation had assured a satisfactory portion of the profitable American market. Finding the essential labor supply under the oppressive working conditions imposed by the plantation owners remained a problem, however. To make matters worse, after Hawaii became a territory contract labor was outlawed. The solution was to canvass willing workers from abroad, and the number of solicited immigrants increased each year.

The Chinese coolies increasingly left the plantations at the start of the new century: they moved to the cities, where many of them had already started small businesses and business combines (huis). Japanese labor was imported in swelling numbers until 1903, when an agreement with the Japanese government ended immigration of workers from that country (but did not prevent an inpouring of so-called picture brides). From then on the planters saw to it that many other nationals were enticed to the islands to work for them in various categories. More Portuguese came—and Puerto Ricans, then Koreans, Samoans, and, increasingly, Filipinos. European stock, such as German and Scandinavian, was added, and Scotsmen proved to be particularly good managers and overseers.

The result of all this, obviously, was a population mixed in ethnic background and race. When the first reciprocity treaty was signed in 1876, signaling the spurt in sugar production, people of Hawaiian ancestry formed over 80 percent of the population, Caucasians about 6½ percent, and Orientals some 10 percent. By 1940, as World War II approached, Hawaiians and part-Hawaiians constituted only 15 percent of the people on what had been their islands. Caucasian residents had increased to 23 percent, Orientals formed a husky

44 percent (six to one, Japanese over Chinese), and various other groups composed 17 percent of the total.[28]

Plantation business, during the territorial period, became the paramount industrial activity. Around the plantation revolved almost every aspect of life in Hawaii. Other commercial enterprises such as banking and transportation, as well as general merchandising to supply the needs of the growing population, depended to a large extent on producing sugarcane and, before long, pineapples. That tasty tropical fruit had been grown in the islands without fanfare (or much success) before 1900, but it was the acumen of James Drummond Dole, a cousin of the political leader Sanford Dole, that made pineapple a successful commodity and an important part of the islands' economy. The local strain was further improved and the product was canned to overcome the spoilage that slow ship transport had caused.

The prodigious profitability of the plantations (dividends paid by the factor firms, which soon controlled most of the growers' businesses, ran 50 percent or more in some years) meant that their dominance inevitably was extended in another direction: ownership of more and more land.[29] Sugarcane and pineapple entrepreneurs recognized that good land for growing was limited on the islands (only about a tenth of Hawaii's surface is "prime" agricultural land)—and *that* good land was indeed good, ideally suited for the crops they were growing. Hence the demand for the limited resource became obsessive. Fortunately, some of Hawaii's land resource was judiciously guarded: an act passed by the Territorial Legislature in 1903 empowered the governor to set aside forest and water reserves, and a continuing preservation program resulted.[30]

The republic's Land Act of 1895 limited to a thousand acres the amount of land that could change hands as a single parcel (a provision carried over into the Organic Act). It became important to the growers and their agents to have this curb lifted: although it was a restriction easily violated, by such devices as dummy owners, it still was a nuisance in acquiring land. In 1919 they lobbied though Congress a Hawaiian Rehabilitation Act that eliminated the unwelcome limitation and, in one of the coalition deals that was supposed to help the Hawaiian people, also created an agency called the Hawaiian Homes Commission. The advantage this act gave the land-hungry planters was quickly obvious. An outstanding example was the purchase in 1922 of the entire island of Lanai—a 90,000-acre treasure of tropical landscape (the land that wears the many-colored lei, says a Hawaiian song)—by the Hawaiian Pineapple Company, which became the Dole Corporation, which was later controlled by the Big Five factor Castle & Cooke. The benefits that the Hawaiians gained from the act were not so clear.

During this time a number of large landed estates, some of which had been set up to protect the income of their founders' heirs, became a major landowning element. With one notable exception and a few lesser ones, these trusts were of haole origin and inheritance. James Campbell, an Irishman who worked with Benjamin Dillingham to acquire major blocks of land for development, established an estate for his heirs amounting to about a fifth of the island of Oahu. Samuel Damon, a missionary son who secured large areas for ranching, left an estate amounting to over 140,000 acres. Lincoln McCandless, who with his brothers engineered the drilling of Hawaii's early artesian wells and who was an active political figure into the 1920s, put together over 36,000 acres for his descendants. In addition to these family inheritances, large blocks of land scattered among the islands were accumulated by the Big Five corporations: from about 155,000 acres held by Castle & Cooke to a mere 38,000 that Theo H. Davies had in fee simple.[31]

Of all these trusts and estates, the largest by far was the Bishop Estate, not at all a haole holding but the lands of the Kamehameha family inherited by the last of that line, Princess Bernice Pauahi Bishop.[32] Other Hawaiian royal and alii lands secured in the Great Mahele were formed into trusteeships (the Liliuokalani Trust amounts to almost 10,000 acres,

some of it in the heart of Waikiki), but the Bishop Estate
overshadows them all. Princess Bernice Pauahi, whose
genealogy showed her to be a direct descendant of Kamehameha I, was an esteemed, attractive, intelligent woman whom
Kamehameha V, as he approached death, tried to persuade
to be his successor. Married to Charles Reed Bishop, who
had way-stopped in the islands and then had stayed to
become one of Hawaii's earliest bankers, she preferred to
avoid the responsibilities and frustrations of the throne, but
she demonstrated her concern for the people by willing her
land, in trust, to be used to its best advantage for the purpose of educating Hawaiians. Some of the Kamehameha
lands had been in the hands of Princess Victoria Kamamalu
(heiress of Kaahumanu) and her father, Governor Keku-
anaoa. These Princess Ruth inherited and passed on to Bernice Pauahi Bishop, along with lands she had been awarded
by the Great Mahele. Nine percent of Hawaii's lands, about
370,000 acres, have been in this single ownership since Mrs.
Bishop's death in 1884, providing a powerful instrument for
affecting the environment and the society.

Another major accumulator of Hawaiian land in the early
years of the century was the United States government. Not
only were crown lands and government lands appropriated,
but additional areas were "set aside" for defense purposes.[33]

Urban Design and Nondesign

Urban expansion continued to increase in the first decades of
the century, primarily around Honolulu on Oahu and, in the
towns that had already begun to develop before annexation,
on the other islands. Several plantation towns grew to sizable
proportions on the central Oahu plains, on the northern tip
of the island of Hawaii, and elsewhere. The town of Lanai,
on that island which had been sold outright for private use,
became a sort of model company town, decently planned and
developed, though built with quite miserable little houses. In
fact most of the plantation homes (sometimes sentimentally

invested with architectural merit by urban historians) were nondescript wooden boxes.

In Honolulu and even in other places influenced by the thriving economy, building construction increased appreciably. Moreover, some attention was now being given to the quality of urban appearance.[34] The cities grew haphazardly as needs arose and land became available, however, not by any kind of plan. Although no town-planning landscape-architect types appeared, several well-known American architects designed buildings in Hawaii. The early years of the century have been termed a Colonial Period in its architecture, since the influence was obvious of styles fashionable on the American mainland, imported to the territory by these visiting designers.

Even by 1910 the central part of Honolulu for a good half dozen blocks in each direction was quite solidly built up, and the expansion of "downtown" continued rapidly.[35] The stores and other commercial structures in those first decades of the century still averaged two or three stories high. Some, like the Alexander Young Hotel—built with modified Renaissance decorative finery in 1902 for $2 million,—were twice that height.[36] Public buildings were added to the burgeoning civic center around Iolani Palace; the central library, typical Carnegie-grant Doric-porticoed neoclassicism, was built in 1911. Up the Nuuanu Valley, where Kamehameha the Great had won his decisive battle for Oahu a hundred years before, one of the earliest American golf courses was stretched across the rolling foothills.

Church buildings—of all religions, sects, denominations, and architectural styles—appeared everywhere. There were such examples as the Central Union Church on the outskirts of Honolulu, designed in 1922 by Ralph Adams Cram, the well-known American exponent of Georgian Colonial religious architecture; the First Church of Christ Scientist, designed the next year by local architect Hart Wood in a remarkably contemporary manner; and the Izumo Taishakyo Mission, closely copied from a Japanese Shinto temple at

about the same time by one Hego Fuchino. Another mainland architect of repute brought to Hawaii for several
commissions was Bertram Grosvenor Goodhue, designer in
relaxed romantic styles, who began in 1925 the planning of
the Honolulu Academy of Arts. Generally considered by
both laymen and critics to be the public building most at
home in the Hawaiian atmosphere, the design was completed
(and simplified) by a local architect named Hardie Phillips.

The residential areas of the city spread first into the lower
foothills and then stretched out in both directions along the
coast. While many of the houses built during the territorial
period were modest (a kind of single-wall simplified frame
construction, used even today, was developed), the new affluence attained by so many during the period showed in the
homes they created for themselves. Two architects of considerable creativity added a good deal of originality to the
work of the 1920s and 1930s. One was Hart Wood, who had
practiced in San Francisco before he moved to Hawaii in
1919; the other was Charles W. Dickey, raised in the islands
but absent for study and practice on the mainland until he
returned in 1934. Dickey devised a residential style with
sweeping, overhanging roofs that fitted the Hawaiian landscape well; Wood had a general practice that produced not
only houses but several distinguished commercial and religious buildings; together they designed one of downtown
Honolulu's most handsome structures, the home building for
the Big Five company Alexander & Baldwin.

Another industry that was to become a major user of Hawaii's lands in many parts of the islands noticeably emerged
at this time: tourism. Recognized as a potential addition to
the territory's primary agricultural economy even in the previous century, the commerical entertainment of visitors did
not amount to much as a business until several fairly large
hotels were built at Waikiki. First the Moana Hotel as early
as 1901 and then the luxurious Royal Hawaiian and the more
modest Halekulani in the 1920s made Waikiki seem a busy
place compared to the restful recreation spot for American

and Hawaiian kamaainas that it had been. Now, however, large aircraft were bringing visitors across the Pacific from the American mainland in a bit over twenty hours. Local entrepreneurs saw signs of a sizable new industry.

By 1940 Honolulu had grown truly to city stature from its small-town size at the turn of the century; a panoramic photograph taken that year might be a picture of any of hundreds of American municipalities of the time. But it was an insular community in more ways than one. As troubled war times approached, Hawaii did not seem to sense them. The only problem that worried the haole elite was the increase in size of the nonwhite population and its growing independence. Both the workers of Japanese ancestry and the more recently arrived Filipinos had begun to form into labor unions, and many of their children, along with those of Chinese and other non-Caucasian groups, were crowding the public schools.

The Hawaiians seemed no longer a problem; they grumbled occasionally about loss of their land, but they provided an interesting cultural-historic background to display as additional enticement to the visiting tourists. Occasional moves toward statehood for the territory were made, but many haoles feared full inclusion in the American juridical-political system more than they wished complete citizenship.

There was little realization that major changes had already taken place in Hawaiian society, changes that would alter the islands' political pattern and strongly affect the way its lands would be used. The workers who had been brought to the plantations had already reached numerical dominance in the population of Hawaii. Now they aspired toward economic and political strength—just as the war with the original homeland of their largest component, those with ancestry in Japan, was about to break violently on the islands.

chapter 3

The Lure of the New

THE bombs that fell on Pearl Harbor during the morning of
7 December 1941 not only destroyed eighteen American war-
ships, they shattered Hawaii's insular complacency as well.
They set in motion forces that altered the islands' social
order drastically; that ended one-party political dominance;
that moved sugar-and-pine agriculture from first place in
Hawaii's economy to a position below tourism and expenditures by the military; that above all hastened the addition of
Hawaii as the fiftieth state in the union of the United States
of America and the inclusion of its people as fully qualified
citizens. And the new forces once more altered the uses to
which the islands' lands were put and again changed the
ways in which those lands were owned and valued.

The period from 1940 on has been a time of rapid Americanization, in every respect, of all the various groups of people that had come together or been brought together on the
Hawaiian Islands. The first touch of American policy and
power was uncomfortable: during the war years Hawaii
was governed by a military commission.[1] Martial law was
imposed and most civil rights were suspended. The islands
became a huge staging area and much more land, of course,

was taken for military purposes. Two-fifths of the population, the Americans of Japanese ancestry (often called AJAs) were at best kept under suspicious scrutiny and in many cases deported to mainland detention camps.

The years between the end of the war in 1945 and the achievement of statehood in 1959 were a time of turbulent readjustment, a shuffling of almost the entire population into new positions in a society that had been shaken awry. To some it meant the first chance for equal advancement and even the settling of old scores. To others it meant new or augmented business opportunities. To Hawaii as a whole, used to slow if steady lineal growth in population and economic stature, it meant the sudden start of an ascending exponential growth curve.

There were several elements in the Americanization process. One of the most important to the future of the islands was consummation of the upward movement of the habitants of oriental ancestry. Although it is often remarked that in Hawaii the nisei (children of first-generation Japanese immigrants, which most adult Japanese Hawaiians were at this stage) did not suffer the same physical and emotional wartime injuries as those on the mainland (how could the territory intern 40 percent of its residents?), there were hardships imposed and insults offered that were not easy to forget.[2] Those AJAs who served with soldierly distinction during the war formed into battalion, regimental, and even special intelligence alumni clubs afterward. Many used their G.I. Bill of Rights benefits to study on the mainland (largely law it would seem) and they were ready to take full advantage of the social shake-up that followed the war's disruptions. It was politics and the professions that primarily attracted the Hawaiian citizens of Japanese descent, and their power over Hawaii's lands as political decision makers became very strong in the postwar and particularly in the poststatehood periods.

The Americanization movements of the Chinese descendants tended more toward business proprietorship, as indeed

it had ever since the first coolies began leaving the plantations to go to the towns. After the war such entrepreneurial
figures appeared as Chinn Ho, Clarence T. C. Ching and
two other Chings, the brothers Hung Wo and Hung Wai,
and Hiram Fong (who mingled careers as financier and
United States senator), many of whom became involved in
land development either directly or through its financing.
These ethnic-group interests were not rigidly distinct, of
course; several Chinese Hawaiians in addition to Senator
Fong became important figures in the political sphere, and a
number of Japanese Hawaiians successfully entered business,
including contracting and land development. In addition, the
increasing number of Filipinos, the Portuguese who had
stayed in the islands from earlier days, and other groups
joined the upward movement to some extent and had their
representatives in political positions and the business world.

It was that world of commerce and industry which became
the second important element in Hawaii's Americanization.[3]
The scope of the activities of the old-time firms increased as
they became involved in many diversified undertakings in addition to plantation agriculture. For this they needed corporate executives with broader experience than island activities
had provided for the local people, and malihini faces
appeared even in the Big Five administrative councils.

Another development was the appearance in Hawaii of
new business organizations, branches of mainland establish-
ments and enterprising individuals, to compete in commercial
activities that were already under way or to begin new industries. Under such impacts, the complacent old understandings
that had divided local business benefits among the kamaainas
were quite quickly replaced with a more typical American
kind of competition.

A third element in the Americanization process was growth
of a true two-party political system in the islands.[4] Revitali-
zation of the nearly moribund Democratic party came from
several factors: hard work by younger progressives who saw
conditions changing; restlessness of Hawaiian, part-Hawai-

ian, and other depressed ethnic groups; political action by
militant leaders of Hawaii's first strong labor union, the
ILWU; and clever manipulation of all these forces, particularly the ambitious AJAs, by a Montana-born, Kalihi-raised
former Honolulu police officer named John Anthony Burns.
The result was a political organization that was to dominate
Hawaiian politics for at least twenty years. In what is known
locally as the Revolution of 1954, Democrats captured the
state legislature and two years later Jack Burns was elected
delegate to Congress.

Earlier ambivalence about the desirability of statehood had
pretty well disappeared by the time Burns arrived in Washington and began the necessary political maneuverings to
bring favorable congressional action. It took several years,
but in 1959 Hawaii did become the fiftieth state. Now the
delegate to Congress would be replaced by two senators and
a representative (later, as population grew, two). The governor would no longer be appointed by a president holding
office in the nation's capital four thousand miles away but
would be elected by the islands' own citizens. Hawaii was
part of America, politically if not physically, and its people
were Americans, by political circumstance if by neither
heredity nor environment. In 1959, those people elected
William F. Quinn, who had been the last territorial governor,
as the first governor of the state. Four years later, Burns
defeated and replaced him.

To a remarkable degree all these paths to Americanism
focused on attitudes toward land. Hawaii's lands had been
through several stages of change since Cook's time, and now,
under the teachings and the pressures of American business
enterprise, they entered a new phase of valuation, utilization,
and even ownership. The American concept of the "highest
and best" use of land appeared a reasonable principle to the
new nationals, and the American method of taxing real property on its assessed potential worth, rather than its present
use, seemed a good way to maximize public gain from this
most plentiful resource.[5] The extent to which values had

changed since the Polynesian Hawaiians had considered that
the best use for land was to support life was now very clear.

In immediate terms the newly introduced precepts meant
that plantation agriculture had to be questioned: was that activity land's highest and best use in an expanding island
economy? An organized labor force was achieving higher
wages; competition in the production of sugar and pineapple
was increasing on the world market; agricultural land, because of its reasonably level, accessible, buildable expanse,
was becoming desirable for new, urban uses. To some landowners, the highest and best use of land, for the time being,
was to hold it off the market while its value increased. Some
complicated economic-social-public policy formulas and some
sophisticated land planning studies were now needed to weigh
sugar-and-pineapple agriculture against diversified farming,
to measure the islands' own needs and the outside markets
for various potential products, to balance loss of arable lands
against mounting demands for housing and community services, to calculate immediate and long-term tax revenues
from alternative land-use possibilities. Hawaii's territorial
government had in time included a Planning Office, but it
had neither the expertise nor the impulse to make the necessary studies of costs and benefits for the public good.

Hawaii's postwar legislators were not blind to the new
trends in land uses, however. Nor were they unmindful of the
effects of concentrated land ownership on the islands' people, their constituents. It was no longer only the land-poor
Hawaiians and part-Hawaiians who worried about land for
housing. The plantation workers of various backgrounds
who had lifted themselves to a new status—which, they felt,
should warrant home ownership—were also having difficulty
finding places to live.[6] In addition, the increasing numbers of
malihini haoles moving to America's tropical outpost were
finding that land for living on was tightly held by the state
itself or a handful of private owners.

Although it always seems to a newcomer that Hawaii has
vast expanses of available land for any purpose, a large part

of it is unsatisfactory for either farming or building. More than half of Oahu's surface is too steep for residential construction; only about 10 percent of the state's land is truly arable. And the best land for farmers to till is also the easiest for developers to build on. As population continued to increase, it was clear that one of the two uses had to give way to the other. As Thomas P. Gill, a leader of progressive forces in the legislature, said during the 1961 session, the land problems in Hawaii were shortage and monopoly.[7]

Thus Hawaii was caught on the horns of a dilemma that was not unique to the islands but seemed sharper there than elsewhere. More land was needed for urban development, particularly housing, and yet there were strong reasons for keeping the plantations and other open spaces intact. The economy of the state, it seemed, was still largely dependent on sugar and pine,[8] and most landowners had no desire to break up their holdings until other uses could be proved more profitable. Land control legislation, in this situation, took two directions: toward broadening of land ownership, ostensibly to make more housing construction possible; toward maintaining the plantation holdings in order to protect agricultural land from urban expansion. These two aims presented a dichotomy that has never been resolved.[9]

With these cross-purposes, land became a major political issue. The legislatures of the last years of the territory and the early years of statehood were so deeply concerned with land that its problems cut "to the very core of Hawaii's polity . . . connected in one way or another with virtually every major political issue on the Islands," as one observer noted.[10] To some the political differences seemed primarily a divergence on party lines: a stand of the Republicans—strongest in the Senate—still favoring the concentration of power (and of land ownership) that had characterized Hawaiian society for many decades versus a position of the Democrats—dominant, now, in the House—leaning toward a more egalitarian division of resources and a more democratic participation in the benefits of island life (including land

tenure).[11] Legislative debates during the 1950s and 1960s
indicated such a distinction between "conservative" and
"liberal" party policies. Indeed, some of the Young Turk
Democrats were seriously concerned with the social aspects
of better-distributed land ownership and better-provided
home ownership, and many of the die-hard Republicans still
spoke in patrician terms. The basic political struggle, however, was between the (weakening) hold of plantation agriculture on the economy and the (increasing) strength of the
forces of urban development—and this issue often cut across
party lines.

The stakes were high in these conflicts; both the power
that accrues to land ownership and the profits that land uses
can bring were at issue. Political figures found it difficult to
be objective. As the earlier territorial legislatures had included many members who were involved in plantation agriculture, now a large number at both state and county levels
were interested, one way or another, with development and
construction.

As singleness of land use was under attack, so was cen-
trality of land ownership. Four estates owned a third of
Oahu; less than a hundred owners held half of all Hawaii's
land, and 40 percent more was in government hands. A
number of legislative moves made at that time were directed
toward greater distribution of land ownership. Governor
Quinn had a program, proudly labeled the Second Mahele,
which proposed selling 145,000 acres of state land, for
private housing construction, at $50 an acre.[12] Some called it
the Great Hoax, pointing out that much of the land involved
was leased to plantations and much of the rest was unsuitable for house construction. The Democrats favored further
changes in taxation of privately held land, changes intended
to penalize owners who were keeping off the market land
considered essential for housing.[13] Legislation to raise taxes
on such "nonproductive" property was offered in various
forms during the 1959 and 1960 legislatures.

The first state legislature, in 1961, saw the most intense

partisan struggle over this type of legislation, Senate and House producing different versions of a land/tax reform bill.[14] A conference committee tried to resolve differences through three time extensions of the session made by the governor, but they failed. In succeeding years, as the Democrat majority grew larger, further bills intending to break up the large holdings were passed, but they had small effect. Some estate lands were made available as fee-simple house sites and a great deal more were opened up as leaseholds. In the main, however, the large landowners have succeeded in keeping their land intact while that is to their advantage, letting it go in increments as land values have increased.[15]

All these moves, whether Democrat or Republican, had the basic intention of forcing land development—the endeavor that seemed most desirable in that period of expansion. Republican Governor Quinn, urging his Second Mahele on the 1961 legislature, argued that selling state land would be "sometimes the only way to attract developers."[16] Democratic representative David McClung introduced a bill for a double-taxation system on private land (the so-called Pittsburgh law, where land is assessed at a higher value than buildings on it)—intending it, he explained, to "give a tax break" to the most highly developed land.[17] Soon after this system became law in Hawaii, it was apparent that there was no need to attract developers. The problem might now be to restrain them, and in 1977 the state legislature repealed the proviso.

Moves to Manage the Land

The other kind of land legislation that Hawaii enacted during this transitional period had to do with the ways land was used rather than who owned it. Land use management at the state level was a new concept at that time. It obviously required analysis of the most appropriate (not necessarily the economic highest and best) uses for specific land areas. It needed careful land use planning, in short. Planning of this kind had been recommended by a firm of planners, Harland Bartholomew & Associates, in 1957, in a study sponsored by both government and private land-owners.[18] The firm's report urged that data be gathered from the federal Soil Conservation Service and other sources for preparation of a territory-wide land use plan. That same year a Land Study Bureau was established, to be operated by the University of Hawaii, to classify all lands in the territory by scientific methods; an act was passed that extended and regulated land uses in the forest and water reserves; the island-counties were mandated to prepare long-range land use plans; and a Territorial Planning Office was set up and assigned the task of preparing a general plan to guide physical and economic growth.[19]

The general plan was completed as Hawaii became a state, the first such statewide plan in the nation. It was a remarkably forthright, laudably progressive document, with the great flaw that most general plans have: it lacked any potential of implementation. One important recommendation in the body of its text was, however, carried out—a proposal that the legislature devise and adopt land-use and land-classification legislation with the teeth the general plan lacked. The lawmakers acted on this recommendation in the 1961 legislative session, and Hawaii became the first state in the nation to legislate land use management on a broad basis.

Act 187 of 1961, which became known as the State Land Use Law, established a Land Use Commission, to be appointed by the governor, with the primary function of districting and classifying all lands in Hawaii in three categories: conservation, urban, and agriculture (a fourth category, rural, was added several years later but has been little used). The law required that after all lands had been so classified—zoned, in effect—classifications and regulations be reviewed "comprehensively" every five years. It empowered the commission, moreover, to act on applications for changes in classifications (district boundaries, in the law's terminology) at any time it saw fit between reviews. The law also revised methods of appraisal for taxation purposes, incorporating elements of the Pittsburgh plan, and provided for dedication of land to agricultural purposes for tax benefits.[20]

Hawaii's people, even its legislators, did not seem to recognize at the time the importance of the law that had been passed.[21] During the busy 1961 session, Honolulu's two newspapers scarcely noticed its passage. A study of the politics of land in that session, published by two intelligent observers, concentrated on the land ownership bills and virtually ignored the passage of Act 187. The Democrats seemed content to let Governor Quinn take credit for the "greenbelt bill," as it was first called, and to explain its purpose as "a pioneering step in the effort to achieve logical and orderly urban growth."[22]

It is difficult to understand how this advanced land-use legislation, almost a decade ahead of its time, found its way through a legislature so tangled in the politics of land ownership. One of its promoters insists that few people, including most legislators, understood its intent. Introduced by a coterie of the "revolutionary" Democrats as "A Bill for an Act Relating to the Zoning Powers of the State" and looked on by many simply as a means of putting Pittsburgh-law principles into effect, it was referred first to the Committee on County and Municipal Affairs and only later to the Committee on Lands. After three readings it passed, along with a number of other bills, at 2:53 A.M. on the ninetieth day of a session intended to last sixty days. The vote was 27–22, with the ayes including 26 Democrats and 1 Republican and the nays comprised of 16 Republicans and 6 Democrats.

Partisan politics continued to cloud any lofty purposes the law had. When the first commission, appointed by Republican Governor Quinn, began the process of land use classification, it was quickly "fired" (nonconfirmed) by the Democratic legislature.[23] This commission and a second one appointed by Quinn antagonized those who were protecting planned developments that might be hurt in the zoning process, and it was not until Democrat Burns was elected gover-

nor that the first working commission began its appointed
tasks. At first temporary land-use boundaries were set up by
the commission's staff, and in 1963 Harland Bartholomew &
Associates, with planner Donald Wolbrink as local partner,
was commissioned to recommend boundaries of permanent
land-use districts.[24] The zones were delineated by a combination of pragmatic observations and decisions and by what
scientific analyses could be made quickly from existing data.
By definition of the law, Urban districts were "areas characterized by city-like concentrations," and when these had been
determined they were increased to accommodate an estimated
1980 population. Agriculture districts were formed from
lands already being farmed and grazed and lands which the
university's Land Study Bureau had classified as arable. Conservation districts included the forest reserves that had
previously been set up, with additions and modifications (to
guard against flood and erosion, for instance). It was recognized that revisions would be necessary for some time "to
provide the opportunity for adjustments . . . which necessity
may demonstrate"—an accession which has provided
welcome excuses for affected landowners to request changes
for years to come.

Although land questions had become political issues before
passage of the Land Use Law, a new, nastier kind of land
politics now was invited. For the first time in Hawaii's
history, an attempt was being made to regulate by law the
uses to which land could be put. When a government adopts
regulatory policies, it stimulates those whose activities are being regulated to find ways to control the decisions that are
made, no matter what amount of intrigue that might entail.
Inevitably, in this case, those whose business was development of land or speculation in land would try to influence
the commission's decisions.

The commission's record of objectivity has been far from
unblemished, although the net effect of the law has undoubtedly been to constrain, if not, as one consultant firm
noted, to "minimize" the amount of "new lands converted

to Urban zoning on Oahu."[25] It protected prime agricultural
land to a considerable extent in the first decade of its operation and restrained land speculation somewhat for a while.
There was a drop from 2,000 open-space acres shifted to
urban uses in the four years before passage of the law to
1,600 in the first four years afterward—but then applications
for rezoning to the Urban category zoomed up to an *annual*
rate of more than 1,200 acres.

The law gave to the commission—a politically appointed,
nonprofessional body—very broad regulatory powers. There
were no policy guidelines to follow.[26] The original land
classification and the two five-year reviews that have been
held were made by professional planners who had to set certain policy criteria for themselves and their clients; but the
free hand allowed the commission for boundary revisions at
any time between reviews inevitably invited political persuasion.[27] Except in very broad terms, the original legislation set
no goals or objectives; it simply established procedural functions. Not until 1977, sixteen years later, was an attempt
made to establish policy guidelines.

In these circumstances different understandings of the
intent of the law were embraced by conservation and
proagricultural groups of citizens on the one hand and by
prodevelopment groups on the other. The commission was
left to choose between them. Generally speaking, decisions to
release land to the speculative market as a commodity, presumably for ultimate development, have been more rewarding and less costly in a political sense than decisions to
conserve land as open space. Hence many reclassifications
from Agriculture and even Conservation to Urban have been
made, decisions which not only reduced the amount of
agricultural land but often destroyed important scenic and
recreational areas.[28]

Although the zone recommendations made by Bartholomew were not unduly "affected nor influenced by property
ownership" or "specific plans for development," the commission's decisions "were contrary to [their] recommenda-

tions in a few instances" in the original border-setting, the
planners noted. Almost immediately after that job of land
classification was completed the commission was faced with
an important and difficult decision. Oceanic Properties, the
development arm of Castle & Cooke, had for some years
been making plans to develop a large community of homes
on the upper-central Oahu plains at Waipio, just below the
old plantation town of Wahiawa. The proposal had attracted
much attention and no little controversy when it was first
advanced in 1960, a year before the Land Use Law was
passed. A "new town" was planned (well planned, in fact,
by an experienced mainland group) on two thousand acres of
land—this community, it was promised, would provide
homes costing only $15,000 and would include all the other
essential urban appurtenances: recreation, education, even.
employment. All this was to be on land which the commission zoned, in its first classification Agriculture, since it was
arable plantation land. To his discomfiture, the developer-
landowner had to take his proposal to the Land Use
Commission, when that body was set up, and apply for
reclassification of the land. At the first go-round the commission members, five to three, disapproved the application.
One member, Robert Wenkam, a conservationist photo-
grapher and writer, argued against the petition long and, it
seemed, successfully. If this change in use should be granted,
he said, it would be "only the beginning," would "open the
gates," would in fact "make the Land Use Law meaningless."[29] Nevertheless, after there had been time for suasion
and reconsideration, the commission reversed its decision and
granted the reclassification, by a vote of six to two, of some
seven hundred acres.[30]

As this development has grown through the years (by 1977,
1,435 acres had been granted on six approved petitions), it
has provided attractive homes for many of Hawaii's upper-
middle-class citizens; but the promise of $15,000 homes has
of course never been fulfilled, and the industries which were
to provide local employment have never appeared. Mililani

New Town, as it is now known, is a huge bedroom community whose residents must travel on clogged highways to their work and entertainments elsewhere. The Land Use Commissioners had concluded arbitrarily that the most appropriate use of a large part of Oahu's plains, which they themselves had just decided should remain as agricultural land, became, when a developer asked for it, a site for suburban home building. The commission had set its own policy guidelines.

The commission has indicated through its life how impossible it is in contemporary Hawaii for a public agency to be objective about land use questions: its members are almost certain to be biased, if not involved personally in activities connected with the land. Conflicts of interest have been charged against four Land Use Commission members. When Shiro Nishimura of Kauai was appointed to the commission in 1963, he boasted that he now would be able to "get things done." One thing he did accomplish, in 1969, was to form a hui which bought 136 acres of land on his home island for $325,000, land which the commission rezoned to urban uses later that year and was sold, then, for $900,000. Governor Burns had to ask Nishimura to resign under these circumstances, which he did "for reasons of ill health." Commissioner Wilbert Choi, a landscape gardener, participated in a vote which made possible his continuing use of land on Oahu as a nursery. Commissioner C. E. S. Burns voted on a number of occasions when firms with which he was connected were involved (as an instance, on lands at Lahaina and Kaanapali owned by American Factors, of which he was a vice-president), as did Commissioner Alex Napier (voting to rezone lands of the Kahua Ranch on the Big Island, of which he was an officer).

In 1960, the attorney general of the state was asked by Governor Burns to investigate these incidents. His report "pulled no punches," as a newspaper story said, in labeling many actions of these commissioners as instances of "conflict of interest."[31] It did, however, draw back from considering them criminal wrongdoing, even though it noted that

some of the votes in question had been "critical," in the
sense that the rezoning request would have been denied without them. In any event, no action was taken as a result of
the inquiry.

On the original commission, Robert Wenkam continued to
be an obstreperous member. He voted, for instance, against
rezoning land that would have permitted a cluster home
development on Pacific Heights in which some political
figures were reputedly involved. He failed to receive recon-
firmation of his appointment in 1966: his name was held in
committee in the Senate until it was too late to go before the
floor.[32] Later appointees were more willing to bend with the
varying winds that swayed Hawaii's land use decisions in the
1960s and into the 1970s. In August 1969, Eddie Tangen, an
ILWU executive officer, was appointed to the commission by
the governor. Tangen quickly became the strong voice on the
commission, and before long he was made its vice-chairman
and then its chairman, serving until 1977. From time to time
he too was accused of voting with a conflict of interest in the
outcome.[33] The ILWU (sometimes working for continued
agricultural jobs and sometimes for additional hotel employment) could undoubtedly benefit by having one of its top
executives in a land-use decision-making position. In 1973 the
State Ethics Commission cited Tangen for unethical practices, but a court ruled that the charges were unfounded,
since it would be unfair "to leave agricultural workers
voiceless while the lands on which they work are being swept
out from under them." The good judge, in his eloquence,
forgot or ignored the fact that Tangen could vote to sweep
land in either direction that he and ILWU chose, toward
farming or toward development.

In 1968 the first review of land use classifications was
made. Professional consultants (Eckbo, Dean, Austin & Williams) did a thorough, analytical job: their report included
recommendations for a number of changes in the law's
operation that would have tightened up procedures and
defined more closely the commission's duties, but none were

adopted. On the contrary, early in the 1970 legislative session
a bill was introduced (known to many, irreverently, as the
God Bill) that would have broadened the commission's
powers to an alarming extent.[34] It was not passed nor yet
rejected; it was simply allowed to lie quiet for the time.

The effect of Hawaii's Land Use Law, once studied as prototype legislation by other states, is now widely questioned.
In judging "effectiveness" of this legislation, however, the
changes that have taken place in value judgments of land use
must be remembered. Even in economic terms the impulses
for land preservation have changed sharply in the past decade. "New concepts of land-use management are emerging
with the current awakening of ecological principles and the
realization that land is a finite resource," notes a 1975
publication of the Council of State Governments.[35] The purpose of the Land Use Law of 1961 was set forth in its preamble: "Inadequate controls have caused many of Hawaii's
limited and valuable lands to be used for purposes that may
have a short-term gain to a few but result in a long-term loss
to the income and growth potential of our economy."[36]
There were other phrases about "uses best suited for the
public welfare," but the key words are "loss to the income
and growth potential of our economy." There is nothing
about the contribution of nonurban spaces to the unique
physical quality of Hawaii, about their scenic, aesthetic
worth or their recreative value—and certainly not a word
about the environmental harm that accelerating loss of green
open land would bring. If goals had been set to guide the
commission in 1961, they likely would have been ambivalent
then and unsatisfactory today.

The plantations devoted to the production of sugarcane
and pineapple, limited as the basic agricultural importance of
those crops is, had constituted an "industry" that by its
nature had kept vast expanses of Hawaii's lands open. When
the economy changed and urban development of those lands
became, in commercial terms, their highest and best use,
there might well be "loss to the income" of the state in try-

ing to keep them open. The premises on which the landmark law had been drawn had changed by the 1970s; in a way, the law itself was out of date. Land use legislation by then had other bases, some social and environmental, some built around totally different economic understandings than had prevailed in the early years of Hawaii's statehood.

Hawaii's 1961 Land Use Law is generally considered a strong forward move in land management legislation: an advance action in "the quiet revolution" in land use controls.[37] In another sense, though, it must be thought of as a last-ditch effort to protect agriculture as a commercial enterprise. In Hawaii, that meant protection of the grip that sugar-and-pine agriculture had so long held on the islands' economy, whether the plantation landowners still wanted it or not. The sponsors of House Bill 1279, which became Act 187, considered it an important step in the succession of land planning measures that had begun in 1957; they were anxious to keep farmlands green in land use plans, which is what the label "greenbelt" meant to imply. The plantation landowners did not originate or support the legislation, but neither did they actively oppose it. For some years after the law's passage, they were pleased to benefit from its taxation provisions. After all, when they were ready they could apply for reclassification with reasonable assurance of success. Efforts in the legislature to "repeal" Act 187, for several years after its passage, were instigated by land developers, not agricultural landowners.[38]

The Surge in Population

The pressures for urbanization of additional land were not based on unfounded speculation alone but resulted from a tremendous surge in urban population, along with the expanding economy, in the early years of statehood. Hawaii's population, after a long period of near stability, had begun rising on a steep path at the turn of the century. The number of residents was about 150,000 in 1900, having risen from some 85,000 in 1850; but in the next half century, by 1950, it had increased to approximately 500,000. That growth total, accounted for largely by importation of plantation workers, had enlarged to more than 750,000 people by the time of the 1970 census, a 50 percent rise in two decades produced by a very different kind of immigrant, mostly from the mainland United States.

Much of the population increase during that period was on Oahu and a large part of that in the previously rural areas outside Honolulu proper. The Hawaiian and part-Hawaiian percentage had dropped, as had the Japanese-descended proportion, while the Caucasian share of the populace rose from 25 to 40 percent. For a number of postwar years the neighboring islands lost permanent residents and Oahu gained them sharply, as plantation workers moved to city jobs in the changing economy.[39]

While the major urban centers on the other islands grew in size, rather slowly, the City and County of Honolulu (encompassing the entire island of Oahu) spread out further into new suburbs as it also increased in height and density in its older sections. Urban tentacles stretched along the coast to Makapuu Point at the island's eastern end and crept around to the windward side. Along these extensions nodules grew: Kahala, an area of former pig farms just beyond Diamond Head, had already become a fashionable suburb; Henry Kaiser, leasing Bishop Estate land, began development of a huge master-planned project at Koko Head, known as Hawaii Kai; in between, middle-class American-type tract houses surged up the valleys as far as safely buildable land allowed, and sometimes further; at Kaneohe and Kailua, around the eastern point, suburban growth was so rapid that two highways were built across the Koolaus to serve them and a third to be called H3, was planned.[40]

In the other direction, the civilian military activities at Pearl Harbor and various other defense installations in that area pulled population that spawned suburbs at Aiea, Pearl City, and Waipahu. A light industrial park development at

Barbers Point by the Campbell Estate drew more people
westward, and Castle & Cooke proceeded rapidly to build
Mililani Town. In most cases the State Land Use Commission and the counties' planning commissions and councils
obligingly reclassified and rezoned these lands from agricultural to urban use as they were requested by landowners and
developers.

In Honolulu itself the growth was upward. While some
enclaves remained much as they had been in the previous
period—the early settlement called Kaimuki, once the end of
the streetcar line; the haphazard small-business stretch adjacent to downtown known as Kakaako; the old residential
areas of Kalihi and Palama on the other side of midtown
(once admired by Mark Twain as the prettiest part of town,
destined later to become a Model Cities poverty area)—and
while downtown itself remained for some time a sleepy backdrop for the harbor, other parts of the inner city boomed.

The Dillinghams, for instance, used a stretch of reclaimed
swampland called Ala Moana, just on the downtown side
of Waikiki, to build one of the world's largest and most
successful shopping centers in 1959. The first high-rise
apartment house appeared in Waikiki in 1954, and in 1961
mainland architect Minoru Yamasaki designed a handsome
apartment cluster, the Queen Emma Gardens, near downtown. By the early 1960s the city was losing its moderately
low, reasonably uncrowded look and starting on the road to
metropolitan densities. The condominium ownership technique became popular even on leasehold land, where in the
long run no one except the original trust could own anything.
High-rise apartments began to appear in unlikely, scattered
places, since the city's zoning map had ignored visual considerations. Valuable sight lines and view planes were lost as
tall, often bulky, generally unrelated structures were built—
up the sides of Punchbowl, into Nuuanu Valley, back of
Waikiki, on the close-in slopes of lower Makiki Heights, at
the base of Diamond Head, in Kahala, and of course as part
of the burgeoning Hawaii Kai environs.

Downtown developed in the late 1960s as an office center rather than a commercial core, and high-rise office buildings joined the new apartments to mold the three-dimensional character of Honolulu toward mainland models. In Waikiki the change was rapid from a restful retreat for visitors in a few hotels to a bustling center of tourist-shuffling activities. Kamaainas shuddered and remembered Waikiki's old days; hordes of happy travelers filled its new rooms as quickly as they could be built; the tourist "industry" could not have been more contented. Regular air service had boosted the early trickle of vacationers and sightseers to a steady stream in the first part of the century, and the first jet planes that flew between Hawaii and the U.S. mainland in 1959 opened the floodgates. In the 1950s there were fewer than 100,000 visitors annually; by 1976 that figure had grown to 3 million. Such an influx demanded space accommodations, of course, and the approximately 1,000 hotel rooms that had been available after the war (an astronomical figure *that* had seemed at the time) jumped to over 40,000 in 1976. And more continued to be built.[41]

Waikiki's phenomenon was based on high-density land use, but elsewhere the new hotels and resort complexes spread out over miles of the most attractive oceanfront land. Much of the agricultural and conservation land that was changed to "urban" uses by the Land Use Commission, to be administered by the counties, was developed to attract tourist visitors, not to satisfy needs of the local population. As physical development increased in the towns and resort areas, and especially as Honolulu grew to metropolitan magnitude, building design and city planning arrangements should have become important considerations, but in these respects the urban quality worsened in the 1960s and 1970s. Outside Honolulu, some of the earlier unsophisticated charm remained. In a few places (Lahaina on Maui, for instance) it was retained consciously through preservation; elsewhere it became, in time, haphazardly mixed with the new construction.

In Honolulu the trend was toward mainland big-city

modernism—without benefit of the creative talents that megalopolitan architecture needs in order to have form and visual organization. Many island youths studied architecture in mainland schools and some returned to the islands converted to new design fancies. Mainland architects founded practices in Hawaii in some numbers, either permanently or to establish outpost offices to capture local commissions. Few, of either local or off-island origin, succeeded in designing anything in Hawaii that seemed to belong in Hawaii. In the way it used its central-city land, Honolulu, which could have had its own colorful tropical character, matured as carelessly and as drearily as any other American metropolis.

As the 1970s became Hawaii's present reality, with the postwar expansion years of the '40s, '50s, and '60s now left behind as part of the islands' past history and the 1980s looming as the start of a problematic future, it was clear that once more in Hawaii "an era had come to its end." That was the phrase used in the state legislature's 1974 session as retiring Governor Burns, aging and ill but still an erect and distinguished figure, made a farewell address. Several of the House and Senate members who had sat there since the 1954 political revolution also said good-bye.

Already there were restive signs of opposition to the unrestrained growth which had marked the era. But there were also indications that any such movement would meet strong counteraction. In April 1974, a heated hearing that lasted fifteen hours during two days brought out advocates and opponents of the proposed third freeway—up a third green valley rich with early Hawaiian artifacts, across land classified as conservation—to provide a new link that everyone knew would encourage further development on the windward Oahu coast.

One of the speakers was Luka Nalui, representing a Hawaiian and part-Hawaiian community in Kahaluu near the windward end of the intended highway. She was head of a group that called itself Hui Malama 'Aina O Ko'olau (Those Who Care for the Windward Lands), some of whom lived on kuleanas their families had held since the Great Mahele. She feared, in a voice moved with emotion, that another remainder of the old Hawaiian life on the land would be lost to more high-priced suburbs.

But David McClung, then president of the State Senate (a native of Michigan who had joined the resurgent Democrats in Hawaii and been admitted to the local bar in 1957) and later a losing candidate for the governor's office, testified in favor of the freeway. McClung spoke with a different kind of emotion. If the construction's opponents were so worried about Hawaii's population growth, he said, "they should help solve the problem by resigning from the human race and allow the rest of us more room to breathe."[42] While this may have been an exaggerated comment on the polarities that existed, there were clearly sharp differences between values that motivated Hawaii's people as the postwar decade drew to a close, a time which had started with such promise of true aloha.

chapter 4

Memories and Expectations

AS Hawaii prepared to enter a new era in its history the people were torn between two opposing desires. One was a wish to save as much as possible from a past that was remembered with fond nostalgia; the other was a hope to gain as much as possible from a future that promised unparalleled prosperity. Hawaii's old customs and their settings were still revered in memory while Hawaii's new activities and the environments they needed were replacing them in fact. When the islands officially joined the New World as an American state they carried with them many memories and much material from their past. A nagging problem has been what to do with this cargo: how to save much of the old without having it interfere with the new.

The past that Hawaii's people recall is as oddly mixed as their origins. To those of Hawaiian descent, it is the Polynesian time that is revered and the monarchy period that is remembered with pride. Many kamaainas have recollections of a more recent patriarchal time. One charming elderly lady, an ardent conservationist, reminisced in a talk to a gathering at the Honolulu Academy of Arts about the rice fields that once lay close to the city's heart, where Chinese plowed with slow-moving water buffalos. She recalled this stage in the movement of the Chinese Hawaiians away from contracted labor on the plantations as a "picturesque" time that provided "amusing sights" to her and her haole friends as they rode by in their carriages.[1]

The aspect of preservation that has caused most soul-searching is the presence, in sizable amount, of early Hawaiian artifacts. Heiaus, house platforms, various walls, rock slides and other sport places, salt production ponds, remnants of wells, petroglyphs, burial caves pocking the hillsides—these and other remains of different times and diverse types, in varying conditions, can still be easily seen on all the islands if one wants to look for them. The watchful wanderer can even pick up smooth game stones, poi pounders, and such small relics. Without a preservation program, of course, these things are as easily lost as they are found.

Some parts of the islands, not yet exploited because of their inaccessibility, have changed little over the years. The route taken by the missionary Reverend William Ellis in an exploratory trek around the Big Island in 1824 was followed in 1973, in a reminiscent reenaction, by a group which the descendant of another missionary family, Thurston Twigg-Smith, headed. The assemblage included journalist Robert Krauss, who wrote an account of the trip, as Ellis had done 150 years earlier. These two described many places and objects, even people and their life-styles, in remarkably similar terms.[2]

On the other hand, where modernism has intruded there has been a distressing deterioration of artifactual history. Even Ellis' journal of his trip, written soon after the death of Kamehameha I, reported neglect of earlier structures. At Kukaniloko on Oahu stand old Hawaiian "birth stones" where royal mothers bore those destined to be alii—dating, one authority believes, from the twelfth century. Today, beer cans and broken bottles are cleaned up periodically from the site by members of a local Hawaiian Civic Club.[3] On the island of Hawaii a landowner concerned with Hawaiian history keeps as her own secret the existence of burial caves on her property. She is afraid of pilfering.

The presence of artifacts cannot generally be ignored or concealed like that, however. They are so common that they become a nuisance to development activities, and there is constant conflict between the temptation to bulldoze ahead regardless of what aboriginal remains might be destroyed and the restraints of conscience or, in some cases, of law. Legislation does require field inspection before the construction of highways and certain other public works so that archaeologists may try to save any found objects. Moreover, environmental impact statements assessing potential harm to historic spots are called for under certain circumstances. What happens after that, though, is problematical. The Bishop Museum, institutional guardian of Hawaiian history, has a staff capable of identifying and evaluating items that might be located, and they continuously catalog classified material. Sometimes this information is requested and is gratefully received before development goes ahead; at other times it is deprecated or ignored. Even public agencies anxious to proceed with pet projects are impatient with the need for preservation; the State Department of Transportation has worked very hard to refute the testimony of archaeological experts about the worth of historic places and things that stood in the way of the projected H3 freeway in Moanalua Valley.[4]

Some few important heiaus and petroglyph sites are protected and maintained by county, state, and federal government, but capital acquisition costs and maintenance and operating expenses force such projects to low-priority positions in public works budgets. The outstanding historic conservation in Hawaii is the City of Refuge National Historic Park at Honauna on the south Kona coast of the Big Island—which includes the restoration of a heiau built by Keawe, ruling chief of the area several generations before Kamehameha's ascendancy, and expert reproduction of a number of other structures. It provides not only an illustra-

tion of the worth of such an effort but also an example of
the great cost involved, the need for professional control if
inaccuracies and superficialities are to be avoided, and the
risks of vandalism even when supervision is careful and
constant.

Tourism in Hawaii should be a potential force for preservation of artifacts, since it provides a commercial reason for
keeping them available and visible. Unfortunately the visitor
industry has not worked well as a guardian of history. The
restoration it has sponsored or tried to accomplish itself has
seldom been scholarly or thorough and the maintenance it
provides tends to be careless.[5]

The likelihood of a full program of conservation of
artifacts *in situ* that would be satisfactory to historians,
archaeologists, and serious conservationists seems dim. The
scope of the job is too great, costs are too high, official
interest is too low. The historic sites branch of the Division
of State Parks was mandated in 1969 to prepare such a program, but one of the nine professionals who resigned from
the activity by 1975 said that it was impossible to work "in
an atmosphere of distrust, lack of communication, misunder-
standing and annual threat of no funds, no jobs."[6] In 1975
the state legislature adopted an Environmental Policy Act
which bespoke a vague aim to "reserve scenic, historic,
cultural parks and recreational areas . . . for public recreational, educational and scientific uses"—without explaining
what those words meant or voting any funds to implement
them. An Environmental Quality Commission with no real
powers was also established.

The difficulty is a basic problem of value conflicts. To
preserve physical history, the land on which that history was
made and on which its artifacts remain would also have to be
preserved. In too many cases that would obviously interfere
with development.

Hawaii has also had its problems with preservation of
worthwhile *structures* from periods later than Polynesian
times. Like mainland America, the state has been wasteful

with its buildings, following the habit of tearing down in a few decades most of the urban construction that was earlier built at great cost and sometimes with great care. But in Hawaii the term "historic buildings" has somewhat different connotations than in mainland America and other western countries. For one thing, the time span is unique: anything built before 1900 is an aboriginal artifact; on the other hand, structures put up as late as the 1820s are considered historically significant.[7] Hence it is not easy for a conservationist to use conventional criteria in deciding what to keep and what to let go. Iolani Palace has undergone extensive and expensive restoration in recent times, not by reason of its design excellence (it is "pleasant, make-believe architecture,"[8] says its restoration architect) but because it is the only royal palace in the United States of America. It is easy to sympathize with bewildered lawmakers. During a crowded public hearing on a proposed city ordinance that would designate the capitol environs a historic-cultural-scenic district with special protective zoning, a councilman admitted his puzzlement to a community leader who was testifying. "It doesn't seem to me," he said, "that any of these buildings you want to preserve are old enough to be 'historic'." The witness agreed, but he added: "If we don't leave them there long enough to *get* old, they never *will* be historic."[9]

If there were contentions about saving the individual objects that covered the land with some evidence of historical continuity, they were small compared to the disaccord over preserving communities of people living in traditional and ethnically different ways. New developments must often destroy places where those older life-styles still exist, and the people living in them are seriously hurt—even though the land, by contemporary values, may be "improved."

Hawaiians and part-Hawaiians still furnish the most tragic instances of the destruction of earlier social and physical environments. Inevitably the Hawaiian population and the Hawaiian culture have become pocketed in the more remote parts of the islands where western man and his mores have not yet deeply penetrated. Into the 1960s and 1970s it was still possible for students of the Polynesian culture system to find viable remnants in places like Kau on the Big Island, Waihei on Maui, Koolau Loa on Oahu—and the island of Niihau, where the land's owners, the kamaaina Robinson family, will allow no non-Hawaiians, even as visitors. No program for continued preservation of this culture is even being considered, however. Only the more visible and audible parts of the struggle to maintain a special Hawaiian kind of life on the land are noticed—the people of Kahaluu, Waiahole, and Waikane fighting highway construction and subdivision development that would force them from kuleanas they dated back to the Great Mahele; the people of Niumalu on Kauai working to prevent development plans of a land estate (ironically, a trust benefiting wealthier Hawaiians) that would mark the end of their very old community; the pig farmers of Kalama Valley on Oahu forced out by Kaiser's development on Bishop Estate land, moving to the Waianae coast to be turned away again by highway construction leading to Chinn Ho's Makaha resorts; the small farmers on the Kona coast of Hawaii losing their coffee lands to retirement home developments.[10]

When immigrants from other countries began leaving the plantation company towns to find new opportunities, they grouped for some time in ethnically defined neighborhoods.[11] The Japanese seemed more venturesome than most, and parts of their early communities remain on all the islands, some still with traces of their original quality. The Chinese tended to move near Honolulu's harbor (although Chinatown, located there, soon became ethnically mixed), but they founded enclaves on other islands too. Their wish was to be close enough to established towns to find patronage for their new businesses yet far enough out to grow rice or taro or raise ducks. Portuguese, Koreans, Puerto Ricans, and others at times formed their own neighborhoods, but before long most of them were absorbed into the large communities or towns. As in cities on the mainland, waves of low-paid immigrants followed and replaced one another; the Filipinos, for example, took over large parts of Honolulu's Chinatown at one point and now Samoans are occupying many of the old buildings there.

As these neighborhoods lost much of their distinctive quality, the desire to maintain a life-style came to mean a wish to preserve a more rural and independent, less regimented and replicated (and certainly less costly) life on the land than the new developments allowed. The struggle against change became a battle against new development per se—and the argument that special cultures were threatened was used as an understandable, and forgivable, pretext.

As an instance, attempts in 1973 by the Honolulu Redevelopment Agency to make Chinatown's in-town real estate more productive were opposed by local residents (abetted by sentimental conservationists) who had learned to use the cliché terms of "preserving life-styles" and "keeping the Hawaiian way of life" when they really, and reasonably, wanted a continuance of cheap residential and commercial rents. In its turn the agency promised, with tongue in cheek, to preserve the "indigenous quality" of the area by pinpointing a few old buildings to be kept.[12]

Further muddling the confusion, malihinis bring with them to the islands other concepts of a "Hawaiian life-style." For the most part they want a life in Hawaii lived in single-family houses in single-family-house suburbs—just like the ones they occupied on the mainland, but with a lanai added. As more high-rise apartment houses and condominiums are built in the towns, the haoles (and the Orientals who follow them) are happy to find the same room arrangements they had in New York or Detroit or San Francisco, again with the outdoor appendage called now a lanai rather than a balcony.

To a certain extent, Hawaii is also ambivalent about preservation of the indigenous biota that its lands support. Only to a certain extent, however, because there are few besides scholars and specialists who really care, or even know, very much about the meaning of that word which has become so widely adopted in the conservation movement: ecology. Even for scholars there are subtle distinctions, for there have been several Hawaiian ecological systems. There was an ecology of sorts before the Polynesians arrived, whatever hard scratching was needed for existence. This ecology, as we noted, was radically altered when new plants were taken to Hawaii from other Polynesian islands further south and altered again when the white man came.

Since then there have been constant shocks to Hawaii's ecology; flora and fauna brought from many places through the nineteenth and twentieth centuries have continuously altered the balance that existed and destroyed species that were or had become locally adapted. Once there were a thousand or more plant species and at least a hundred birds endemic to the islands—that is, to be found nowhere else—and many more that had become indigenous—fully at home there. If endemic species disappear, they are gone forever, of course; and Hawaii has lost many, forced out of existence by newly imported exotics.[13]

This deprivation has distressed scientists and naturalists and the conservation societies. The responsible state agencies have done their best to check it, but ordinary citizens in Hawaii give little sign of caring. Fishermen and pet collectors continue to deplete the reefs of their many-colored, multi-shaped indigenous fish types, with only mild community concern. At one time some colorful parrots were imported to the Diamond Head district and at another an attempt was made to introduce a beautiful Brazilian toucan. They seemed appropriate, handsome additions to the local landscape, and the fact that they would endanger the existence of certain endemic but not too attractive birds stirred little local concern. The parrots stayed, but the State Board of Agriculture stood firm on forbidding the toucan. People who enjoy hunting as a sport have been trying for years to get permission, over the opposition of conservationist groups, to add axis deer to the quarry available on the Big Island (including feral goats and sheep). The state remains firm on this issue, too, since the import would be disastrous to much endemic plant material. The state even has plans to eliminate the goats and sheep in time, but no great popular support has been evident.[14]

Because all these nostalgias had to do with things that happened on and to Hawaii's lands, they clearly focused on the ways those lands themselves were treated. In recent decades there has been a growing awareness of the effects of pollution from so much building for so many people: awareness of the physical spoilage of the land, sea, and air that truly formed the "Hawaiian way of life." It had seemed impossible through the decades that the quality of the land in this Pacific island paradise could ever be impaired. Its ownership might shift from one proprietor to another, its uses might change, restrictive legislation might even be required, as in the Land Use Law, to protect its economic value. But vast open spaces and wide beaches would always remain, it was believed, kept green by the periodic rains and blown fresh by the constant tradewinds.

Yet suddenly, inconceivably, unhappy changes began to take place, and toward the middle of the twentieth century they were becoming sharply visible. Ugly scars appeared on prominent hills, formed by construction crews who, to flatten the slopes, pushed around the soil that thinly covered the lava and left it there—no longer able to guide the rain's runoffs but ready to erode and be carried along the valleys and into streams and estuaries and bays.[15] Low-lying areas where people lived began to flood for the first time in their history. Sandy coves started to fill with murky drainage running down from new tracts built above them.[16] The meaning of ecological systems was becoming clear by demonstration: Kaneohe Bay began to die, its coral reefs, which supported schools of particular fish, killed by sewage and construction wastes in the waters where the coral had lived.

At first only the serious-minded groups called in aspersion "environmentalists" protested, but soon the tangible evidences of spoilage of land and pollution of sea could no longer be ignored by anyone. Waikiki itself, key to visitor-industry income, found its beaches sometimes reaching dangerous bacterial-count levels. Incredibly, something approaching the nature of smog could be seen hovering over parts of the landscape; even the constant trade winds could not blow away all the increasing automobile emission. There was still reluctance to give the change its proper name. On a smoggy day in 1976 the *Advertiser* noted that "lack of the normal trade winds caused smoke from the Ewa Plantation to move over the Pearl Harbor–Pearl City area in a blanket effect." Nonetheless, protest over careless, harmful development on the land began to widen. Old-line organizations that had politely urged "beautification" of the environment over the years became almost belligerent over its salvation; new citizens groups were formed, some still reasonably respectful, others angrily activist.

When the story of public concern over pollution of the land is told about any place, however, one must always remember that only a minuscule segment of the citizenry is being described. Most of the people in Denver or Pittsburgh or Los Angeles or Honolulu are not concerned at all. Or else they are concerned only with the quality of their own immediate environment. This has certainly been true in Hawaii. The residents of Hawaii Kai have protested development of the shore near Hawaii Kai; those living in Lanikai have stormed over development on Mount Olomana above Lanikai; people living near Salt Lake have banded together to oppose the filling in and development of Salt Lake. Very few of them have worried about one another's troubles, and even fewer have thought about the long-term implications of the overall loss of open space on the islands. When one of Ralph Nader's "raiders" spent some time in Hawaii in the early 1970s and wrote a reasonably accurate description of the increasing environmental pollution, which he broadcast to travel agencies on the mainland, the general popular reaction was that such defamation was most unfair to the beauties of the tropical isles—not that an alarm had been sounded and should be heeded.[17]

The state administration and the state legislature reacted in

several ways to the increasing evidence of land spoilage and
land loss and to more insistent prods from the environmentally conscious (some of whom were managing to get themselves elected to Senate and House). Governor Burns'
response was to set up an Office of Environmental Quality
Control within his own office. It was to have, however, only
suasive powers, even though it was later bolstered by
appointment of an advisory commission.[18] The State Department of Health developed a pollution control "plan" with no
force.[19] The legislature's answer was to establish commissions
and appoint commission consultants to make studies of the
problem. None of these moves committed anybody; nor did
they stop anything. They were the discreet reactions of those
pressured on two sides by a society divided between a love
for what it saw it was losing and a yearning for what it
hoped it might gain.

The Yes . . . But Syndrome

This conflict between an emotional tug backward and a pragmatic pull forward not only results in many inconsistencies
and absurdities: it also makes life in Hawaii a euphoric
experience, lived in a sort of advertising-agency promotional
atmosphere. Hawaii's people are used to hearing a new condominium in Hawaii Kai described in television commercials
as being near "gentle waterfalls" and "secluded beaches,"
when they know that the community is becoming daily more
densely developed and heavily trafficked. The future is seen
through amber-tinted glasses because the vision of sustained
expansion looks better that way. There is a blind belief that
soft breezes will continue to blow away most of growth's
fumes and rolling surf will still lap up its wastes. Unwilling
to make a choice between conservation and expansion, the
state and its people want to believe that a kind fate will
somehow allow them a share in the best of both attractive
worlds. Since responsible people must face facts, the realities
of environmental deterioration have resulted in a reluctant,

qualified admission of loss. Hawaii is suffering from a
"yes . . . but" syndrome.

The growth of tourism is alarming, yes . . . but the visitor
industry is now the major source of the state's income. It
would be foolish to restrict it.

Population projections have become frightening, yes . . .
but (with an almost audible sigh of relief) everyone knows
that, constitutionally, nothing can be done about it. In 1972
Dr. Earl Babbie, university researcher, wrote a treatise which
he called *The Maximillion Report*.[20] Babbie demonstrated the
connection between an increasing population and a decreasing quality of life in Hawaii and suggested ways for the state
(even without testing possible constitutional restrictions on
limits to environmentally damaging growth) to hold the
number of its residents to one million people. Since the current total was something less than 800,000, that seemed to
give enough leeway to make the goal reasonable and even
possible.

Babbie's paper was thoughtful, well documented, and persuasive. As population had grown on the isolated, separated,
circumscribed island chain, he showed in charts and tables,
so had crime rates and taxes, while recreational potential
and other quality-of-life indicators declined. Babbie showed
causal connections and described means for stabilizing
population growth and arresting its social and cultural
damage—means ranging from contraceptives to land use
policies. The argument gained much attention for a time, and
the local ILWU even adopted a Maximillion Policy at one of
its conventions. Yes . . . but progrowth proponents in private
industry and government said that such a goal was neither
achievable nor desirable. Wesley Hillendahl, director of
business research for the Bank of Hawaii, expressed in a
symposium discussion on Babbie's paper a common belief
that more people meant more, rather than less, modern-life
benefits.[21] As Honolulu's population densities had swelled,
the number of night clubs and "places to eat out" had increased, he noted, and local residents could now even see live

mainland sports events on their TV sets via satellite. None of
the candidates for the governor's post in the 1974 campaign,
Democrat or Republican, liberal or conservative, believed
that Babbie's maximum million target was feasible.

Concerned people in Hawaii were not unmindful of the
increasing worldwide conviction that there must be limits to
growth—that trend lines of unchecked increases in people,
with their demands, and of consumption of irreplaceable
resources are on a course of inevitable collision. The Club of
Rome's book *Limits to Growth,* reporting on a computerized
study conducted at M.I.T. with international sponsorship and
showing dangers ahead unless growth could be stabilized,
received a good deal of attention for a time in Honolulu
circles. The work's findings were debated in a number of
well-publicized sessions at the University of Hawaii and
under other sponsorship, and in 1974 Dennis Meadows, director of the research, and his wife Donella, principal writer
of the book, were at the East-West Center in Hawaii and explained the study in several local talks. The limits-to-growth
thesis is convincing to all save those who believe either in a
divine providence or in a technological utopia. In essence its
findings are that the down-curving supply of world resources
will before long meet the upward exponential growth curve in
population, production, food consumption, and pollution—if
the world continues its present physical, social, and economic
habits. If that should happen, the "standard run" of the
study's computerized charts indicates that catastrophe would
occur, probably not long after the turn of the century. If the
world's inhabitants should act to control their own fate,
however, and should achieve, in time, a state of equilibrium
between resources and consumption, disaster could be
avoided perhaps indefinitely.

The study was found interesting, especially by intellectual
and conservation-minded groups, yes . . . but even in those
circles the findings were looked on not as well-documented
warnings but as "doomsday" prophecies with conclusions
"that should not be given much weight at this point."[22]

Some University of Hawaii faculty members pettishly attacked the book on technical, pedagogical points rather than evaluating its purpose and its undertaking. One of the sharpest critics was a professional futurist, Dr. James Dator, who wrote a lengthy essay on "The Limits to *The Limits to Growth*." Among other comments Dator offered the optimistic credo that technology might lessen dependence on natural resources with new breakthroughs "just in the nick of time, like the U.S. Cavalry in an Indian raid." He pointed out, for example, that the authors of *Limits to Growth* "apparently do not anticipate a rapid shift to synthetic food production" but "expect the continuation of current farming techniques which require extensive farm lands."[23]

Even if the world could achieve such a land-free state as Dator hoped for in the next thirty or so years, the argument seemed inept and inapt in the islands at just that time. It certainly gave support to those who would rather use the arable land resource for urban development than farming. Castle & Cooke's president, Malcolm McNaughton, had recently said, for instance, that preserving lands for agriculture "doesn't make much practical sense" because of escalating land values, which, he pointed out, become the overriding consideration when land is employed at its highest and best use.[24] And Theodore and Harvey Meeker, prominent kamaaina businessmen, had written not long before that even "the large-scale agricultural industries . . . are no longer essential to the economic well-being of our island." Because of "marketplace realities," they explained, "much of the agriculture on Oahu is in fact economically and socially undesirable." That was a good statement of the economic change since the Land Use Law had been adopted to protect Hawaii's agricultural lands: no longer could such preservation be justified on the grounds of economic necessity. Now technofuturists were adding the argument that it could not even be defended on a functional, food-production basis.

Another radical change in Hawaii's land economy has worried some but to others has seemed just one more aspect of welcome growth—the quickening rate and increasing volume of capital investment from outside the islands.[25] Since the mid-nineteenth century Hawaii has needed capital for its burgeoning businesses. By local bootstrap methods, the establishment of banks (authorized first by a bank charter bill passed during Kamehameha III's reign) solved the problem for a time. Money has flowed from the United States mainland in increasing quantities over the years since then, at first as investment in the plantations and their offshoot enterprises. It reached massive size in the 1960s and 1970s, most of it now going to land acquisition and new construction. Other out-of-state investments also, almost unnoticed at first, became appreciable during that time. British-Canadian Grosvenor Estate, for instance, increased its stakes in open lands on Oahu and even in urban property in downtown Honolulu. Canadian investors bought several hotels and financed construction of some office buildings. Then suddenly appeared a sizable amount of investment money from Japan. For a long time just one store, Shirokiya's, in the Ala Moana Shopping Center, had been owned outright by Japanese interests. Now Japanese investors started to absorb through purchase completed hotels, resorts, condominiums—and raw land.[26] The first trickle reached the proportions of a stream, if not yet a flood. By 1974, Japanese from Japan had a controlling interest in twelve hotels comprising about four thousand rooms—11 percent of the state's total. By 1976 that number had grown to nineteen. Before long, conflicting reactions were surfacing in Hawaii.

For a time, this threat to the old tightly and locally controlled island economy seemed, to the business community, as great a challenge to "the Hawaiian way of life" as loss of older buildings and earlier life-styles was to the conservationists. The local tourism entrepreneurs were particularly worried; they saw the possibility of a "package" invasion, with Japanese airlines bringing Japanese visitors to Japanese-owned hotels, to sightsee on Japanese-controlled buses, eat in Japanese restaurants, and buy souvenirs in Japanese shops.

The president of the Hawaii Visitors Bureau felt that "there is a very real fear that they will try to hog it."[27]

Most of the worry was about impact on the economy, not on the environment. A state senator objected to the sale of land to foreign owners because "he who controls land controls the political and economic life-blood of any community."[28] But former Lieutenant Governor Tom Gill commented soberly that "when we let outsiders buy into our tourist industry we're also selling them our clean water and air and our scenery . . . so let's insist that they use us properly."[29] An excellent idea, certainly, but no such caveats were added to any of the sales agreements.

Soon, however, the excitement subsided and the volume of Japanese investment decreased. The Japanese government itself placed temporary restrictions on moving capital abroad and, noting the adverse reaction in Hawaii, advised its countrymen to make their new enterprises seem to "grow out of the Hawaiian soil, as the earlier Japanese immigrants became an important part of Hawaii." Many local businessmen still sensed a threat to home control, but not all did. When a Japanese financier bought the Sheraton Waikiki, including the proud old Royal Hawaiian Hotel, in 1974, kamaainas were outraged. But Chinn Ho, defending his sale of part of the Makaha development to Japanese interests, said of the inflow of Japanese capital that "economic stagnation" would come to the islands without it. George Kanahele, a part-Hawaiian, in 1973 secretary general of the Japanese-American Economic Council, commented that "the amount of Japanese capital in the islands [some $350 million in 1975, compared to several billions of U.S. mainland money] is so minuscule that I sometimes wonder why there's all the fuss." Anyway, Kanahele added, "I submit that the benefits are far greater than the costs." He counted as benefits "needed capital . . . jobs . . . new professions and skills . . . and a counterbalance to U.S. mainland investment."[30] On that note of acceptance—more capital for more expansion, to provide a kind of symmetry with other new capital for other new expansion—the arguments seemed to rest for a time. Yes, foreign investment was dangerous to conservation of Hawaii's traditional qualities . . . but it was necessary for further priming of the production pump.

Trying to Look Ahead

While there seemed to be a consensus that the best of both worlds, old and new, could be grasped and held, there was not much examination of the likely future the state faced if present trends continued. A Governor's Conference on the Year 2000 was held in 1968 and a program based on the new discipline of futuristics was instituted at the university. These were attempts to study desirable alternative futures for the year 2000 and beyond, assuming that present-day aims, ambitions, and attitudes could be changed. There were few analyses, however, of the real probabilities for the years immediately ahead. For land use, there were several ways that a potential protraction of the growth curve of the past few decades could be estimated, and some attempts were made to draw lines into the approaching future. One could, for example, add up plans already in the minds of landowners, developers, and investors and calculate what part of total future reality they were. Trend lines could be drawn from some distance in the past and projected for some distance into the future for an extrapolated guess. And if these more or less mathematical methods of forecasting were not sufficient, one could listen to the hopes (or fears) of those who felt they had some special means for foreseeing Hawaii's future.

Oahu provided a model for the pragmatic method (simply toting up plans that developers had announced or were obviously preparing) and several people who took the trouble to calculate in the early 1970s came up with about the same figure: between 30,000 and 35,000 additional acres were planned for development by their owners, most of them still classified and zoned for agricultural use. At that time only 37,000 acres were zoned for civilian urban uses.

Ramon Duran, a planner who had been staff officer for the State Land Use Commission until he resigned in the early 1970s in protest against the indiscriminate reclassifications, used a device in talks he made later to civic groups: he would pin cardboard cutouts representing planned developments on a blown-up copy of the general plan of Oahu.[31] As he proceeded around the map, placing more and more swatches on the areas zoned for agriculture or preservation, his audience always gasped with disbelief. Starting at Hawaii Kai, showing its major planned expansions inland, along the shore, and on to Makapuu Point at the island's eastern tip, he covered next with cardboard the areas that were planned for development in the suburban districts of Kailua and Kaneohe—almost 2,000 acres. Then he put a piece on 700 acres already rezoned for development at the rural community of Kahaluu, a larger one on the several thousand agricultural acres which developer Joe Pao later bought from the McCandless Estate, and another on 600 acres further on the windward coast where Lewers & Cooke had development rights.

A huge piece of cardboard would fit over most of Kahuku Point at the northeast tip of Oahu—land that had been a sugar plantation and the source of Hawaii's watermelon crop until it began "phasing out," as the term went—where a large hotel had already been built as the start of a resort community. Further along the north shore, over 700 acres of Bishop Estate land and some 2,800 acres owned by the Dillinghams, land planned for withdrawal from sugar production and slated for development, had cardboard placed on them.

Duran would then move across the map to Makaha. (The western end of the island around Kaena Point was too rugged for profitable development; yet construction on its conservation-zoned land was planned by the state itself, which intended to push a highway along the shore.) There he would show the 2,000 or so additional acres that Chinn Ho was ready to develop or sell for development as soon as he could get it reclassified. Comparatively small cutouts would dot the shore leading toward the agricultural central plains until the Campbell Estate holdings were reached. Then expansion of an existing industrial park would be shown, and further on a huge piece was added to represent a proposed new town on about 4,000 acres still zoned for agriculture at Honouliuli.

In this central area, containing most of Oahu's arable land, the Robinson Estate had 350 acres already zoned for urban uses and intended to ask for rezoning of another 2,000 acres of sugarcane land; Castle & Cooke, builder of the huge suburb Mililani Town through its development arm, Oceanic Properties, had plans for three more increments that would take that bedroom community in the heart of the cane country to 3,500 acres; above the town of Aiea the Bishop Estate and the Austin Estate each had some prime agricultural acreage already rezoned for development; and finally the Bishop Estate was requesting reclassification of 4,500 more acres of the Wahiawa slopes (much of it plantation land) for its own version of a new town. On toward downtown Honolulu and the already urbanized sections, additional cardboard pieces were tacked on the map—at Waipahu, Pearl City, Salt Lake. And as Duran's demonstration worked back to Hawaii Kai, he stopped to pin bits of cardboard on the hills along the already congested Kalanianaole Highway—at Aina Koa, Aina Haina, Kuliouou.

These were developers' intentions, and of course not all of them were certain to go ahead. The State Department of Planning and Economic Development, concerned about the implications of the proposals for the central Oahu plains area, made a study in 1972. They estimated that if the landowners and their developers did what they said they were going to do, more than 10,000 acres of land would be built up in that area alone to contain some 55,000 living units.[32] The report strongly recommended against expansion of that magnitude, primarily because of the tremendous cost of public services and transportation that would be required. The study was gratefully received by the legislature and filed.

In the meantime, the University of Hawaii announced plans to build a major second campus in this area. The three principal landowners (Bishop, Castle & Cooke, and Campbell); hoping to sweeten their intentions and hasten the rezoning they wanted, vied to have the campus located on their properties. The only problem that the university saw was choosing among the offers (Campbell ultimately won out); there was no doubt in anyone's mind that removal of any of the lands from agricultural uses could be had on request.

Intentions of large-scale development appeared also on the other islands.[33] For a forecaster, a difficult problem was to guess what the immediate plans of the buyers and sellers of land really were; speculation rather than building seemed to be the purpose in many cases. Requests that the state reclassify and that the counties rezone were often made only to escalate assessed valuations so that the land (or rights to its development) might be sold at a greater profit, often after it had been held idle for some time. An example was the reclassification in 1968 of some 3,500 acres of the Molokai Ranch Company's land at Kaluakoi on Molokai, ostensibly for a huge resort community development to be completed in ten years. Six years later construction was still promised but not yet begun, although a number of major land sales and leases had been transacted. (Construction of a large hotel has since gone ahead.)[34]

In many other cases it was not easy to know real intentions unless one was somehow privy to corporate plans, which were often formulated elsewhere than in Hawaii if foreign or mainland American money was involved.[35] It was impossible for people in Hawaii to know what might really happen to about 1,000 acres of Kauai land that Grove Farm Company planned to sell to a development corporation headquartered in Florida, to two major parcels on Maui and Kauai that Amfac, Inc. sold to out-of-state resort developers, to 1,500 acres on Oahu's windward side and 15,000 acres on the Big Island (rich with koa forests, sandy beaches, and fertile land, scattered with heiaus, slides, house platforms, and other artifacts) that the Bishop Estate negotiated to sell to mainland investors presumably planning residential resort development.

No one could be sure that all the land which seemed to be planned for development would really be built upon, even over a long period of time. Plans to develop the land often sounded as impossible, in their way, as hopes to save the land from being developed often seemed, in theirs, to the conservationists. On Kauai, a multimillion-dollar resort was announced for the old cannery site of Kapaa; on the Big Island a consortium of Laurance Rockefeller, Eastern Airlines, and Dillingham, (later split up) announced a multimillion-dollar extension of the Mauna Kea Beach resort, and later in that same area Boise Cascade and a Japanese joint-venturer asked for rezoning to permit the first, $50 million stage of a huge planned development; further south on the coast a development consortium announced plans for six hotels, four thousand apartment units, and a residential village with six thousand homes; the Lanai Land Company announced plans for a multimillion-dollar development on that island; back on Kauai, the Hanalei area was rezoned to allow a multimillion-dollar grouping of residential resort communities; and rezoning for the thousand-acre development that Joe Pao planned on the windward side of Oahu was requested by the McCandless heirs. Each week, almost each day through the mid-1970s, new multimillion-dollar "announcements" were released. It was difficult for a reporter to keep up with them all.

Even a conservative prognosticator could assume that ultimately much of this announced residential and resort development would take place, after enough speculative gain had been milked from the land through the shuffling of ownerships. Most forecasters did not depend on stated intentions, however, but used the method of extrapolation of past trends into the future—projecting certain variables whose behavior in the known range could be charted into the unknowable time ranges ahead. Those who did this became sure that at least double the number of acres for which plans had been announced would ultimately be developed.

The state had a capable statistician, the Department of Planning and Economic Development from time to time made its own demographic and economic projections, and, in the area of land uses, the Overview Corporation, headed by Stewart L. Udall, former secretary of the interior, included a prognosis of development prospects to the year 2000 in an open-space plan it prepared for the state in 1972.[36] Most of these predictions were based on modified extrapolations, going back as far as statistics were available to develop trend lines that could then be projected into the future with some degree of confidence.

The underlying factor for all future projections is, of course, the number of people whose demands must be met. The food required for sustenance, the industrial capacity to produce all the things needed (or wanted), the resources that would have to be used to provide for this production, the construction on the land surface to house people and their activities, the resultant creation of wastes and pollutants—all these variable factors depend on the numbers of people who generate them. In Hawaii this is more clear than it usually is, because all the related activities take place in close, highly visible surroundings. There had been a drop from the 250,000 or so Hawaiians who lived in the islands at the time of Cook's arrival to a low point of some 57,000 total residents in 1870. But then, as new arrivals increased, the population had begun rising rapidly, not only in numbers of people but in rates of increase. By 1970, with 770,000 residents, Hawaii's population was growing at an annual rate of about 2.5 percent compared to a mainland U.S. rate of increase of 1.4 percent.[37]

Four-fifths of these people lived on the island of Oahu in the early 1970s, although that island contained only 9 percent of the land in the state. Hence Oahu's densities had grown to be great: in 1970, for the entire island, there were 1,058 persons living on an average square mile of land; in Honolulu proper the ratio was 3,550 to the mile; one census tract was populated at the ratio of 35,000 persons to a square mile and another at 60,000. (Chicago and San Francisco each has

about 15,000 people per square mile, Manhattan some
70,000.)[38] The trend toward relative concentration on Oahu
was continuing, despite the state administration's desire to
disperse people to the other islands and despite a rise in the
absolute population on those islands after a period of
decline. Extrapolating from these trends, the state's statisticians estimated that by the year 2000 Hawaii's population
would reach somewhere between one and one and a half
million. At one time Honolulu's city planners predicted a
population for Oahu alone of two million, but that figure
frightened everyone and it was later revised to one and a
quarter million by 1995.[39]

Estimates of economic growth were based largely on an
assumed continuing increase in tourism.[40] The three top
"industries" on which the islands' economy had long
depended—agriculture, the military, and tourism—had been
reduced to two with the decline in sugarcane and pineapple
production and the lack of real interest in other kinds of
agricultural activity. The military was an unpredictable
source of revenue and local employment. Defense agencies
spent $350 million in Hawaii in 1960, and the sum grew close
to $1 billion by 1975, creating by far the largest part of total
personal income in the state. The Oahu Development Conference suggested stimulating even more activity by the
defense departments to make the military a "growth industry" for Hawaii.[41] The idea never caught on, primarily
because plans from Washington are apt to run hot and cold
and are an unsafe, unsure base for an island economy. At
one moment there may be talk of moving major divisions
and their dependencies complete to Oahu and at another
threats of curtailing military land uses and transferring command posts to another location.

The visitor "industry" as such is by no means the only
other economic activity, but it is the hub around which
revolve many of the businesses that provide income and produce jobs. Prognostications about tourism were important,
then, as statisticians and others tried to foresee the future.

Past trends were clear: in 1950, visitors spent maybe $40 million in the islands, which seemed a sizable sum then; by 1960 that had grown to $130 million; and then the exponential curve steepened. Expenditures by tourists were $550 million in 1970, $645 million in 1971, and over a billion dollars in 1974.[42] Surprisingly, the income from tourism held up even during the big slump of the 1970s although during that decline growth was minimal compared to the earlier increases (about 10 percent annually rather than 25 percent). As we have seen, the number of people who spent that money had increased from a few thousand in the first decades of the century to more than three million a year by 1975. A Tourism Advisory Committee appointed by the governor foresaw five million visitors by 1985, just ten years ahead. Increasingly they were arriving in tour groups, shipped by prearranged schedules from one island to another, from one hotel to the next, guided to the sights to see, the places to eat, and the shops to patronize. This development resulted in the continually increasing number of hotels on the land, along with more roads leading to them and more facilities serving them. Projections considered conservative in 1975 indicated that sixty thousand rooms would be needed by the tourist trade in 1985, an increase of at least twenty thousand in ten years.

By 1975 and 1976 there was general agreement in Hawaii's business community that tourism was the most certain—if not the only—industry that could be counted on to continue, into the future, supplying revenues for the state and jobs for its people. An Economic Advisory Task Force reported to the governor its conviction that agriculture would keep on declining, the military would remain unpredictable, and the development of other industries would be minimal—while "the travel industry appears to be the only area in which there is a distinct substantial growth potential." At the same time the governor's Tourism Advisory Committee told him that its primary worry was whether enough new capital would be available to meet tourism's demands.[43]

Other trends that might be taken as growth indicators (most of them, of course, stimulated by the visitor influx) achieved increases in the ten-year period between 1960 and 1970 that, extrapolated, would produce almost absurd estimates. Personal income rose from about $1 billion in 1950 to $1.5 billion, approximately, in 1960—and then jumped to $3.5 billion by 1970 and over $5 billion in 1975. From a modest increase during the 1950s, completed construction grew from $275 million to $784 million during the 1960s (and then sagged badly during the middle 1970s, partly due to the national recession but largely because developers had greatly overbuilt high rises for the condominium market). Bank deposits rose during the 1960s from $670 million to $1.5 billion and by 1974 had reached $2.5 billion.[44]

Several attempts were made to extrapolate the amount of land that would have to be converted from open-space uses to urban development purposes to accommodate all these proliferations. While preparing its open-space plan, Stewart Udall's Overview Corporation made projections of acreages of presently open land that would have to be reclassified to urban uses if the growth curves continued. Its forecasts were a doubling of urban districts between 1970 and 2000—from 145,000 acres to over 300,000. Since there were in 1970 only about 330,000 acres of plantation lands (the primary source which new developments drew upon), Udall's figures would indicate a great reduction in the state's farmlands. For Oahu alone, with about 60,000 acres of plantation land, Udall estimated 46,000 additional acres added to urban-zoned districts by the year 2000. Overview Corporation and others foresaw further loss of open space on the other islands in sizable amounts, but not at the same pace as on Oahu.

Large as these acre and dollar and people projections were, time after time local demographers and economists hedged their estimates, pointing out that all previous appraisals had been surpassed by the actual turn of events in recent years. An important reason for uncertainty about the rate of growth was that Hawaii was no longer a distant, isolated island territory whose future was fixed by a small band of local businessmen. It had become part of a wider universe, affected by events originating outside its borders and over which it had no control.

Increasingly, then, hard-nosed, experienced social and economic planners turned away from the carefully calculated trend charts and began estimating the state's future by the course of world changes and Hawaii's potential place in new global relationships. Some saw a surge of population and business to the islands from the continental United States. Others looked further, toward a flood of additional people and new enterprises from both East and West, as Hawaii sat in the center of their freshly opened concourse.

Among those predicting a great inflow from the U.S. mainland was Dr. John Craven, head of the university's Department of Oceanography and state coordinator for oceanography, who foresaw hordes of "refugees from the mainland" in the decades ahead. He based his reasoning largely on a belief that Hawaii's islands would always offer more comfortable and attractive living than the increasingly polluted continental metropolitan areas. Craven envisioned a much greater population density than any official forecast predicted. And he saw only two possible ways to contain it. One was to begin planning huge megalopolitan concentrations in the manner of "arcologies" of architect Paolo Soleri. The other, which Craven advocated instead, was to start designing and arranging to build additional "floating city" islands off the shores of the Hawaiian archipelago—these would provide a skillfully engineered and tightly planned living environment for a tremendous future population and would allow much open space on land to be preserved. The imaginative idea caught the fancy of a number of people, but Craven did not explain how the artificial islands would benefit from better planning or more careful development than Hawaii's land surfaces had received.[45]

A number of serious and experienced political-economic-physical planners also foresaw a much greater population and business expansion for Hawaii than Hawaii itself dared count on. One who stirred local business imagination was Fred Smith, an official of the prestigious National Planning Association who visited Hawaii often in the mid-1970s as a representative of Laurance Rockefeller, then planning the expansion of his Mauna Kea Beach complex on the Big Island. Smith contended, in one statement he made, that "Hawaii cannot escape becoming the primary staging area for a growing army of pilgrims moving in both directions to build an unprecedented and crowded bridge between East and West." He felt that Hawaii would have no way to stop growth or to stabilize it. "Hawaii," he reminded his audiences, "is America's front door." As eastern nations broadened relations with America, he said, Hawaii would be "the one strategic stop on the only Pacific sea and air highway to Western society, to the Western economy, and to Western institutions." Smith warned his listeners that plans should be made to benefit from the "inevitable fallout" of this traffic.[46]

Hawaii's disinclination to face the problems that further unprecedented growth on its limited land would bring is the topic of the last part of this book. Unwillingness to choose between limiting growth or welcoming growth has resulted in an inability to plan for either alternative. The best scheme, in political terms, has seemed to be to wait and see what happens.

Thus Hawaii was approaching its next decade of development ill prepared for the *expanded* expansion it was told to expect. Historian-environmentalist Gavan Daws lamented that "we're sleepwalking with a dreamy smile on our face."[47] The only thing that seemed clear in that dream of the future was that every estimate of growth which was made would be exceeded.

The thousand rooms and endless ballrooms, convention halls, restaurants, and night clubs of the huge Sheraton Waikiki, when they were thrust into the sky between the genteel Royal Hawaiian and the comfortable Halekulani, had seemed about as much as the tiny Waikiki peninsula could take. But then the Waikiki Biltmore Hotel, built with great fanfare in 1953, was dramatically demolished in 1973 to make way for a twin-towered resort planned for intensely greater density: an aggressive haole developer named Chris Hemmeter announced that it would be a $100 million combination of hotels, condominiums, and commercial enterprises which "would make the [Waikiki] Sheraton look like a small thing" and would eventually overshadow Chinn Ho's complex around the Ilikai Hotel. By 1976 Hemmeter had completed a twin-towered hotel—the Hyatt Regency—whose additional thousand rooms were quickly absorbed by the island's visitors.

Chinn Ho himself was looking toward expansion of a different kind. The Makaha Inn, where a Hawaiian haole couple had watched the parade of handsome Hawaiian ladies to the Sunday meeting of their Civic Club, had been sold to a Japanese investment company. That did not mean the end of Ho's interest in the lush Makaha Valley, however. There was more land to be developed, sometime, and more land to be sold at augmenting prices in the meantime.

Chinn Ho, among others, saw the great surge ahead primarily as financial bounty from land sales. "There's no money in hotel operations any more," he told an interviewer in April 1974. "The money is in real estate."[48] It was still possible to gain fortunes from caring for tourists in hotels, but that was a transient, depreciating source of wealth. The Biltmore had lasted only twenty years before it was sold and its land rebought for a new and larger capital investment. Land for development, not the development itself, was "the basis of all wealth," reaffirmed the real estate salesman on Honolulu television.[49]

In two hundred years Hawaii had not only condensed the history of people's uses and misuses of the earth that had always supported them. It had also begun to demonstrate, for everyone to see, what further exploitations of the land might lie ahead.

PART 2

The Worth of Hawaii's Lands

THE worth of land has been measured in many ways throughout history, and in Hawaii most methods of valuation have been used, from simple to sophisticated. For many people (especially those whose lives have not been fully absorbed into urban surroundings) the greatest regard one can have for land is a sense of belonging to it, a feeling that we are part of the earth we live on: by tramping through it and resting on it; by seeing a sunset give it brilliance before it darkens or watching the moon lighten it later; by appreciating the variety of the forms it assumes and marveling at the myriad growing things it supports. Perhaps that was land's first assessment by humans—as a living thing itself, progenitor, stern parent, mother earth. The Polynesian people chanted of earth rejoicing, earth thirsting, earth giving, earth mourning.

But people have also made practical use of the land, and through the ages its worth has been measured in terms of how useful it might be. Different people have wanted to use land differently, however, so "usefulness" has been defined in many ways. In a time when there is almost daily confrontation between those who want to conserve land and those who want to develop it, there is a tendency to oversimplify and consider only the extremes of the ways land is used—at one extreme, kept open and natural; at the other, developed and thereby altered. One tends to think only in terms of "good" uses and "bad" uses according to one's particular bent. In planning parlance, the term "land use" has a purely pragmatic connotation; it is based on functional classifications like residential, recreational, commercial, industrial land—even, dispassionately, urban land and conservation land.

A more useful way than this to consider the worth of land might be to think of the underlying social reasons (social in the broad sense, encompassing economic and political motivations) for which the land is esteemed. In these terms there seem to be three basic types of valuation: the first considers land as a resource, the second as a commodity, the third as an instrument of power.

When land is valued as a resource, it is looked on as a treasured store to be drawn on carefully as human needs arise. The portioning out can have a number of essential purposes: to satisfy the need for pleasure, to supply emotional re-creation or physical recreation, to provide essential sustenance, or to furnish shelter from the elements. In any case, the finite, irreplaceable nature of land is apt to be recognized when it is valued as a resource, and its inherent qualities are likely to be understood and respected. Land thus considered is often looked on as a public asset to be guarded by society against depletion.

Land valued as a commodity is more likely to be considered as personal property: capable of being bartered, bought and sold, or transferred in some way to another owner or user in order to make a gain from the transaction. With this valuation, land is looked on more as a source of wealth than enjoyment or sustenance.

The third valuation of land's worth, as a source of power, regards it as a tool that can create or bolster personal influence or political potency. Through history there seems to

have been conviction that mastery of a region's land meant
control of its destiny. It was primarily to secure influence
over more of the earth's surface that the great explorations
of the eighteenth century took place, one of which opened
Hawaii's lands for transfer of power from kings and alii to
later political elites.

These three ways of gauging the worth of land, and the
ways of treating and using land that result from them, are
not always clear-cut and rigid, although it is easy enough to
find instances of each. More often evaluations and intents
are blurred and overlapping. That is what makes land planning and land management the difficult disciplines they are.
Nevertheless, in Hawaii perhaps more clearly than in most
places, one can see the effects of the different ways land has
been esteemed on the way land has been treated. The following chapters examine the result of considering land's greatest
worth to be that of an essential resource, a valuable commodity, or a useful instrument of power.

crop up, with rules and regulations and bills and budgets. Since political issues always have two opposing sides, there are inevitable conflicts between the public upholding conservation of land and the public supporting development of land.[1]

In a world peopled by ever more numerous habitants on ever more precious land, the conservation-minded are bound to be considered visionary in their political position and the development-disposed regarded as practical. Often the opposite is true. In Hawaii, tourism illustrates the dilemma: is it possible to maintain the beauty of the islands as tropical paradise, mecca for vacationers, when the hordes of visitors who are attracted and the development that must be built to satisfy them destroy the very values that lured them? Even Hawaii's open-land plantation agriculture finds itself in conflict with conservation's ideals at times. On the island of Maui, the Hanawi stream is not only a beautiful sight to see in the Hana district: it is habitat for a number of native fish, crabs, and shrimp that are becoming increasingly difficult to find. When the East Maui Irrigation Company, a subsidiary of Alexander & Baldwin, asked permission to draw ten million gallons of water a day from the stream for seven months a year, ecologists, zoologists, marine biologists, and plain citizens protested, but permission was granted by the state's Board of Land and Natural Resources. The company's vice-president allowed that "we realize that we will be altering the stream," but he was happy that its water would now be raised into an irrigation ditch to supply sugarcane fields.[2]

When Hawaii's Land Use Law set up the "conservation" classification, it seemed an easy enough category to define, but through the years it has been subject to innumerable definitions, interpretations, and administrative regulations. The trouble is that the state itself defines conservation as the practice of protecting and preserving natural resources "by judicious development and utilization."[3] Hence the state has for the most part considered conservation policy to be a judgment about the way conservation land should be used and when it should be developed, rather than how it should best be preserved. Lands classified as conservation by the Land Use Commission are administered by the Department of Land and Natural Resources, governed by a so-called Land Board, further complicating the already fragmented government controls over land uses.[4] Originally the standards for inclusion of lands in Conservation districts were clear enough: forest and water reserve lands were included; some scenic and historic areas were selected; generally, those parts of the islands that did not seem to be in the path of urban development and were unsuitable for agriculture were incorporated in this category. But over the years so many ways were found to "develop and utilize" conservation land that a complicated set of regulations was drawn up for its administration and "subzones" of the Conservation districts were established. In the early 1970s there was such general dissatisfaction with the administrative regulations that several attempts were made to revise them, first as a commission given to Stewart Udall's Overview Corporation and later by the administrative agency itself. In each case the suggested changes were found too restrictive by developers and too loose by conservationists, so the special zones and subzones described in Regulation 4 remain a tangled mess. Within the broadest use category, the General Use subzone, almost any conceivable activity is permitted: not only logging, quarrying, and such, but even the building, under certain circumstances, of residences, resorts and hotels, military structures, and airports.

Thus the Conservation districts have become, in a sense, a catchall for various uses that are neither agricultural nor truly urban. In another sense they are a kind of holding stage until landowners have other plans for their lands and the Land Use Commission is ready to reclassify them.[5] Each year the Land Use Commission reclassifies districts from Conservation to Agriculture and Urban on individual petition. Even more approvals of applications for diverse uses are granted by the Department of Land and Natural Resources. So far neither the administrative agencies nor the legislative branches of the state government have been willing to face up to the basic problem of clearly defining and then firmly maintaining Conservation districts.

Playing political games with these districts is a sport almost as popular as parceling out acreage from Agriculture districts. In 1975, an area of conservation lands on the slopes of Diamond Head was allotted to the university as a site for a junior college, and then a bit later a parcel of that site was leased to the producers of the television series called Hawaii Five-O. Conservation groups and nearby residents protested that there would be noise and constant traffic as a result, that the use was far from conservation-oriented, and that at least an environmental impact assessment should be made. But the NBC crew, from top officers and public relations personnel to actor Jack Lord, mounted a political campaign that the city council members could not resist. The lease stood.[6]

When either state or county officials have decided that an area really deserved perpetual preservation, other means than classification as Conservation have had to be found. In one instance the Big Island's county council even bought an important heiau site from the Bishop Estate to be sure that it was permanently preserved.[7] In 1972 the legislature created a Natural Areas Reserve system to save some of the state's own valuable open space.

The other major problem that always faces conservation of land in an unspoiled state is the difficulty of explaining, in sufficiently clear terms to have legal validity, why certain places have scenic, historic, cultural, or ecological values worth preserving. The first task that must be undertaken by any region considering land conservation is to inventory its natural assets in both quantitative and qualitative terms. Hawaii has never taken on this job; not even the extent and characteristics of lands classified as Conservation under the Land Use Law are inventoried.[8]

In pre-Cook times Hawaiians had understood and classified, by memory and name, variations in land form and land characteristics. There was one name for central mountain ranges and other names for hills that rose alone, hills that were clustered, and hills that stood in line. Below the mountain top, soil qualities and bearing capacities were known and named: the belt where small trees grew, that where forests of larger trees occurred, and the stretch that supported giant species. Wilderness areas and rain forests were recognized, and further down the slopes descriptive names were given to various kinds of arable land. The classification continued down to the sea: a hard-baked, sterile belt was named, a belt where flowers naturally grew, a slippery strip above the principal habitable lands, which were the dry, open-country areas, and finally the shoreline stretches.[9]

In contemporary times there has been considerable study of the basic geographic and geologic nature of the islands' lands. Most recently land and soil characteristics have been analyzed by the University of Hawaii's Land Study Bureau and, under the guidance of the Department of Land and Natural Resources, by the Soil Conservation Service of the U.S. Department of Agriculture. This work, using a new soil classification system, was the first such classification to be completed for any state in the union.[10]

As many planners have discovered, however, the material is too academic in some respects and too difficult to apply in others to be useful as a guide for specific questions of conservation or development or for political-administrative judgment between the two. To decide the appropriate use of a parcel of land on the basis of its natural resource characteristics, the data available would have to be translated into pragmatic terms—into an index of what is where supplemented by a great deal more information that is not now available. Not only soil classifications, watershed areas and water supply sources, forests and wildernesses, and places of value because of mineral deposits should be included, but also scenic views and vistas, historic spots, places laden with cultural artifacts, and many other categories.

Several starts in this direction have been made. The "interpretations" made by the U.S. Department of Agriculture from its 1972 soil survey analysis supply maps for "soil limitation ratings" (slight, moderate, or severe constraints for community development and recreational uses) in broad terms. In preparing the open-space plan he presented to the legislature, Stewart Udall used such data—as well as available information on slope gradients and natural vegetative cover, along with scenic and historic qualities—to pinpoint areas that should remain as open space. An ambitious, computerized mapping of natural data as well as social characteristics for a limited area around Kaneohe Bay has been under way for some time by an environmental research branch of the university (Hawaii Environmental Simulation Laboratory). Whether they are considered inadequate or, perhaps, all too informative, none of these efforts have been used for decision-making purposes by state or county agencies—certainly not by the Land Use Commission in classification or reclassification of conservation land. Several methodologies for environmental resource analysis have been developed on the mainland; among them Hawaii could find a useful prototype. Any of them, however, must begin with complete data in usable form—and this comes back again to the need for an index of natural resources.[11]

The Meaning of Recreation

Conserving land as open space, in as natural a state as possible, does not always mean that it must be kept totally unused. Even the most ardent conservationist must admit that land has assets beyond its qualities of visual beauty and ecological vitality. The simplest functional use to which we put it, which demands the least change in land's natural order, is for recreation. Since its earliest habitation Hawaii seems to have used its lands generously for recreational purposes. The Hawaiians whom Cook discovered must have had their passive enjoyment of the landscape, but their best-documented recreations were active, sometimes violent, games played in special places set aside for them. Some sports were individual, competitive exercises; some were group games; and at specified times there were gatherings for large festivals. One manifestation of the culture shock that helped destroy the Polynesian society in Hawaii when the white man began coming in numbers was the almost complete, almost immediate, discontinuance of the sports that had been developed. There was a good deal of gambling associated with game competitions. David Malo reported that after losing smaller possessions in a game like *noa* (where the location of a small piece of wood or stone hidden in a bundle of tapa had to be guessed), a man might wager his property and "perhaps risk everything he had and become beggared." As haole concepts of personal possession of sizable, valuable goods became established, such betting could be disastrous. And of course the whole idea was repugnant to the missionaries when they arrived.[12]

Popular contests included sliding down slopes at great speed on a sled with oiled runners called a *holua* (or, in a different game, on ti leaves or coconut ribs), bow and arrow shooting, wrestling, boxing, and foot racing. Among the alii, the art of spear throwing was practiced, and even of dodging or catching spears thrown by others. (Kamehameha the Great was reputed to be highly skilled at this demonstration of strength and bravery). Less dangerous were games where a disk or dart was skimmed along the ground toward stakes set thirty or forty feet away. Group games ranged from variants of hiding the noa to a sophisticated game of lovemaking called *ume,* with male and female partners picked by lot from a circle of participants.

The great time for fun and games on the land was the festival of *makahiki,* beginning about the middle of October and lasting four months. During this time no work was done, normal religious observances were suspended, and relaxation and recreation were mandatory. The celebration was in honor of the fertility god, Lono, and the time of "the growth of plants and the spawning of fish." There were other events than sports festivals during the makahiki, the most important being collection of taxes by a representative of Lono who circled the islands to check with the konohiki landlords whether all taxes had been paid. For the common people, however, the big thing was the continuous enjoyment of sport, tournaments, dancing, and singing—with flower-decked crowds numbering into the thousands attending the scheduled events.[13]

During the nineteenth century, the more affluent members of both native and haole groups tended to organize their recreation along social lines. Several private clubs were early formed in the outskirts of Honolulu. Waikiki remained a pleasant resort spot for the alii elite, who were joined in time by haoles who built homes there.[14] A great swath of open space near Diamond Head was set aside and developed as Kapiolani Park—not, at first, as public recreational open space but for landscaped drives and a race track.[15] On a less organized basis many people, from the early haole days on, enjoyed walking and camping in wilderness and forest areas. The Hawaii trail system remained usable for a long time, and later arrivals developed paths and trails of their own, sometimes overlapping with the earlier ones. By the 1870s there were four hundred miles of trails available to hikers.[16]

Recreation for the less well-to-do malihinis, including the successive waves of imported plantation workers, was not well taken care of during the early years. These people found what relaxation they could, with no land especially set aside for it, through much of the nineteenth century. The concept of public parks grew slowly in Hawaii, at first through public benefaction. Samuel M. Damon, an amateur horticulturist, carved a magnificent park from his estate lands around the turn of the century, furnished it with authentic Japanese structures, and made it a public park called Moanalua Gardens. A civic-minded group naming itself the Pan-Pacific Club did its best to establish an area along the Nuuanu stream close to downtown Honolulu, to be known as Liliuo-

kalani Gardens. The city of Honolulu itself (having allowed
both the Moanalua and the Liliuokalani park gardens to be
"cannibalized," as one historian puts it) tried for years to
get estate lands to make an oceanfront park in town back of
Ala Moana Beach—a job that the New Deal's Works Progress Administration finally did. Even today a nonprofit
foundation, together with heirs of the Damon Estate, is
struggling to develop Moanalua Valley as public park space.
It has been handicapped, however, by the determined efforts
of the State Department of Transportation to build a freeway
through it.[17]

When Hawaii became part of the United States, spaces formally designated as parks, based on national standards,
began slowly to replace the earlier haphazard uses of land for
public recreation. Today Hawaii's total of federal, state, and
county park systems is impressive (even though it may be de-
ficient in meeting acres-per-thousand-persons standards used
on the mainland). And, generally speaking, the spaces are
jealously and zealously guarded. Recreational needs and the
lands necessary to satisfy them were studied in the first
general plan of the state and then again in the first revision
to that plan. An additional study of recreational land needs
was begun in the late 1960s as a State Comprehensive Outdoor Recreation Plan (SCORP). Updated several times, most
recently in 1971, it is a serious study of needs, using generally accepted standards and modifying them by an analysis of
available resources and of demands indicated by the local
people.[18] To some extent the state has followed the SCORP
recommendations, although budgets have not allowed true
implementation and conflicts with development desires have
prevented acquisition of all the necessary land.

The open-space park system in Hawaii includes federal
parks under jurisdiction of the National Park Service
(designed primarily to preserve natural and historic areas of
national significance); state recreational reserves (classified as
state parks, state monuments, state recreation areas, and
state waysides); and county parks (almost entirely designed

for local community recreation). The national parks total
207,000 acres and include several important preserves with
very high user counts: Haleakala National Park, centered
on a dormant volcanic crater on Maui; Hawaii Volcanoes
National Park, encompassing a crater system that is still very
much alive on the island of Hawaii; and the City of Refuge
National Park, also on the Big Island.[19]

The state park system, with all its components, totals
about 16,000 acres and includes such magnificent scenery as
Waimea Canyon and Kokee Point on Kauai, Akaka Falls on
Hawaii, and Iao Valley on Maui, as well as certain separate
spots designated as monuments, among them Diamond Head
and even several heiaus and other historic sites.

Many county park areas, particularly important on Oahu,
are beach parks. The islands have 934 miles of tidal shoreline, but only about 185 miles are classified as sandy beach
and only 13 percent of this mileage, or 24 miles, is considered really good for beach recreation use (which means
that if all the 33 percent of the population who say they enjoy beachgoing were to decide to sun themselves at the same
time, there would be about 12,000 people on each mile of
good sandy beach).[20] While it seems to a visitor driving
around the islands that there is a plenitude of beach park
space, on a sunny weekend the beaches are filled and the
roads leading to them are clogged.

Indeed, while Hawaii seems to have a large park reserve, it
is really not too great for the present population, swollen as
it is by several millions of visitors annually. The great problem now is how to keep adding to it as numbers of people
and their recreational demands grow, with ever greater competition developing for open lands. For those who see a need
for further urban expansion, particularly more housing for
the growing population, setting aside large expanses of open
land for "unproductive" recreational use is socially wasteful.
At the same time, to those concerned with preservation of
the natural environment, many recreational uses are ecologically damaging.

The competition between public needs for recreation and private desires for development is most acute along the ocean shore. Theoretically, all beach is state property back to the vegetation line, but in reality private owners facing the shore preempt much of the beach use. Honolulu's deputy parks director estimated that about half of Oahu's sandy beach frontage is being used for nonrecreational purposes. Access to good beaches is made difficult; there is little use in saying that the shore is everyone's property when private holdings block the way to it. Not long ago on Molokai, a great public march across private lands and an all-day luau on the island's best sandy beach effectively protested the way a landowner was making access impossible through his property; the beach is now accessible.[21] Even in Waikiki, access ways that by law are supposed to be kept open are blocked. The Royal Hawaiian-Sheraton complex, among others, makes the required public routes past the hotels invisible and almost unusable.

Urban recreation spaces, especially in Honolulu, are a special problem. The Honolulu Parks and Recreation Department admits that national standards for urban parks of various categories are by no means met. And as the population increases, the amount of parkland per person—or per thousand people, as the standards are measured—drops further each year. The municipal budget for acquisition, development, and maintenance of parklands is inadequate, and competition for desirable spots exists as it does on open lands and beachfronts. Since the costs are very great (land for parks suffers from the same inflated valuation as any other real estate), there is an understandable wish by government to hang some of the price tag on the shoulders of private developers. In 1972 the state mandated the counties to pass "park dedication" ordinances requiring developments of certain sizes and kinds to set aside land for parks to be developed and maintained by the counties.[22] The great fault with such a procedure is that it inevitably produces segregated park enclaves—the favored residents are allowed and the adjoining, often less well-to-do neighbors are forbidden. Another disadvantage is that the overall result, in time, could be a pattern of almost private park sites located wherever new developments occur, rather than a recreational program planned objectively for the full population, in the older ethnic neighborhoods as well as in the new subdivisions.

One of the most outrageous instances of the political jockeying of private developments and public parks was the filling in of Salt Lake, an inland body of water lying in the cone of a volcanic crater on Oahu, by entrepreneur-financier Clarence Thing Chock Ching, a master of political logrolling. Alia-pa'akai, as the early Hawaiians knew this "salt pond," was in legend formed by Pele as she traveled around the island. Her eyes watered as she worked at the task and drops fell that formed the salt in the pond. Geologists explain its origin in more scientific terms as the result of a subsurface hydromagnatic explosion that thrust up a cone of ashy limestone pellets some 150,000 years ago.[23] In 1957 the heirs and trustees of the Damon Estate, modern-time owners of that part of the island, were not as concerned with historic preservation as they were with cash flow. Clarence Ching negotiated a purchase of 1,200 of their acres, including the lake.

This was before the Land Use Law had been passed and such areas had been formally classified as Conservation districts, but various state and county permissions were nevertheless required before development plans could proceed. Ching was Democrat Governor Burns' financial campaign chairman and at the same time a heavy contributor to Honolulu's Republican mayor Neal Blaisdell,[24] so there seemed to be no problems ahead for him. Before long he had ready a handsome presentation of plans for use of the land and the lake, and in September 1959 planner George Houghtailing (a former city planning director whom developers found a useful translator and effective advocate for their plans) submitted it to the Honolulu Planning Commission.[25] The plan showed that the lake was to be dredged and developed for water sports. On its shores there would be 2,500 individual homes and forty landscaped acres of hotels and "deluxe" apartments. An additional twenty-two acres would be developed as apartments for middle-income families, and the plan showed a shopping center and other neighborhood amenities. One of the most attractive features was to be a private park with Japanese and Chinese gardens and a marina on the lake. As the greatest gratuitous gesture of all, Ching offered to set aside a ten-acre public park space.

Such promises were irresistible, and the commission readily approved the zoning request.[26] Soon subdivision houses and suburban apartments began to appear on the land. From time to time further rezoning requests were made and approved (the 40 acres of apartment-zoned land grew to 135 acres)—but the lake remained uncared for, even partly silted with fill from the construction areas, and neither of the promised parks was built. Then, in 1966, in petitions to the city's Planning Commission and the board of the state's Department of Land and Natural Resources, Ching discarded his earlier plans: he now asked permission to level the lake. He wished to fill it in so that he could build on its surface a private golf course.

There was no more difficulty in gaining the essential permissions this time than there had been earlier. The Planning Commission (chaired at that time by an architect) consented to loss of the lake—despite pleas from the local neighborhood that its need was for public parks, not private golf links, and conservation arguments that the lake was unique and irreplaceable although the golf course could be built elsewhere. ILWU officer Eddie Tangen, speaking for his union, testified that "we will do all we can to prevent this destruction." The Land Board (which by then had jurisdiction over use of Conservation land) proved no more difficult to convince. Its own staff recommended approval, and the board's vote on 9 September 1966 to grant Ching's request was unanimous. Even a member who was an ILWU business agent abandoned the union's previous position.[27]

That might seem victory enough, but Clarence Ching had

more ideas. The golf course/lake was sold to a local automobile dealer (suspected by some of being a front for Japanese interests, though Ching's attorney denied that),[28] and Ching turned his attention to other projects. Sales of condominium apartments in the Salt Lake development had been so successful—despite wide recognition that the crowded buildings were badly placed and poorly designed (Ching himself has been quoted as agreeing that the neighborhood has "a cluttering effect")—that more space for more building could obviously be used.[29] In 1972 a request was made to city and state that twenty-nine more acres of conservation land adjacent to the community be rezoned to permit high-rise development.

Once again Ching promised that if his application was granted he would provide park space—sixteen acres for a regional park, this time, and two smaller parcels (three and a half and four acres) for neighborhood parks. Local residents, who by that time had formed a community association to keep vigil on the developer's various moves, were understandably torn between those who wished to keep the conservation land as a shield against further development and those who were willing to compromise to gain some of the park space that had so long been promised.[30]

By now the government end of the political fulcrum had changed somewhat. Ching's Republican friend Neal Blaisdell had been succeeded as mayor of Honolulu by Democrat Frank Fasi, who, during his successful 1968 campaign, had named Ching as one of the city's "fast-buck operators." Nevertheless Ching contributed to Fasi's campaign fund ($8,000 according to one reporter) and Fasi strongly supported the proposed apartment-zoning/park-dedication operation.[31] It would be "a good deal for the developer, the residents, and the city," he said.[32] An additional change in strategy was needed, however, to complete the deal: the Department of Land and Natural Resources was not involved now, but the Land Use Commission would have to approve the further change in land classification from conservation to

urban use. Something slipped up for the first time in Salt
Lake's progression from natural resource to high-rise suburb.
This step was too much for the commission to allow to be
taken. In February 1973, the application was disapproved.

So, for the time being, the story seemed to end. Clarence
Ching, of course, withdrew his offer to make parklands
available, until such time as the Land Use Commission might
change its mind. Like other developers who have suffered
rezoning setbacks in the commission's continuing series of
arbitrary decisions, he is content to wait. Conditions and
characters will change again. The parkland is badly needed
and is available at any time the developer's terms are met. It
is almost the only area of conservation land near the center
of the city that could be used for recreational purposes, but
neither the state nor the city government, for a long time, indicated any intention of acquiring it so long as the possibility
of a political arrangement remained. Finally, late in 1976, the
Honolulu city council asked the state to release funds ($2.5
million was suggested) for purchase of a site from Ching for
the public park that he had once proposed to provide.

In fact, as the population continued to grow at rates that
seemed to justify more Salt Lake–type developments, it was a
good question whether enough additional Hawaiian land
could be preserved anywhere for the local people's enjoyment
and recreation, without a radical change that would replace
politics with policy. It was not difficult to demonstrate the
problem. A professor and a student in the university's architectural department made some calculations in 1974 showing
how recreational needs in the broad sense (re-creational was
the word form they preferred) could be made a measure of
the state lands' capacity for carrying a load of human population.[33] They proposed using the three common methodologies for planning recreational space—standards, demands,
and resources—not as checks on one another but as factors in
a single formula. They calculated the need, the *demand* of
people in Hawaii for recreation of various sorts, and
measured it against accepted standards to determine how

much land space would be required for each person. They then figured the amount of land that could be reasonably used for recreation of the kinds required—the total available resource—and divided this by the space needs to calculate the number of people who might be accommodated decently by the resource. The figure came out very close to one million persons: the number that others had used intuitively as an optimum maximum population for the islands.

There was little likelihood, however, that the politics of land use in Hawaii would support such an objective conclusion as policy. Rather, the approach to relating people and recreational space continues to be first, satisfying the land needs of building for urban growth and then examining state and county budgets to see how much of the land left over might be acquired for the unprofitable, nonessential purpose of human pleasure. Everyone knew it would not be enough.[34]

chapter 6

Source of Sustenance

THERE are numerous additional ways in which land functions as a vital asset, none more important than its support for life's essentials of food and shelter—as arable agricultural land and as buildable urban land. The competition between these two demands on its limited supply and their mutual contest for conservation land constitute the largest part of today's land management problem.

There may come a time in the future when agricultural lands are not of such prime importance, when, as many biochemists believe, chemical or microbiological synthesis will supply our essential nutrients. For a long while, however, it seems likely that we will continue to depend on foodstuffs grown in or raised on land. As needs increase with population growth, they will be met for some time to come by increased land yields rather than technological substitutes.[1]

Hawaii's history is peculiar in this respect, and it may presage some of the difficulties that lie ahead for the rest of the world. It is a story again of rapid change, in this case a shift from a satisfied dependence on local products for the necessary food to dependence on imports. Each situation has

involved risks. The Polynesian Hawaiians worked hard for
their crops and chanced damage and drought. "Food was a
child to be cared for, and it required great care," wrote an
early native historian.[2] Food in Hawaii is now, to a large
degree, a child of the shipping industry and the airlines, to
be cared for, when it arrives, by supermarket distributors.

The Hawaiians before Cook were good, proud farmers.
They understood their land and they knew where it would
bear well and what things and when. To provide for a
limited but ample diet, their methods of cultivating foodstuffs and raising livestock were crude but skillful. From preparing the soil to harvesting its produce, agriculture was an
integral part of life on the land, an inseparable aspect of the
union of nature, man, and deity. The word for land, *'aina,*
comes from the verb *'ai* (meaning to feed) with the suffix *na*
and has been translated as "that which feeds."[3] For the sustenance that work and the land's productivity provided, the
Hawaiian paid feudal tribute to the chief and made grateful
offerings to the gods, many of whom were respected in
particular ways for help in growing food.[4]

The primary farming tool was a crooked stick *('o'o),* treasured and preserved when it had proved to be a particularly
good one, supplemented by the farmer's own hands and
feet. Irrigation was carefully planned: taro patches, which
required water, were formed by earth banks reinforced with
stones; carefully selected stones were used to construct fish
ponds (some, credited to the earlier, smaller inhabitants
remembered as Menehune, of extremely skillful construction); stone irrigation ditches were formed where they were
necessary.[5]

The time of planting was carefully considered, and the effect of dry, rainy, warm, and cool seasons on the crops was
well understood. In addition, planting was guided by phases
of the moon; leafy produce was put in the soil when the
moon was full, root vegetables later in the lunar cycle. Soil
qualities were comprehended and capably utilized. Land that

supported wild growth (under the jurisdiction of the god
Laka) was best for most produce, and it was well understood
that weeds and wild materials held within them the vital
essence of good land; they were carefully dug in or left to
mulch. Taro, a food staple, needed wetlands for some varieties and drier but well-irrigated soil for others. Sweet potatoes grew best on dry land (known as *kula,* which was also
the word for a bald man). Farm plots were planted with
successive seasonal crops, so that some produce was always
ready to use. If the soil became sour (because Laka was dis-
pleased for some reason), it was covered with wild growth
and allowed to improve until the god was satisfied and the
farmland could be used again.[6]

These products of the soil furnished a diet that was simple
but adequate and remarkably nourishing. Its basis was taro,
breadfruit, sweet potato, and yam, supplemented by certain
leafy vegetables. The taro was eaten in several ways, as it is
today, but most commonly as poi, produced by pounding the
root and cooking the resultant pulpy substance. Coconut and
sugarcane provided succulent variety for the fare and certain
fruits, including bananas and mountain apples, were plentiful. Seafoods of many kinds were included in the diet, of
course, and edible seaweed grew plentifully along the shores
and on the reefs. For meat the choice was limited: there was
pig, chicken, and dog, and that was about it. Fresh water
from streams and springs was no problem, and a headier,
narcotic drink called *'awa* was brewed from shrub roots.[7]

The land provided not only foodstuffs but the means for
preparing them as well. Cooking was done in the *imu:* an
underground oven still used for roasting the pig and steam-
ing other ingredients of a luau meal (hot stones are placed in
or around the well-salted animal or leaf-wrapped victuals).
Quite clearly the Hawaiian diet was heavy in starchy foods,
but it provided sufficient protein and also furnished vitamins
and the essential minerals, amino acids, iodine, and other
nutrients we work so hard to add to our fortified foods. In

addition, of course, it contained plenty of calories. The Hawaiians were (and still are) a sturdy, well-built, often overweight folk who were nevertheless generally healthy—until the white man came.

For the newcomers the diet was neither appealing nor satisfying. Poi is always difficult for a malihini to learn to like, and the haole taste for beef, white potato, and green vegatables is hard to change. Captain Cook on his second trip (knowing by then what the local limitations were) brought with him not only goats but sheep and a different kind of pig and seeds to propagate onions, pumpkins, and melons. As other ships began to arrive, they too carried food offerings. Vancouver made a major change in the available fare when he introduced horned cattle. Captain Charles Berkley added turkeys to the diet. Don Francisco Marin introduced many vegetables and a number of fruits now considered indigenous: guava, lime, lemon, mango, and probably the pineapple.

By the time the first missionaries came in 1820, then, the islanders were accustomed to many new fruits and garden vegetables, and additional importations continued. David Malo, recording the changes, noted in the 1830s that "among the kinds of food brought from foreign countries are flour, rice, Irish potatoes, beans, Indian corn, squashes, and melons, of which the former are eaten after cooking and the latter raw." He also reported that "many new intoxicants have been introduced from foreign lands, as rum, brandy, gin."[8]

In political-economic terms, this importation of exotic products marked a shift in emphasis in the agricultural use of Hawaiian land from raising essential food to developing an industry. Vancouver and others admitted their purposes were several. In part they were self-interested, wishing dietary improvements for themselves; to some extent they were generous, because no foreigner could believe that the Hawaiians did not need additions to what seemed a meager fare. But they were also farsightedly businesslike, for these pioneers saw that an expanded base of food and cattle production could go a long way toward taking Hawaii into the growing pan-Pacific trade as an important producer and exporter.

Turning Agriculture to Profit

The new values that were being introduced to Hawaii and its people required that an economic footing be found for the islands; otherwise they would be a picturesque but useless addition to the modern world that had discovered them. The first search, very reasonably, was for ways to turn agriculture to profit.

Many products were tried in the early years of the nineteenth century.[9] When Ladd & Company leased the Koloa land in 1839, they planted five thousand coffee trees, an equal number of banana trees, and taro in forty-five well-irrigated patches. The missionaries saw the need not only to improve food supplies but to make the "wasted fertile land" productive—and sent back to New England an appeal for experts to help them raise cotton, silk, indigo, sugar, and other edible goods, avowing that their activities would be based on "Christian and benevolent principles," with their aim primarily "teaching the people profitable industry."[10] Soon, however, missionaries themselves were finding profit in raising certain crops (primarily sugarcane) and their principles and purposes shifted somewhat.[11]

During these early times unsuccessful attempts were made to raise silkworms and cotton and there were sporadic tries at producing and exporting kukui nut oil, arrowroot, mustard seed, tobacco, a fern product called *pulu,* and even goatskins. None of these efforts caught on well enough to warrant further development. In the 1850s, wheat was grown for a time and several flour mills were built. These experiments and the foodstuffs they produced were almost entirely for local benefit until the whaling industry, growing in size and making more use of Hawaii as a fueling and resting place, provided a new market. The first whaling ship arrived in

1819, and during the 1840s and 1850s more than four hundred were coming annually.   In addition to relaxation and amusement their crews needed supplies of all sorts, including food.[12] The opening up of California and Oregon, particularly during California's gold rush, provided a further stimulus to Hawaii's commercial agriculture.

That western U.S. market was a particular spur to potato growing in the islands. In the 1840s, 80,000 to 100,000 barrels of potatoes were exported annually, and then the activity began to decline. Coffee trees were introduced early and grown successfully in several places, most notably on the Kona coast of the Big Island. Coffee immediately proved to be a profitable export item and continued to be a successful activity for a long time. However, the small farms on the Kona coast have never abandoned hand picking (until recently requiring school schedules to be arranged to suit the harvesting season), and now they are unable to compete with mechanized activities elsewhere.[13] Commercial fowl and egg production, and the raising of pigs, began slowly from the original Hawaiians' supplying their own needs and increased through the years.

Raising cattle, for both food and hides, began auspiciously soon after Vancouver carried the first horned beasts to the islands, and it continues a profitable activity to the present time. In the early days cattle raising and crop farming were not compatible activities—most of the cattle brought early were allowed to become wild and the farmers suffered from their depredations. Even when ranching became organized and grazing was controlled by cowboys (*paniolos*) brought from Mexico and Spain the trouble continued for some time, and in 1841 a Law Respecting Mischievous Beasts was enacted.[14] (In the highlands above the ranches on the Big Island some wild cattle still wander quite visibly.) Nevertheless, ranches grew in number and size and many of them continue to thrive today. In 1848 there were about ten thousand head of cattle in Hawaii; in 1970 that number had grown to around sixty thousand head using over a million acres of land—one fourth of Hawaii's area—for grazing.[15]

While the planters had their attention focused on agriculture as a commercial activity, the food needs of the growing local population were increasingly overlooked. The plantation workers brought to Hawaii from other places (to help grow crops of little nutritional value) added sharply to the need for food supplies. What they wanted to eat was often quite foreign, once again, to the crops that the lands of the islands were growing. Vegetables such as bitter melon, eggplant, gobo dasheen, wonbok, and daikon were imported and planted at that time and have become staples of home-grown agriculture. New exotic fruits such as the persimmon, lychee, and pummelo were added to the local orchards.

The primary new food requirement in the late nineteenth century was rice. Efforts to grow rice had been made earlier. Oriental varieties did not do well, but grain from the southern United States flourished and produced a small boom in the 1850s. For some time rice was such a success that it replaced taro on many of the wetland fields and became an important exportable item. At one point some 6,400 acres were devoted to rice growing. In the long run, however, it could not compete with California's machine-processed product and its cultivation declined until today it is a rare crop on the islands.[16] It is still a major food staple but, absurdly, its great local usage must be satisfied by importation from outside.

Gradually, in the latter part of the nineteenth century, this downtrend spread to one kind of local food crop after another. Before long it was clear that sugarcane had become the most profitable crop. Raising sugarcane and manufacturing sugar from it began in earnest in the 1830s. Cane had been brought from the south by early Polynesian settlers and had long been grown by the Hawaiians on small plots and used for chewing as a sweet. The white settlers soon saw its commercial possibilities, but for a long time attempts to grow it in quantity were not successful. The first large-scale enterprise was that of Ladd & Company at Koloa on Kauai. After their difficulties, others took over the operation, and that plantation remained through the years one of the largest and most productive on the islands—until the present owners decided in the 1970s to develop large portions of it for resorts.[17]

As Koloa succeeded, other plantation enterprises were undertaken and land was acquired for increasingly large-scale production. In 1836, 8,000 pounds of sugar were exported; by 1860 it had reached 1½ million pounds; a decade later the export poundage had grown to 19 million; just before annexation in 1879, the total was 500 million pounds. (Hawaii's peak year, 1968, had exports of 2¾ billion pounds.)

From Sustenance to "Industry"

Aside from the continual need for good farmland there were other problems in a rapidly growing economy on islands so recently changed from an aboriginal state. There was a chronic shortage of capital during the early plantation days, along with the continual difficulties in finding sufficient amenable labor. The U.S. Civil War caused a boom during its duration, but later in the century production began to overreach available profitable markets. There was pressure for a reciprocal tariff treaty with the United States that would give Hawaii preferential access to the American market, an aim that was successful in the 1870s. The next push was toward annexation, which the growers saw as an even more secure way of supplying sugar to meet American needs. That goal took a little longer to achieve, but when it was reached in 1898 little stood in the way of sugar plantation dominance of the islands' economy—and of course its land. The number of plantations grew to fifty-two in 1900 and then leveled off as they consolidated and increased in size and productivity. Growth in the industry continued through the years until its very recent decline.

Raising pineapple and developing ways of exporting that fruit and its succulent juice began as a serious enterprise much later than did sugarcane growing.[18] Before the 1870s occasional shipments of the fruit itself were made, but the first canning was done on the Big Island in 1882. Although the quality of the fruit was improved and the canning process was further developed during the 1880s and 1890s, the industry really got under way only after annexation. Acquiring land for growing pineapple became as important, and as ruthless, as finding it for cane growing had been. When James D. Dole formed the Hawaiian Pineapple Company in 1901 one of his first—and continuing—needs was land, and in 1922 he managed the purchase of Lanai.[19] Like the sugar plantations, pineapple lands and canneries proliferated and then, in time, consolidated. Along with sugar, pineapple has remained a profitable, growing activity until the last decade. Before production began to slide in the 1960s, Hawaii supplied 80 percent of the canned pineapple and all the pineapple juice sold in the United States—and 75 percent of all the pineapple juice drunk anywhere in the world.

For about a hundred years—from the 1860s to the 1960s—ever more land was needed to support these two agricultural uses. In 1875, less than fifteen thousand acres had been devoted to growing sugarcane and a great deal less to pineapple. As the peak of activity was reached in the 1960s, a third of a million acres, or one-twelfth of the state's surface and almost three-fourths of its prime agricultural land, was devoted to the two crops. By contrast, all the green vegetables grown in Hawaii use only six thousand acres.[20]

The days when the islands' arable lands had been used primarily as a source of sustenance—essential foods to supply the needs of the local people—were long since gone. As the sugar-and-pine agricultural economy had expanded, almost all other kinds of farming on Hawaii's richly fertile soil had declined, for many crops almost to the point of extinction.

Slowly, during the plantation time of the first half of this century, the distinction between agriculture as sustenance and agriculture as business had become blurred. For a very long time data on farm production has been given in terms of amounts exported and dollars earned, never in degrees of satisfaction of consumer needs. Decisions to plant one thing or discontinue the planting of another have been based on profitability of export, not on essentiality of product. In fact, there is no longer much understanding that there *are* the two different agricultural functions of food supply and commerce. The term "agricultural industry" is used now by both government and the private sector to describe the state's soil cultivation activity. To designate specifically the growing of foodstuffs, another phrase, "diversified agriculture," has been devised.

"Agriculture," says the dictionary, is the science and art of farming, the work of cultivating the soil, producing crops, and raising livestock: tillage, husbandry. An *industry,* on the other hand, is any branch of trade, business, or manufacturing, often involving production—but, Webster says, production of a kind "as distinguished from agriculture." Thus the combination of the words in one descriptive term is a revealing distortion of diction. This contrived usage of the language became necessary when sugarcane and pineapple, as commercial export items, assumed the use of almost all arable land in Hawaii. Defining either of the activities as "agriculture" is an extension by courtesy of the meaning of that word. Sugar is indeed a part of our diet, but certainly not an essential nutrient; pineapple is a luxury fruit providing some food energy (from *its* sugar) but composed of 85 percent water. Describing the state's farming activities as an agricultural "industry" simply recognizes the fact that Hawaii put its arable lands almost exclusively at the service of the commercial producers and merchandisers of these two commodities.

Several interesting problems result from this change in agricultural emphasis and the redefinition it has required. One is the fact that Hawaii has been far from self-sufficient in food supplies during the twentieth century. Another is that arable land has become valuable not by reason of its food-producing qualities but in relation to the income it can generate. A third is that arguments for protecting open land from development because of its fertility—one of the primary justifications worldwide for greenland conservation—are specious in Hawaii. It is unconvincing to urge preservation of agricultural land when its "agricultural" use has long been commercial production of a crystal sweetener and a sweet fruit.

As the politics of land shifted—from strategies designed to protect the plantations from the spread of urban growth to tactics planned to encourage urban development and permit the phasing out of plantation agriculture—some worried citizens and some anxious politicians began to rethink the results of the loss of local crops. Even as the population had been growing, the islands had become gradually more dependent on food supplies imported by sea or by air. Hawaii's people had thus been placed at the mercy of shippers and their unions and were paying just about the highest food bills in the nation.

In the 1970s, only 40 percent of the fresh fruits and vegetables consumed in Hawaii was produced locally. About half the beef used in the islands was local (with the remainder sent about equally from the U.S. mainland and from New Zealand and Australia) and slightly over a third of the pork.[21] An odd feeling had developed that local things should be looked down on as provincial and common; imported items were more precious, hence more desirable, therefore better. This despite the fact that the quality of most of Hawaii's homegrown products was excellent: Manoa lettuce, Maui and Molokai onions, Kahuku and Molokai watermelon, Chinese bananas, Ewa poultry and eggs, local potato, yam, turnip, celery, cucumber. The local beef, less tender perhaps but certainly more tasty than the artificially fattened mainland product, is ignored by most haoles and western-oriented Orientals; its sale is primarily in out-of-the-way local stores in the native sections.

Under both Governor Burns and Governor Ariyoshi, directors of the State Agricultural Department, Fred Erskine and John Farias, worked seriously to bolster diversified production. Ariyoshi continually stated as principle his belief that agricultural lands should stay in agriculture and should remain productive, even when they were abandoned by the plantations. Some truly diversified crops were already being raised and exported. Of the ones that early growers had produced in the nineteenth century for export, few remained. Potatoes are still grown—but the lands that produce the best yields are prime targets for urban expansion. Coffee is still raised and handpicked on Kona farms—but its future is very uncertain. Commercial fowl and egg production remains a viable activity, supplying a sizable part of the local need, although it has never become an export item. The same can be said of pig farming, with the big difference that the poor souls in that enterprise have been more harried and harassed than any other food suppliers on the islands. Guava and passion fruit, ginger root, and other luxury items with fringe food value have shown signs of catching on as commercial export items. Macadamia nuts are becoming an important crop: the amount of land devoted to this crop has increased from four thousand to nine thousand acres during the decade of the 1960s. The product with perhaps the greatest sign of successful export is papaya, long enjoyed locally and now shipped in greater quantity all the time and finding increasing markets on the U.S. mainland and in Japan.[22]

The Move to Save Farmland

As the plantations threatened to close or gradually shut down, state-appointed agencies known formally as Task Forces were set up to encourage employment substitutes that would not always require land-use zoning changes to permit building development. Various ways were tried to bolster local industry by these groups, from establishing group-farming activities in agricultural parks to encouraging nurseries for tropical plants or orchards for tropical fruits, and even, in one instance, deserting agriculture altogether to subsidize a controversial and not too successful plastics manufacturing plant.

The task that these forces faced, with state and county government input and advice from many segments of the private sector, was well-nigh impossible. No preparations had been made or long-range planning undertaken for replacement of the plantations in any of the places where task forces were formed. At Kohala on the Big Island, at Kilauea on Kauai, on Molokai, and in other locations, ad hoc decisions were made to lease land or subsidize operations that were seldom well thought through. At Kohala, where one of the earliest plantations had been established in missionary days, most task force efforts failed, but the state stubbornly kept putting money in those that remained.[23] The county, however, was not so optimistic. Early in 1976 the Hawaii Planning Commission approved land rezoning in south Kohala for a huge resort development planned by a Japanese investment group: it seemed a more certain way to stimulate local industry and guarantee local employment.[24] On Molokai, where the task force had blocked out an agricultural park for small-farm enterprises, the sole tenant, a potato farmer, gave up and canceled his lease. He had found, he said, that it was not possible to farm successfully on such a small scale, and a larger acreage was not available to him in Hawaii. He planned to move his operation to northern California.[25]

On Maui a different sort of state-county political conflict developed, in this case over what were known as agricultural subdivisions. The Land Use Law permitted the sale of good agricultural land to individuals in parcels as small as two acres, presumably to allow small-operation farming in subdivisionlike groupings. At one time the idea was appealing (as homesteading always has been, in principle) and a number of local people eked out a living that way on long-familiar land. In recent years, however, developers had taken advantage of the proviso, finding it a loophole in the land

classification system: they sold sites in agricultural subdivisions as two-acre estates to wealthy buyers who had no intention of farming. The scheme rapidly became another political
game played by state and county agencies with the developers; players on both sides knew that the label of agriculture
on these plots was a deceit.

When Ariyoshi's state administration began making moves
to protect farmlands, this trickery turned on the government
that had allowed it to develop. Denied a large-scale rezoning
of fertile valleys on windward Oahu, developer Joe Pao
used agricultural subdivisions as a threat: give me an urban
classification for these agricultural lands so that I can build
moderate-priced homes there, he said in effect, or I will
develop the land anyway as high-priced estates.[26] On Kauai
in the mid-1970s some twenty such subdivisions were in the
planning stage, most of them by small-scale operators. On
former Kilauea Sugar Company land, where the state's task
force hoped to establish an agricultural park one of these
high-class tracts reached the stage of application to the county Planning Commission. It was approved. Under the law,
the commission contended, it had no other choice. The state
brought suit against the Planning Commission and the mainland couple who hoped to subdivide seventeen acres of arable
land, as a test case, to see what the courts would say about
the rights and wrongs of this mismanaged bit of state land
management.[27]

So sure were plantation landowners that they would eventually gain urban zoning for their farmsteads that they often
had no hesitation in dropping their own insufficiently profitable tillage, or canceling nonremunerative leases to others for
farm uses, and simply waiting. In 1975 Ariyoshi's administration made plans for another court test to experiment with
an innovative way of preventing this kind of loss of agriculture on fertile land. An investment company named Kilauea
Management moved to cancel leases it had extended to farm
and ranch operators and a number of truck farmers on C.
Brewer & Company land, which had once been the Kilauea

plantation, even though its application for partial rezoning had been turned down by the Land Use Commission. The state's scheme to counter the cancellation threat was to condemn not the land itself but the leasehold interest in the lands—and not permanently but for a term of ten years. The intention would be, when the state had acquired first leasehold rights, to sublease the farms and ranches back to farmers and ranchers, at reasonable rates, in reasonably sized acreages.[28] It would take some time to test the idea in the courts and there was sure to be opposition and counterlitigation. The ubiquitous Eddie Tangen, for one, testified against the state's intention immediately (whether as chairman of the Land Use Commission or an officer of the ILWU, news reports did not make clear).[29] If the move worked, it would be less costly to the state than outright land condemnation, unquestionably, but it appeared to be a circuitous, temporary device that would hold farmlands from development for ten years at best. By then the pressures for rezoning could have become too strong to resist. The scheme was never tested in court, however. In 1976 Brewer announced a well-planned long-range use of its land which would keep a "major part" in agriculture (guava raising) and aquaculture (prawn farming) and the next year the state dropped its plan to condemn the leasehold interest.

Those Hawaii citizens who believed that plans should be made for the future—carefully considered, not quickly contrived; as a matter of determined policy, not political expediency—kept their fingers crossed as they watched the operations and listened to the quarrels about task forces, subdivisions, and lease condemnations and heard the governor reiterate his intention to save agricultural land. It was encouraging that some moves were being made; they seemed to mark a clear change from the consistent prodevelopment approach of the previous administration. Yet there was not an equal consistency evident in the new proagriculture stance. While the state's Agricultural Department set up task forces to preserve agriculture, the Land Use Commission continued

to approve applications to abandon it. The political support
for the new administration was the same as it had been for
the prior one; few of the faces in state offices had changed.
The new state director of agriculture, John Farias, vowed to
keep windward Oahu's lands in agriculture (as the previous
director had also promised) while the director of transportation, E. Alvey Wright, held over from the former regime,
continued to press for a new freeway to open them for
development.

What was wanting was firm policy, consistently pointing to
an assured future for agriculture in Hawaii. There was no
lack of foundation for such a position, but the political will
was absent. The University of Hawaii has a respected College
of Tropical Agriculture which over the years has done what
it could—in inadequate facilities and with a small budget—to
help improve and bolster local growing capacities and techniques. It has never found the same enthusiastic support
from the business community that, for example, the school
of Travel Industry Management enjoys. A new dean was
appointed in 1976, the former head of a United Nations
agricultural agency, and he arrived full of enthusiasm. "I see
Hawaii as an agricultural-commercial center for the Orient
and the Pacific," Dr. William Furtick said. "One of the
most important problems facing mankind is developing a
strong agricultural capability in the tropical areas, the only
major untapped reservoir of food production left."[30] Those
were exciting words. One wondered, though, whether the new
dean—an employee of the state now—realized that Dr.
C. Peairs Wilson, the man he succeeded, had once arrived
with equal enthusiasm . . . and had left with a sense of
frustrated hopelessness because of the state's coolness to the
college's programs.

To direct his school to the broad goals he outlines, the new
dean would also have to contend with the attitude expressed
by two economic study groups at about the same time he
arrived, one appointed by the governor and the other privately sponsored. They agreed in their findings that Hawaii's

economic future lay with tourism, not agriculture. Both concluded that the plantations were indisputably on their way out as a major economic and employment base for the islands and could not be replaced in that role by other kinds of agriculture. Small support for farming could be expected from the business community, then. And in the face of those predictions little hope could be held for a political policy of protecting agricultural lands for agricultural uses.

The problems that serious farmers faced in this situation were manifold. Land was costly and in competition with other uses. The local market was unstable and tempted by more stylish imports. There was not the government activity in finding wider markets that there had been during the lush days of sugar-and-pine export. An example of the difficulties in farming's way was the experience of an ex-architect named David Curtis, son of a mainland rancher-farmer. Curtis saw great agricultural potential on Molokai, gave up his architectural practice in Honolulu, and leased from the state two hundred acres of fertile but tough, windy land. Curtis was realistic. He knew that he must produce profitable exports to make his venture work in the long run and he decided that they were to be macadamia nuts. Until those trees matured and bore, and as a move toward true food farming, he raised onions, of the sweet variety that grows quite well locally. In a few years he was producing and shipping to Oahu 17,000 bags annually, but then his crop was struck by a blight (which the University's tropical agriculture experts frantically worked to cure for him) and in 1973 his onion output dropped to 3,000 bags. Then he grew cabbage, which did well, and beans, which proved to be a good crop, and hung on until his onions revived. Still he faces continual, unpredictable competition in the Oahu markets from imports of produce from off the islands, such as Texas onions, that at times arrive in distressful quantities.

Curtis is a medium-sized farmer (twenty people at times work for him), not a large corporate enterprise but certainly not a homesteader. He and a few others like him know what they are doing, what they need, what the soil will produce, what mechanization is essential, what capitalization is required. Farmers of this kind, whether experienced oldtimers or newcomers, represent the enterprise that would be needed to keep Molokai's agricultural land, as well as similar lands on the other islands, in agricultural production.

"There is so much talk about Molokai's being the breadbasket of Honolulu, but it's not a very well thought out idea," says Curtis indulgently. "The market so easily gets out of balance."[31]

In Hawaii's present mood, there seems little likelihood of achieving the sort of balance that Curtis and others need—a stability that only a firm policy of government support consistently implemented could provide. The political preference is for a balancing act that juggles arable land back and forth between various uses as conflicting economic pressures develop.

chapter 7

Source of Shelter

EVEN though Hawaii is threatened with overbuilding on its open green lands, there are not enough homes to shelter all its people properly. Every few years someone makes a new study of the "housing problem" and comes up with a fresh version of an old set of facts: for its own residents, Hawaii's supply of living places is insufficient in numbers, inadequate in quality, and overly expensive in cost. It appears, then, that the lands of Hawaii are not being well used for provision of shelter. This seems to be another case where the Polynesian inhabitants of the islands, with their primitive technology, were better able to acquire life's necessities from the land than are today's residents with all their vaunted know-how.

The early Hawaiians constructed well what quarters they needed, placed them in the most suitable and convenient locations, and built them of materials that the land provided. The contemporary dwellers on Hawaii live, typically, in houses built very carelessly, located wherever a subdivision developer finds unused space for sale, and manufactured of products brought from many places by commercial suppliers. The original natives knew their lands well enough to grow their food in one place and build their houses in another, separated but conveniently near. Today's people of Hawaii allow houses to be built on thousands of acres of the land that is best for growing foodstuffs.

The comparison is totally unfair, of course. There were only some 250,000 Polynesian Hawaiians when Captain Cook found them; today there are three times as many inhabitants. Then, because they lived an agrarian life, farming and fishing, they were able to scatter their buildings on the hillsides so that a village of perhaps ten thousand people was almost invisible to the discoverers when they came.[1] Today's urban centers and residential subdivisions and the wide roads connecting them are obtrusively visible. People must assemble to work wherever the businesses that employ them are located. They must have their homes built where utilities are available and where schools, shopping centers, and service stations can be provided. It is a different kind of life. Dwelling units are not made individually by hand but are mass-produced in suburban rows or in high-rise tiers as they are everywhere else in the industrialized world—with not much consideration for how people really want to live in the islands or how their lands want to be used.

The early Hawaiians (who probably, at first, lived in caves) had a carefully developed construction system for their houses by the time Captain Cook arrived.[2] The primary materials they used were stone, timber, pandanus leaf *(lau hala)*, and pili grass. The stone adz, the principal construction tool, was supplemented with shaped shells and bones. Structures were cleverly lashed together (these were sailors as well as farmers) with occasional use of wooden pegs fitted by bone drills. The basic construction system was post, plate, and rafter, highly stylized, with descriptive names for each member. The timber skeleton, secured to a stone foundation platform that was sometimes earth-filled, was thatched with pandanus or strong grass. The typical building had a single low entrance. There were no windows or other openings. Students of early Polynesian history have provided detailed descriptions and drawings of the many construction details that were developed and carefully followed. A number of studied reconstructions have been made to demonstrate the system, too, so this aspect of the Hawaiian life-style before the white man came is well documented.[3]

The home of the typical household (a unit within the expanded family, or *'ohana,*) consisted of several buildings. Considered as fundamental were a living and sleeping building, a house where the men prepared food and ate, and an eating place for the women of the household. More pretentious places included a separate building for menstruating women (usually a comfortable thatched house) and other structures that might be needed for work: a canoe house for a fisherman, a tool house for a farmer, buildings for tapa makers, mat weavers, and so on.

There was no profession of home builder as such, but skills in the art were developed and appreciated and experts were much in demand for guidance and help.[4] The location of the home was so important that it required the services of another specialist: a diviner who knew, for instance, that if a house faced the road illness would result, if it was situated above its neighbors, wealth might come, whereas disputes would develop if it was placed behind others. Great care was given, then, to location as well as to the planning and construction of the buildings; even death might occur, it was believed, if major alterations had to be made to a home after it was completed. While home building of this nature was, by all evidence, the common tradition until the white man came, Ellis described other kinds of shelter he saw on his travels: spacious caves in some places; larger family residences, "quite open," in others.[5]

Malo and other early writers refer to "villages" and "towns" and Cook described villagelike gatherings of houses that he saw, but these were not commercial or political centers as we know urbanized places. Homes were built in clusters because land for housing, even then, was a limited resource considering the size of the population. The population was widely dispersed, nevertheless. Some of the village-like complexes were inland or on the slopes, if occupations such as farming made this reasonable; others were on the shore near good fishing places.

Although political control might change as a result of battle or inheritance, towns grew up inevitably around the chiefs' residences. The town of Napoopoo on the south side of Kealakekua Bay, where Cook and his men saw more than a thousand homes, was one of these. It clustered about the court of Kalaniopuu, the king who ruled that part of the island of Hawaii before Kamehameha's rise to power. John Ledyard, one of Cook's officers, described the community as attractive and the houses as having "an air of elegance and comfort." These groupings close to court became more urban in character, Malo notes, and their inhabitants developed characteristics quite different from people in the more rural settlements. Whereas country folk were industrious and "humble," enjoying simple games, inclined to "gathering together for some profitless occupation or pastime for talk's sake," and enjoying casual personal and sexual relations, those gathered around the chiefs were likely to be "overbearing, loudmouthed, contentious," searching for more sophisticated pleasures in a more tense atmosphere, with prostitution and even homosexuality common. Undoubtedly different kinds of personalities were attracted, to begin with, by urban excitement and rural contentment, even as they are today.[6]

This tradition of building communities of houses did not survive for long the advent of the white man.[7] Soon after the first haole arrivals, houses and other buildings constructed with boards nailed to studs, fitted with glazed windows and trimmed door openings, began to appear along the rough streets of the new towns. Not only did Kamehameha build himself European-style residences: his royal family and the alii who gathered about his court felt that they also must improve on the houses that had once satisfied them. Shortly before 1800 Vancouver's men visited a kingly family in its compound of sleeping and eating places and other houses built carefully in the traditional manner. But soon after the turn of the century a visiting dignitary called on Queen Namahana, one of Kamehameha's wives, in her "pretty little house of two stories, built in the European manner." Already Honolulu was boasting many frontier-style wooden buildings.[8]

Construction materials became an important item on the bills of lading of the ships that began making Honolulu a regular port of call, but it was a long time before anything like enough timber and fittings were available. Some buildings were constructed of blocks of coral stone or lava rock, but these masonry materials were difficult and time-consuming to use.[9] Thatched structures were still built for some years, distasteful as they were to the foreigners, and early drawings of Honolulu, Hilo, and Lahaina show an odd structural hodgepodge.[10] The common Hawaiian native was not likely to enjoy either a "pretty" or a well-built home in town when he left his thatched house. With the influx of newcomers and the movement of the Hawaiian people away from the land toward the new communities, Hawaii's perpetual housing shortage had begun.

During the years of the monarchy, as some of the towns grew to substantial size, the construction industry prospered and thousands of solid homes were built. But the deficiency in housing for the natives and other less affluent members of the community was never solved. The troubles of the ordinary Hawaiian had to do with loss of contact with the land. In a new urban life removed from the sustenance of the soil, the Hawaiian people learned that jobs and salaries were necessary for subsistence, but their dispositions were disinclined to this social pattern. Food, which had grown so readily from Hawaiian soil, was now often hard to come by. Homes, which had been built so easily on the open land, were now often difficult to find in the native quarters of the new cities. The problem was carried into the government administrations that followed the overthrow of the kingdom and it increasingly involved more of the population than the Hawaiians and part-Hawaiians. Chinese, Japanese, and then Filipino plantation workers moved to the cities to seek jobs or start businesses that they hoped would improve their lot—and they needed places to live. Inevitably, workers from the mainland and abroad came to find employment in the increasing commercial activities in the towns, and not all of them were well fixed or well paid; they too needed urban dwelling places.

Hawaii went through all the phases of the "housing problem" and tried all the solutions the U.S. mainland had tried in the early twentieth century. Honolulu and to a lesser extent other towns allowed ghettos to develop and tenements to be built. Company towns were established at the plantation sites. Endless efforts were made to encourage homesteading. None of these panaceas worked in other places and they all failed in Hawaii as well. The underlying difficulty was modern man's inability to relate land, as a resource, with shelter, as a need, when land was considered a commodity.

The plantation towns were no better than company-owned communities usually are; one chronicler describes them as "ugly and harshly uncomfortable places," segregated living places for non-haole workers.[11] When living conditions became so bad that it was difficult to keep workers in the fields, paternalistic improvements and some rehabilitation of crowded and unsanitary quarters were often undertaken.[12] (When the Hawaiian Sugar Planters Association was formed, this was one of its first recommendations to its members. At best, however, life remained strictly controlled and income was often mortgaged. It took union organization in the 1940s to begin real improvement in plantation-town conditions (with the militant organizers, at first, evicted from their homes) so that later some plantation communities could boast of excellent living conditions and fine recreation, health, and education facilities. Dependency on the company remains a socioeconomic problem, nevertheless; as the plantations phase out, the worker-dwellers often find themselves with neither job nor living quarters.

The Homestead Experiments

From the time when Kamehameha III worried about the Hawaiians leaving their land to live in town, there were periodic tries at some form of residential subsistence homesteading. After the revolution that overthrew the monarchy, Sanford Dole, guided by Jeffersonian ideals of a resident yeomanry, was determined to advance the homesteading concept.[13] The republic's Land Act of 1895 made possible small acquisitions for homesteading from the bank of public lands, and some eight hundred people asked for and received about forty thousand acres for that purpose.[14] After annexation, the Organic Act attempted to make homesteading more attractive and the Land Commission of the territory was mandated to survey, open up, and sell public land to any association of twenty-three or more eligible citizens who applied for it. Partly because of bureaucratic difficulties, disappointingly few such applications were received, however, and few of those granted showed signs of success.[15]

The most serious homesteading attempt of that period was made in 1918 at Waiakea on the Big Island. When the lease of the Waiakea Mill Company ran out, the government took back six thousand acres, in 216 lots, of good agricultural land and offered them to "serious, bona fide" homesteaders. Over two thousand applications were received and the plots were distributed by lottery. Serious or not, there were few experienced farmers among the recipients and they received little advice. Within a short time the plantation had most of the land back again.[16] The failure of the Waiakea experiment did not discourage homestead enthusiasts, however. Congres-

sional Delegate Prince Kuhio, Territorial Senator John Wise
(a part-Hawaiian), and others continued to push for more
favorable legislation.

By the time of the 1920s these continuing efforts to help
the Hawaiian people regain a foothold on their native soil
were joined in an unhappy political linkage with the plantation owners' wish to gain more land. A large number of
government land rentals, many of them negotiated during
Kalakaua's reign, were about to expire, and the planters
wanted to be in a position to dicker for more acreage than
they had.[17] Particularly, they were anxious to have the
ownership limitation of one thousand acres removed. To
accomplish this and gain several other aims (making it
difficult for local Japanese to acquire land was one of them)
the landholding oligarchy was willing to make some apparent
concessions toward placing Hawaiians on the land. They felt
sure that the homestead plots would again, before long,
revert to the plantations. A lobbying delegation to Washington worked out a bill that finally passed Congress—the
Hawaiian Rehabilitation Act (often known as the Hawaiian
Homes Commission Act) of 1920,[18] which was "conceived in
almost purely political terms," as one analyst has put it.[19]
The thousand acre limit was removed, Japanese were forbidden federal jobs (making it hard for them to gain land), and
gestures were made toward homestead housing. All "highly
cultivated lands" were to be leased to the highest bidder, and
some 200,000 acres were earmarked for the "rehabilitation"
of the Hawaiian people.

The moral pretense of this politically conceived legislation
was obvious at once. The best lands went to the top bidders,
which meant the wealthiest, as John Wise noted, and they of
course were the plantation owners. The lands set aside for
homesteading were seldom good agricultural plots.[20] There
was no more attempt now to formulate a workable plan
through helping the homesteaders in farming and marketing
than there had been at the time of the Waiakea fiasco. The

temptation of the new homestead owners to lease workable plots back to the plantations (whose managers then put Filipino laborers to work cultivating them) was still great.[21] There were some successful experiments, particularly on the island of Molokai, but in general it was true, as a later official analysis of the act concluded, that not only was the immediate rehabilitation program a failure but "the demand for the opening of new homestead tracts practically ceased" with the passage of the bill.[22]

By the time of statehood, there was agreement among most groups that despite the efforts that had been made over the years homesteading attempts just would not work in a competitive society where agriculture had become big business. Certainly there was little likelihood that such rehabilitation efforts would furnish the housing that the Hawaiian people, along with other unaccommodated groups, needed. Yet even today a Department of Hawaiian Home Lands, established in the 1960s as successor to the Hawaiian Homes Commission, continues to administer remnants of a government homesteading policy. Billie Beamer, a part-Hawaiian director of the department appointed by Governor Ariyoshi, has made valiant efforts to improve use of the lands that remain in the program. Many lie unplanted and unbuilt upon, some are almost unusable, a good quantity has been leased for other purposes (including the Hilo and Molokai airports), a portion was early "set aside" for federal government uses, and of those that were being farmed by resident homesteaders, as intended, a sizable number are in serious rental arrears. In a report to the legislature in 1975, Beamer called for a reevaluation of the entire program—from objectives to implementation. "We search for directions," she said, admitting that less than 10 percent of eligible Hawaiians were then on homestead land and only 13 percent of them were using their plots for farming or ranching.[23] The legislature has not yet indicated directional guidance (failed, in fact, to act on Beamer's recommendation in its 1977 session), and family farming, pleasant as it may be as a way of life to some, remains a small and unimportant solution to the overall problem of housing Hawaii's people.

Once it was obvious that homesteading was not going to be an important method, the attitude of most territorial governors toward ways to use the land for housing was ambivalent. Generally a conservative succession of appointees, they tended to defend concentrated land ownership, but as time went on it became increasingly clear that homesites for the growing population would have to be subtracted from plantation acreages. Governor Stainback (1934–1942), disturbed by the fact that so few held so much of the territory's lands, proposed a forward-looking Hawaiian Homes Development Corporation to tackle the problem—a move that the legislature considered communistic and defeated. He did, however, appoint a Land Revision Commission which recommended against any further homesteading efforts and advocated sale of public lands for single-family homesites and other urban development purposes. Although the governor supported his commission's proposals, little effective legislation resulted. Governor King (1953–1957), a part-Hawaiian, made one last effort to revive interest in homesteading, still without success. When Governor Quinn (1957–1959 and then, after statehood, 1959–1962) proposed his Second Mahele, its major intention was to have the private trusts sell some of their land for fee-simple home ownership. After the Democrat takeover of the legislature in 1954, much of the land reform legislation, proposed or adopted, had to do with forcing more land to be available for housing construction. A Hawaii Land Development Authority, somewhat similar to the one Governor Stainback had wanted to create, was appointed in 1959. It was not as strong in potential as some legislators had wished and was never used to the fullest of what promise it did have.

The problem that was faced then, and was not solved, continues today. With so much of the buildable land held by a few owners, a great proportion of Hawaii's homes are necessarily built on leased property. The leasehold land system has developed its own set of customs, rules and regulations, and legal sanctions. Leases are negotiated for a period of years and must be renegotiated at the end of that time if the lessee wants to stay on. Lessees pay taxes and assessments on the land they use just as though they owned it. "Improvements," including the house itself, can be built on the property with the permission of the landowner and, under most lease arrangements, can be removed at the end of the lease period. Absurd as that provision seems, it makes financing home construction easier and provides a kind of lever at the time of renegotiation.

In recent years pressure on the landed estates to allow fee-simple land sales in place of leasehold tenancies has increased. Inability to own one's own land has been galling to middle-class malihinis from the mainland indoctrinated in the great value that America attaches to the ownership of the land one lives on. More seriously disturbing, lease negotiations have resulted in greatly increased payments as the valuations assigned to urban land have risen sharply. On the average, land in Hawaii has grown in market and assessed value to seventeen times its 1950 worth—in some areas as much as fifty times.[24] The fact that rises in residential land costs would give landowners a reason to be tough in their renegotiation of leases—to a point that might make home ownership on leased land precarious—had been evident to the legislatures concerned with land reform measures in the 1960s. A right-to-purchase law, known as the Maryland law because it was similar to legislation adopted in that state, was passed as Act 307 in 1967. It turned out to be an ineffective measure and, because of built-in administrative difficulties, was seldom used. The state was supposed to be able to buy, at a minimum, five-acre tracts for resale to leasehold owners, if enough of them in the five-acre area wanted to buy their plots. This law raised certain problems, however: no one was

sure whether it was constitutional, and no one really wanted
to test it.

When lease renegotiations conducted by inflexible landlords guided by cold-blooded tax appraisers began to make
it impossible for many families to live in the homes they
themselves had built, pressures for more effectual land-lease
reform increased. There were a number of reasons for the
rising cost of urban residential land which resulted in the
larger appraised values which seemed to justify the greater
sums asked for renegotiated leases. The limits on land available as homesites, in a market where demand was increasing,
was obviously one reason. Desire for speculative profits on
the part of homeowners themselves was another. During the
1970s house-hopping became a common practice.[25] Some
houses in more desirable areas had FOR SALE signs displayed several times a year. The ability to sell one's home at
as much as a 100 percent "profit" made many families
overlook the fact that any new house or apartment they
might move to would be burdened with a similar arbitrary
increment. Not only greedy homeowners but professional real
estate speculators recognized the inviting ability to buy and
sell houses at a handsome gain within a matter of weeks.

Whatever the causes, the higher evaluated prices, even if
they were not true values, seemed to justify greatly increased
land rents. For lower-income people in rural areas, like the
farmers living on leased land in windward Oahu's valleys, or
the townspeople in older areas like Kalihi and Palama, the
situation was tragic: they could not afford the new rents they
were asked to pay and had no other place to go. Some were
preparing to fight eviction. As a community leader said,
emotionally, "This is the stuff revolutions are made of."[26] In
more affluent neighborhoods problems of a different scale
were faced, but their results could also be disastrous. In the
Waialae-Kahala area, where an upper-middle-class suburb
had been formed from pig farms in 1950, the Bishop Estate
land had been valued at about thirty cents a square foot then

and was leased at around $90 a year per lot. After fifteen years these rates were renegotiated—to $250 or $300 a year. But after a decade or so of speculative inflation, the estate set "renegotiated" lease costs at ten times those rates, boosting them to $2,500 or $3,000—a jump in the family budget from perhaps $25 a month to $250.

Faced with such increases, more owners of homes on leased land wanted the privilege of buying the property they were occupying. In 1975 the legislature passed two new measures and amended the 1967 act in several ways.[27] In effect, the law now says that annual lease rents must be limited to 4 percent of "fair market value" less certain off-site improvement costs (which still allowed many leases to be boosted by several hundred percent) and that landowners must buy improvements on the land at their full value if the lease is not negotiated. It also includes provisions making it more possible for the state to carry out the intent of the so-called Maryland law.

No one is sure what the long-term effects of this legislation will be. Local people are now accustomed to lease arrangements. (Almost two-thirds of Hawaii's residents, until recently, rented their homes, compared to one-third in the mainland United States.) Spokesmen for the Bishop Estate first said that it, for one, would be happy to get rid of its small leased properties (under "equitable" conditions, of course). But later the estate challenged the new lease ceilings in the courts and declared a moratorium on all lease extensions until the whole matter was "clarified." The restrictions on lease rents and the encouragement of sales to lessees "changed the rules of the game," as one estate trustee put it, making it necessary to "adjust policies" to protect the estate's income.[28] Still later, in early 1977, both the Bishop and Campbell estates expressed willingness to discuss ways to sell off their residential land parcels.

How many homeowners will really want to "own" their homes will be known only over a long period of time. One group of lessees of land on a smaller estate in Niu Valley moved quickly to take advantage of the new provisions, with careful legal advice, and succeeded in arranging a satisfactory purchase agreement, but not many others planned to follow suit immediately. If the law has the effect that was intended, a larger question will remain: will fragmented rather than concentrated ownership be helpful or harmful to effective planning and reasonable use of Hawaii's residential lands?

From "Problem" to "Crisis"

Aside from questions of leasing or owning land, or of paying rent or paying off a mortgage on a house, in the larger sense of adequacy and availability of accommodation the housing situation in Hawaii reached a truly critical stage during the first decade of statehood. From then on it has been referred to as a housing "crisis" rather than a "problem." In 1970 a penetrating report entitled *Hawaii's Crisis in Housing* was prepared by the state's then lieutenant governor, Tom Gill.[29] The study made these points: 70,000 to 100,000 additional dwelling units were needed just to meet current demands; more than half of Hawaii's citizens were exceeding the commonly budgeted 20 percent of income for shelter; the cost of new houses in Hawaii was 60 percent above prices for those built on the mainland (even though no heating systems were needed); residential land costs were three times the national average; the local housing industry was tightly controlled and in many ways inefficient.

Gill recommended four government actions. One was to make suitable public land, state and federal, available for housing construction. Another was for the state to enter into contracts with competent developers to build large-scale, well-planned, cost-controlled communities (on nonagricultural land). A third was to develop government-sponsored financing arrangements so that the new units would be available to all socioeconomic groups. And, finally, the

Gill report recommended that the state—in order to forestall
the speculation in built homes that was boosting original
prices—buy back at original cost plus interest any units that
the first owners wanted to sell.

Under the rising pressure, Burns' administration proposed
and the legislature adopted in that same year, 1970, a grab-
bag housing measure, Act 105, that promised great things
but produced few of them. It followed many of the suggestions in the Gill report: it gave authority to the state to
condemn land, help finance construction costs, guarantee
mortgages, contract or joint venture with developers, and
build innovative communities. It also permitted the state to
issue revenue bonds to finance the program, although for
many years no bonds were floated. Implementation of the
program was put under the jurisdiction of the Hawaii Housing Authority (HHA), an agency with no great record of accomplishment. There it languished, partly due to insufficient
staff to administer it, partly because of lack of administrative
enthusiasm. Since the provisions of the act were very little
used after its passage, it was inevitable that cynical citizens
came to believe that Burns, through sponsoring the measure,
had simply made a political gesture that helped him succeed
in his campaign for reelection that fall. After all, his unsuccessful opponent in the Democratic primaries had been Tom
Gill.

In 1972 the state commissioned another comprehensive
study of the housing crisis. This one, made by the consultant
firm of Marshall Kaplan Gans Kahn & Yamamoto, was
entitled *Housing in Hawaii: Problems, Needs and Plans.*[30]
Although the data gathered for this study were more
complete than Gill's, its findings were much the same. It
documented a great deficiency in housing for middle and low
income groups and showed in detail why it would be impossible for private industry to meet those needs. The report
indicated that fifty thousand units would be required in the
next five years to fill the existing lack, meet the additional

anticipated demand, and replace the worst of the deteriorated places. A program of action was proposed, including establishment of a state land bank, state financing to write down land acquisition costs, use of air rights and other devices to lower land costs for planned communities in urban areas, and a number of other innovative moves. The report was applauded by all who read it, was widely quoted (and is still the best source material available)—and was shelved.

Hawaii cannot be blamed more than any other part of the United States for its inability to house the middle and low income sectors of the population. This is an unanswered challenge in all of industrialized America. Costs of land, construction, and financing under a building-for-profit system have created a burden that a great proportion of the citizens on the mainland as well as in Hawaii can carry only with government assistance of some kind.[31] As Hawaii became fully Americanized it inherited all those contemporary difficulties while it was still struggling to unravel its own tangle of shelter problems produced by the quick changes of the nineteenth and early twentieth centuries.

Along with the problems of modern America, of course, the islands also gained the opportunity to try the mainland's solutions to them. From time to time in its history Hawaii has experimented with procedures developed under the Housing and Urban Development administration—and generally has discovered that they did not help very much. Redevelopment agencies, under the federal Urban Renewal Program, were set up in Honolulu and in Hilo, and some of the more colorful areas in those cities were demolished, as slums, to make room for typical American commercial and residential developments. Some good things resulted from these programs: Queen Emma Gardens, an apartment complex handsomely designed by Minoru Yamasaki, Detroit architect, but priced beyond the low-income families for whom it was intended; Kukui Gardens, a lower-rise grouping of lower-priced units designed by a more matter-of-fact firm (Daniel,

Mann, Johnson, and Mendenhall) in a more prosaic manner; several commercially successful shopping areas in the two cities; office buildings, public and private; and even a hotel in Hilo. But they were by no means answers to the widespread, deep-seated housing deficiency.

The various FHA programs of the 1960s for subsidies and lower interest rates were used by some developers until those aids were eliminated under the Nixon administration. The HHA had been established as a public housing authority very early after statehood, and it had succeeded in building about a thousand living places under the federal public housing program. One, Kuhio Terrace, an ugly, ill-planned high rise, could challenge St. Louis's famous Pruitt-Igoe project for unsuitability to the life-styles of its tenants. Pruitt-Igoe was ultimately demolished, however, while Kuhio Terrace remains, miserably visible and unhappily occupied.

Facing other legislative sessions with no additional moves likely, a number of citizen groups, brought together by the local chapter of the League of Women Voters, formed a People's Housing Coalition in 1974 and proposed a comprehensive program of housing action. This program included measures to curb speculation in the short housing supply through buy-back and owner occupancy provisions, controls over unwarranted rent increases, establishment of a semipublic housing development corporation similar to New York's Urban Development Corporation—and strengthening and implementing Act 105. The legislators at first seemed impressed by the proposals and the extent of their public support: they debated a number of the suggestions, including the development corporation concept, at some length. In the end, however, they backed off. They did little more to attack the basic problems than their predecessors had done.

All the studies, recommendations, debates, and occasional bits of legislation about housing dealt with the *economics* of providing shelter, certainly one of the toughest parts of the problem. By 1975 the average sales price of a new home in

Honolulu was $83,000—in a state where the median income of a civilian family was around $10,000.[32] The average citizen of upper middle income, to say nothing of the lower-paid worker, was finding it increasingly difficult to pay the monthly costs of either a mortgaged or a rented house on either mortgaged or rented land. An updated study by the state in 1977 noted that 55,000 homes had been added to the supply since the 1972 *Housing in Hawaii* report, with most available units "not within price ranges which can be afforded by those residents who have the greatest housing needs."[33]

In such a crucial situation, land, the restricted resource on which all shelter, high-priced or low, must be built, also has to be thought about in primarily economic terms. How much of it will be available for new housing? At what prices? How can more be obtained and how can its cost be lowered? Questions of what lands were most *appropriate* for residential use were seldom considered and seemed almost irrelevant. Stewart Udall, preparing his open-space plan, recognized that "on the surface" his proposals for conserving open space seemed to "contribute to and perpetuate" the lack of low-priced land to build houses on. He hopefully argued that better planning would solve the problem and make the proper distinctions among proper uses.[34]

It did not require a professional planner to see what a drastic choice faced Hawaii's decision makers in the land-housing relationship. If more homes were to be built to loosen up the tight market that helped to force costs to impossible figures and perpetuated the use of unfit places, there were only two directions for them to go. They could be built in districts already classified for urban uses, at increasingly high densities, on land that was usually costly. Or they could spread out on undeveloped, less expensive land, at densities as low as desired, where reclassification from agricultural or conservation uses would be required.

Since there seemed no likelihood of a decision to limit population growth, Hawaii's people had to choose, then, between living more closely together, to save their open spaces, and living dispersed, in suburbs which consumed that open space. In the 1970s the decision was being made by default. Developers went ahead with their developments wherever they could find land that would attract a market that could afford their product. Some were happy to build in-town condominiums on land zoned for urban uses; others preferred to seek the zoning that would allow them to build on raw land outside the central city.

As for the citizens who needed a place to live, they still seemed to prefer "the Hawaiian way of life" in mainland-style subdivisions. The number of high-rise apartments (generally condominiums) built annually began to outpace new single-family house construction, but many of them were for transients, retired mainlanders, and speculators; local people who lived in tract-home neighborhoods still out-numbered the in-city dwellers. In addition, not all the condominiums were really in town. A number of new apartment developments were built in suburban areas like Hawaii Kai or Salt Lake—even as far out as Chinn Ho's hillside high rises in Makaha Valley.

Neither in the outer stretches of the islands nor within the towns and cities, however, could a way be found in modern times to make Hawaii's lands serve well as a resource for its people's shelter. There had been enough attempts to combine a way of living on the soil with the process of farming it to demonstrate that *that* simple solution could not work here and now as it had in primitive places. To live comfortably on the land by even the simplest modern standards it was necessary to make arrangements with a myriad of owners, vendors, and agents. It did not seem to make much dif-ference whether the land itself was offered for lease or outright sale, whether the offerer was a profit-oriented entity or an eleemosynary institution, whether or not government interceded in the transaction. The result was almost always the same: acceptance of living accommodations that were

priced above a proper share of family income and placed
where economics, not suitability, dictated. There were, of
course, degrees of discomfiture resulting from this process—
from the distress of less-favored families to the inconvenience
of the better-advantaged. All, however, suffered from the
same basic disadvantage: the intrusion between dweller and
dwelling of a long series of profit-generating stages. The
citizen of a modern capitalist industrial state, which Hawaii
has become, is accustomed to this process in every aspect of
life, from securing food to finding entertainment. In Hawaii,
however, the stretch between the ability to buy and the price
that must be paid is nowhere so great as it is for the commodity we coldly call "housing"—a living place on the land.

chapter 8

Source of Wealth

ON an August morning in 1965, Henry Kaiser, the industrialist who had made a worldwide reputation for building huge engineering projects and then building his own construction and development empire, had a meeting in Honolulu with the trustees of the Bishop Estate. Kaiser had gone to Hawaii to vacation in 1950 and decided to stay and introduce mainland American methods of land development and construction. He was now leasing six thousand acres of Bishop Estate land at the eastern end of Oahu to build a small city and was in a hurry to get started. This stocky, solemn, but restless malihini had to satisfy the kamaaina trustees of the estate of Princess Bernice Pauahi Bishop that his plans were feasible and would produce a satisfactory income for the Kamehameha Schools. To him the procedure was an unavoidable nuisance.

Kaiser sat at the end of a long koa table in a large koa-paneled room along with the trustees (all selected by Hawaii's Supreme Court justices as the will of the Kamehameha heiress provided, most well along in years, only one with a tinge of Hawaiian blood) as though he were one of them. No one seemed to question his right.

Several members of the firm of planners and architects who had made Kaiser's plans for him explained the extent of the proposal. Graphs and charts were tacked on the walls and maps and drawings displayed on easels. It was an impressive presentation of a development that would change the character of a major part of the island. The trustees and their own technical advisers looked, listened, nodded from time to time, and at the end congratulated Mr. Kaiser. For him, that was enough. He stood, nodded in his turn, with satisfaction, and moved to leave the room. At the door he stopped and as though in afterthought asked no one in particular, "How soon can we get started now?"

Frank Midkiff, one of the most down-to-earth of the board members, smiled and said, "Henry, we have a few steps to take yet, even after we have informal approval from the City. A change in the general plan, zoning revisions, other formalities that we will all have to go through."

Kaiser thought a moment. "All right," he said then. "But let's see that it doesn't take too long."[1]

It did not, as those things go, but to Henry Kaiser, anxious to re-form that part of Oahu in the image he pictured, it seemed an interminable process. Taken by the beauty of the islands—and the tremendous profit potential of that beauty—he had transferred his personal interests from the numerous mainland Kaiser industries to development activities in Hawaii. He had already altered the character of Waikiki by building a hotel at its far western end, tremendously extending the reach of tourism there, and had started a new industry for the state in the production of cement.

Now Kaiser's consuming enterprise was this plan to make the entire Koko Head end of Oahu into a resort-residential town to be called Hawaii Kai. What a remarkably fortuitous coincidence that the first syllable of his name was the Hawaiian word for the sea! Hawaii Kai, reached from Honolulu only by a narrow road winding between sometimes steep foothills and often sharp drops to the ocean, was nevertheless to have endless tracts of suburban homes, a large shopping center, communities of condominiums along the ridges, numerous hotels on the beaches, a marina, several golf courses—all on those six thousand acres of Bishop Estate land that were not at that time zoned for such purposes, but were classified for open-space conservation uses by city and state.

In the end, there was no problem and the impatient Mr. Kaiser did not have to wait very long. By another of those happy coincidences that seemed to bless his career, the General Plan of the City and County of Honolulu was undergoing revision just then and it was very convenient for the public planners to incorporate Kaiser's consultants' plan, with some revisions, in their final document.[2] When the city's new long-range plan was approved by the Planning Commission and adopted by the city council, Hawaii Kai was an integral part of it, as Henry Kaiser had never doubted it would be.

The story of Kaiser's project illustrates handsomely the contradictions and counteractions in the determinations of Hawaii's land uses. Land development today provides necessary homes for an upper-middle-class segment of Oahu's population; in that sense the land is being used as an essential resource. The rental income that the Bishop Estate receives helps to educate children of Hawaiian descent; to that extent some of Hawaii's lands still benefit the Hawaiian people. But Hawaii Kai has also made a small fortune for the Kaiser enterprises and Henry Kaiser's heirs (as well as decent profits for numerous subcontracting developer-builders). Considered in that way, it has used for private monetary gain land that had once been set aside as a great park for the public.

Many questions are raised by these conflicting values—questions that were not asked when government agencies simply approved Kaiser's intentions and allowed the eastern end of Oahu to become a huge suburb. Have those houses really satisfied a need that existed? Or, by being built, have they created one, just as a new highway generates additional

traffic and a new airport increases the wish to travel by air?
If they were necessary, was that the best place to put them,
or would they have been better located on other land? And
assuming still that they are essential living places, are they
the kinds of homes in the kind of community that Hawaii's
people really need, or are they just Henry Kaiser's idea of
the sort of shelter for the sort of resident he wanted Hawaii
to have? Are the answers to these questions ones that an
economist can supply, or a sociologist, or a land planner?
Or would they best be furnished by the people of Hawaii
themselves? No one asked those questions in 1965, and there
is no indication that the people now living in Hawaii Kai are
bothered by them. Their concern is how to have a wider,
faster road to downtown Honolulu.

Economists in Hawaii as in other places have not provided
very useful answers to such questions—they disagree on the
ways to estimate the worth of land and the income that may
be derived from it. Not many students of economic theory
would endorse the simplistic distinction between land used as
a resource, satisfying certain human needs, and land used as
a commodity, providing someone a monetary profit or loss.
In economics, everything must be capable of quantification
so that it can be put on one side or the other of a ledger. It
seems impossible to assign dollar values to all of our needs,
but attempts to do so are increasing.

Even social theorists and citizen activists today are shying
away from the defense of physical environments as spiritual-
ly, aesthetically, or even socially essential for individual
fulfillment or the public good. The tendency is to develop
economic rather than social or even ecological arguments for
keeping some lands open. Cash-flow analyses are beginning
to replace emotional reasons to defend husbandry of other
lands for sustenance and shelter.[3] Ways are being sought to
meet, on their own ground, the Henry Kaisers who want to
make money from land.

This new approach, of course, has to consider two aspects
of land use management: one for land we should leave alone;

another for land we must lay our hands on in some fashion. To use to their best advantage places where it would be most appropriate to grow food or build housing, the argument has been the familiar plea for good planning—land is limited and must not be used wastefully. The early Hawaiians knew, better than we do, where those appropriate places were and how to protect them. But even though no economist, not even a thoughtful developer, would disagree with that principle as a premise for land usage, it has not prevented thousands of acres of essential farmland from being removed from agriculture and developed carelessly. The pressures for using land as a source of immediate, visible income have just been too great.

During the 1960s and 1970s a counterforce to the compulsion to make land pay quick profits began to appear. It even had an economic validity of its own that was useful to environmental planners. It was a growing realization that *public* costs are generated by *private* land uses and that sometimes these become excessive financial loads on all taxpayers. The public costs come from the need for roads to new subdivisions; sewerage and water supply to developments on raw land; schools, libraries, and parks for neighborhoods being formed; protection by police, fire fighters, and other public servants for communities that developers developed, sold, and then left.

On the mainland several cities which retained consultants to advise them about the course of future growth received unexpected findings. Their analysts sometimes discovered that unless expansion was carefully limited, controlled, and planned it would be better not to have it at all: costs to the citizens would be too great. Palo Alto, California, was told by a consultant team that every new house built on a stretch of undeveloped hill land would cost the city much more in services than it could ever get back in taxes.[4]

In Hawaii itself, a central Oahu planning study made by the Department of Planning and Economic Development indicated that if developers went ahead with their plans for an additional 55,000 homes on Oahu's central plains, the costs that taxpayers would have to bear just for new highways, schools, and sewer and water supply (not even considering such municipal services as fire and police protection, local roads, and so on) would run to about $723 million—three-fourths of a billion dollars that no one had thought of at all. It pointed out further that the state would lose $25 million annually in income from the built-over plantations. In total, by any calculations, this would be far more than any feasible real-property taxes and other public sources of income from the development could possibly bring.[5]

In 1973, under University of Hawaii auspices, a conference was held to study this aspect of development economics: "The Public Costs of Private Development."[6] One of the Palo Alto consultants, an analyst for the central Oahu study, and others presented their findings. The information gathered was impressive, but it seemed to affect no one but those attending the conference sessions. Lawmakers from the state and the counties were invited; almost none attended.

The reasoning in studies of this kind had to do primarily with the most economical, least wasteful ways to allocate and use lands for farming and housing. The problem that remained, a more difficult one, was how to estimate hard cash costs and benefits of keeping land truly open for historic, scenic, cultural, or even recreational reasons.[7] Some economists would not even listen to the possibility that economic costs and benefits might be calculated, in cash terms, for open-space preservation. They saw little evidence that there could be monetary as well as spiritual or ecological losses when pristine beaches were lined with hotels and farm-lands were covered with condominiums. A report made to the state legislature by economists at the Economic Research Center of the University of Hawaii in 1971 grudgingly admitted that there might be "some real wealth enhanced" by keeping a certain amount of space open—for "residents and tourists who enjoy driving through [sic!] farm and conservation lands on the urban fringe."[8]

With this limited understanding and valuation of the natural environment, the report contended that the amount of private profit, not the degree of social need, should determine land use. If developers are willing to pay more for land than are farmers or others, then their intended use must be the best. After all, "retention of land in less than its highest-valued uses reduces the welfare of society." Even speculation in land ("risk-bearing for profit") performs an essential function, the report said, in holding land off the market and out of use until its development is profitable.[9]

To a critic who objected that values were changing and new social attitudes could alter such an economic theory, Louis A. Rose, author of the Economic Research Center's report, insisted that he had no way "to know society's valuation" of open space. Perhaps, he allowed, "some day economists, psychologists, and ecologists will come up with such an estimate." In the meantime he had no reason to believe that either preservation of agricultural lands or prevention of speculation in land are "economically desirable goals." Economics is a hard-boiled social science, he said, which "simply tells it like it is . . . not like it ought to be."[10]

Other economists, even in Hawaii, did not agree. Some had begun developing methods of calculating the overall economic return to society when certain lands were kept open. Even other members of the local university's Department of Economics studied ways to figure nonpecuniary, long-range, public economic costs and benefits along with immediate, private cash input and outgo.

Some factors, even environmental costs, were easy to translate directly into dollars: additional water supply needed when open lands were urbanized, for instance, and valuable natural drainage ways that were lost and had to be replaced. Others were less tangible but nonetheless provable public deficits: increased erosion and surface runoff into coastal estuaries and decreased amounts of topsoil with its oxygen-producing vegetation. Mineral resources and land-related sources of power are often lost to the public when land tenure becomes private.[11] Factors such as mental and physical health are even more difficult to express in terms of either public or private budgets, but the researchers believed it was possible. At least a start had been made in developing a further argument and a new point of view. And in the conservation temper of the times there seemed no doubt that it would be pursued further. For the time being, however, land in Hawaii remains a profitable commodity, its speculative manipulation defended by social custom, by economic principle, and, with certain restrictions, by law.[12]

The Speculating Game

Using land for other than basic needs and treating it as an article of commerce was a concept that haoles had to implant slowly in Hawaii. Among the Polynesians, land changed hands at times, but what manipulation there was came from a desire for power or prestige, more than profit. There was, of course, full understanding of the value of one ahupuaa compared with another, and great care (even jealousy) attended the distribution of land after a victory or on a new accession. Once assigned, however, the land stayed in the care of one chief until death or war brought a redistribution.[13]

As for the *makaainana,* the commoner who lived on the land and worked it, he could leave his kuleana if he wished, although there is evidence that great pride attached to long tenure of one family through generations, "until the coconut trees grow old." But at no level was there anything comparable to selling or even bartering land, and it took some time for profit, one of the most radical concepts brought from abroad, to be applied to land transactions. It was enough to gain what the soil produced.

Although the haole newcomers were happy to acquire land, and early monarchs were generous, for some time full personal ownership was not terribly important. Even when questions of tenure became so confused that the pressure for change resulted in the post-Mahele legislation that allowed both aliens and natives to own their properties, there is little record of land immediately being sold simply for speculative profit. It was desired, and its value increased, because it was needed for specific uses: for homes, farms, businesses, and, before too long, for large-scale plantation agriculture. Leasing, even very early, made it possible to use land profitably without acquiring ownership;[14] leases from government and crown lands were the basis for first formation of the largest, most lucrative plantation operations, from Ladd & Company's enterprise on.

Eventually, operators were inevitably attracted to the islands. They wanted to barter the precious land rather than use it. All speculation in commodities depends on some ultimate consumption, though, and the "risk-bearing for profit" during the first half of the twentieth century was based on faith in easy markets for sugarcane and pineapple. For an environmentalist, there is reason to be happy that the lands of Hawaii, once they were valued as a commodity, found their most profitable use for so long in the plantations; no great long-range physical harm is likely to come to farmland. Agricultural fields are open space, ecologically altered, perhaps, but not irretrievable for other uses. Their natural qualities can easily enough be restored if anyone wants to take the trouble, whereas concrete-paved urban spaces can be returned to an open-land state only with the greatest difficulty.

Not until after World War II did that same land become doubly valuable as the need for land to support urban growth increased. Then the consumer contest for land that was both arable and buildable brought about the Land Use Law, with its attempt to classify the state's lands according to their most economically productive uses and preserve the plantations. For the speculative dealer in real estate, it does not matter too much how land is going to be used, what may go on it, or how it will be treated, and in the land boom of the 1950s and 1960s great fortunes were made in real estate.

Chinn Ho has described how in 1955 he was offered, for $2.25 a square foot, the property on which the Ilikai Hotel now rests. He thought that was high for land so far from Waikiki proper and did not buy it. Two years later, when he was interested, the asking price had gone to $25 a foot. (In the meantime Henry Kaiser, willing to extend Waikiki's growing hotel strip, had put together the deal that gave him the present Hilton Hawaiian Village property for less than $7 a square foot.)[15] Ho bought the land and after some complicated financing built a 500-room hotel on the seven-acre site, which has now grown to 680 hotel rooms, a thousand condominium units, convention and banquet facilities, and fourteen restaurants and night clubs. The Capital Investment Corporation, which Chinn Ho heads, finds it an extremely successful enterprise, but Ho himself, considering that land in the area where he and Kaiser bought and built is now, twenty years later, worth close to $50 a foot, knows of what he speaks when he concludes that the truly great profits are now in real estate—in buying and selling the land itself—not in the businesses performed on the land.[16]

As the boom continued into the 1970s, as manipulation rather than utilization became the most profitable way to make money from land, new malihinis with fresh capital were increasingly attracted. The polite word for their purpose was not speculation but *investment*. The investment of mainland and local American money, and then funds from foreign countries, sent real estate prices further skyward.

Often the game was quite frankly trading in a negotiable article whose value was obviously increasing, as in any bear market. Nonbeachfront land that did not seem desirable to local investors was sold abroad for $2,000 an acre. More attractive land brought $3,600 an acre.[17] No one believed that such properties would be immediately developed; they would be likely to change hands several more times before reaching some useful purpose. In other cases the process was to buy the land, build something on it to indicate its income potential, and then sell land and improvements.[18] Many of the hotels purchased by foreign investors have been bait of this kind designed to lead to land sales. The Japanese purchasers of the land on which the Makaha Inn rests brought suit against the Capital Investment Corporation in 1976, claiming that the hotel's income potential had been misrepresented in order to sell the improved property. (In 1977, as though to prove their point, they went into bankruptcy.)

In the mid-1970s it seemed as though every other person in Honolulu was selling real estate. A parcel of land on the Big Island was advertised on television by Jerry ("land is the basis of all wealth") Assam. He noted that there was no worry about near neighbors: the land was in a conservation district and could not be built upon anyway.[19] A buyer could only assume capital appreciation. Newspaper ads touted land in unlikely places, supposedly ripe for subdivision, assuming that people had forgotten some postwar fiascos on the Big Island that had left about 75,000 acres subdivided but undeveloped.[20]

Many who were looking for ways to gain wealth from land continued to find profit in leasing it without bothering to try to purchase it. As an example, the Sheraton hotel chain obtained a lease on Bishop Estate land in Waikiki, on which sat the venerable Royal Hawaiian Hotel. To provide an income above the tremendous rental the lease called for, the lessees built the huge, tasteless, highly successful Sheraton Waikiki Hotel on the property, dwarfing the relatively re- served Royal Hawaiian. Then, having proved their combined income potential, Sheraton sold the hotels to Kenji Osano, a Japanese financial (and in a shadowy sense, political) wizard who has invested heavily in Hawaii. Many kamaainas were infuriated. "When we can sell the historic Royal Hawaiian to a foreign [buyer] I have to believe that some in this commu- nity would sell anything for a buck," fumed one.[21]

Not only were kamaaina landmarks sold for eager dollars and yens, however. Kamaaina landholdings, once considered by the big estates almost as "inalienable" as the crown lands had been, were also disposed of. Even the Bishop Estate began to reconsider its long-held policy, presumably imposed by the princess' will, of leasing the Kamehameha properties of which it is composed but never selling any of them.[22] As the temptation grew to gain high-percentage interest from invested capital rather than sometimes unsatisfactory income from leased land, disagreements developed within the estate's board of trustees and among people in the community of Hawaiian descent. The Hawaiians, by and large, wanted to see their ancestors' lands, dedicated to the education of their children, kept intact.[23] One of the trustees, Richard Lyman, Jr., insisted that the terms of the will be literally followed. He accused his fellow trustees of being poor businessmen and letting the estate's lands go for less than they could bring on the booming market.[24] Nevertheless, sales were consummated for 15,000 acres on Hawaii, 4,000 acres on Molokai, 1,500 acres on Oahu, and more. Some of the arrangements have been embarrassing to the estate and some harmful. According to a real estate broker on the Big Island, one purchaser of Bishop Estate land resold it quickly for a 300 percent, $9 million, profit.[25] At Keauhou on the Kona coast, a deal with mainland financier-developer Troy Post, intended to permit the estate to finance a huge resort development without harming its tax-free status—a complicated financial arrangement which would have allowed Post to buy 1,200 acres of Bishop Estate land at far below its likely value after the resort was build—was castigated by the courts (where trustee Lyman had taken it). A circuit court judge said that the majority trustees had failed to act "in a manner which might reasonably be expected of ordinary, intelligent and prudent businessmen." And the State Supreme Court upheld his harsh judgment.[26]

Although the trustees, by these sales, succeeded in raising cash which they felt was needed, it is likely that they will stay away, in the future, from the hard-boiled huckstering of Hawaii's land surface that sales in today's market involve—at least until the hunger for land produces even greater pressures. Other estates and trusts, however, governed by more astute men of business, continued to sell large blocks of once tightly held land to gain quick profits (or show book losses) while the easy opportunities remained.[27]

The Trouble with Taxation

As more and more land was bought and sold for capital gain rather than continuing income, many people in and out of government began to wonder about the use of taxation— to control speculation, to gain some of the newfound wealth for the public purse, and, possibly, to make an appropriate *use* of land more profitable to its owners than selling it would be. Slicing some of the gain from selling real property off the top, as public or private tribute, is certainly not a new concept: tithing goes far back in the history of land-based human relationships. But the idea of manipulating capital gains taxes and tax assessments so as to influence the way land might be utilized—really a first step toward land management—is a fairly recent notion.

In Hawaii's early days, taxation was a form of profit drawn from the land by its owner (the king) and its assignee (an alii) and collected by a kind of estate manager (the konohiki). The commoner who lived on and from the land was entitled to what he could raise after he had paid his taxes in goods (supplemented sometimes by tributary labor). Taxes were not light. The early Hawaiian historian Kamakau found that even before the white man's influence became strong, Kamehameha's "uniting of the land" increased taxation to an "excessive" point (an early instance of the fiscal effects of centralized government). And although he recalled a good, plentiful life in those early days, he also remembered very heavy taxes.[28] Taxes on land, direct or indirect, levied against the Hawaiian people, continued into the monarchy years. During the time of the desolating sandalwood trade everyone was taxed a certain weight of wood to be taken from the forests.[29] Kamehameha III's Constitution and Laws of 1842 included regulation of taxation on farmlands: for a large farm, a swine one fathom long; for a small one, a beast one yard long.[30]

When haoles began to make use of the lands they received as gifts or grants, they largely avoided payment of taxes on them for some time, and what little was paid did not much help the government's finances. Even those dues were considered objectionable —"unequal and unjust, bearing hard upon the poor natives" *(sic)*—and in 1852 were eliminated.[31] Soon after a real-property tax was imposed (in 1859, at the rate of ¼ percent of assessed valuation) and was made law in 1877.[32] During the territorial period land taxes remained light; necessary revenues were derived from more widely distributed sources than the few landowners. They came from poll taxes and road taxes, for instance, and an excise tax on all kinds of enterprises. The territory's income tax was regressive: it levied a flat percentage on everyone. It is improved today in that regard, but it remains one of the nation's highest. The excise tax, a tax on the gross income from almost all business and professional activites, continues as an important source of state revenue.[33]

Real-property taxes as such are still moderate in Hawaii for individual homeowners; they revert to the counties rather than the state, although a state tax department assesses valuations. Land taxes, based on land uses, have been the most difficult form of tribute to levy equitably and have become a particularly controversial political issue as the idea grows that they might be a land-use-planning tool. The estimated "highest and best" tax system adopted in the 1960s has worked hardship on small farmers whose properties are near urban areas and likely to be absorbed for development. It is almost essential for the owner of fertile land toward which urban growth is pointing to apply for reclassification that would permit development—if he wants to avoid paying high urban taxes on land producing a lesser agricultural income.

This tax system and the so-called Pittsburgh law, until it was repealed in 1977—political moves that had been intended in the 1960s to prevent properties from lying idle by forcing their development so that they would become productive resources adding to the public revenues—were, in the 1970s, making it more difficult to keep essential green spaces open.

There seemed an obvious way out of the dilemma that had developed: to base taxation of agricultural land on agricultural use, if that was a serious operation, rather than on its most profitable potential. For some time it had been legally possible for owners of small farmsteads to "dedicate" their land to agricultural uses and gain a promise of continued low taxes, but the process was a complicated one and the long-term commitment frightened most farmers. In 1974 a law passed that applied the same principle to larger parcels. It allows land acreage to be dedicated, committed to agricultural uses for ten or twenty-year terms, and thereby gain assurance, during that time, of taxation at a farmland rate. The law provides that if the owner should make application for rezoning at some time in the future (so that he could then develop his land, or sell it profitably, or market development rights), he would pay the accrued back taxes that would have been levied if the land had been put to urban uses earlier, plus a penalty for having changed his mind.

There was no doubt that this legislation helped financially those who honestly wished to farm their agricultural acres. For instance, at a small scale, a hog farm of nine acres in Waianae had its assessed valuation dropped from $4,900 an acre as potential urban space to $1,750 an acre as dedicated farmland. At a larger scale, several thousand acres at Kilauea on Kauai, used to raise grain, were taxed at $140 an acre after dedication rather than at the former rate of $1,050.[34]

This legislation offered convenient loopholes, however, to those owners who looked forward to future capital gains from selling their farmlands. It provided, for example, a convenient tax shelter until the most advantageous time came to sell. Then payment of a tax differential from previous years, even with a penalty added, would not seriously stand in the way of a rezoning application. It would simply add one more

item to the sales price and the ultimate development cost.
Such an assumption of the use of tax legislation that seemed
on the surface well meant was not overly cynical. Tremendous windfall profits can be made through the reclassification and rezoning process. Land with a market value based
on agricultural uses can instantaneously—at the stroke of a
commissioner's pen—increase to a new book value based on
urban uses and make millions of dollars for a successful
applicant when sold. There were instances where cane land,
with a possible sales price of $5,000 an acre at its current
use, was reclassified to urban use and suddenly became
worth something like $40,000 an acre. This unearned incre-
ment of $35,000 on each acre would amount to $35 million
for a thousand-acre parcel. It was clear that a tax penalty at
the time of sale would not be an important deterrent to the
rezoning application in a case like that.[35]

An illustration of the political maneuverings that resulted
when such sums of money were involved is the case of
Robinson Estate lands at Waipahu, east of Honolulu proper.
A sizable acreage of good cane land found itself in a corner
formed by two intersecting freeways. The obvious conflicts
developed. The landowning estate saw great profits in the
sale of development rights if the land could be rezoned. Conservationists, agriculturists, and, for a time, the lessee, Oahu
Sugar Company, and its workers, unionized members of the
ILWU, saw a great loss to the plantation potential of central
Oahu if the lands were rezoned. The location was such that
changes in the use of this key area could trigger development
all the way up Oahu's central plains to the old settlement of
Wahiawa and the new suburb of Mililani Town.

The first request for reclassification of the property came
in 1967. At that time the commission's staff recommended
against approval and the commissioners denied the application. But then the firm that wanted to develop the land
(HMS Ventures, headed by a builder-developer named
Herbert Horita) used persuasion, and second thoughts came
to the sugar company, its employees, and the members of the

commission. When a new application was made in 1968, Oahu Sugar and the ILWU supported it. Union executive Eddie Tangen was appointed to the Land Use Commission in August 1969. In September the commission approved the application and the land became developable—and extremely valuable.[36]

The role of the unions, particularly the ILWU, in deals of this kind was interesting. When the union movement in Hawaii that had begun among the plantation workers in the 1940s made headway, after rough struggles, the union members depended on continuation of sugarcane and pine-apple growing for their livelihood, and it was on that basis that their organizers and negotiators operated.[37] As hotel workers were added to the union rolls, and then construction workers, conflicts in self-interest began to appear in labor's position on land use and development. The plantation owners and the developers well understood this friction, and it often appeared that the workers were being manipulated along with the land. As the unions sought their own greatest financial benefits from the land-based enterprises their members were engaged in, they inevitably became instruments in the overall search for the greatest wealth the lands could produce for their owners.

In the spring of 1972, an application was made to the Honolulu Planning Commission to rezone a parcel of land at Kahuku, on the northwest corner of Oahu, to allow a pro-moter, F. R. Schuh, to build a commercial "theme park" there. (The *theme* was to be an imitation Polynesian settle-ment with an accompanying amusement area to attract pay-ing tourists.) The area was prime cane-growing land, but the sugar company operating it wanted to close out, the local people feared for their jobs, and the state's Land Use Com-mission had agreed to reclassification.

A member of the city's Planning Commission who, in preliminary hearings, had indicated his skepticism of the pro-ject and its requested rezoning, received a phone call one day from the ubiquitous Eddie Tangen, by then vice-chairman of the Land Use Commission and still an ILWU official, asking him to change his mind because "our boys really need jobs out there."[38] The commissioners were about evenly divided on the question, and its outcome was uncertain. But a few weeks before the final vote another ILWU officer received an appointment, this time to a vacant seat on the city's Planning Commission—and his vote for the development made a decision to recommend approval certain.[39] As many had suspected, the jobs the local people had been promised never developed; the entrepreneur could not finance his scheme and gave it up. But in the meantime the land had tremendously appreciated in value, and it was now rezoned to permit any urban uses that the owner, the Campbell Estate this time, might find profitable.

Another kind of land taxation was urged at that time by citizen groups and some legislators; it was to tax directly as capital gains the unearned money, the windfall, that accrued to a piece of land when it was rezoned. The theory was that since the act of rezoning produced wealth, some of it should be returned directly to the taxpayers, at least to help pay for the public improvements that development on the rezoned land would require. Some thought this might inhibit speculation in land prices and its concomitant political implications; others disagreed.

A bill for an act to this end was introduced in the 1971 legislative session.[40] It was a study of this proposal, made for the legislature by a university research economist, which resulted in the report referred to earlier, questioning whether maintaining open land or preventing land speculation were "economically desirable goals." The report's conclusion about the capital gains tax was that it would "hinder the construction of housing and hold up the price of housing."[41] Since the buyers of homes built on rezoned agricultural lands, not the land's owners or developers, would be asked to absorb the capital gains tax on top of the new artificially escalated land valuations, the economists' conclusion was undoubtedly correct. The lawmakers believed so, anyway, or at least they used the argument as a good excuse not to impose this forfeit on profit from the rezoning-selling-developing destiny of Hawaii's fertile farmlands.

The difficulty encountered by this and other attempts to control land use and land management by taxation was that no one, from legislators to low-income citizens, really wanted to interfere with the wealth-producing land development process. The private incomes to be made from buying and selling, speculating with, and ultimately building on the land could always be justified as rewards for making raw land available for essential housing and needed employment, thus contributing to the public wealth of the state. These myths persisted even after it had become clear that the jobs were often illusory and the housing, when it was produced, was beyond the means of the native population. Planning commissioners learned to turn off their ears when applicants for zoning and general-plan changes based their appeals on promises of "low-income housing." They knew that the requests, when granted, always resulted in additional high-priced subdivisions.

It was naive, in any event, to expect the state legislature to inhibit speculative land profits. A majority of its members was in some way professionally concerned with the income to be derived from real estate—directly as developers, indirectly as attorneys, insurance brokers, consultants to developers, or managers or salesmen of developers' land.

The Tourist Trap

One of the major wealth-producing land-use activities in the state was difficult, as it expanded, to classify in terms of land's worth to the island society. It was the building of physical facilities for the movement, storage, and protection of the staples of the state's top industry—tourism. Those staples, or commodities, were of course the visitors: the articles of commerce in the business of moving people from one location to another. Tourists had to be transported from place of origin to place of destination and then back again, with transfer stops along the way, just like any wares handled in any industry. They required container vehicles to convey them and roads to move them over. At storage and loading points they had to be kept in prime condition like any other fragile article. That required hotel rooms, restaurants and banquet halls, swimming pools, golf courses. They could generate profits all along the route they were moved on, so boutiques, night clubs, and commercial entertainment facilities of various kinds were indispensable parts of the industry.

Was this use of Hawaii's lands responding to public needs? Or was it merely another way of exploiting the natural resources of the islands for the profit of a small group of entrepreneurs? Did it provide enough jobs of a desirable kind for the local people? Did it furnish enough public income of sure continuance to justify the increasing amount of irreplaceable open space it was consuming? Were the travelers themselves really enjoying a worthwhile vacation time with recreational and cultural benefits? Or were they being moved onto and off of Hawaii's lands like so much valuable merchandise?

These questions were becoming increasingly important. The land this industry needed for its operations in growing amounts was the most desirable in the state—the most beautiful long stretches of white sand beach and the most verdant valleys—and the public costs of satisfying this activity were obviously increasing. A definitive socioeconomic cost-benefit analysis was needed. Several had been made, but none had satisfied enough people to settle the questions, either in the public mind or in regulatory legislation.[42]

The state had assumed from the first days of tourist arrivals that its role should be to promote this developing industry. As early as 1903 the territorial legislature appropriated $5,000 for advertising the beauties of Hawaii as a place to visit and in 1904 the Honolulu Chamber of Commerce added $500 to the promotional kitty. Even today the Hawaii

Visitors Bureau is a quasi-state agency receiving regular appropriations from the legislature in addition to money raised from private business—its task to attract tourists and build tourism as a source of income.[43] Not until very recently has there been any recognition either by the industry itself or by the government that there might be disadvantages as well as advantages in the growing influx of visitors.

On the plus side, it would seem, were the two standard apologies: jobs and revenues. Unquestionably, employment was produced by the traffic in tourists: at high levels, for hotel managers, travel agency executives, and such; at intermediate ranks, for specialists like tour operators and guides, restaurant managers, maitres, and chefs; lower down and in greater bulk, for bellboys and busboys, waiters and waitresses, maids and janitors. In the early 1970s, around 18,000 work functions were created in hotels,[44] another 25,000, perhaps, in other tourist-related activities. And, one analyst calculated, for each of these jobs one and a half more was generated in other sectors of the economy.

There were questions about these raw data, however. Although statistics were confusing, it appeared that more than half the executive-level employees were trained people transported to Hawaii from the mainland as positions opened (although the local university tried to draw them, earlier, to its School of Travel Industry Management)—and the un-skilled jobs were not that desirable. Lower-level hotel work was not very well paid, even with action by the unions, and it was a vocational dead end for sometimes ambitious local people. Hawaiians and part-Hawaiians were finding it difficult enough to move up the socioeconomic ladder. For other natives with plantation-worker backgrounds it was not very inspiring to see their children acting as servants to tourists.[45] "The travel industry," wrote one commentator, "furnishes the lowest-paid and socially least desirable employment for local people of any industry that the state might encourage."

The housing situation seemed to be worsened rather than

.helped by tourism. It was always hoped that construction of hotels would include provision of housing for employees, but that seldom happened. New employees needed new houses, and in most cases they had to shop in the already sparse local market. When home people were employed, they usually found that they had to travel from what homes they had.

As for bolstering the state's economy and even providing direct revenues for the public treasury, there was no doubt that tourism was generous. Visitor expenditures passed the billion-dollar mark in 1974 and kept on growing. More than $100 million in state and local taxes was generated annually by the industry. Countless fringe benefits came from the tourists: construction, for instance, and of course merchandising of all kinds increased in volume because of the visitors' vacation extravagance.[46]

Peculiar factors were turned up in some analyses of the income-producing aspect of tourism. On the one hand, not all the money spent in Hawaii stayed there, perhaps not much more than half. On the other hand, the cash that visitors left in the islands multiplied as it was passed around, in a way difficult to pinpoint. What was termed the "catalytic effect" of tourism on the state's economic growth was the subject of several controversial studies, at least one of which questioned the weight of its impact on the state's economy.[47]

The stability of the industry that Hawaii had come to depend on so greatly was also examined by analysts. Tourism is a fragile business. It depends on a stable economy and steady levels of personal affluence in the places where tourists come from. Further, to continue drawing paying guests, the location must remain more attractive (both to travel agencies and to the traveling public) than other places that might be visited. Although they may be handled like so much merchandise once they are on their way, vacationing travelers are fickle in their choice of destination. There was plenty of evidence of this for Hawaii's entrepreneurs and legislators to study. And they lived with the knowledge that islands further south in the Pacific were ready to tout their fresher, and often less expensive, attractions.

The immediate physical effect of tourism on Hawaii's environment was evaluated by impact-analysis methods in several studies. As public costs of services had been found at times to outweigh the revenues provided by residential subdivisions, so the facilities that the state and the counties had to furnish for visitors were obviously mounting seriously. Roads, and good ones, had to be built to the resort areas, often far from urbanized places. Water, sewerage, and protection services of various kinds were necessary.

The possibility of levying a separate occupancy tax on hotel rooms to ease the public cost became a political issue, with the industry spokesmen protesting that it would kill the visiting geese now laying their golden eggs so lavishly.[48] Unpleasant arguments developed between state and county officials as the problem of public expenditures became more pressing. There was a perennial question how state and city funds should be allocated to bolster the decrepit services in Waikiki and plan the necessary new ones, a dispute which prevented anything at all from being done there for countless years.

There was a large increase in the early 1970s in the number of packaged tours—prepaid tour groups traveling together in great guided numbers—and many who feared the block impact of these tourist herds suggested that "quality" tourism should be stimulated instead. In practice this would mean encouraging and building for visits by wealthier people than those now generally arriving. A few expensive places like the Mauna Kea Beach Hotel on Hawaii and the Kahala Hilton outside Waikiki on Oahu already drew people who had more money to spend and presumably more regard for the environment than the tour-type tourist. On the face of it, there seemed to be much greater benefits in this kind of trade than in catering to the low-budget groups.

Aside from the interesting social questions these proposals

raised—is it right to discriminate against the less wealthy traveler?—it appeared that there were economic complications involved. A report made for the state pointed out that the high-income visitor needs more land for his hotels because he does not like to be crowded; he requires more physical services and more lavish appointments, which are costly and space consuming. With all this, he may or may not spend more dollars per day locally; in fact, "there is evidence that [he] is characterized by a slightly lower cost-benefit ratio than the middle-class visitor."[49] That is, the corporation head may not return as much money to the state while he is in Hawaii as the once-in-a-lifetime retired shopkeeper, although he unquestionably demands much more space and imposes a more intensive use on the land.

The social impacts of tourism were found to be as difficult to evaluate as the economic effects. The lives of people living on the islands' lands, interrupted by "visitors," were affected in several ways. The most violent impact on local residents was that they were often asked to leave when tourists were invited to come. The displacement of native people by resort development was not great in numbers of individuals disturbed (the new hotels were likely to be on raw, vacant lands). But when it occurred it caused acute social pain.

More subtly damaging was the effect on the people leading natural lives in tranquil communities when they found sightseers peering over their shoulders. Affluent citizens could ignore the visitors if they wanted to but, as so often happens, it was the least wealthy who felt most sharply the social stress. It was bad enough to be segregated de facto at playtime, with one beach for the transient tourist and one for the home folks, but it was worse to have one's "quaint" lifestyle photographed at any time. The people of Koloa, one of the oldest of the plantation towns, on the road to those hotels that preempt Kauai's Poipu Beach, were having hard enough times in the 1970s. The Grove Plantation was threatening to close and leave them without livelihood. Jobs that were offered by the Sheraton Kauai and other hotels on the shore helped some. But busloads of strangers—driving through their quiet town, stopping to take pictures, poking into the local store, wandering up the neighborhood streets—made tourism's benefits doubtful. Normal living habits stop under such circumstances and are replaced by a kind of living performance. In 1976 another assault by tourism on local neighborhoods began to cause concern. It resulted from a shortage of hotel rooms in some key spots and a glut of condominium apartments (overbuilt to the extent of 16,000 units, one source said).[50] Many of the apartments were rented to short-term visitors—upsetting the balance "not only in terms of the services provided but also in the life-style of the community," as one planning director put it.[51]

What was happening to the land? This was the ultimate question that had to be asked about tourism after all the economic and social effects had been analyzed and debated. Again, quantitative measurements did not mean much. Only a small percentage of the lands of the islands was being given to resort use, but that was not the point: they were obviously the most beautiful places of all, and the most unspoiled, when they were taken over. Otherwise the industry's finger would never have been put on them. And it was the best of these best lands that were the most profitable for tourism and the most overbuilt and overcrowded.

Once the highway had been improved to the first few hotels on Amfac's beach land at Kaanapali on Maui, once water lines had been laid and a sewer system installed, it made economic good sense to build as many hotels there as possible.[52] The restaurants and stores did better business, then, and soon a proprietary shopping center could be built with guaranteed success. Anyway, people liked to see more people; if they did not, they felt they had gone to an unpopular place. The path toward the greatest profit potential of the land was clear. Before long the original good intentions to keep densities low and vistas clear, formalized at one time by a team of architect-planners, went by the boards.

Condominiums and hotels nudged one another along a new resort strip on one of the islands' greatest beaches.

The report made to the state legislature in 1973 by a Temporary Visitor Industry Council recognized the dangers to the very environment that had attracted the tourist hordes that were now overloading it. It based a suggested controlled-growth policy for tourism on the premise that "the unlimited expansion of the number of tourists in Hawaii is something which the fragility of our social and physical environment cannot tolerate."[53] But by that time the ability of tourist-serving land to generate wealth for private pockets and the public purse had been demonstrated so convincingly that it was difficult to keep in mind its other values.

The 1973 report of the Temporary Council resulted two years later in appointment of a governor's Advisory Committee. Its further analysis, in turn, pointed to the many more hotels that would be needed to accommodate the great increase in visitor traffic required to make tourism Hawaii's economic mainstay. The legislature began, finally, to recognize the need to plan for such growth and started to consider legislation to that end. However, a "fact-finding" trip to Latin America, the Caribbean, and other resort areas, made by a group from the state House and Senate in that same year, discovered, not surprisingly, that places like Miami can become physically unpleasant, that others, like Puerto Rico, can turn visitors away by being socially unpleasant, and that, in general, tourists are fickle and tourism is flighty.

The traveling legislators unanimously admired Bermuda's careful control of its beauty along with the continuing success of its tourism. One of them felt "good vibes" there; another noted a pleasant "retained image"; all were impressed with the income figures they saw. Few, however, had any wish to apply any of these lessons to their own islands. Bermuda is "a Utopia," one solon said, "as far as authoritarian planning is concerned . . . but what they do is not applicable to Hawaii." Another concluded that it was "a tremendous place to visit,'' but ''the government calls the shots'' and ''in terms of government, Hawaii can never be in this position.'' Others who had made the trip concurred with this conclusion. A newspaperman agreed editorially: ''Tourism in Hawaii doesn't want government controls.''[54]

What that judgment seemed to imply was that those who were profiting from tourism's use of Hawaii's land might welcome a growth plan for their industry, but they would not tolerate government action to protect the environment upon which the growth depended.

chapter 9

Source of Power

MASTERY of a region's land means command of its destiny, and nowhere has this truth been more clearly demonstrated than in Hawaii. In early days, the kings knew they had to secure the land to gain authority—and hold it to keep control over their people.[1] After the kingdom was established, the gradual loss of governmental power by the alii and its transfer to white foreigners came about with changes in the system of land ownership. The final forfeit of the throne became inevitable as the plantations assumed increasing power over the land. After the overthrow of the monarchy, the provisional government and then the United States itself asserted authority by taking title to the lands the kingdom had owned.

The oligarchical powers of the planters and their agents during the time of the territory came from their domination of the land—and the overweening command of the federal government was demonstrated by the setting aside of great areas for national, primarily military, use. The war years after Pearl Harbor, with martial law invoked, saw even greater parts of the lands of the islands absorbed by Washington for the defense establishment, to remain permanent witness to the national power.[2]

As private control over land shifted, in the postwar years, to those who owned or secured development rights, this new group's influence began to show itself in actions of agencies at the state level and (since the state had no firm policy regarding land use) increasingly at the plane of county zoning. Today there is widespread, cynical understanding that "the developers," as a class, pretty well control the state's politics.[3] The new worry is whether the increasing transfer of land tenure to investors outside the state may mean that these new owners will, in their turn, use the powers that go with land to control the islands' future.

While certain civil laws obtained in ancient Hawaii, primarily as religious taboos, basically "everything went according to the will of the king."[4] Government and land were closely related in the old days, writes the historian Kuykendall.[5] Acquisition of power by the principal chief of an island meant sole ownership of all the land, and the allegiance of the king's chiefly supporters depended on their receiving grants of land parcels. The authority that an alii might have came from his dominion over the common people, the makaainana, who were living in their kuleanas on his allocated property.

The king's need for a diplomatic adviser in the distribution of land was clear; the nature of the areas that were apportioned determined the relative power of the alii. Mokus and ahupuaas varied in size and even in shape and some gave greater scope and authority than others. Jealousies were inevitable, and there were many wars inspired by a desire for better distribution of land power before Kamehameha drove Kiwalao off his short-held throne. When the fighting stopped after these contests, as when a chief named Umi-a-Liloa succeeded in taking over a section of the island of Hawaii several generations before Kamehameha's rise, "the lands were apportioned and chiefs set up over each district, land section and ahupuaa, and all was at peace."[6]

When a new chief did assume command, civil wars were likely; those with land tenure did not want to relinquish

control and those who had been with little or no land wanted
to gain the power they had lacked. It was the maldistribution
of land after the death of the old king Keawemauhili that
inspired Kamehameha's thrust for power on the Kona coast
of Hawaii. In the traditional manner, after his wars were
over, Kamehameha made sure that close friends and relatives
were first rewarded with land. He then gave to a political
adviser the duty of distributing authority—"dividing the
lands to the chiefs and commoners, to all those who had
used their strength for the victory"—in a manner that would
avert later disputes.[7]

With the chiefs wielding such power and the common
people so beholden to the will of the landed alii, intraclass
rivalries would seem unlikely, but apparently they did exist at
times. When a makaainana felt he was being treated unfairly
he had just one recourse: to leave his land and find another
kuleana under a more just owner and manager. The chiefs,
on the other hand, could be more ruthless when they thought
a commoner was exceeding his prerogatives.

"It was not for a commoner to do as he liked," wrote
Samuel Kamakau. "If a chief saw that a man was becoming
affluent, was a man of importance in the back country, had
built him a good house, and had several men under him, the
chief would take everything away from him and seize the
land, leaving the man with only the clothes on his back."[8]

The haoles who arrived early in Hawaii remarked how the
chiefs used land control to maintain their prestige and noted
with what tenacity they held on to this mark of authority. An
old chief's unhappiness at the kuleana grant of 1849 was
described by a missionary writer: "If we cannot take away
their lands," he asked, "what will they care for us?"[9]

Apparently the idea that land might give it political or
personal power did not immediately occur to the foreign
population. As an early trader wrote, "the white men, who
hold extensive lands, derive little benefit from them unless
they cultivate the ground."[10] The early missionaries had no
thought of using the land they were allowed to occupy for

any purpose other than living on it themselves and building on it churches and schools for teaching their beliefs to the natives. There is little suggestion in the history of the increasing influence of the missionaries of any wish to acquire land for the power it might bring.[11] Those who stayed in the church's service were anxious from the beginning to see the native people themselves become more "self-sufficient, free and enterprising" in the way they used their land. The thought that their kanaka converts occupied kuleanas only at the will of often heathen konohikis was repugnant to their New England freeholder tenets.

The records of those missionaries who left the fold to enter government service have also pretty well satisfied later historians that their motives were unselfish. Generally they did not work to their own advantage or that of their religious band in seeking wealth, assuming personal political power— or acquiring land. People like Richards, Bingham, and Judd, who had tremendous influence on the successive kings and their governments, tried their best, according to their standards, to bring Hawaii to a sense of Christian social morality and an ability to govern itself; they did not, except perhaps in a few instances, reach for self-serving power.

Gerrit P. Judd, the most hardworking adviser to the monarchy, was firm enough in his beliefs to antagonize many and sure enough of his abilities to annoy many more, but he never achieved a secure position. After his enemies succeeded in seeing that he was "retired" from the kingdom's government he had difficulty supporting his family for the remainder of his life.[12]

The haole contingent outside the religious fraternity, however, had no such restraints. (Nor did the second generation of the missionary families, many of whom stayed in the islands and started or joined business enterprises.) In fact, the burgeoning business community was increasingly annoyed at the pro-Hawaiian position of the missionary advisers to the government. Seeing that these good-hearted public servants were intent on strengthening the hold of the Hawaiian

kings and the alii on the islands' lands, they began to
move into politics themselves, often with more selfish purposes. Many of the haole cabinet members whom the later
Kamehamehas and then the last monarchs added to their administrations were objective advisers, a few were adventurers
who gained the royal families' confidence, but an increasing
number were established professionals and businessmen
who wanted full control of the lands of Hawaii, and the
political power they carried, to be in the hands of the white
island residents.

What signaled the end of the monarchy was in essence a
series of adopted and proposed changes in the kingdom's
constitution attesting to the shaky nature of haole land
politics while the Hawaiians were even nominally their own
rulers. There was a fairly authoritarian Hawaiian constitution
which Kamehameha V sponsored, a weak, so-called bayonet
constitution forced on Kalakaua by his cabinet, and another,
projected constitution prepared by Liliuokalani, which would
have strengthened native control again.[13] This last one the
queen's cabinet balked at; to the by-then proannexationist
members of the business community it was insulting. They
were, after all, the people of Hawaii who now governed its
land, and that fact, they felt, should give them authority over
its civil polity as well. Their proclamation of 1892, justifying
the revolution, said of the queen's proposed constitution that
it would "disfranchise over one fourth of the voters [viz.
white] and the owners of nine tenths of the private properties
of the kingdom."[14] When a band of local businessmen
walked the few blocks from the office of one of them to the
government building to tell the queen that her rule was
ended, she made no resistance: she yielded to "the superior
force of the United States of America" in 1893,[15] as
Kamehameha III had to yield to Britain's superior force fifty
years earlier. Although America's might did not officially
support the revolutionaries, this time the submission was
permanent. The Hawaiians' power over the life of their
land was now gone, no longer with hope that it would be
returned.

After the Haole Takeover

The story of the passage of national power does not end quite at that point, however. What followed is important to the claim of today's people of Hawaiian descent that retribution is due them for land illegally taken from their forefathers. The takeover had almost seemed a simple, polite accession by a group of nice people. Sanford Dole, who agreed to lead the new government, was a kindly gentleman, a lawyer, well enough liked by the Hawaiians despite his association with the haole hegemony. He and his provisional government were anxious now for the next step they foresaw: annexation by the United States.

President Benjamin Harrison's first term of office was in its last days when the revolution took place; when Grover Cleveland succeeded him, one of his first acts was to send an emissary named James Henderson Blount, former chairman of the U.S. House Committee on Foreign Affairs, to investigate at first hand in Hawaii what had happened. Blount reported that the taking of power had been with the assistance of the United States—it would not have been possible if the U.S. minister, John L. Stevens, had not helped out, primarily by ordering American troops (from the USS *Boston,* under command of Capt. G. C. Wiltse) on shore at the crucial time.[16] The president was disturbed at Blount's report and moved, at first, to put Liliuokalani back on her throne. When the provisional government in Hawaii remained adamant in its power, however, and the former queen was stubborn about hers, he referred the problem to Congress. That body set up its own investigation in Washington under Chairman John Tyler Morgan of the Senate Committee on Foreign Affairs. Morgan's final report concluded, contrary to Blount's findings, that the landing of U.S. troops had been only for "the preservation of law and order" to protect "the rights of American citizens resident in Honolulu." With that patriotic justification, Congress decided to wash its hands of the affair and, for the time being, let Hawaii work out its own fate.

Agitation for annexation increased, however, despite concern about the results of universal suffrage.[17] It finally succeeded during the administration of President William McKinley, when on 15 June 1898 Congress passed a joint resolution remembered by the name of its sponsor, Senator F. C. Newlands. By then it seemed "manifest destiny" that the islands be annexed, as one enthusiastic congressman put it.[18] When, two months later in Honolulu, Dole ceded the Republic of Hawaii to the United States of America in a formal ceremony, the flag of an independent Hawaii was lowered and the islands finally became a territory of a distant power. Former President Cleveland, looking back on the earlier stages of "this miserable business," said "I am ashamed of the whole affair."[19]

Land and power went together in these moves. Each succeeding government made sure that it had acquired not only political control but possession of the lands which were its token. The provisional government barely had time to turn itself into a tightly controlled "republic"—to say nothing of adopting a constitution and deciding what laws of the kingdom should be retained and what new ones should be considered—before annexation became a fact.[20] But time was found in that short interim for the most important act of all: making sure that all the monarchy's lands passed into the hands of the new government.

The republic established its land policy in the Land Act of 1895.[21] Crown lands and government lands were merged, in this legislation, as public lands to be administered by a commission. Where the control over land uses really lay was made very clear in the charge to the commissioners: they were authorized to "lease, sell or otherwise dispose of the public lands, and other property, in such manners as they may deem best for the *protection of agriculture* and the general welfare of the Republic."[22] It followed naturally that during the time of the republic large areas of these public lands were disposed of to the plantations, some by sale, more by long-term lease.

At the time of annexation the public lands that remained were "ceded" to the United States, which thus acquired about 1,800,000 acres of mid-Pacific territory with no bloodshed and with not a penny of payment.[23] Under terms of the Newlands Resolution and then of the Organic Act that regularized the annexation, the president of the United States was supposed to appoint another commission—a five-man body to study Hawaii's peculiar land situation and make recommendations to the Congress on its regulation.[24] This was never done. Tacitly it was agreed by all parties that management of the now federally owned public lands would remain in the hands of the territory, with full understanding that sovereignty over them had passed to the mainland government. Hence the interim administration (a continuation of the regime of the republic, still headed by Sanford Dole) and then the first appointed governor (the same Sanford Dole) continued to operate under the Land Act of 1895 until the Organic Act was passed. At that time it was stated clearly that all public land was property of the United States but remained, for administrative purposes, under the "possession, use and control of the Territory of Hawaii." When Hawaii became a state the Statehood Act provided for a division of the public lands—a new kind of mahele—between federal and state governments. Much of the ceded land was transferred back to the state,[25] so that at the present time approximately 400,000 acres remain with the national government and almost 2,000,000 acres are in state ownership.

The plantation owners and the businessmen whose fortunes depended on them saw that things were still working to their advantage. Nothing stood in the way of their assumption of the powers over the islands that had been so tantalizingly close during the last years of the monarchy. The one part of the new legislation that made them unhappy—the proviso in the Organic Act which limited anyone's possession of land to a thousand acres—they would have to work to remove. This they succeeded in doing with the 1920 Rehabilitation Act.[26]

One other restraint stood in the way of handling all land as the local haoles wanted during the territorial period. The military establishment and some congressmen were worried that if public-land management were left entirely to the local government, even bound as it was to the national administration in Washington, the United States might not be able to take what it wanted, when it wanted, for national defense purposes. After all, securement of the islands as a defensive outpost had been a main reason for annexation. (A garrison of troops arrived in Hawaii four days after the annexation ceremony and bivouacked alongside Waikiki.) President McKinley, stimulated by a military report in 1899,[27] issued a series of executive orders and proclamations ordering that certain lands which the military wanted be "set aside."[28] About 287,000 acres thus became specifically engaged as federal property for defense and related purposes. None of this transfer disturbed plantation lands, however; in fact, the new military population and the old industrial-agricultural society got along very well together, each in its way utilizing Hawaii's lands to enhance its own authority.

Although much more land was set aside for the military than it could immediately use, a good deal of defense construction did take place soon after annexation. A system of defensive forts was established which required sizable land areas: Fort Shafter on high ground above Honolulu harbor and Fort Armstrong at its entrance; Fort Kamehameha and Fort Weaver near Pearl Harbor; Fort DeRussy in an attractive beach location near Waikiki and Fort Ruger on the slopes of Diamond Head. The greatest land take was for Schofield Barracks, high in the central plains of Oahu, one of the largest of all U.S. garrisons.[29] The lands that had earlier been ceded at Pearl Harbor were prepared for intensive use for the first time: the channel mouth was dredged to allow entrance of large ships; docks were constructed; ancillary shore work was begun. By the time America entered World War I the harbor was usable as a major naval base. Other smaller acquisitions followed during the early years of the century, such as Wheeler and Hickam airfields. No one foresaw then the competition for land that would develop after World War II, but the presidential executive orders from 1898 through 1900 "have contributed," as one study puts it, "to land use problems that remain unresolved to the present."[30]

One of the most visible problems finally erupted as a violent protest by an angry group of Hawaiians over use of the island of Kahoolawe as a target for military bombing practice. Kahoolawe is a volcanic dome forming a small island lying off the Kihei shore of Maui, its highest parts once covered with deep soil and its beaches used during Polynesian times by fishing villages. Now it is pocked with the remains of live ordnance deposited there during years of persistent bombing by the Navy. Several times members of a protesting " 'Ohana" paid forbidden visits to the island, to occupy it as a demonstration of their concern for this misused part of their native soil. On one trip two young men were lost from the surf boards they were travelling on. The Navy, however, continued to insist that the most important use of this island was for military training, no matter how destructive to the land.

Many accounts have been written describing the great powers that the plantation oligarchy possessed during the first half of the present century in Hawaii, but the story is still hard for a later generation to credit. It is difficult to understand how the government of the United States, which had devised its own constitution to guard against focalization of power, could have allowed its Pacific territory to fall so completely into the hands of a small group of colonial planters. There were reports sent back from time to time, but Hawaii was pretty far away in those days (it took the sons and daughters of the kamaaina elite ten days by ship and train to get to their mainland colleges, one of them recalls). Moreover, the occasional investigating bodies that Congress sent to see what was happening were well entertained in the islands.

Even during Franklin Roosevelt's administration and
the New Deal, Hawaii was still largely ignored. Political
lobbying machinations by the planters' representatives in
Washington, involving even Harold Ickes and James Farley,
precluded any real governmental concern for the way Hawaii
was handling its politico-economic affairs—and its land.[31]

The Polynesian Hawaiian land-tenure system is often
referred to as feudal, and in many respects the aliis' control
of land, in an authoritarian society of simple technologies,
did give them a hold over the commoners that was not unlike
a lord-vassal relationship. And in some ways the white
kamaainas who owned the land in territorial times exerted
just as great a power over the common people (especially on
the plantations), in a more industrialized, democratic society,
through such devices as political appointments and interlock-
ing directorates. In other terms, the powers and life-styles
of the elite in Hawaii are often likened to the antebellum
plantation-centered society in America's south, and there
were in fact many similarities. In both cases the economy
was based on a nearly one-crop agriculture, produced on
land controlled by a genteel aristocracy, and farmed by an
imported labor force. In America certain democratic principles that had been adopted by the founding fathers prevented the southern plantation-owning class from becoming a
true political oligarchy, although it approached it at times in
ways that helped lead to the Civil War. In Hawaii, however,
the transition from a monarchy (itself so recently an
aboriginal society) to a territory of a democracy was so
rapid, and the distance from the national seat of government
so great, that it took a half century before the powers of the
landholding oligarchy could be challenged.

The scope of the hegemony included every aspect of
Hawaii's economic, social, and political life. In the economic
sphere the arrogation of power was through the medium of
the Big Five factors, or agents, who not only marketed sugar
but began early to develop additional commercial enterprises
and assist in the formation of others. The agricultural in-

dustry required banking support, trust activities, and related financial facilities; ships were needed for transport of the plantations' products; construction of all kinds was required by the plantations and their offshoot enterprises; stores and all sorts of merchandising businesses grew up around the central industry; insurance companies, advertising agencies, and all the professions found clients in the correlated activities.[32]

Perhaps never in capitalist history has there been such a maze of meshed directorates—certainly never one so tightly woven—as the network of board members that ran Hawaii's commercial companies in the 1920s and 1930s. The same names repeated themselves as directors: of the Big Five, of Matson Navigation and Inter Island Steam Ships, of Oahu Railroad and Land and Honolulu Rapid Transit, of the Bank of Hawaii, Bishop Trust Company, International Trust, and Hawaiian Trust, of Liberty House, of hotels, insurance agencies, all kinds of wholesale and retail business firms, even of the utilities, the Honolulu Electric and Honolulu Gas companies and Mutual Telephone.[33] Social historian Lawrence Fuchs has calculated that one kamaaina family had members on the boards of eighteen companies and another was represented on ten.

In a political sense the elite group was able, almost until Pearl Harbor, to influence appointment of the territorial governor, to control election of the territorial delegate to Congress, and to make sure that the actions of the territorial legislature were not detrimental to elite interests. All this required adroit political maneuvering because the haoles were still, for a time, outnumbered by the Hawaiians.[34] If they had been prepared, and if they had had sophisticated leadership, the Hawaiian people would have had a remarkable opportunity under democratic American procedures to regain control of their islands. This did not happen, however. Increasingly, they were landless in a territory where authority lay with the land.

The social domination of the white elite was as complete as it has historically been in any colonial territory. Occasional marriages with Hawaiians who had royal connections (and often alii land) added some color to a few of the kamaaina families, but other than that the social and cultural activities were confined to the ruling clique. For that gentry it was a fantastically pleasant life in a tropical paradise, lived with the aplomb, the assurance, the dignity of a landed aristocracy. Even half a century later the detachment of the old families remains. Their social clubs and their cultural associations have been breached by newer newcomers, just as the old-line companies have had to admit new administrative talents. But they are still the kamaainas, the native-born. The ethnically mixed non-Caucasian population calls itself the "locals," and the haole kamaainas are willing to accept that termi-nology.[35] New arrivals are malihinis (strangers or guests), and after a short time in Hawaii every new resident wants to graduate from that rank. But there is no name for the great group of people who have more recently been attracted to the islands and have remained, many of them more thoroughly involved in social, political, and cultural affairs than either the kamaainas or the locals.

The Breaking of Plantation Power

In a political sense plantation power lasted into the 1950s. In economic terms the Big Five and the related businesses they spawned during territorial days still control much of the local activity, since they still own major parts of the land on which income is produced. Socially, the oligarchy began to lose its absolute grip during the 1940s when the plantation workers, particularly the Chinese and the Japanese, started to move up the ladder of American-type success.

   The first break in socioeconomic paternalism came with attempts to unionize the plantation workers. Early moves to protest working and living conditions were not very suc-cessful. A man named Pablo Manlapit organized Filipino workers in 1924, but their attempt to strike resulted only in mass arrests and Manlapit's forced departure from the islands.[36] A decade later, encouraged by the National Labor

Relations Act, Filipino plantation laborers organized again (and struck again fruitlessly). Organizers from mainland maritime unions who came to Hawaii with slogans of class, rather than ethnic, solidarity were more successful, however.

After struggles, strikes, and settlements the ILWU (CIO), having unionized first the dockworkers and then the sugar and pineapple plantation laborers, emerged as a powerful factor in island political as well as economic affairs. The American Federation of Labor, many of whose craft union members had found work in Hawaii, also sent its organizers, and before World War II almost all major industries were unionized.[37] The planters' complete control over the way their plantations and the businesses allied with them were to be operated had been broken.

In the meantime, many of the early plantation workers who had moved to the towns had not only established their own commercial enterprises but had formed their own social and business organizations. The Chambers of Commerce in Honolulu and Hilo had always been haole kamaaina organizations. Now separate Chinese and Japanese chambers were formed. Against some quite strong haole opposition, the public schools were opened to the socially upward-moving groups, and the Japanese particularly took quick advantage of the educational opportunities.

Even before the war, the end of the exclusive social, economic, and political power of the select kamaaina class was in sight. Yet the absolute control it had held over the island lands allowed it to maintain authority for some time. Sugarcane and pineapple production still dominated the economy and the economy controlled the government. The unions had become powerful in their right, but they held no land and had not yet learned how to exercise control over the way land was used. The major transfer of control came about after the war. With rapid urbanization, power began to shift from those who farmed land to those who manipulated it.

The kamaaina landowners tried to maintain a measure of control over their lands into the 1960s and 1970s. When the

Big Five and the trusts and estates sold land they lost contact
with it, of course, just as the Bishop Estate did. To avoid
that they devised several methods of gaining profits from
development without losing tenure. Sale of development
rights was one common means; joint venturing with a
builder-developer was another.

Once in a while an old-line landowning company itself
became the development entrepreneur. Oceanic Properties,
development arm of Castle & Cooke, planned and developed
Mililani Town; in that same central Oahu area the Campbell
Estate proposed to joint venture, for another new town project to hold 85,000 persons, with Grosvenor International,
subsidiary of a British financial trust anxious to spread its
activities.[38] And still in that agricultural district the Bishop
Estate sold development rights for three thousand acres to an
association called Amfac-Trousdale.

An interesting power struggle among these three combinations resulted when the University of Hawaii decided it
wanted to build a new central Oahu campus—each of the
landowners and his partners realized that locating it on his
property would be of tremendous assistance in getting cane
land rezoned for urban use. The combination of pressures
from a kamaaina landowner, an aggressive developer, and
the board of regents of the university, they figured, would be
found irresistible by the state and county zoning agencies.
Maneuverings went on for years until finally, in 1974, the
regents decided in favor of Campbell Estate's Honouliuli
land on the far western edge of Pearl Harbor. There seemed
no question in anyone's mind that the necessary reclassification and rezoning would be obtained; that was considered
just a final formality which would have to be observed.

It was hard to say, even for someone watching the inner
struggles from a close vantage point, what power pressure
had been most effective in the final choice.[39] It was obvious
that such decisions were no longer comfortable arrangements
between friendly members of a colonial cabal. The chairman
of the board of regents at one point was Harold Eichel-

berger, retired president of Amfac, but he refrained from
voting on the question. One of the petitioners was Frederick
Trotter, a Campbell Estate inheritor and trustee, but the
estate let Hirano Brothers, its selected developer, apply much
of the pressure.

If the question had been only selection of a land parcel
from among three offers, one could almost believe that
political power plays had little to do with the choice. A quite
thorough analysis of the advantages and disadvantages of
each location was made for the regents by a responsible planning firm. Although no specific recommendation was made,
the findings seemed to point to Honouliuli as the best suited
of the three sites.[40] A number of other power struggles im-
pinged on the campus-site selection process, however. The
university's regents had all been appointed by ex-Governor
Burns, who had made it clear during his administration that
he favored placing any new campus on the Big Island. In this
case Burns' influence over his usually loyal cohorts had
failed; the board of regents was adamant through the years
about its preference for central Oahu, where the three influential landowners were vying for it. The State Land Use
Commission's consultants for its first five-year land classification review said that a campus on those agricultural plains,
with its urban-generative effect, "could well negate one of
the most significant purposes of the State Land Use Law."[41]
The State Department of Planning and Economic Development issued several memoranda and a strong report opposing
the proposed location. They insisted that "no further
encroachment on agricultural lands in central Oahu be
allowed"[42] and, going further, suggested eight alternatives—
from building on the island of Hawaii to planning a more
imaginative system of small liberal arts colleges on the
neighbor islands. One alternative was not building any new
campus at all but intensifying use of the existing, inefficiently
organized Manoa campus facilities.[43]

Not only were the state administration and the state
university in conflict but the continual struggle between state

and city over control of Oahu's lands was also involved. Honolulu's planning department was urging growth in the Ewa direction, where the new campus would be located; the state was pushing for the H3 freeway, which would lead to growth in the other direction, toward the windward coast.

The stubbornness of the university's position was difficult to understand, unless it was intended to be a sheer demonstration of power. When a central Oahu campus had first been suggested in a 1967 consultants' report,[44] the university's enrollment of four-year and graduate students was increasing quite rapidly; by the mid-1970s those registrations were decreasing. The location proposed for a new conventional campus was only nineteen miles from Manoa, an absurdly short distance between major duplicated facilities. No recent analysis had been made of educational needs that might justify what looked like fiscal and educational extravagance.

The university seemed as obstinate in pushing for this change in land uses as the state was in insisting on building the H3 freeway; both were outdated concepts kept alive and moving by the sheer momentum of institutional force. Governor Ariyoshi stayed neutral on the issue. The legislature, excepting a few of its members, seemed content to let the university play out its game and appropriated enough funds for it to begin classes in temporary quarters (which it did, with dismal enrollment). But in 1974, to everyone's surprise, the State Land Use Commission denied Campbell Estate's application for reclassification of two hundred acres of agricultural land to urban uses. The campus now seemed unlikely.

In no way did this rejection alter the university's intentions, however. Instead of pulling back and reconsidering the effect its intended move would have, the university administration began thinking of ways around the unexpected rezoning obstacle: asking for a conditional use permit from the city, perhaps, which would bypass the state's commission.[45] It might now take "two, three, four, or even five years" to

get started, said University President Fujio Matsuda, but few
doubted the end result. Even though all considered judgments about best use of land opposed the campus proposal,
the combined strength of its proposers seemed likely, in time,
to prevail.

In other cases, the transfer of power from early landowners to later land brokers was more clear. When the Land
Use Commission agreed to reclassify the land occupied by
Oahu Sugar Company in 1969, it was developer Herbert
Horita, not the Robinson Estate, who engineered the deal. It
was developer and new owner Clarence Ching who obtained
approval to fill in Salt Lake, not the original owner, the
Damon Estate. During the 1950s, '60s, and '70s the pressures
for urbanizing open lands came from developers with names
new to island politics, seldom from the familiar missionary-
descended or haole oligarchy families. By the time of the
1974 land-use boundary review of the Land Use Commission,
letters of intent to develop open lands were sometimes signed
by Alexanders and Baldwins and Castles and Cookes, but
most were submitted by the new owners and developers and
their planners and attorneys: Ing, Sakoda, Minder, Palk,
Omori, Calilao, Freitas, Agena, Nakamura, Yuen.

Many odd combinations came about in the actual development process also, in the rush to urbanize long-held
kamaaina lands. A planning consultant familiar with
Hawaii's land history remembers sitting in a meeting in 1965
between Clarence T. C. Ching, landowner and developer,
born on a Kauai plantation, and representatives of the
Dillingham Corporation, builders, a business descended from
the Benjamin F. Dillingham who had organized the Oahu
Railroad and Land Company in 1889, as they negotiated
prices and divided anticipated profits from a housing project
to be built on land acquired from the estate of Samuel
M. Damon, who had helped found Hawaii's first bank in
1850 and later took part in Queen Liliuokalani's ouster.[46]
They were strange bedfellows that Hawaii's lands were bringing to couch.

A Time of Consensus

The division of power in the decades of the 1950s and the
1960s has aptly been called a "consensus."[47] Although the
successful revolution of the Democrats that started in 1954
had had elements of reformism, particularly in land control,
the state administration soon found it convenient to collab-
orate with a number of oddly diversified elements. The
consensus before long included not only the nisei and union
constituency which had made the original political victory
possible, but also certain still powerful Republicans and
many newly powerful members of the developer-builder
group. A very cozy concord on most matters was reached.
The Republican mayor of Honolulu, part-Hawaiian Neal
S. Blaisdell, shared friends, supporters, advisers, and even
policies and programs with the Democratic governor, main-
land-born John Burns. An architect moving to Hawaii from
the mainland in the early 1960s, anxious to make useful contacts, was introduced by one of his clients to both the mayor
and the governor—to whose campaigns, he explained, he
contributed equally. The local builder advised the malihini
architect to do the same; favors could come equally from
both ends of the capitol district.[48]

The ILWU and the Sugar Planters Association no longer
had any serious conflicts during that time (strikes are easily
arbitrated in an atmosphere of consensus). Both were
prodevelopment and ready to work together to promote
Hawaii's expanding urbanism, even when it meant expanding
onto the agricultural lands where the union had once struggled to survive. With most members of the state and county
legislative bodies also development-oriented, the consensus
was complete. As a cynical observer puts it: "The wheels
were greased and the machine rolled between the Capitol, the
Land Use Commission, City Hall, and the Planning Commissions. Everyone was everybody's friend and everyone made
out."

As political power increasingly centered in the new types

controlling land, opposition to unlimited expansion began to develop in the 1960s and 1970s, not so much from a break in the consensus among political figures (there were no substantive differences in the programs of Democrats and Republicans in the legislature in these years) but from an awakened public concern about Hawaii's lands. Citizen participation in the political process assumed new strength across the mainland nation in the 1960s, particularly on issues affecting land use. Moves toward citizen-participatory political action and participatory planning were felt in Hawaii, too, and to some extent introduced a new force in land-use power manipulation.

In one sense citizen activism is a reaction to the growth of bureaucratized, centralized government and an attempt to recapture some of the control the political establishment has appropriated. Hawaii's people could certainly find cause to react to a long history of concentrated power over land. In some ways it is a sophisticated move: it recognizes that purely political considerations, swayed by power groups, have a strong effect on decision making—and tries to create a counterforce with its own political power. In other respects it forms what has been termed a "third public" of ordinary citizens affecting policy. It is a loose, amorphous, and unorganized public, yet one to be reckoned with in decisions such as land use allocations in addition to the more professional development-oriented and conservation-minded publics.[49]

One must recognize that citizen articulation is often a self-solicitous move; beneath much of the new activism lies a desire to see that everyone gets his share of a good, affluent life before options are closed. In Hawaii, this desire has often translated into an insistence on tropicalized American suburbanism. Increasingly, of course, fear and frustration have inspired the citizen-initiative movement. Pollution, the environment, that vague thing called ecology—these matters really concern more and more people, in Hawaii as much as anywhere else.

Because of its various motives, this attempt to reassert popular power had mixed results in the islands, as it did elsewhere. Much of the new political populism centered on the question of how land was used—and particularly what was happening to Hawaii's open spaces. The old-line organizations became more belligerent: the Outdoor Circle, the League of Women Voters, and even the Junior League began monitoring commission meetings and issuing position papers on land planning matters. The Oahu Development Conference, an influential, primarily businessmen's organization directed by a nationally respected professional planner, Aaron Levine, centered more of its attention on land management problems, and Honolulu's Downtown Improvement Association took the lead in urging a lethargic city planning department toward central-city land planning. Similiar moves, on a smaller scale, were made in Hilo and Kailua on the Big Island and in some few other places. Conservation societies such as the local branch of the Sierra Club, the Conservation Council, and even the Audubon Society found fresh adherents and compatible colleagues. New organizations were created. Some formulated positions and lobbied for consumer interests and others more aggressively demanded environmental protection measures. In a few instances, organized local citizen councils prepared planning studies and made informed approaches to government bodies: the most effective, Windward Citizens Planning Council, was guided by a professional planner-administrator, Leonard Moffitt. Heads of a number of the locality groups combined, in 1974, to form a parent organization they named the Council of Presidents. This council exerted considerable influence on such issues as shoreline protection.

In most cases, however, the grass roots movements were unorganized or were put together for a single campaign on an ad hoc basis. Students of the subject have pointed out that well-organized, well-informed environmentalists are generally in favor of areawide (state or regional) land use controls and professional land planning,[50] while the more irregular citizens coalitions tend to be interested in decentralized, locality-oriented issues. This characteristic of much citizen activity is evident in any public hearing before a government decision-making agency. Each local group is anxious to protest actions that it feels may harm its community, but has no evident concern for the problems of any other place or the overall area. Even within that limited interest, constructive suggestions are rare unless there is expert guidance; commonly, only arguments *against* some proposed action are heard. Planning commissioners, in Hawaii as in other jurisdictions, become inured to the testimony of neighborhood organizations opposing every new development, no matter how essential, well placed, and well planned, especially when it might bring "new elements" into a closed community.

Nevertheless, in Hawaii the antidevelopment protest movements had a cumulative effectiveness as they grew in size and volume. In the 1960s there came a threat to a revered environment that stirred the entire Oahu public: a serious proposal was made for resort development at the makai foot of Diamond Head. A huge gathering of ordinary citizens crowded the council chambers in Honolulu Hale, the city hall, to remonstrate at a public hearing against that environmental sacrilege. The city council was properly impressed: it promised that there would be no development there and that ways would be found to make the majestic mound a state, possibly a national, monument.[51]

After this success (Diamond Head *is* now a national landmark, and the city has designated it a special scenic, cultural, and historic zoning district) other public protests followed, some with uncertain results. In 1969 a large outpouring testified against Joe Pao's attempt to develop the side of Mount Olomana, a handsome 1,600-foot-high peak to which a legendary giant is supposed to have leaped from the island of Kauai.[52] The Planning Commission recommended disapproval of the project to the council, which still, after all these years, remains undecided. Another scenic, cultural, and historic district around the state and city capitols and Iolani Palace, approved by the Honolulu Planning Commission, was threatened with emasculation by the Council at the behest of adjoining property owners. A great outpouring of citizens protested, and much of the plan was saved.[53] Other public remonstrations have resulted in an ordinance protecting views toward Punchbowl, where the National Cemetery of the Pacific is located, and, for a short time, moves to prevent high-rise construction adjacent to Thomas Square, the intimately scaled and landscaped park marking the place where Kamehameha III received Hawaii back from the British in 1844.

The citizen organization with the broadest effectiveness on land matters has been a group called Life of the Land. Staffed by a small coterie of ardent, youthful environmentalists and led by a tireless, single-mindedly devoted individual, a former writer on land planning matters named Tony Hodges, LOL grew through the 1970s in size, respect, and impact. Continually in financial straits, as are all such organizations that depend on support from a citizenry larger than its active membership (and randomly irritate elements of that community by their actions), it has learned to use what power the public does have in environmental protection. The National Environmental Protection Act (NEPA) and Hawaii's state counterpart (HEPA) establish certain requirements, assessments, and scrutinies for public works, at least. If they are not observed properly, the projects can be challenged in the courts. The process is costly, time-consuming, and often frustrating, and those who make the effort are seldom popular in the community: they are "troublemakers." By scrounging funds, gaining the help of many capable volunteers, and ignoring the inevitable epithets, Hodges and LOL succeeded in restraining a good deal of potentially harmful public development and bringing into litigation or challenging a great deal more (including the H3 freeway). By late 1976, however, both LOL and Tony Hodges were completely out of funds. Then in 1977 a sizable federal grant

allowed a reorganized Life of the Land to proceed in a totally different direction (as aid and adviser to community planning groups). Hodges had to seek new outlets for his
dynamism.

The Sound of Vox Populi

The public which began to assert itself during the 1960s
included those of Hawaiian descent. For a long time the
Hawaiians' only extrinsic association with the use of their
ancestors' lands had been through the Bishop Estate,
established to employ income from its landholdings for the
education of their children. The community of Hawaiians
and part-Hawaiians protested, at times, the fact that few
trustees of Hawaiian lineage were appointed to the estate's
board (appointments are made by the Supreme Court).[54]
There were, moreover, occasional rumblings about the quality of the curriculum (improved, when a former president of
the University of Hawaii, Thomas H. Hamilton, was added
to the advisory staff), and, as we have seen, serious objections were raised when some of the estate's land was sold. By
and large, however, the beneficiaries of Princess Pauahi's
will accepted with little question the academic benefits of the
income from the Kamehameha family's lands—which were
provided in handsome school buildings on a hill above
Honolulu, segregated from the rest of the community's
educational system.

In an odd, indirect way, the Hawaiian people thus exert a
tremendous, though not always salutary, power over the
lands of the islands. The estate has been called a second
Hawaiian government; it has the ability to improve or
destroy the quality of large parts of several of the islands.
With the advice only of a rather small technical staff,
trustees can make arbitrary decisions on the use of 10 percent
of the lands of the state—subject, of course, to agreement of
the normally amenable state and county zoning agencies.
When the board of trustees was plantation-oriented, land was

often leased to sugar interests at low rates and investments were made in sugar-related paper like plantation bonds and plantation-railroad stock. When the economic temper of the trustees changed along with that of the rest of the business community, they turned their influence toward land development enterprises. Their only objective in making land use decisions was the goal that Princess Bernice Pauahi had established in her will and the courts rigorously protected: providing the maximum possible income for the Kamehameha schools. Through the boom years of development on Bishop Estate lands, the only protests heard from the community of Hawaiian people (aside from expressions of concern about loss of income when land was sold) have been isolated objections from some younger activists when pig farmers were ousted from their leaseholds to make room for construction.

The strongest manifestation of interest by twentieth-century Hawaiians in the overall status of the lands that had supported their ancestors has been a movement to gain reparations for native lands taken by the United States government. A Hawaiian Native Claims Settlement Act was introduced in Congress in June 1974. It asked for a cash settlement of $1 billion and a return of 2½ million acres of land, the income to be administered by a native corporation.[55] The sponsoring entity, an organization called ALOHA (acronym for Aboriginal Lands of Hawaiian Ancestry), was formed in 1971 through the activity of an ardent part-Hawaiian named Louisa K. Rice, a taxi driver who had become inspired by reading Queen Liliuokalani's account of her last days as monarch. As time went on, with advice from local and mainland attorneys as well as those who had led successful reparations movements of native Alaskans and American Indians, the group became more sophisticated. In 1973 it incorporated itself as the Aloha Association. Demands were added to the original request—most importantly for income from all public and private revenues derived from Hawaii's natural resources—and a resolution was adopted (on advice of the association's Alaskan- and

Indian-experienced friends) declaring Hawaiians to be "a people who are still a sovereign nation."[56] Louisa K. Rice was made a lifetime director of the association, but she resigned in 1976, impatient at what she termed "stagnation" of the movement.[57]

Congress has taken the claim with sufficient seriousness for the House Interior and Insular Affairs Committee to travel to the islands in early 1976 to hear testimony on its justification.[58] Hawaii's congressional delegation has at times been lukewarm in its support for the legislation: Senator Inouye has proposed that a commission be appointed to study the validity of the claim before any serious decision is made one way or another.[59] This suggestion is simply considered insulting by ALOHA's leaders. The pertinent history is well-enough established, even if its interpretation may be disputed. It begins with the statement in Kamehameha III's constitution of 1840 that Hawaii's lands did not really belong to the king any longer, but "to the chiefs and the people in common." It notes the Great Mahele's division of land between the ruler and his chiefs and the legislation that allowed fee-simple land ownership to all residents of the islands. It involves the declaration, in the act of 3 January 1865, that the crown lands were "inalienable" from the crown. It takes account of the Blount Report of the overthrow of the monarchy, a lawful government, "through the agency of the U.S. government"; the Organic Act of annexation, whereby all of Hawaii's public lands were ceded by a haole republic to a haole American nation with the question of equitable settlement left unresolved; and the Articles of Statehood under which the United States government retained some of the public domain as federal property and returned the rest to the State of Hawaii.

Emotionally, the settlement claim is based on Queen Liliuokalani's passionate insistence that "to prevent the shedding of the blood of my people . . . I quietly yielded to the armed forces brought against my throne and submitted to the arbitrament of the United States."[60] Historically, it focuses on the fact that the United States never did "arbitrate" the disputed domain's unresolved problems but rather, quite quickly, annexed it in all of its landed parts. Legally, most experts agree, the case rests on the further fact that these Hawaiian ancestral lands, held until 1893 by an independent, sovereign government, were taken away with absolutely no recompense or compensation.

There are many sticky questions that will have to be resolved if a commission does investigate all the ramifications of Hawaiian land tenure. Who really did own what at the time of the revolution? Royal ownerships, crown land rights, government land possession, and private holdings, as we have seen, were never clearly resolved. (One scholar has even disputed the genealogical successions which passed on to Princess Bernice Pauahi the Kamehameha lands now held by the Bishop Estate.[61] Both commoners and chiefs in many cases sold lands they had acquired after the Great Mahele. Queen Liliuokalani sued the U.S. government for income from the crown lands which she thought, to the end, should provide income for her personal use.

Some present-day descendants of the royal lines want the ALOHA claim to distinguish among kingly, chiefly, and commoner land rights. Aside from the quality of lineage, it becomes difficult to define a Hawaiian today. Should compensation be made to those with any part of Hawaiian blood? What fraction—half, one-fourth—should prove the descendant's equity? Since the federal government never distinguished between the rights of the people to public land and the rights of the state, does that imply that the natives held no rights? Or does it signify that they were deprived of their rights? All but 400,000 acres of public lands were returned to the State of Hawaii by the federal government in 1959. Does that limit the extent of damage that can be sought from the United States? And someone will surely ask whether, despite the Blount Report of U.S. involvement in the overthrow of the monarchy, America took land from a native nation or, after a hiatus, received it from a haole republic.

Forgetting all these quandaries and quibbles, two salient
facts seem clear enough to justify a claim for settlement. One
is that Hawaii was a sovereign nation when the revolution
took place, a nation with whom, indeed, the United States as
well as other countries had negotiated treaties as an equal—
and it was certainly not so treated in the succession of
governmental changes that took place between revolution and
statehood. ALOHA's advisers point to five recorded treaties
and agreements between the Kingdom of Hawaii and the
United States to establish that point, including the treaty on
tariff reciprocity and the agreement on Pearl Harbor. Proposals have been made that this issue of the "constitutional-
ity" of America's acquiring Hawaii might be tested in the
courts.[62] Other land acquisitions by the U.S. federal government were by undisputed cession, through purchase, or as
treaties. Western American lands were ceded by the colonies.
Texas, a nation, voluntarily gave up its sovereignty to join
the union. The United States bought Alaska from Russia in
1867 for $7 million. The Alaskan situation was further
different from Hawaii's at the time of claim settlement in
the fact that much of the federally held land there was
unassigned. In Hawaii, by contrast, all the land that the
federal government now retains is assigned in some way to
particular agencies for specific uses.

The other, and most persuasive, justification for a com-
pensatory settlement without looking too deeply into historical complexities is the fact that Hawaii's lands were taken
with absolutely no payment. All questions of compensation
were indefinitely postponed and then conveniently forgotten
by Congress. ALOHA's guides have pointed out that in
Alaska's case the original recompense was inadequate and in
the case of the American Indian lands it was unfair, but for
Hawaii it was nonexistent. Awards were made in the other
two instances to "extinguish" any further claims, as the legal
phrase goes, and in this respect the Hawaiian people seem to
have the strongest argument of all.

There is a disturbing aspect of ALOHA's action, however.

The claim is for money and for land which would produce money. There is no attempt to set up a land management procedure, only a financial distribution agency. In the discussions there has been no mention of land use planning or land use controls, no insistence on restoring to those of Hawaiian descent some power over the way their ancestral lands are used. Looked at that way, the ALOHA movement could be seen as the latest instance of the Hawaiian peoples' willingness to accept money, as their government did during the monarchy, for the loss of their land. Alaska does not present an inspiring precedent in this regard. Shareholders in the native corporations which handle the benefits established by the Alaskan Native Claims Act of 1971 receive cash payments and look forward to further income from exploitation of their land and its minerals. Conservationists in Alaska find themselves not at all pleased with the newly gained power the natives have over their land; rather, they are apprehensive. Whether the Hawaiian people will offer reassurances on this point to their fellow inhabitants of the islands remains to be seen.

The ALOHA action is a unique bid for new land power by today's Hawaiian people—now, unhappily, only a segment of the present population of the islands. Ideally, in a democratic society, the power of the public should be expressed through the actions of elected government officials. Redress of wrongs as great as the taking of their land from a sovereign people requires special effectuation, but scattered citizen protests against individual misuses of the land and isolated citizen court actions delaying certain treatments of the environment are costly and inefficient ways to effect the public will. Too often they are merely nuisances to those whose actions are challenged, nuisances which eventually can be overcome.

Expressions of direct political will of the kind that LOL has made have become necessary. There is no clear "public" policy position, expressed in unambiguous terms, which could direct official action, if elected officials wanted such a guide, or force it if they demurred. In most cases there is

little wish for such guidance. Our administrators and legislators, as representatives of an amorphous constituency, must
recognize a numer of organized publics whom they represent.
And, as pragmatic politicians, they are likely to be responsive
to those with the greatest immediate power. Firm public
policy can hamper the freedom of political action.

There are, fortunately, exceptions to this unhappy rule of
the political science thumb; there are some candidates for
office who possess and express intrinsic convictions (that we
must respect our environment, perhaps) and who *become*
public officials for that very reason. Sadly, in Hawaii there
has seldom been strong political leadership on land matters.
After speaking enthusiastically at a conference in Oahu about
the land controls he would like to see adopted, Shunichi
Kimura, then mayor of the Big Island, lapsed into pessi-
mism: "Our problem is that now we go back and face the
so-called realities, and we give up."

If a popular ground swell were to develop in Hawaii,
indicating a strong desire for careful management of the
islands' lands, these political realities might change and the
worries of people like Kimura could vanish—but no such
general wish has yet appeared. In the 1974 gubernatorial election three candidates vied for the Democratic party nomination: Frank Fasi, mayor of Honolulu, who insisted through
the campaign that further growth on the land was desirable
and inevitable; Tom Gill, former representative, both in
Hawaii and Washington, and later lieutenant governor of the
state, who had been an important participant in the passage
of Hawaii's progressive land legislation during the 1960s; and
George Ariyoshi, current lieutenant governor, "slow growth"
advocate, whose campaign was effectively organized by the
still-active Burns machine. Ariyoshi won the nomination,
with Fasi second, and easily carried the general election. (The
Republicans, with a kind of death wish, had nominated a
slate of two figures from territorial history.) Fasi remained
mayor, biding his political time. Gill, for now, has with-
drawn from politics.

Since his election, Governor Ariyoshi has indicated a desire to control careless land development and save agricultural land. Effective land management, however, does not come about through good wishes. It has to be based on popular insistence that land again be valued as a finite resource, not as a commodity for financial and political barter. Hawaii's people, if they have that wish, must find ways to express it more manifestly than any of their predecessors since Polynesian times have done. Their will, their ultimate power, will determine the fate of their lands, in ways which the final part of this book discusses.

The Fate of Hawaii's Lands

THE Hawaiian people used land in the ways for which it was best suited. This was a simple land management policy, dictated by the requirements of people and the mandates of nature, not by any government decision. Control over the land might change as an alii nui suffered military misfortunes or alterations of allegiance, but uses of the land stayed the same unless floods, volcanic eruptions, or tsunami waves interfered. There was no need for people to debate land use issues; they were solved by experience, translated into custom, and codified, if at all, as religious taboos. And there was no need to find ways to enforce these accepted policies: the population of the islands by Cook's time was fairly dense and the land was clearly limited; to have abused it at that stage of technological development would have been disastrous.

The white man, however, taught the Hawaiians that land could be adapted to purposes that did not appear natural. Meadows that had always stood open could be used for building construction. Wells could be dug to provide water where none seemed to exist. Before long it was not necessary to save the best farmlands for growing food, the best forests

for timber and vines and tapa, the best hunting grounds for a
meat supply. Technology, even in nineteenth-century non-
sophisticated forms, furnished the means for changed uses
(essential products could be imported, or manufactured, or
replaced by substitutes). A desire for profit from the land
furnished the motive.

Suddenly, then, it became necessary to make choices about
the ways land should be used. And since the person who
owned the land seemed to control those decisions, it became
necessary in this new world to decide who could be the
owners. And ultimately, since the new land uses produced
public costs as well as private profits, it became necessary to
consider new ways to assess taxes. That is, policy decisions
were necessary, whether by decree or by ballot. Then, if
policies were adopted, plans would be needed to carry them
out, and designs to effectuate the plans.

To a limited degree Hawaii has faced up to these modern
necessities. There have been brief periods when government
enunciated strong land policies in the public interest, longer
periods when private owners seemed to control policy decisions, and many periods when no firm policies were at all
discernible. Today Hawaii seems to be in a time of indecision, deliberating over various land policies that might be
adopted, without adopting any. The initiative that the state
had when the Land Use Law was passed seems to have been
lost, relinquished to others.

In recent years, a number of other states have enacted
legislation for land management; by the end of 1974 more
than twenty had some form of land use program under way.[1]
Very few followed Hawaii in attempting direct statewide zoning and regulation of overall land uses. Vermont passed a
Land Use Development Law in 1970 establishing criteria for
specific sorts and sizes of development (commercial, on more
than ten acres; housing, of more than ten units). That same
year Colorado adopted a promising Land Use Policy Act,
which was weakened in later legislation. Florida, through its
Environmental Land and Water Management Act of 1972,

designates areas of "critical state concern," overriding local
land-use regulations and establishing its own when that
becomes necessary. Oregon, in 1973, passed a law which
received wide acclaim but, in practice, seemed to be a well-
meaning statement of policy without application to any
specific plan.

Most state land-control laws are even less comprehensive
than those. One category follows Florida's lead in pinpointing areas where the state seems to have particular reason
to be concerned about local land-use controls. Delaware's
Coastal Zone Act, California's recent Coastal Zone Conservation Act, Michigan's Shorelines Protection and Management Act, Maine's Site Selection Law (intended largely to
protect the shoreline)—all concentrate on waterfronts as areas
of most critical concern.

Another kind of land control statute was adopted by a
number of states in the late 1960s and remains tempting to
others; it is delegation of unusual authority over land uses in
specific areas to regional agencies, usually with supervisory
authority and ultimate right of approval held by the state.
The philosophical as well as constitutional basis for such
acts is a state's right to control the uses of land (failing any
federal assumption of power) and its traditional delegation of
land-use zoning authority to local governmental jurisdictions.
Wisconsin's Water Resources Act of 1966 led the way in this
direction, mandating to the state's cities and counties the
duty of protecting land uses near lakes and rivers. Minnesota
established a Twin Cities Metropolitan Council in 1967 to
regulate land uses in the Minneapolis–St. Paul area; in New
Jersey the Hackensack Meadows Development Act of 1968
gave a local commission the authority to develop and enforce
a master land-use plan for that valuable real estate. Various
urban development corporations, notably New York's, established in 1968 and highly successful until it overextended
itself and expired in 1975, fall in the same category.

That checklist, hardly complete, indicates the many
directions that state land-use regulations have taken since

Hawaii's 1961 law was passed—and makes the important
point that none of the later acts have dared be as broad in
scope as Hawaii's earlier one. Recent legislation differs from
Hawaii's in basic intent: its aim is directed more toward conservation of "environmental resources and natural beauty,"
as Vermont's law puts it, and less toward "income and
growth potential of the economy," as Hawaii's does. Yet,
having studied Hawaii's experience, the others shy away
from statewide management controls; most refer to particular
regions or specific uses. Sometimes they establish policies; in
other cases they fix regulations. Seldom do they span, comprehensively, the full process from setting goals and developing plans to implementation. Hawaii's law, at least in intent,
is still the only one that is truly comprehensive.

Yet Hawaii also fails to provide an example of effective
land management techniques. The reason is easy to state but
hard to solve: the opposition of political influences (crudely
put, developers versus conservationists) has a neutralizing
effect. Clear-cut policy statements and firm decision making
are inhibited. When other states planning land legislation
sent delegations to Hawaii to study the operation of the
islands' landmark law, they quickly saw this defect in its
draftsmanship. "Although procedures were established the
[land use] commission was given no guidance in law on the
relative emphasis to place on such major controversies as
tourist-related development versus the preservation of natural
and scenic attractions, or agricultural land versus the supply
of land for reasonably priced living accommodations," says
a report from Oregon State University.[2] Yet the visitors went
back home and fell into the same faults themselves. Most of
the legislation their states produced was strong on procedures but weak on goals. The purposes the laws intended to
accomplish were generally put in ambivalent terms that
would offend neither developers nor conservationists.[3] Inevitably the execution of such laws has tended to hurt no one.
Opposing groups have been granted at least some of their
desires: some conservation land saved, some development

allowed. Firm decisions are avoided and long-range consequences are ignored.

Having moved so quickly from aboriginal land-use mores to leadership in modern land control legislation, with documented experiences under various conditions, Hawaii remarkably demonstrates both the need for a comprehensive approach to land control and the difficulties that lie in the way of achieving that goal.

chapter 10

Programs and Policies

IN early human history the concept of a land "policy" was unknown. None seemed necessary; land was limitless and was there to be used. Flood and frost, bane and blight, might reduce its functions for a time, but there was always a greener valley across the mountains or over the seas. Ancient history is a story of migrations, first in search of better hunting grounds and then in hope of more fertile farmland—and they could always be found.

So long as the population was small and the world's vast face was largely unexplored, any restrictions on land's uses were nature's, not man's. When there were only a few million persons scattered on the earth, aboriginal people could not seriously worry about land depletion; but when there were a billion, around the time that Captain Cook landed on Kauai, modern men and women were finding it necessary to govern the uses of their home territories—and to reach for more. The great explorations of the seventeenth and eighteenth centuries constituted a continuing search for additional lands with additional resources.[1] Cook's sponsors wanted him to find the elusive northwest passage to connect the Atlantic and the Pacific oceans, so that distant places and the incomes they could provide might be brought closer to home.

But then as the explorers found new lands and settlers colonized them, they carried along the problem—and the policies that were supposed to solve them—they had become used to at home. The questions about land that Europe and, to a certain extent, America found pressing toward the end of the eighteenth century were created by the industrial revolution and enhanced by the urban growth it brought. They were primarily issues of tenure, use, and taxation, none of them worrying Hawaii in the early 1800s. Imposition of land policies that were products of an industrial-age capitalistic society on a people emerging from a stone-age feudalistic era produced some of modern Hawaii's first major cultural conflicts.

Policies regarding tenure that had been developed in western Europe and carried to America were based on the concept of individual private ownership.[2] Hawaii, of course, was still functioning under the concept of central, kingly ownership; and any distribution of land further into society was revocable at the king's will. To the Hawaiians this was natural and workable; to the newcomers it was an unacceptable policy that had to be changed.

Policies governing land use had become troublesome issues in capitalist Europe, but they were of little import for a long while in Hawaii. In an industrializing, urbanizing society it was easy for fair land to be fouled by misuse; ugly towns and slums developed quickly with the industrial revolution, and competition between open-space uses and urban development began with the building of the first factory.[3] Hawaii, on the other hand, had seemingly endless expanses of land little developed, and its population, far from expanding, had begun to shrink.

How land uses were planned in Europe's older areas and America's new ones is another story, but the fact that they *were* planned, as policy, quite ardently during the eighteenth and nineteenth centuries, is part of the history of land

management and land policy.⁴ The land use policy questions
that had to be settled abroad were procedural—how much
liberty the individual possessed and how much control the
public, through its government, might exert. They were also
substantive—to what uses, in what proportions, land should
be put. Some of the early settlers of Hawaii had seen English
towns like Nottingham restricted and crowded because they
were surrounded by inviolable agricultural lands; on the
other hand they had seen fertile fields invaded by expanding
industry. Hawaii did not have to face any of these problems
yet. One can imagine that some of the pleasant sense of
abandon the foreigners found in the islands came from seeing so much land with so few problems of competing uses
and no need, apparently, to worry about policies in this
regard.

The Hawaiian people themselves were confused about land
use concepts after the white man came. They were torn between a desire to hold to the old, logical system of letting the
nature of the land itself determine how it was to be used and
a conflicting wish to follow the new idea of finding its most
profitable use. The period of the sandalwood trade demonstrated how income could be created by a policy of exploiting
land's assets. It showed also how quickly that policy could
deplete resources. The Hawaiians, bewildered by many innovations, did not appear to learn much from either lesson.
The newcomers, however, were willing to continue looking
for more land-generated income and defer any policy formation that might restrict their freedom.

Taxation policies had also become a bothersome matter in
the industrializing countries. New land uses, greater concentrations of population, and rising standards of health and
sanitation all demanded greater outlays for public services.
Ad valorem assessment, based on the imputed value of a
property such as land, was the kind of tax policy Hawaii's
early settlers had been used to at home. And although this
was another penalty of modern civilization they were glad to
forego for a while, before long real-property taxes were

applied in the islands. Although Hawaii's monarchy did not need much monetary revenue in its early years (the government budget in 1842 was $41,000),[5] public services soon demanded a larger public income. A mild tax law passed in 1877 continued as policy until the territorial government revised it after annexation. The first clearly stated policy decisions about land in Hawaii, then, dealt almost exclusively with matters of tenure. Questions of ownership forced the so-called land reform movement of the 1840s, brought about the land division of the Great Mahele, and effected legitimization of individual ownership and the rights of sale and inheritance. After these policies were established, all the concomitant problems that private land ownership entails had to be faced: questions of private property rights versus public rights as well as eminent domain, regulation of transfers, sales, and inheritances, and all the statutory tangles that can be wound around realty law and the economics of property.[6] Very little in the way of formal public land policy was adopted during the monarchy period, however. Government lands were most often leased, sometimes sold outright, but the dealings were made with few set criteria or established policies, as an editorial in the *Islander* complained in 1875.[7]

By the time the monarchy was overthrown, the New World's values had been sufficiently consolidated in Hawaiian life. The opportunities as well as the restraints they posed were so clear that the new political leaders felt a need for stating them as explicit policies. This they did in the republic's Land Act of 1895, so clearly in accepted American land-commodity terms that the Organic Act did little to change its provisions. In Washington, Congress seemed to wish to slow the concentration of Hawaii's lands in the control of the plantation owners (though not prevent it) and there appeared to be a real desire to encourage homestead farming. To these ends the terms of leases of public land were restricted to five years, the thousand acre ownership limitation was imposed, and various attempts to stimulate family farming were pursued. The oligarchy in Hawaii felt sure it could overcome the inhibitions to plantation expansion these new policy measures posed, and after several decades of politicking, pressuring, and compromising in Washington and Honolulu it succeeded. The Hawaii Rehabilitation Bill set basic land policies for some time: no serious opposition to concentration of land ownership; an acceptance of plantation agriculture as the most-favored land use; gestures toward residential homesteading as a subsidiary use.

If the social consequences of these policies were questionable and the political result was partriarchal control, there was no doubt that the economy of the islands benefited. Whereas the monarchy had always been in debt and its exports of capital and goods had fluctuated widely, the territorial government (accepting high consumer prices and business monopolies) was able to stabilize the agricultural industry and bring the economy to a state of development that was the envy of other plantation-agriculture countries.[8]

What ended this economic idyll and presaged the need for a revision of land policies was another stage in the constantly rising population curve. The pleasures and the penalties of a planters' empire could continue only so long as there were no seriously competing demands on the land. And that condition could last only while the population was just large enough to supply the needed labor force, sufficiently docile to be stationary, and so constant in numbers as to be controllable. But around 1940, about the time when the world reached its second billion of inhabitants—and Hawaii had tripled its turn-of-the-century population, from 150,000 to 450,000—the islands began to feel the pressures of urbanization that other countries had already experienced.

New policy questions started to arise during the terms of the later territorial governors. One was the increasing need for lots on which the growing populace could build homes, a problem that many realized for the first time to be distinct from providing estates for the haoles and homesteads for the natives. Governor Stainback wanted to force sale of idle lands from large owners to prospective home builders, and the commission he appointed recommended the development of subdivisions on public land.[9] Stainback and his successor, Governor Oren Long, foresaw an increasing demand for urban lands, for commercial as well as housing purposes, and urged public-land policy changes in that direction.

Another question about land use began to surface. Should land with no profitable use at all, land preserved as a natural resource, be protected as a matter of policy? Although the conservation movement was well established in mainland America,[10] in Hawaii there still was so much unused land that its preservation seemed almost an absurd proposition. The idea of "conserving" some land crept into discussions of public land policy from time to time, but never very seriously until after the war. Governor Stainback's commission, for example, suggested that public lands "not suitable for residential purposes be conserved."[11] But the definition and purpose of conservation were unclear at that time (as they remained during the drafting of the state's Land Use Law). Those conserved lands, it was felt, might later be "disposed of only upon lease" and for specific kinds of development. But at least the thought that policies might be needed regarding urban land uses, on the one hand, and land conservation, on the other, was not a totally new idea when Governor Quinn brought it forward after the war and then when the Land Use Law established conservation districts as a kind of holding category.

New Pressures, New Programs

It would be interesting to speculate on the changes that might have come about in Hawaii in the 1940s if World War II had not produced the transformation it did. Changes were obviously inevitable. And the needs and demands of the growing, restive, ethnically mixed population were bringing them constantly closer. But the war with its impacts did come, and when it had gone, leaving scars on the society and military garrisons on the land, the old policies no longer worked. There were many more people, who needed places to live and jobs to work at and schools to attend. And there were new types among those people, who were willing to break sugar-and-pine agriculture's grip on the land in order to develop new uses for it that would satisfy the new urban needs.

The Land Use Law of 1961 recognized those new pressures and noted that there are many uses for land in a modern society. Its declaration of purpose said it was the state's *policy* "to preserve, protect and encourage the development of the lands of the State for those uses to which they are best suited for the public welfare."[12] That sounded at the time like a high-minded purpose, relating land uses to land qualities, even though it said little of substance that would guide administration of the law.

The basic intent of the 1961 legislation, then, was to set new policies regarding land *uses,* whereas the legislation of the 1840s, at the time of the Great Mahele, had been directed exclusively to questions of land *ownership.* Although other so-called land reform bills have surfaced from time to time, the principle of concentrated land ownership has never been seriously challenged as policy until very recently, as residential land-lease rates have become excessive. The great holdings of the comparatively few landowners have not been disturbed, in fact or by plan, except as the owners themselves have begun selling off pieces of them.

Increasing population pressures and the expanding needs they produced again led Hawaii to a reexamination of land policies in the mid-1970s. At the time the world approached its fourth billion of people and as Hawaii passed a de facto population of 800,000, it became obvious that no present policy could save the islands from rapid environmental deterioration. For the first time the concept of "conserving" land began to mean something specific. Now it was a pressing need. New words and phrases that were common parlance on the mainland were heard too in Hawaii: "ecology" and "environmental protection" as imperatives; "pollution" and "congestion" as perils.

The first element of environmental policy to receive attention in the legislature was open-space planning. By the late 1960s several other states had adopted formal open-space plans.[13] Techniques were well developed for determining what parts of a region's land should remain undeveloped, not only for agriculture and grazing but as forest reserves, watersheds, protected ponds and streams, essential shorelines, natural landmarks, scenic and historic areas, and recreational space. Having led the way in land control legislation, the Hawaii legislators did not wish to lag too far behind in this new process. In 1969 they called for preparation of an open-space plan for Hawaii.[14]

The following year Governor Burns commissioned Stewart Udall's Overview Corporation to prepare this plan. Burns had known Udall in Washington when the Hawaii politico was territorial delegate to Congress and the mainland politician-cum-environmentalist was congressman from Arizona. Within the conservation-minded groups in Hawaii there was speculation at the time of the appointment whether Udall's plan would take as strong an open-space position as his recent writings had expressed or whether it would be designed to satisfy the governor's progrowth and prodevelopment position. In an odd, unintended way it did both.

The Udall report, entitled *From the Mountain to the Sea: State of Hawaii Comprehensive Open Space Plan,* was issued in 1970. It tried to accomplish two things. One was the job that the Overview Corporation had been hired to do: prepare a plan for the state indicating what spaces, for what reasons, by what means, should be preserved as open lands. The methodology used by the professional planning staff Udall hired for the project and located in Honolulu for the duration of his contract was based in large part on a system that had been developed by the much-admired mainland ecologist-planner Ian McHarg. In essence it consisted of identifying as accurately as possible ecological features such as forests, marshes, and beaches, geological properties like rock and soil formations, physical characteristics including rainfall and climate, and factors of scenic, historic, or cultural worth. These findings are mapped in graduated value tones on transparent sheets and overlaid on each other—the resultant darkness or lightness indicates the suitability or, conversely, the inappropriateness of any given land for certain uses.[15]

Ideally, using such a method, a planner should be able to tell what areas are best kept as conservation or farming lands and which are most suitable for development of various kinds. This rather simplistic system caught the imagination of ecologically enthusiastic planners, and indeed it is a much more objective and reliable process for determining land uses than the arbitrary decisions that political agencies generally depend on. Udall's report included specific plans showing areas recommended to be kept open, undeveloped, on each island.

But Udall went further than that: he explained in the preface to his report that he was "committed to holistic planning." Overview was a "generalist organization," he said, and no good open-space plan could be prepared without a comprehensive analysis of all environmental factors—"such as population policies, urbanization patterns, resource uses, transportation alternatives, and other man-engineered growth vectors."[16] Certainly Hawaii needed, at that time, just such a broad review of its total planning process. It is rather tragic that the efforts of Stewart Udall and the competent team he put together were largely wasted; in the end they turned out to be a futile effort even to guide Hawaii to an environmentally oriented land policy. The plan did not achieve acceptance by the administration that had commissioned it, by the legislature to whom it was addressed, by the community at large, or even by the citizen organizations which eagerly awaited it.

There were several reasons for this lack of success. In the first place, Udall's estimable wish to broaden his study so as to be comprehensive diluted his particular open-space recommendations. Attention was distracted, for example, from the advice that Salt Lake and Mount Olomana, among other places, be given first-priority conservation status—distracted by a controversial, detailed proposal for rearranging the state's entire zoning, planning, and environmental protection organization. Then for some reason Udall avoided any attempt at participatory planning and instead adopted the method of the self-assured planner of the early days of city and regional planning. This approach for many years had been to accomplish planning as a personal creative act in the planner's sanctum and then, when the plan was completed, to make an impressive presentation to the client and "sell" the community at large on the plan's merits. As a result of Overview's reversion to this process the political leaders, the general public, and active citizens' groups were largely ignored during the plan's preparation and found, when the handsomely printed final report was presented, there were parts of it they did not like.[17]

The greatest disappointment was with the incomplete way the report handled an important part of its commission: recommendations for legislation and other ways of implementing the open-space plan. The report suggested that the state should "adopt quality growth as its official policy" and also "adopt as a long-range policy the goal of stabilized population." Beyond those two rather inconsistent generalities there was a somewhat vain proposal that "legislation be adopted to make Overview's . . . Plan the State's official growth policy for the future." Specific recommendations for the reorganization of state planning were listed, but no further detailing of legislation was attempted.

As means for preserving the open spaces that the plan indicated to be important, in four stages of priority, the report broadly discussed methods that had been tried elsewhere, at times with a degree of success, at other times with only a measure of hope—easements, zoning, development rights, compensable regulations, lease, dedication, gift, purchase, eminent domain, and so on.[18] The report ended by recommending that the state create a land acquisition fund of $100 million by marketing general obligation bonds. Since the state's bonding authority was already stretched, this proposal placed Udall's plan, in the minds of the legislators and many other pragmatists, in the blue-sky realm. The community was left with a hopeless feeling. It now had an open-space plan that no one, apparently not even the expert who had prepared it, knew what to do with.

Policies, Goals—and Delays

Another important study of land use policies was made in 1973 by a Temporary Commission on Statewide Environmental Planning which the legislature authorized Governor Burns to appoint for the purpose of exploring further the policy of quality growth the governor had enunciated. The report of this study group, issued as a brochure entitled *A Plan for Hawaii's Environment,* dropped the phrase "quality growth" and suggested a new kind of policy for the state, one that it termed an "environmental ethic." It called for the adoption of two goals: conservation of Hawaii's natural resources by controlling pollution and "safeguarding the State's unique natural environmental characteristics"; and enhancement of the quality of life in the islands by "developing criteria" and "adopting strategies" to hold population at an optimum level, encouraging economic activities "in balance with the physical and social environments," and planning communities "in harmony with the physical environment."[19]

In presenting these goals and thirty-seven policies that amplified them, the temporary commission chaired by Adam A. Smyser, editor of the *Honolulu Star-Bulletin,* carefully avoided the errors that Udall's firm had made. No appointed task force agency had ever been so diligent in taking its proposals to the public for suggestions and reactions or in detailing legislation that might implement its recommendations. As soon as the commission had a tentative set of policies ready to talk about, it published and disseminated them as a draft for general discussion. It arranged open forums in each county. It sent teams to any meeting of any organization that wished to learn about or debate the proposals. This proved to be much more than a gesture of goodwill; the public's reactions were strong and surprisingly effective.

The group's first set of policies was overly general and became progressively weaker as the report moved from basics to specifics, but major improvements were made in redrafting and most weak wordings were changed or omitted. A policy to "protect the shorelines of the State from encroachment of man-made improvements" finally said just that, whereas the first draft had added the mangling words "except those for public use and public benefit." In short, the final report was a much stronger public-policy proposal than the first draft had been.

In addition to improving its language, the commission's ultimate report added a concept that gave great dimension to the policy proposals. It was the idea that a physical environment can "carry" just so much people-imposed burden without being overloaded; that any area's "carrying capacity" can be determined by environmental-ecological measurements; that overloading environmental capacity will inevitably result in ecological damage.[20] The report recommended strongly that the governor initiate a program to analyze Hawaii's environmental capacity and advised that any area found to be overloaded or in danger of overload be protected against further development.

This concept, already recognized elsewhere as a good rationale for land management policies, was a quite radical notion to Hawaii. It pleased those who were plugging for limitation of developmental growth. It alarmed those who believed that continued expansion was essential for the state's economic health. In a way the idea was an extension of the requirement for the environmental impact statements (called EISs by the cognoscenti) that national and many state governments (including Hawaii's) were already calling for in certain circumstances; it carried to more sophisticated levels the thought that the environmental effects of loading additional development on the land should be analyzed before permits were issued.

Even those who liked the idea realized that its ultimate effectiveness, as with other parts of the report's recommendations, would depend on the seriousness with which state officials took it and the strength of any implementation measures that might be adopted. In this case, the commission left nothing to chance when it suggested legislative action. Its major recommendation was adoption of a State Environmental Policy Act, and this was drafted as a proposed bill for the legislature, as were three additional bills and two proposed concurrent resolutions for House and Senate.[21]

In retrospect it was apparent that an error of judgment was made in the legislation drafting process by segregating the Policy Act as a separate bill from the other legislation which carried the teeth that would make policies bite. Particularly, one of the implementing acts proposed was an extension of the state's requirement for environmental impact statements (at that time simply an executive order asking for statements only for work by the state or on state land) into a law that would require such environmental assessment for all major work, public or private, anywhere in the state. There was a great risk, many felt, that the legislature would willingly adopt a motherhood-type policy statement but refuse to father effective action measures.

The legislature did pass the separated Policy Act, as had been predicted. And then, later, it enacted an environmental impact requirement weaker than the commission had recommended.[22] (For instance, it did not require the state or the counties to insist on EISs when changes were proposed in land-use classifications or in zoning.) Among the conservation-minded members of the community there was considerable disappointment and some bitterness at the legislative results: it seemed as though little had been accomplished beyond an expression of good intentions. Yet an environmental policy had been adopted for the state for the first time. Up until then all land-control and land-use policy had used economic value as its premise. Now, at least in words, there was a stated policy on the books that promised protection of lands and shorelines because they were irreplaceable resources. Whether the words would have any real weight remained to be seen.

Another pro tem study group established in that period was a Temporary Visitor Industry Council headed by Dr. Thomas Hamilton, who had been president of the University

of Hawaii and later executive head of the Hawaii Visitors
Bureau and now was a consultant to the Bishop Estate. It
worked closely with the commission on environmental
planning. Its major recommendation was that a ten-year
growth plan for tourism in the state be developed—taking
into consideration the jobs and the revenues that visitors
could provide but also assessing carefully the carrying capacity, the "load-bearing factor," of the physical and social
environments.[23] It took some time for its report to bear fruit.
Not until 1976 did the legislature ask for further analysis of
its findings and begin considering implementation.

That Question of Growth

The most difficult and inevitably the most controversial
policy any state must consider in this period of environmental concern is that dealing with growth. Hawaii, like most
other political jurisdictions, has hedged on the question.
Some attempts have been made to "develop criteria" for an
optimum population limit, as the Environmental Policy Act
proposed, and Governor Ariyoshi believed that his administration was pursuing a "slowed growth" policy. Yet whenever the visitor count dropped to less than a solid advance
over the previous year's figures there was concern. In mid-
1976, economists for the leading banks saw the state's economy doing no better than continuing on a "high plateau,"
and that worried them.[24] Hawaii's citizens seemed ambivalent
on the subject, although a survey conducted in 1974 by the
Honolulu Advertiser discovered that more than half of voters
wanted *some* kind of restriction on growth.[25] A 1976 state
study reaffirmed this finding.[26] Governor Ariyoshi, after his
election, referred from time to time to a report from the
Department of Planning and Economic Development recommending restricted growth. Ariyoshi spoke as though it were
state policy, although no policy position on the subject had
been adopted by the legislature.

It has long been obvious that there would not be state and
county cooperation on the question. Kauai had adopted a

comprehensive zoning code based on growth limitation. Maui
and the Big Island were somewhat indecisive on the subject
in their general plans; they seemed to believe that further
growth, of a desirable kind, could be controlled by such
devices as impact assessment. With no clear policy, of
course, this hope rested on decisions of the local legislative
bodies being miraculously guided by objective values of environmental analysis instead of the political criteria they were
used to. On Oahu, however, where more than 80 percent of
the state's population was centered, the city administration
recommended to the people that they accept growth as it
might come and plan always to accommodate rather than
limit it.

After years of delay the city's Department of General
Planning brought forth two volumes of a proposed revised
general plan in the fall of 1974. A section called "Population
Assumptions" explained the policy regarding growth on
which the plan was based. It was to assume no fixed figure
or "target" for any given time but was to use a range of
estimates based on "high and low rates of growth attained in
the past years." Using estimates of continuing trends was the
only "practical" way to make plans for what growth might
come, the city's planners said. With this fatalistic approach
to setting goals there was no attempt to calculate the island
environment's carrying capacity, as the state's policy advocated. In fact, the general plan document said, "in a practical [that word again!] sense 'capacity' is not an absolute
fixed number."[27] For instance, the text explained, "capacity
can be increased as long as one more chair can be squeezed
into a classroom or one more car onto the highway."

In the meantime the state planning office had taken a very
different tack. The Department of Planning and Economic
Development, as part of *its* general plan revision program,
produced a document in the spring of 1974 entitled *Growth
Policies Plan: 1974–1984* which described four growth alternatives among which Hawaii's people might choose. One
was a continuation of existing trends (the likelihood that
Honolulu's city planners considered inevitable), another was

an attempt to stop growth, the third was a slowing down of the rate of growth, and the last was promotion of accelerated growth.[28] Dr. Shelley Mark, the department's head, recommended the slowed growth alternative: a policy to "slow the rate of growth in the State's population, as well as to slow the rate of growth in certain sectors of the economy while accelerating the rate of growth in other sectors." It was this recommendation that Governor Ariyoshi seemed to assume as policy.

The report reviewed Hawaii's history of growth and its results. The income of the state had increased, it pointed out, and to a certain extent the quality of life had been improved. Now, however, various measurements indicated that rapid growth's harms were outweighing its benefits—particularly in environmental deterioration and the per capita costs needed to try to control it, but also in the growing burden, for each state resident, of providing services for an expanding population.

The slowing down of growth rates that was recommended would allow an annual civilian population increase of some 1⅔ percent (a drop from the 1970–1973 rate of 3.2 percent but still about twice the national growth rate). It was felt that this decreased rate of growth could be achieved by reducing both birth rates and in-migration. Birth rates might be lowered through educational programs and by tax reform to reward small families rather than encourage large ones as at present. In-migration might be checked by such means as "selectively slow" employment growth (for instance, encouraging industries that would provide jobs for local people and discouraging those that would require skills and employees brought from outside), and "modest" housing supports (manipulating the delicate housing supply so that new units would be provided for residents who needed them while second homes and speculative purchases by nonresidents would be discouraged).

The policy recommended—slow growth—was admittedly a compromise. Loss of agricultural lands would not be stopped; it would become "relatively slow." There would be "possible reduction" of traffic congestion, not elimination. Difficulties in meeting educational needs and supplying essential services would only be "reduced." There would be a "relatively healthy" economy, with "most citizens" sharing the economic prosperity.[29] Nevertheless, another policy statement with potentially important effects on the future of Hawaii's environment had been thrown in the long-range legislative hopper. Questions had been raised and courses of action suggested that could never again be completely ignored. Sharp conflicts lay ahead—not only in the community, among citizens with differing values, but also in the political realm. Whether growth of the population and economy should be slowed had obviously become a political issue. The administration of Oahu, the dominant island, contended that it could not be done, directly opposing the state government, which said that it could, and should at least become public policy.

In his State of the State message to the legislature in January 1977, Governor Ariyoshi made what seemed a bold statement on population growth. "Too many people can spell disaster for this state," he said. "Hawaii is a very fragile treasure, one which can be destroyed by overpopulation and excessive demands on its resources. . . . We need bold and innovative ideas and actions now if we are to achieve what we must achieve."

That sounded good, but in his extension of the proposition and his proposals for implementing it the governor indicated that his concern was socioeconomic rather than environmental. The too many people would mean "too few jobs and too much competition for them . . . too much pressure on all our governmental and private institutions." Ariyoshi's proposals had nothing to do with the danger of overloading the *environmental* capacity of the islands. They were limited to asking the federal government for a "more equitable distribution" among the states of immigration from abroad (and for financial assistance for those states receiving more than their share); and (probably implying a constitutional amendment) state legislation requiring a year's residency before government employment or welfare benefits could be obtained. The legislature, without much enthusiasm, agreed only to the public-employment residency requirement, and that move was rejected by a federal court as unconstitutional.

For environmental policy, recent sessions of the legislature have limited moves to the seeking of advice in preparation for later action. Most significant of the projections and presentations called for was a comprehensive policy plan to be ready for consideration at the 1978 legislative session. Its scope was to be ambitious: setting the basis for a fresh general plan, providing guidelines for direction of the Land Use Commission, even delineating policy about growth. A coordinated state-county planning council was established to oversee preparation of the plan, which, the legislators hoped, would "serve as a guide for the long-range development of the state." There were those who held great hopes for this brave attempt to set state policies, including land policy for land planning. There were others who could not believe that in such a short time all the conflict that had prevented effective management of the islands' environment over the years could be so readily resolved.

Nevertheless a start had been made toward a new land policy. Hawaii's land reform movements of the 1840s and the early 1960s had served their purposes at their times, and now again times had changed. New policy considerations had been introduced in the tentative land legislation of the mid-1970s, especially questions of ecology and growth. They were certain to affect land ownership, use, and taxation patterns in some ways. In the meantime, with or without articulated policy statements, plans continued to be made for using the lands of the islands. Over the years land planning in Hawaii had proved to be as indecisive, in most respects, as the setting of land policies had been.

chapter 11

Plans Without Purpose

IN the absence of policy guidelines it has not been possible for effective plans to be made and satisfactory designs drawn for the handling of Hawaii's lands. To plan is to give conscious purpose to actions that might otherwise be random. A plan's purpose can become *conscious* intent only when firm objectives have been chosen and determined policies guide the actions which will lead to those goals.[1]

Everyone has a certain ability to plan his or her own life, limited as that freedom may be at times, but in a community those individual plans are affected and often frustrated by the plans of others. Hence groups of people, societies, towns, states, and sometimes even nations try to make plans which at least many of their members may agree to. Broad-based planning of this kind is a risky enterprise of fairly recent origin (still considered a romantic notion by some and a radical idea by others). And to have any degree of success it must try to find mutual purposes and common principles. For land planning to be effective, then, there must be a reasonably wide agreement about the ways a community's environmental resources should be consciously employed.

Through Hawaii's history many disparate sorts of individuals living in the islands have planned their own lives well and designed their courses of action firmly, sometimes successfully. Seldom since the white man's arrival, however, has there been enough agreement on policies, or even objectives, to make possible societal planning. At those times when goals were widely accepted, as when a plantation society in the early 1900s had little doubt about the best uses of the islands' lands, there seemed no need to plan. In those pleasant, prosperous days the path to the future appeared clearly enough marked, the design of the tropical paradise sufficiently satisfactory.

In an organized society plans must be made to reach social, cultural, and economic objectives as well as goals of physical development. Planning the husbandry of resources so that all these desired ends can be achieved has become, in modern times, a complicated job requiring a high degree of sophistication in techniques. Early primitive societies had neither the skills nor the needs for meticulous planning. For the same reasons that land management policies were unnecessary—goals were simple and resources ample—land use plans could be primary, almost instinctive. But the people who maintain primitive cultures today (most of them, as the African nations, trying to leap directly to a place in the modern industrialized world) find an acute need to plan. New objectives must be reached quickly, often with resources shrinking as populations rise.

Hawaii in the nineteenth century was in a peculiar position in this respect: hurried and harried in its changeover from a primitive society which had sufficient resources for its simple technology, it yet lacked any clear picture of where it was heading or what its needs would be. When the white man came to the islands with his new social and economic concepts, his strange ideas about the ways land should be used, and his early hints of technological advancement, the *need* to plan became suddenly acute. But the absence of any desirable, discernable future restricted the *ability* to plan—and resulted in the confusion and confoundment that destroyed the early society and then undermined the monarchy. The Hawaiian people of that time could not plan; the haoles saw no reason to.

Before Cook's arrival, however, the Polynesian Hawaiians managed over the centuries to define overall land uses carefully and arranged their settlements logically and conveniently. The division of an island into mokus, ahupuaas, and kuleanas was not only a scheme that fitted the simple social relations: it also resulted in land being used in the most appropriate ways. The ahupuaa—the island slice that encompassed stretches suited for every purpose—was the most intelligent division of real estate any planner could have devised for an island society that lived from the land it loved. When war came or death intervened, land changed hands; but the fertile areas were still set aside for farming, and the villages, near the farms and the fishing grounds, remained where the earth, the climate, and such necessities as water had suggested their locations. The plan held.

What seemed to some a lack of planning in the villages was in fact thoughtful if innate: individual houses were placed where they had communication with one another but privacy of their own; temples were positioned where they could command respect; recreation places were located so that they were convenient gathering spots. To the newcomers this arrangement appeared aimless nonplanning. Cook wrote that "the houses are scattered about, without any order, either with respect to their distances from each other, or their position in any particular direction."[2] On the other hand, his lieutenant Ledyard found the town grouping of Napoopoo "very compact," and although the house arrangements "do not seem to have been the effect of much design," he noted, there were nevertheless "a number of little streets that intersect one another very happily . . . generally paved." Further, there was attention to what we self-consciously call amenities these days: "There are coconut and other trees interspersed artificially among the houses all over the town, and in the middle of it there is a level course for running and other exercises, which is very beautifully skirted with trees from end to end, and is kept very clean."[3]

The haole settlers who followed Cook and the other explorers had, themselves, very rudimentary understandings of land use planning and town design. They showed no desire, at least for some time, to substitute another basic land-division system for the one the Hawaiians had developed, but they did want to see orderly settlements built in place of the rambling villages. Yet the only background that most of them could draw on was the New England cluster of houses on a gridiron street pattern reaching out from a central square where town hall and church stood.

Unquestionably this was the model on which the nineteenth-century Hawaiian towns were based; how they grew from that form to their later, larger shapes is a separate, peculiarly undocumented story ("crying for elucidation," says one environmental historian).[4] For a less detailed survey, it seems enough to note that the Hawaiian people were not forced directly from their nonurban condition into modern concepts of urbanism. The change came slowly in plan arrangements, as it did in construction methods, but it did in time come. Toward the end of the nineteenth century Honolulu was bragging about being "a modern city, laid out on the best American and European plans,"[5] and Hilo and a few other towns were growing pridefully larger.

The later, more sophisticated haole immigrants to Hawaii brought with them knowledge of town planning developments abroad which had no pertinence whatsoever in the tropical islands but which ineluctably exerted an influence, particularly on the development of Honolulu. The eighteenth-century prototypes with which they were familiar were the monumental city-planning concepts that had produced polite, classically symmetrical urban spaces like Grosvenor Square in London, the Rue de Rivoli in Paris, and the Capitol surround in Washington. This phase of design-oriented planning, carried to American towns, had resulted in formal features overlaid on essentially ugly places—grand boulevards with no true grandeur and focal squares on which nothing of significance focused. Honolulu in its turn gained from this period the Ala Moana and Kapiolani Boulevards and some open space around Iolani Palace. Essentially it remained an unplanned city. From "the best American and European plans" it had learned only a few superficialities.

During the early decades of the twentieth century, the Territory of Hawaii was subjected to contemporary American city planning influences by visiting professionals and immigrant residents who had watched new developments on the mainland. Ebenezer Howard's and Sir Patrick Geddes' garden city concept in England, transplanted to America and adopted eagerly as part of a city-beautiful, municipal-art movement, was one such development that Hawaii learned about. Another was the broadening of landscape architecture as a profession to form the new discipline of city planning. On the mainland Frederick Law Olmstead, a landscaper, and Daniel Hudson Burnham, an architect, indicated how well urban open spaces could be planned, as in New York's Central Park and on Chicago's waterfront, and then how "the art of town arrangement" could be extended, at least on paper, to entire cities like San Francisco. Several mainland architects and landscape architects, inspired by this new vision, found commissions in Hawaii and held high hopes for a tropical version of the city beautiful.[6] In the end, however, its interpretation in the islands was limited to a few parklike areas. Honolulu and Hilo gained some breathing spaces in their increasingly clogged cores and along their compacting waterfronts, but any hope that new tropical garden cities might develop proved vain. Several plantation towns—notably Lanai's one "city"—were drawn with formal prettiness but built with practical plainness.

In Honolulu, Kapiolani Park, the magnificent stretch of green between Diamond Head and Waikiki, was acquired in time, under popular pressure, and Honolulu's civic and administrative center went through several planning stages that had sufficient effect to ward off much of the impinging commercial construction.[7] The in-town waterfront, however, despite the classic focal point of Aloha Tower, built in 1921, became too crowded with miscellaneous commercial activity even for decent functional arrangement of harbor spaces, to say nothing of allowing concern with civic beauty.

When the city of Honolulu finally took steps to make urban planning a part of municipal government, the reasons were not aesthetic but purely practical. The first commission on planning, appointed in 1912 as an advisory panel to the board of supervisors, was concerned primarily with matters of sanitation and health (the classic reasons for planning of cities, in Europe and in America) and then with rudimentary zoning to protect property values (the original impetus for zoning, on the mainland). It was not until 1939 that a planning commission with some authority to plan was installed and began to consider allocation of land uses for the island as a whole.[8]

In the meantime, the only public agency seriously concerned with orderly arrangement of the city's parts was Honolulu's Park Board, for whom Lewis Mumford, even then an eminent urban critic, prepared a report in 1938 that contained such informed and literate comments as "Honolulu is a little like a beautiful woman, so well assured of her natural gifts that she is not always careful of her toilet; she relies upon her splendid face and body to distract attention from her disheveled hair, her dirty fingernails or her torn skirt."[9] He was particularly distressed at Honolulu's evident lack of planning, because he saw such great opportunities to form a remarkable city in that setting. "No other city that I know of would proportionately yield such high returns to rational planning as Honolulu," he wrote.[10]

Steps toward such rational plans were slow, however, even though Mumford as well as several local architect-planners made specific proposals for immediate improvements.[11] During the 1950s and into the 1960s both the city of Honolulu and the state of Hawaii followed the lead of mainland American jurisdictions in establishing systematic planning

procedures.[12] On the mainland, the concept of an overall
plan for an urban area indicating how land should be used in
its various parts—a master plan, or general plan as it was
named in the federal government's Housing Act of 1949—
was becoming well established as a municipal or county land-
control device (although there was a great deal of confusion
for a long while about how much of what kind of information the plan should contain).[13] The general plan was
ordinarily followed by a zoning map (usually adopted as an
ordinance) establishing very specific uses and often densities
of the municipality's parts, almost parcel by parcel. Zoning,
or detailed classification of land uses, was not used as a procedure in statewide planning until Hawaii's landmark general
plan suggested it and the 1961 Land Use Law adopted it.

For some time Honolulu's Planning Commission tried to
use zoning alone, without general planning as a first step, for
direction of urban development and disposition of public services such as schools and parks. In 1954, however, a city
charter was adopted that mandated the preparation of a comprehensive physical plan for the city. The first such document, quickly put together to meet the new requirement, was
as quickly found by the courts to be inadequate.

What Is a General Plan?

It was not until 1964 that the first general plan in Hawaii
that followed all the current rules and practices was completed and adopted—by the City and County of Honolulu. It
too had its troubles in the courts, primarily because it was
excessively specific and consequently inflexible, unable to
meet changing conditions.[14] The city's charter was revised in
the early 1970s and, like the earlier version, this document
had a good deal to say about city planning. It pointed out
that planning procedures had changed in America since the
1964 plan had been drawn; general plans were now more
comprehensive in content but less rigid in format. Unfortunately, Honolulu's department of general planning never suc-

ceeded in translating the charter commission's injunctions into a workable plan. Rather it has been bogged down, from that time on, in apparent confusion and uncertainty about the general planning process.

In the meantime, the Territorial Planning Office, which had been established back in 1939, had long ago begun work on a comprehensive plan for the totality of the islands. When that office became the State Department of Planning and Research, it continued its work and produced the nation's first statewide general plan in 1961. Passage of the Land Use Law and appointment of the Land Use Commission, which followed, were the principal results of that 1961 plan, which was quickly outmoded and outgrown as a planning document. It was revised in 1967 and is in process of a second revision—without ever having succeeded in providing a usable land-management tool for the state or even policy directions for the Land Use Commission.

The reasons why Hawaii's state plan and Honolulu's city plan have been documents with little value to purposeful action are worth analysis. The islands simply demonstrate more pointedly than most locations, because of the containment of their population and the limitation of their land, the difficulties that have universally developed in city planning. Hawaii is suffering, perhaps more sharply than other places, because the planning profession is having a hard time making up its mind what a general plan should be. Lacking professional leadership, the general public, naturally apathetic about the formal planning process, has become even more disenchanted. In the islands, the state and city planning departments are in accord with one another and in agreement with public planners elsewhere in taking a dim view of earlier general plans made by their predecessors in office, but they are in complete dissent over what should be done to replace them. The result is a kind of planning vacuum—just when urban growth is at a stage where it desperately needs planning direction.

One reason for this confoundment is that it became

fashionable in America in the 1960s and 1970s to deprecate "physical" planning. The argument went that city planning in its infancy, through the first half of the twentieth century, paid too much attention to map planning and not enough to the social and economic situations that lay behind the mapping. Time was taken up drawing lines on paper, showing where physical things like houses and schools and parks should go. Not enough interest was shown in the way people lived and how their lives would fit into the plans that were being drawn.

That was undoubtedly true. And the change that began to take place around 1965 or so came partly because planners themselves, as well as their public and private clients, realized that cartography was an inadequate tool for shaping the future of a city, a state, or a region. There was another incentive too for a new kind of city planning at about that time: the federal government was handing out funds to local agencies for overall planning—provided the plans were broad in scope and considered social and economic needs as well as physical arrangements. There was a new meaning for the term "comprehensive."[15] Many hundreds of plans were made that at least gestured toward broad socioeconomic backgrounds to justify their arrangements of physical things.

A bit later on, as the 1970s approached, a new worry produced another shift in attitudes about planning and a recasting of the methods city planners used. It was the sudden great concern over change: the awareness of its rapidity and its unpredictability. There was increasing realization that exponential, explosive growth in people and people's needs was forcing change on us faster than we were able to plan for it. A master plan intended to be achieved over a decade became obsolete within a few years as requirements multiplied.

Comprehensive planning, then, became in its turn a somewhat obsolete term, and the new words for up-to-date general planning were "evolutionary" and "dynamic." With people and the buildings they needed increasing so quickly in numbers and with social values being transformed so rapidly and so radically (and nowhere faster than in Hawaii), it was clear that any master plan, no matter how comprehensive in scope, had to be subject to almost constant revision if it was to be at all helpful. Planners began to see their job as a continuing *process* rather than a single act to be repeated only at some point in the future.

These changes in planning attitudes seem very sensible when one understands the reasons for them. The search for ways to put them into planning practice, however, had disturbing results in Hawaii and many other places. Forsaking physical map planning so quickly, so completely, not only confused the general public, who should benefit from planners' plans; it also disarrayed the professional planners themselves. In trying to make plans comprehensive, planners had lost the ability to reach any definite goals. And as general plans had once been too rigid, unable to adapt to conditions as they changed, now they were so pliable that they provided no timely guidance at all.

In Hawaii this sequence of planning postures was mirrored faithfully on state and county plans. The state's first general plan in 1961 had a concept of continuing growth as its tacit underlying policy, and it included very specific plans for land use, economic development, tourism, transportation, and other factors that such growth would affect. Later state planners deprecated it as illustrating the "common urban planning theory of the 1950s," based on the belief that "most economic and social problems could be handled by making man's environment efficient, esthetic and functional."[16]

When this plan was revised in 1967 a step forward was made, according to later state planners, although the ideal had not yet been reached. "The old 'general plan' approach was discovered to be archaic and had given way to the 'planning process,' " they explained.[17] The first revision program was largely an outline of this process. It included descriptions of a state economic model, a land use model, a recreation planning methodology, and so on. Models, in planning terminology, are accumulations of data on which plans can be tested. There were no plans to be tested, though; plans had become symbols of an antiquated approach.

To demonstrate the dynamic aspect of the new planning process, various "planning projects," as they were termed, were subsequently undertaken by the state planning office, producing numerous reports, analyses, studies, sometimes recommendations and proposals, but seldom plans. The best of these were an Oahu Transportation Study in 1967, a Hawaii Tourism Impact Study in 1972, and a Central Oahu Planning Study that same year. Any specific plan proposals that crept into the process, such as Udall's Open-Space Plan of 1972 and a consultant's State Comprehensive Outdoor Recreation Plan (SCORP) in 1971, were wasted: principles were preferred. Dr. Shelley Mark, the state's director of planning and economic development, vigorously protested this evaluation of the work of his office, contending that the SCORP study had stimulated federal funds, that the central Oahu study had influenced the Land Use Commission, and that other planning "facts and figures" had "halted the planned use of hundreds of acres of agricultural land for urban development."[18] Granting the so-called planning projects credit for certain immediate results, the fact remained that no overall state plan had been developed to which they could be related and so, in the end, they had to be shelved. The next stage in the state's history of planning was a second general plan revision program. So little had been accomplished by 1975 that the legislature, in essence, called for a fresh start at that time.[19]

More Compromise and Confusion

Of the counties, the Big Island of Hawaii evolved the most firm general plan, since it had set the most defined policy goals. Under the capable direction of a determined planning director, Raymond Suefuji, with sympathetic guidance from the then mayor, Shunichi Kimura, Hawaii's general plan, completed in the early 1970s, won a well-deserved national planning award. Development plans—detailed land use proposals for particular parts of the county—began to follow as neighborhood discussions determined local goals.

On Kauai and on Maui private consultants were retained to help the county officials do general planning. In both cases plans were drawn that were compromises between the wish to stay rural and natural and the desire to benefit, in jobs and revenues, from the development of conservation and agricultural lands. Such a straddle required the plans to be quite specific in indicating where things should happen or not happen on the land, and the general plans of both counties were sufficiently old-fashioned to indicate land use in some detail. Within a few months, unfortunately, they had demonstrated the havoc that quick change, uncontrolled, can indeed bring to a rigid, nondynamic plan: in its 1974 boundary review the State Land Use Commission altered many of the land use boundaries the counties had fixed.

For the island of Oahu, containing most of the state's population, there was no hesitation about abandoning old methods. Its first general plan, in 1964, had also had ongoing growth as its policy goal, and it was specific in its plans for the way land should be used and facilities distributed. Later city planners disparaged it, as the state's planners had criticized the 1961 state plan, terming it "primarily a land-use plan, focusing on 'where' activities should occur," rather than why or how.[20] The city charter adopted in 1972 mandated that the general plan, when it was revised, should be both comprehensive and dynamic. Charter Commission members intended that *general planning* should primarily determine policies; then *development planning* would carry policies forward toward implementation in specific land-use and other plans.[21] However, the plan revision documents that began to appear in 1974[22] (following a long, wordy, abstruse study of the purpose of general planning)[23] were a mélange of fluid "evolutionary" policies and rigid "physical" land use arrangements.

The first two reports in this general plan revision program described the new process being used by comparing it defensively with the old methods. It was, the text said, not "comprehensive" in the traditional sense, because "an effort to be 'comprehensive' by analyzing all of the community's major objectives and policies at one time is not a viable course of action."[24]

In an effort to be viable, then, the new plan focused on residential objectives. It compared basically two alternative residential growth policies. One was to concentrate growth in the central city on land that was for the most part already zoned for urban uses (the "intensive development" alternative). The other was to let growth extend on toward central Oahu, even though that would involve the conversion of "a minimum of 10,000 acres" of agricultural lands when the population reached 1.4 million people (the "directed growth" alternative).[25] After an analysis of the two choices offered, based almost entirely on a study of the current cost of building houses under differing conditions and the long-range cost of supplying municipal services to them in different locations, the directed growth alternative was recommended. The city council was unhappy with the study and refused to consider it a complete general plan document. Through the community, opposition developed to the "directed growth" plan, reaching as it did beyond the the present urban areas. Those 1974 plan attempts remained, then, quite useless exercises. They were never accepted by the general public and never adopted by the city's legislative body.

If Hawaii's planning *documents* seemed ineffectual, its planning *procedures* appeared, to many observers, to be disorganized. Within the Honolulu city-county government there had been a restructuring of planning when the charter was revised: the planning department was split into a section dealing with general planning and one concerned with more immediate problems. The planning director, controlling both, became the chief planning officer, working directly under the mayor with a rank above the administrative line departments.

A result of this well-intentioned arrangement was that the chief planning officer, Robert Way (formerly a principal in a local planning firm), became a spokesman for the mayor's political policies, all too ready to do battle with the city council on political issues and before long launching violent personal attacks on anyone who might dare criticize the city's planning procedures.[26]

The state's organization for planning had moved since territorial days in a fragmented direction that many observers considered unfortunate. At the time of statehood the Territorial Planning Office was succeeded by two departments of the state government, one on planning research and one on economic development. Later these were combined as a single Department of Planning and Economic Development (DPED). The result of this fusion (which incidentally eliminated the office of state planner) was not a gain through better coordination, but a loss through dispersion of the new department's powers. There were now "blurred" responsibilities, "diffused and divided," as the department itself attested.[27]

The DPED is a line agency of the state, along with many others. It has no authority to enforce its plans on the actions of its sister departments, and as a result planning at the state level is actually scattered among many agencies: the Department of Transportation, off on its own planning highway systems unrelated to any land use plans that might exist; the Department of Land and Natural Resources, charged with so much land management responsibility that a legislative auditor's report told of complete confusion of function;[28] the Department of Taxation, achieving an "assumption of planning powers," as a consultant's report noted,[29] through its ability to assess land values; the State Land Use Commission, able to assume broad planning powers because of its right to classify and reclassify basic land uses; the University of Hawaii, choosing sites for new campuses with no reference to existing or planned land uses; the Department of Education, similarly making its independent plans for primary and secondary school facilities; the Office of Environmental Quality Control, moving in on the planning process through the use of mandatory environmental impact statements—and so on.

The division of rights and responsibilities between the state and the counties had become even more muddled. On the mainland the trend has been toward centralization of land planning in state hands to achieve overall coordination of efforts and find greater objectivity in managing land uses. American municipalities and counties are likely to consider only their own local interest and to think of land development primarily as a tax source. Hawaii, when it became a state, had set up a centralized government structure, including the planning function, but for quite different reasons.

Hawaii's counties are separate islands, not adjacent land areas, and except for Oahu were quite rural in fact and in feeling at the time of statehood. The process of planning, along with administration of the educational program and most other social and economic concerns, fell almost necessarily into the hands of the central state government.

As time went on, however, the county governments were strengthened and some remarkably capable and powerful political figures assumed local leadership—Anton Vidhina on Kauai, Elmer Cravalho on Maui, Shunichi Kimura on Hawaii. Planning departments were established in the counties and drew as directors planners who were at least as capable as those in the planning offices of the state—and with much of the authority in their bailiwicks that the state planners had lost in theirs. To a large degree, it was the local people and often the county governments who wanted most seriously to use their land well and preserve it in as natural a condition as possible. The politicians in the State Capitol were the ones pressing plans for growth, tourism, and urban expansion.

Originally, as a strong state government was established, the state planning office was supposed to prepare a statewide general plan and then break it down into separate county plans.[30] This was never done; no state general plan was ever sufficiently solid to be frangible. As time went on and the

county governments gained competence, it began to seem
that exactly the reverse might be the better procedure. If only
the state could determine firm enough goals on which to base
plans, each county might develop its own general plan (as
they were doing anyway, in view of the planning vacuum at
state level) and then these might be combined into an overall
state general plan.

Legislation was introduced in 1974 and again in 1975 that
would have accomplished just about that result. But presented by minority Republican legislators (albeit with advice
from an impressive, informed task force), it got nowhere.[31]
Instead, the 1975 bill calling for a policy plan referred the
job back to DPED—in a measure that confused polity and
planning while confounding county programs and state
policies.

Planning Means Politics

Another reason why Hawaii has produced no usable general plans is that it finds formal public planning politically
undesirable. Since the politics of land is so dominant in
Hawaii, land planning has inevitably become a political
game. Landowners and developers traditionally want public
plans to be loose enough to allow manipulation when pressure is applied. Legislative bodies customarily chafe at being
restricted to the setting of policy; they want to plan the results of their policies, as well, and see the plans implemented.
That is where the action is—and the benefits of action. In
Hawaii, since administrative plans have been lacking, or confusing, or indeterminate, there has been little to prevent the
state legislature and the county councils from taking over the
planning function. The legislature has not been able to resist
controlling actions of the Land Use Commission, retaining
control over the planning of tourism, and dictating plans for
development to the University of Hawaii—all to an extent far
beyond its policy-setting prerogative.

In the city of Honolulu, where the administration's plan-

ning department was demonstrating inability or unwillingness
to produce a general plan, to such flagrant measure that one
newspaper editorially called for removal of the chief planning
officer and a columnist for the other proposed that a competent consultant firm be retained to do the job, the temptation
for the council to act was irresistible.[32] Answering the council
president's inquiry, the city's corporation counsel expressed a
doubt that the 1974 plan-revision documents of the planning
department would hold up in court.[33] In 1976, then, the
council itself decided to move into the vacuum that had been
created: during the spring, summer, and fall it prepared its
own general plan. First it reduced the budget of the official
city planning department far below its current level as admonition;[34] then it produced a 47-page manuscript of objectives and policies—its own general plan—as exemplar. The
work was done by the council members, divided into
appropriate subcommittees, and a meager permanent staff
with the nominal help of unwilling planning department professionals and a kind of casual compliance from a sixty-
member citizens "advisory" group. The work was inspired
and largely accomplished by the then council president,
George Akahane, who had become seriously concerned about
the city's need for planning and the ineffectiveness of the
general planning department in producing a plan.

It was a remarkable document that the council produced.
A special kind of indeterminate language has developed
around political policy statements and the council's policy
plan made full use of it. The first objective was "to control
the growth of Oahu's resident and visitor population . . . ,"
but *control* meant simply use of "the most satisfactory" population projections available (1,039,000 people by the year
2000). No goal setting, only acceptance of the expected, and
no speculation, even, about what effect this number of people might have on the city's social and economic future. No
reminder, certainly, that this was a prediction plucked arbitrarily from one point in time on a continuing growth curve.
Most of the goals set down in the sections that followed were

careful exercises in avoiding the key issues: goals so general
as to be meaningless. As public hearings continued and controversies developed over major points, the wording became
increasingly obscure. There was one objective to "maintain
the viability of Oahu's resort industry," another sought to
"maintain the viability of agriculture on Oahu," a third to
"increase the amount of federal spending on Oahu." There
were the three existing economic supports, with no priorities
given. No advice was offered to help the land-classification
decisions that lay ahead.

There was a policy affirmed to "preserve the island's well-
known and widely publicized beauty," and one to "protect
the island's well-known resources," such as the mountains
and the shorelines. (Apparently public relations was the
criterion rather than ecological, historic, or scenic value).
An urban design plan was called for as one policy, without
definition; nothing was specified about establishing heights,
bulks, view lines—only a wish to form "attractive, meaningful and stimulating environments."

The council's catalogue of objectives and policies did
include two affirmative statements, however. One was a
specific bit of political land use allocation: "designating appropriate areas of the island for resort use"—areas arbitrarily selected by the councilmen. They included several
areas (West Beach on Campbell Estate land at Honouliuli
and Queens Beach on Bishop Estate land at Hawaii Kai)
which were strongly opposed by segments of the community.
The other definite decision made by the council in its plan, if
it could be taken seriously, was where future growth might
occur on Oahu. The policy posited was somewhat of a compromise between the *contained* and the *extended* growth
alternatives which the planning department had earlier
described; it was to "facilitate" development of the primary
urban center, to "encourage" development in the suburban
Ewa area, and to "reduce or at the most maintain" present
percentages of the total island population in the rural and
urban fringe areas.[35]

The council's own conviction about this new policy, unfortunately, did not last even until it had adopted its own plan. In August of 1976, while a draft of the proposed plan was still in its public hearing stage, the council, with just one dissenter, overrode a veto by the mayor and decided to grant urban classification to 510 acres of prime agricultural land at Waipio, an "urban fringe area," on the central Oahu plains for a housing development by a corporation called Gentry-Pacific Ltd.[36] No policy to "reduce or maintain" population levels was mentioned when the chips were down. It was quite apparent that nothing in the vague generalities of the new plan, a plan produced politically rather than professionally, would be likely to interfere with the political gamesmanship that substituted for land use planning in Hawaii.

The agency which had taken greatest advantage of the planning void at the state level was the Land Use Commission. Intended originally only to establish and then police land use classifications in the broadest terms, by the middle 1970s the commission, under labor leader Eddie Tangen's aggressive chairmanship, was in fact acting as a planning agency, examining and holding public hearings on detailed development proposals. In the 1974 classification review process, it listened to arguments about the kinds of housing that should be built in the Waiahole-Waikane valleys on the windward side of Oahu and even debated the costs at which the housing should be sold. At a meeting in March 1975, one application for a change in classification on Maui was rejected and another was approved because of the type of housing proposed. While the commissioners might be making commendable decisions about housing policy, residential planning was clearly not their rightful job. Many such irrelevant specifics considered by the commission during that period gave the appearance of a planning base to arbitrary land use decisions.[37]

The Land Use Commission tried for even greater planning powers at one point. One piece of legislation that failed of passage but continued to return for several sessions would have allowed the agency almost absolute authority over any lands it judged to be areas of critical state concern.[38] Instead of ordering land uses on the basis of an adopted plan, this bill would have permitted the commission to overturn policies or plans of any state department, plans that had been prepared by any county, regulations set forth in codes and ordinances, even decisions of local county councils, in whatever places it adjudged to be "critical."

The tide turned against such moves, however, when the commission's assumption of ad hoc planning powers unexpectedly hurt a number of landowners and developers. In 1974, several members of the commission were dilatory about attending hearings and lost their votes at crucial times in the final decisions. In addition, two ex officio members (the head of the Department of Land and Natural Resources and the director of the Department of Planning and Economic Development) were on the point of leaving office and suddenly decided, with restraints of allegiance to the administration removed, to vote against urbanization of agricultural and conservation lands in a number of cases. The result was that several landowners' plans were frustrated and some developers who had put big money into planning for anticipated developments were hurt financially. It suddenly became obvious to many people, who up to then had been content with the haphazard process, that unpredictable, uncontrolled decisions by a group of individuals basically uninformed about land management was not smart land use economics.[39] Enough pressure was put on the legislature (by developers as well as conservationists) so that the 1975 land planning bill mandated DPED to prepare "guidelines" to direct the commission in its decisions.[40]

Hawaii's unsatisfactory situation in land planning in the 1970s was not generally recognized outside the state. The Land Use Law remained impressive to most mainland planners for a long while and kept the myth of Hawaii's leadership in land use control alive. In 1972 a study conducted at the Georgia Institute of Technology found Hawaii the most successful of all states in the union in meeting criteria of what was called "an emerging model of state planning." Challenged in his conclusion, the professor who had led the study said that his evaluations had been based on "empirical findings" from the states themselves, checked by a "content analysis of the publications . . . of the official state planning agencies."[41] Clearly Hawaii's state planners had done a better job of self-serving publication than others had: DPED's list of publications issued as part of its "dynamic planning process" is indeed impressive.

Those who came to see for themselves were not taken in so easily. While making his open-space study, Stewart Udall found a "fragmentation" of the planning process and little evidence of planning results. A study group from the national office of the American Institute of Architects, sponsored by the Ford Foundation, reported back that it had discovered "lack of coordinated State-wide land-use planning" and "conflicts between Counties and the State" resulting in "piecemeal" actions. This group saw great planning opportunities in Hawaii, as Lewis Mumford had thirty-five years earlier. The state's "frontier status" in land management, its report said, "will raise the kinds of problems and create prototypical opportunities for furthering the state of the art and advancing the impact of planning upon development that we are unlikely to find anywhere else."[42]

Another task force from the AIA a few years later, however, found no evidence that the opportunities had been recognized. Its members still saw distressing gaps in the planning process, this time in the City and County of Honolulu as well as in the state itself, and they discovered that the lack of state-county coordination their earlier confreres had noted had in no way been corrected. In their turn they reported an "absence of public guidelines" and inadequate planning procedures—in short, "a climate of confusion . . . and inaction."[43]

The Matter of Transit

There was no lack of professional planning expertise in Hawaii to do the job that was necessary in public land planning. Half a dozen firms of planners, several of them branches of mainland organizations, were as proficient in analysis of land use programs, study of the feasibility of intended land uses, and arrangement of land use development and its supporting services as anyone could hope for in a competent practitioner. Among the islands' planners, several went beyond mere competence and could provide a client with imaginative and innovative land management advice. In addition to the trained planners, at least one landscape architect and a number of architectural firms furnished planning services. In the late 1960s an excellent planning curriculum was established at the University of Hawaii and helped raise local standards appreciably.[44] In 1965 only a half dozen names were listed in the yellow pages of the Honolulu telephone book under City and Regional Planners; by 1977 there were forty-four names there.

The most important planning activity in Hawaii in the decade after achievement of statehood, public or private, was the Oahu Transportation Study.[45] With all its faults, the Federal Highways Act accomplished more in the way of overall planning, including land use planning, than any other federal program of that period. In a remarkable way, the highway lobby wrote its own death sentence when it worked for passage of a transportation planning measure in 1962, intending it to justify more urban freeways. The thoroughness that the act required in the studies it called for led inevitably to the inclusion of mass transit modes in transportation plans for many cities—and ultimately to federal funding of rapid transit routes as well as highways. As soon as it became possible, Hawaii secured money for study of a "continuing, comprehensive urban transportation planning process on an intergovernmental basis" for the island of Oahu. Funds were supplied by the U.S. Department of Housing and Urban Development and the U.S. Bureau of Roads; the project was administered jointly by the State Department of Planning and Economic Development and the Department of Transportation, with services furnished also by the City and County of Honolulu. Thus it was a joint and truly comprehensive effort carried out by a specially organized staff that delved into data about population, economics, land uses, and all modes and methods of transportation.

Out of the OTS, as it became known, came a great deal of useful information (unfortunately not later kept up to date), a decision to build a freeway system that would include another trans-Koolau link (the controversial H3 route, ultimately), and a recommendation that a sophisticated rapid transit system be built to carry the people whom Oahu would contain by the 1980s.

Although the OTS was supposed originally to be a continuing activity, its staff was disbanded and its director released after the first study was completed. Nothing more was done in the way of transportation planning until the 1970s, when the city of Honolulu retained the firm of Daniel, Mann, Johnson & Mendenhall to study in more detail the need, character, and cost of a mass transit system.[46] This firm's contract called for another comprehensive look at transportation needs for the entire island, but in fact its studies dealt mainly with details of a fixed-rail guided train system along Honolulu's central corridor. In early stages of the work there were some inconclusive and unconvincing stabs at suggesting alternative long-range routes beyond the train line, but obviously no transportation planner could foretell what travel might be necessary toward the leeward coast, the north shore, the central plains, or the windward side of the island when there were no clear policies and certainly no plans to indicate what might happen there.

Although the OTS had recommended a combined rapid-transit and freeway arterial plan, as time went on controversy developed between advocates of the two modes of travel. Some form of fixed-guideway train system seemed a reasonable way to accommodate the heavy traffic along the quite contained corridor that formed central Honolulu, from Pearl City to Hawaii Kai. In fact, as a number of people have pointed out, this lineal urban form seems most suited for rapid transit service. Hawaii continued to benefit from the 90

percent federal handouts for freeways provided by the Highways Act, however, and that was hard to forgo. A network
of freeways—H1 along the central corridor, H2 extending up
into the central plains, and H3 crossing the Koolaus to the
windward side—had already been planned, was well under
way in construction, and was included in the OTS recommendations.

What consensus there had been on the total system began
to fall apart, however: opposition developed to the rapid
transit route because of its cost and its rigidity, while arguments were vehemently voiced against H3 because of its
threatened impact on the environment and the generative effect it was certain to have on development of the windward
Oahu valleys.[47] Both these links in the proposed chain of
travel on the island became political issues. The H3 route—
changed in name by the Department of Transportation to
TH3 as an attempt to appease mass transit proponents, indicating that a bus transit lane (T) could be added to the
highway (H)—planned through a lovely historic valley, was
seriously challenged by environmental groups. Taken to court
on several charges, it met mixed legal reactions which had
the effect of holding up construction through a decade of
controversy. The environmental impact statement which had
justified the project was challenged, but a judge ruled that it
seemed to follow the federal requirements.[48] The history of
Moanalua Valley, through which it would pass, with its still
visible artifacts, was called to the court's attention (the valley
was being seriously considered by the Interior Department
for classification as a national landmark) and a federal judge
ruled that the highway people must prove that no other route
was feasible—thus raising highly arguable questions that
caused further delays.[49]

By 1976, it had become clear that H3 was an outdated
concept if not a lost cause. Doubts about the rapid transit
scheme had dwindled to demands that costs be kept as low
as possible. Proponents of the trans-Koolau freeway were
reduced to those suburbanites who found the two existing

routes between Kailua-Kaneohe and downtown Honolulu congested at rush hours. Still, Hawaii's transportation department planners continued to insist that an additional freeway was essential, defending with almost religious fervor the righteousness of highway travel. The politics of the issue divided state and county, since none of Honolulu's general plan revisions called for great growth across the mountains. It was clear that if H3 did go ahead, finally, it would function not so much as a traffic artery but as a planning device, working to contravene the only policy-plan decision that the city fathers, administrative and legislative, had so far been able to reach in agreement.

Then in late 1976, after years of vacillation, the U.S. Highway Administration was finally convinced that Moanalua Valley should remain inviolate. The agency ruled, in effect, that that route must not be used. Since any other would be much more expensive and probably even more controversial, the community, even including the highway planners at first, seemed ready to accept the demise of TH3. But then in April 1977, the state administration announced that it was making one more, possibly final, appeal to Washington before it gave up the federal largesse. The last judgment was not yet at hand.

Highway construction was not the only substitute for planning that Hawaii found. The environmental impact statement, an excellent tool for guarding a plan's provisions, was too often used in place of planning. Zoning, a way of implementing a plan, was confused with planning itself. Several new concepts that were being tried on the mainland—ranging from transfer of development rights (a useful way to make a plan more flexible) to shoreline protection legislation (grasped as a substitute for total planning rather than considered as one of its parts)—were explained by their advocates to public officials in Hawaii as well as to the general public and were seriously considered in lieu of the missing general plan.

The most ambitious move that the state government made

in its search for planning substitutes was institution of the technique known as PPBS—programming, planning, budgeting system. Adopted in the early 1970s as the State Executive Budget Act,[50] this quasi-planning process (developed by Robert McNamara and the aggregation of "whiz kids" around him in his position as Secretary of Defense from 1961–1968) is intended to relate budgets, and therefore expenditures, to plans for specific programs for action.

As a means of implementing planning and forcing agencies to be realistic about their requests for funds, PPBS, as a report to the legislature said, "can be an invaluable tool."[51] Lacking overall planning, however, the demand that each agency justify its budget request through programs and plans of its own has simply led, in Hawaii, to further fragmentation of what planning does take place. The act establishing PPBS as state policy makes no reference to any general plan or planning agency. As a further disadvantage, the emphasis is on the budgetary outcome of planning. When alternative courses of action are considered under PPBS, the choice is based on costs and benefits—and economic costs are likely to outweigh social or even physical benefits.[52]

Another federal government concept, the environmental impact statement, assumed importance in Hawaii and elsewhere in America as a major replacement for comprehensive planning in the 1970s, The EIS has become a valuable instrument in national land management precisely because there is no national land-planning legislation, despite hopes that have been held out from time to time. If there is no plan for the use of a certain land area, say the shoreline of the Hudson River in New York, or the estuary of the Potomac River in Virginia, or the Moanalua Valley of the Koolau Mountains in Oahu, then when someone wants to build a freeway or an apartment complex or whatever on those lands, the requirement for an environmental impact assessment forces everyone to wonder whether those are really good land uses and what other uses might be better. Thus to some extent it fills the need for land planning.

The reason EISs have proved to be weak substitutes for planning, however, is that when there is no effective land-planning process the proposed action must prove that it is superior to all conceivable alternative land uses—to the universe of alternatives—and no one is wise enough to judge that. When there *is* a land use plan for the area, though, the EIS for a specific project has a much more feasible and useful role. Its job then is to show whether the proposed action is consistent with the objectives of the plan and would not conflict with the environmental policies on which the plan was based. A city with a well-formulated plan for development can accomplish much more when it requires a state or federal highway department to submit a statement of the environmental impact of a proposed highway before it is built through the municipality than can a city with vague, un-formulated plans for its future growth. In the first case, the city's people can evaluate the answers they get to their questions about the construction's impact; in the second instance, they do not even know what questions to ask. The validity of H3's impact statement has been successively upheld and struck down by the courts. Never have they addressed the question of whether H3 is a good urban transportation plan.

More Substitutes for Planning

Zoning is another instrument which serves well to carry out plans but is often used as a replacement for planning. Zoning, in fact, preceded general planning as a method for controlling and protecting real estate values, and the two have often been used independently of one another.[53] Houston, Texas, touted as the city without a zoning ordinance, having defeated at the polls several attempts to impose one, is actually pretty well planned, in fact and in the minds of its people. It just is not zoned. The plot-by-plot division into rigidly defined zoning classifications is the element that is absent—and is not too badly missed.

On the other hand, Honolulu has thoroughly detailed zoning maps for all its districts, even though development plans have been prepared for only some of them and a meaningful general plan is still lacking. Thus zoning maps, which were intended to be drawn from land use maps, which were supposed to be extracted from the policies of a general plan, exist by themselves as a planning proxy. In somewhat the same way, Hawaii's classification of state land into four categories of use, which is in effect the zoning stage, has long been accepted as a substitute for state land planning. Honolulu has a fairly new "comprehensive zoning ordinance," which the council finds too inflexible (that is, too detailed in its land use, height, setback, and other requirements for each type of zone to allow for variations that might be politically useful). The council's solution to this problem for a long time was not to insist on a revised plan but to move to make the existing zoning regulations more malleable.

Several techniques that would relate zoning more closely to land use planning had already been tried on the mainland with some success. For instance, there had been experiments in "impact zoning"—a proposed development's environmental effects were analyzed and weighted and the project permitted only when the impact count was low enough. Another approach was "timed zoning"—development could proceed only at the time municipal services were supposed to be available.[54] Ramapo, New York, became the model for this kind of zoning-cum-planning by adopting a "controlled growth" ordinance in 1969. Developers (even when they complied with the zoning code) were required to obtain a permit indicating that utilities and other services (planned in controlled-growth stages by the city) would be ready when construction started. The Ramapo plan avoided the charge of having a social segregation purpose in its limits to growth by adopting a carefully drawn, long-range, nonexclusionary plan that has been upheld by the courts.[55]

Another way to make the usual broad restrictions of a zoning code more adaptable to changing land uses is to attach conditions to the permission to build, even when the zoning, in general terms, allows it. To make conditional zoning reasonable, not a capricious political agent, a project has to be analyzed more deeply than building permit departments usually do. And to accomplish that, environmental impact statements are often required. If it is shown that an apartment house might bring too many vehicles to adjacent streets, for instance, permission to build might be granted on the condition that more off-street parking be provided than demanded by the zoning code. Conditional zoning might limit the number of units in an apartment house or require more open space around a hotel than the code specified.

The Honolulu city council took these ideas sufficiently seriously to call to Hawaii Robert Freilich, one of the designers of the Ramapo plan, to advise on what to do about Waikiki. Freilich recommended a number of innovative moves, which Robert Way, the chief planning officer, resentfully opposed.[56] Ultimately, the council changed Waikiki's traditional zoning status to that of a "special design" zoning district. By removing it from the standard zoning restrictions, the council gained more flexibility in the permissions that might be granted.[57]

A number of other planning implementation devices were taken to Hawaii hopefully by their inventors or supporters and examined as substitutes for planning. In 1972, Daniel Mandelker introduced the idea that "areas of critical concern" should be the state's responsibility. About the same time, Paul Ylvisaker, educator and adviser to the Rockefeller brothers' study on land, convinced the Temporary Commission on Environmental Planning of the validity of the environmental "carrying capacity" concept. The author of the notion of transferable development rights (known as TDR), land law expert John Costonis, taught at the University of Hawaii for a semester in 1974 and explained his idea to a number of local groups and individuals: that there will always be some property owners, in some locations, who for some reason should not (or might not want to) develop their land as intensively as the law would allow and others who would have good reasons for wanting to do more than the zoning code permitted.[58]

If it could be proved that the swap would not harm anyone and would not be environmentally disadvantageous, Costonis suggested that a transfer of the "rights" to develop which the code conveyed might be permitted, with equitable financial arrangements and under careful government control. Costonis had helped work out a successful plan in Chicago for transferring development rights from historic structures to other sites as a means of allowing landmark buildings to remain.[59] A graduate student at the University of Hawaii studied the potential of a similar use of TDR in downtown Honolulu and found that it could save a dozen or so early landmarks that were threatened with removal.[60]

The council, however, began to eye the principle of transferring development rights as another way of getting around the lack of planning in Waikiki. Costonis himself recognized Hawaii's lack of planning and insisted that TDR was not a planning substitute. Robert Way again protested, writing angrily to a newspaper about this "instant expert" who "appears to be an attorney seeking credentials as a planner."[61] The idea was dropped.

Shoreline protection, a valid enough idea for strengthening an overall land-use plan, became another back-door planning approach that was presented to Hawaii's legislators in the mid-1970s, this time by conservationists. The national government had passed a Coastal Zone Management Act in 1972, which required cooperation from the state. Federal funds were available for the development of plans implementing local legislation on shoreline management. Most states, including Hawaii, rushed to adopt them. California had led the way with an implementation law (known as Proposition 20) forced through by popular referendum vote after two defeats in that state's legislature. That law was considered a successful prototype, and a group of Hawaii's community council leaders (banded together as the Council of Presidents) drew up a similar measure and lobbied for its passage as an interim measure until the state should adopt a full-blown, federally satisfactory coastal zone management program. There did not seem much likelihood that shoreline planning could succeed in Hawaii without an overall land-use plan to relate to, but the community groups felt that it was worth trying to get *some* planning done, even if the whole job seemed unlikely.

There are great physical differences between California and the Hawaiian islands that were bound to make the effects of such legislation quite dissimilar. The biggest difference is that the California shoreline (about the same total length as Hawaii's) lies along the edge of a great continent, while Hawaii's shore is the entire surrounding circumference of each island. The inland, mauka, direction, once one crosses the central mountains, points oceanward, makai. Thus California was protecting a strip of land along one of its edges; Hawaii's legislation could affect most of its usable territory.

Another important distinction is that California's coastal counties are contiguous along the shore: jurisdictions overlap; actions in one affect others neighboring; for coordination a central state authority is essential. In Hawaii the coastlines of the island-counties are separated by expanses of water, and in many cases they are more jealously guarded at home than they are by the central state government. As an instance, for many years the state Department of Transportation has tried to forward plans to build a shoreline highway around the rugged northeast Kaena Point of Oahu, where the county's general plan showed instead an undisturbed preservation district.

A somewhat weakened shoreline protection act, passed by the 1974 legislature, required most development along the coast to prove it would not do any great environmental harm—not asking, however, whether it should be there at all, which would have been a planning question.[62] By 1977 the state's coastal zone management program seemed quite well along and in its preliminary scope appeared to include practically all land in the islands as "coastal"—in effect becoming a statewide land management plan.

In most cases, then, substitutes for planning were proposed simply to keep control over the uses of land in the hands of political agencies, but sometimes as a way to sneak a more considered and conscious procedure into the whimsy of government agency decision making. None of the new ideas, homegrown or imported, received any support from the local business community or from the cohort of malihini developer-builders. The local populace was either disinterested or disenchanted at these covert tries at planning. The islands' planners themselves were outspokenly skeptical, but with no effect. The mood was for action, the wish was for growth. There was no desire to suffer the restrictions that might be imposed by the making of plans, whether by conventional methods or by proxy.

Hawaii was not alone in this temper in the mid-1970s. Much of the advance in environmental protection that had been gained in the 1960s—highlighted by passage of NEPA, the National Environmental Protection Act—had been lost as the threatening energy crisis and the economic recession provided excuses for backtracking. The surge forward that had been made in land management legislation slackened off too.

At the federal level, land management legislation which had seemed close to adoption at the start of the decade was now all but forgotten. At state levels, the "Quiet Revolution" that had been hailed in earlier studies gave way to more moderated moves. Florida's acclaimed advance, for instance, was described in a later analysis as a "Slow Start in Paradise."[63] Only at the home-town level was advance in land planning being made. A number of mainland cities seemed to have tired of the indecision and ambiguity of proposals which vacillated between policies and plans. Chicago instituted a preliminary general-policy stage before drafting its general plan in order to keep the two separate. San Francisco included specific physical-plan elements in its overall policy plan. A new breed of social-environmental designer-

planners moved into the city planning ranks to fill the role
which the dynamic-process policy planners had left vacant.

In Hawaii, at the state level moves were being made
toward a more definitive kind of planning, one which promised even to indicate land uses (if only because the Land Use
Commission so obviously required guidance). The results
might well be worth waiting for. At Honolulu's city level,
however, there seemed to be an unsolvable impasse. The
administration's plan, in many respects, was too precise;
the council's, in most respects, was too vague. Neither was
usable as a guide to Oahu's social, economic, and physical
development.

There appeared to be only one way out of Honolulu's
problem: to reach outside the official city agencies and seek
informed, experienced, professional assistance from among
those who were successfully helping other cities with their
master plans. That solution was suggested from time to time,
but the community seemed reluctant to press for it.[64] The
data that had been accumulated by the administration's planners would be valuable to a consultant, and the reactions
which the council's planners had gotten in their public hearings would also be helpful. A competent professional should
be able to do in a brief time the job that had not been
accomplished in five years in-house. Only one thing more
would be needed: willingness to make planning a social
rather than a political act.

chapter 12

Reshaping Urban Space

IN the early 1970s a practice known as urban design became
a popular conception for sophisticated professional and lay
groups and, to a limited degree, came into political favor.
The move started among the architects, where it was seen as
an aspect of city planning that gave them a chance to utilize
their particular metier, design, in the increasingly complicated problems of urbanization. For members of the
general public concerned with improvement of their cities it
seemed to provide a goal more tangible than "beautification" without requiring too deep an involvement in the in-
tricacies of the planning process. For politicians it furnished
a platform with high-sounding principles that should appeal
to any constituent. On the mainland, urban design became
a requisite element in an increasing number of municipal
general planning efforts, and word of the trend traveled to
Hawaii through reports by several local planning writers and
visits of mainland architect-planners who were sold on the
subject.

Not only did urban design become a stylish concept in
Hawaii: there was an attempt to make it officially mandatory. Understanding vaguely that it promised more attrac-

tive city spaces, the legislature in 1973 adopted a resolution telling the counties to include an urban design element in their general plans (some completed by that time, some still in preparation).[1] Realizing more clearly that a great deal of work was involved and believing that other tasks had higher priorities, the county planning directors for some time quietly ignored the order. Honolulu's city council began to talk about urban design as a desirable ingredient of the planning substitutes it was considering; it seemed to be a modish trend that should be examined. San Francisco's planning director visited Honolulu to describe that city's well-thought-of urban design studies, incorporated in its general plan. Some council members felt that even if their town did not at present have a plan, perhaps it should have a design.

A Honolulu newspaper story in 1974 noted that urban design had become an "in" concept, even though few people seemed to know what the phrase meant.[2] Articles appeared even in professional journals seeking answers to the question "what *is* urban design?" and wondering what the county planning departments would do once they did something about the legislative mandate.[3]

The newspaper piece also described conflicts that were developing between local architects and city planners over the subject. Architects, by and large, look on urban design as large-scale architecture (*The Architecture of Towns and Cities*, as a 1965 book sponsored by the American Institute of Architects had been titled),[4] and they considered it an essential part of the city planning process. Planners, on the other hand, are inclined to feel that design considerations are irrelevant to a policy-oriented general planning procedure and should come, if at all, only deep in the development-plan stage. Neither, during the argument in Hawaii, seemed willing to agree that design (whether or not especially identified as *urban* design) is a means of giving form and structure to a plan (an *urban* plan or any other kind). That is, a design arranges all the actions a plan describes.

There was quite obviously a fear on the part of Honolulu's

city planners that concern with design matters would interfere with attainment of the social and economic goals they
were trying to achieve. When a writer for one of the newspapers chided the planning department for sloughing off the
design element in its general-plan revision program, a func-
tionary with the title of Deputy Planning Officer, Donald
Clegg, replied in inquisitional rhetoric: "Where in the urban
design is the plan for how housing will be financed? Where
in the urban design is the means by which the community
will receive police and fire protection? Where in the urban
design is the plan for getting houses built?" Those functions,
he maintained, are "what planning is all about today." He
agreed that ultimately a design for all those planning goals
would be needed. But to the argument that plans and designs
interact and should be considered together (as in the planning and design of a school, or a space missile, or a suit of
clothes) the planning official replied: "Absolute nonsense."
Whatever it might be, he insisted, urban design "is not the
glue that holds the plan together."[5]

Although laymen may understand only vaguely the function of design, when it is lacking they often miss it. Without
giving it a name, they need a sense of structure in their own
life, in their home, in the community where they live. Behavioral studies have shown that city dwellers *know* their own
cities and can describe them by their physical organization—
their "design"—no matter how haphazard it may be.[6] In
Honolulu there was evidence that opposition to the general-
planning department's recommendation that the city grow on
out toward Ewa and beyond began to appear and increased
in vehemence, to a large degree, because the public (including, in this case, the council members) could not visualize
an attractive, well-designed urban expansion when it was
described only in the cold, policy-planning words "directed
growth." Some well-read, well-traveled citizens suggested on
their own that if the proposed growth plan were adopted a
"Stockholm solution" might be hoped for: attractive new
communities of controlled size and density, separated by

green spaces, extending out from central Honolulu somewhat as new towns like Vallingsby complement Stockholm. Yet these optimists knew in their hearts that never, in Sweden or anywhere else, had such a desirable result been achieved without careful, constant coordination of planning and design by planners and architects. Without the benefit of such coordination Honolulu's expansion would be directed only in its course, not in its form. Undesigned, it would allow the city to "drag its slow growth along," in Alexander Pope's phrase, as more tracts, on past the point where cane fields had so far stopped it.

Honolulu was not the only Hawaiian city with design problems, and the other islands as well as Oahu had been told to prepare urban design plans. The island of Hawaii seemed to take the charge most seriously (and receive it most willingly). Along with regional development plans, with which its planning department followed up approval of its general plan, urban design plans were commissioned and often, as in the town of Kailua, stirred considerable public discussion.[7] Most of Hawaii's urban spaces could have benefited from some design effort. The city of Hilo had been through several planning design studies but remained stubbornly unorganized. Lihue on Kauai and Wailuku-Kahului on Maui had grown through the years with no incentive to design themselves. In some places where development seemed to induce a natural, logical town arrangement, a naive kind of organic design had resulted, achieved by circumstances rather than plan. Lahaina on Maui, formed by the whaling industry after Polynesian times, and Waimea on the Big Island, growing to serve the cattle ranches, were of this sort.

The RUDAT Affair

It was on Oahu, however, where the problems produced by urban growth were the greatest, that resistance to urban design was most apparent. A remarkable illustration of the fear of commitment to designed urban spaces was the area known as Kakaako, a poorly utilized 1,200 acres of land in the heart of Honolulu's core between downtown and Waikiki, stretching from the sea to the hills of Punchbowl and Makiki, crossed by Ala Moana Boulevard and all the other east-west roads running through the urban corridor. A few families remained from an earlier disintegrated neighborhood, but Kakaako was mainly, in the 1970s, a jumble of small businesses and marginal industries scattered along narrow, rutted streets and alleys, clogged with vehicles but somehow finding room, here and there, for a fine tree or a bright spot of garden that gave color and character to the surroundings. The state-city capitol district was almost next door on one side; the highly successful Ala Moana shopping center was a neighbor on the other. Remarkably, the city that was presumably wondering where and how to expand, that was considering growth into fresh farmlands, persisted in ignoring this valuable, underdeveloped territory in its own heart.

The local chapter of the American Institute of Architects, spurred by several of its planning/design-conscious members, saw this ill-used part of the central city as a remarkable opportunity to make a telling point about urban design. On the mainland, the national body of AIA had developed a program called RUDAT (regional urban design team), based on a conviction that many cities throughout the land had unresolved design problems that might be moved toward some solution by fresh expert advice. On invitation, then, AIA offered to provide a team of professionals who would visit a city for a brief time (four, five, six days) to analyze efforts being made locally or to suggest some answers that might have been overlooked. Remarkably, this process had worked well in a number of places. Even a short visit (with sufficient preparation in the background of the situation, after questioning talks with a number of knowledgeable local people, and then a thorough on-site study of the area in question) often made it possible for a team of informed persons, experienced in similar situations but perceptive enough to appreciate local differences, to suggest fresh solutions to old problems.

In 1974 the Hawaii AIA, backed by a number of concerned local citizens and several civic groups, with encouragement from the state administration and halfhearted support from the city, raised the necessary funds, made the essential technical preparations, and requested a visit from a RUDAT team. The subject assigned to the experts for study was the urban design potential of the central Honolulu/Kakaako area. The team that visited Hawaii was of unquestioned expertise: it was composed of seven well-known, nationally respected architects, planners, government officials, and economists.

At the conclusion of their study, the team members positively and explicitly suggested a renewal scheme for Kakaako that could make it, they believed, an attractively functioning new community in town.[8] Their proposal was to begin careful, coordinated planning and design of a neighborhood of some twenty thousand new homes that might be built at prices all income groups could afford, where new businesses and many of those presently there would provide local work for local people, and where large amounts of open space and an expanded waterfront park could be provided. This could be urban design at its best. The plan could be structured to allow the saving of view planes from Punchbowl to the sea, with high buildings kept on the periphery and mauka-makai vistas protected throughout the body of the developed area.

The whole idea was "blue sky," said a spokesman for the planning department.[9] But if any part of the suggested solution was speculative it was the assumption of planning goals for that part of the city. Since neither city nor state had development policies or plans for the Kakaako area, the RUDAT team had to devise its own program for design. Although this was clearly the wrong sequence in the policy-plan-design process, the problem was of the city's making, and the visiting group was experienced and capable enough to feel that it could accept and overcome the handicap. The assumption it made for its study was basically a goal to redevelop Kakaako for high-density but low-rise residential uses, integrated with certain light industries and businesses and a maximum of open and recreational spaces. The experts on the team understood the difficulties that would lie in the way of implementing such a designed plan. There were three principal landowners in the area—the Bishop and Victoria Ward Estates and the Dillingham Corporation—each with its own long-range plan for development. (At one time they had tried to cooperate in formulating a joint plan and had been repulsed by the city planning department.)[10] For the rest land ownerships were a patchwork, sites were confusingly leased for varying terms, property was absurdly overpriced, and the present tenants and residents would need protection if changes were to be made.

The social scramble and economic confusion in the area had worked to discourage public and private efforts at planning and development for decades. The RUDAT team proposed to cut through the tangled urban knot by the formation of the Central Honolulu Development Corporation, a quasi-public body which would be given unusual powers to produce the essential public results without denying private profits. Development corporations such as the one outlined had succeeded in other places, notably, at that time, in New York State, and Edward J. Logue, president and executive officer of New York's UDC, as it had become known, was a member of Honolulu's RUDAT team. Even though Logue's ambitious efforts in New York later ran into both political and fiscal difficulties, the development-corporation suggestion as a method for coordinating Kakaako's scattered ownerships and interests remained one of Honolulu RUDAT's most acceptable recommendations. It was clearly the only way to achieve integrated rather than spotty renewal.

For some time there did not seem to be any tangible effects from the hardworking team's efforts, although it was clear that attention had been called to Kakaako's problems and potentials. The immediate result seemed to be political controversy rather than urban improvement. The city, through its planning officers, expressed stiff-backed rejection of the new community-in-town concept, poking all manner of fun at the visiting "instant experts." Its own general-plan revision documents, when they appeared, made only the vacuous recommendation that "the Kakaako area retain its orientation toward accommodating economic activities."[11] Sensibly, sanguinely, the local AIA chapter turned to the public for support and a Citizens Group for Design of Central Honolulu was formed.[12] Attempts were made to stimulate the interest of both small and large landowners in a cooperative move forward, but without much success. The Victoria Ward Estate went ahead with construction of a low-rise, good-looking, temporary timber shopping-center structure in the heart of the area on Ala Moana Boulevard, and the Dillingham Corporation nurtured its own development plans.

Then suddenly a number of public figures seemed to see Kakaako's possibilities as a sizable political plum. Governor Ariyoshi had long been interested in the area (more than any other public official, he had supported RUDAT's activities), and soon the state's planners came up with a 300-page urban design "demonstration" study of the district. This study presented alternative proposals for land use (one in particular very similar to the RUDAT scheme) and analyzed implementation possibilities (including use of a development corporation like the one RUDAT had suggested). Then the state legislature decided that it should make a proposal for the area, too, and in 1975 it set up a Hawaii Community Development Authority, an entity similar to the one RUDAT had recommended, but as an "authority" without much authority—and no fund-raising power. (Until 1977, no members were even appointed to this body.) In 1976, the city's planning department reexamined its policy for Kakaako and issued still another study, suggesting that Oahu's increasing numbers of tourists, rather than its own residents, might be the best occupants of this urban land.[13] With irrefutable logic the report found, as others had, that a great number of new hotels would be needed to accommodate the growth in visitor traffic that would be required to provide the public revenues and private jobs that would be needed to support the state as its population grew. What would be a more reasonable spot for resort proliferation, the planners asked, than Kakaako, as a spillover from already crowded Waikiki? The local people would simply have to go somewhere else to build their homes, establish their businesses, and find their recreation.

After all this boiling up of interest had simmered down, however, Kakaako remained just as it had been when the RUDAT team arrived. An attempt to demonstrate the value of designing the use of prime urban land had resulted only in stirring interest in its economic worth. That Kakaako would in time be developed, now that its value had been so thoroughly explored, seemed inevitable. Whether its development would be carefully conceived, planned, and designed did not seem so sure.

There were many other parts of Honolulu that suffered from lack of design attention. One of the city's most attractive open spaces is Thomas Square, where in 1843 Rear Admiral Richard Thomas restored the independence of Hawaii after five months under the British flag. The handsome Honolulu Academy of Arts faces the square, as does a dignified old one-story stone school and an agreeable civic theater set back in congenial landscaping. A well-designed Methodist church abuts one corner. The square is nicely planted and has a comfortable, intimate scale. In the mid-1970s its quiet environment was shattered by construction of a bulky medical building facing one corner and further threatened by plans to build a 350-foot-high apartment complex on the property of the Methodist church.[14] This latter move, made to assure the congregation's financial future, seemed a particularly sacrilegious act: it was disrespectful, that is, to a part of Hawaii held sacred by many, and it was vigorously protested. The city council considered various actions to protect the square, and the church's developers agreed to lower their development goals by some stories. But blasphemy was achieved in late 1977 when the Council approved the church's scheme in an area for which a design, based on a plan that implemented an adopted policy, had never been made.

Downtown Honolulu's central business district was a major area ripe for design care as new buildings proliferated, creating new urban spaces and filling older ones, with no thought of forming a cohesive whole. As contemporary malls and plazas were being formed, there remained some of the city's earlier wide streets and a few attractive structures from former times. In many places these individual elements of an urban design almost reached one another and seemed on the verge of mutual acknowledgment and respect, but no effort had been made to help them coalesce. Parking lots surrounded and nearly concealed some of the finest, most usable older sites (like the one where the early Hawaii Hotel had been built and a YMCA now stood) and tasteless new development turned its back on historic neighborhoods like Queen Emma Square, with the St. Andrew's Cathedral which that queen had built to recall Kamehameha IV's Anglican Catholicism, and the Washington Place governor's residence which Queen Liliuokalani's husband John Dominis had put up for his bride.

For a molder of urban form, the sculpting of downtown Honolulu would have been a great opportunity: spaces seemed straining to bring themselves together visually and functionally—with no one bothering to help unify them. The Downtown Improvement Association was truly anxious for its bailiwick to present a decent appearance and had made a number of efforts to bring about development of an overall designed plan. At one time the DIA had retained the services of a local architect-planner;[15] at another time, with the city's cooperation, it had called in a mainland planning firm to study downtown's urban design possibilities.[16] In their times these studies had been tacitly accepted as official plans, without much comment or amendment from the city's official planners, but little implementation resulted. In 1975 the DIA itself, through capable staff effort, produced another quite feasible design study for the business district and its water-front, based on the concept of tying together existing open spaces and adding to them as necessary to form east-west and mauka-makai green corridors through the area.[17] The effort drew wide favorable commentary from the public—and no official reaction from the city. After all, there was no adopted general plan yet. How could there possibly be a design?

The Trouble with Waikiki

No part of Honolulu has been planned more often without ever having been designed than Waikiki. Since the time when the Hawaiian people, even before the Kamehamehas, enjoyed surfing off that sunny, sandy stretch it has increased in pop-ularity and population although, despite endless studies, its growth has been haphazard and indiscriminate. Hotels have been built along the beach and inward toward the Ala Wai Canal with no relation to one another or to the environs. In recent years an indiscriminate surge of costly apartment-house condominium construction has choked the inner streets and rimmed the canal-side Ala Wai Boulevard (witlessly overreaching its own semispeculative market by 1976, so that thousands of units were unoccupied, waiting for population to catch up with production). The city's codes for many years divided the ¾-square-mile area into sections separately designated for resort, business, and residential purposes—in the nature of conventional, use-segregating zoning—with densities that would allow more than triple the 21,000 hotel rooms that were already there in 1974 and a large increase in residential units. Under two mayors, citizen advisory commit-tees drew plans for more orderly growth, the Honolulu Redevelopment Agency proposed an urban renewal plan for part of the district, and the Waikiki Improvement Associa-tion (with a professional planner as its executive head) spent a great deal of time over its own scheme for development.

With none of these plans getting further than the drawing board (federal, state, and municipal governments agreed in seeing no reason to interfere with a growing, financially successful, revenue-producing tourist quarter), Waikiki had become a deteriorated part of Honolulu by the 1970s despite its new construction—with inadequate sewerage and drainage systems, narrow streets that were a dangerous maze for autos, taxis, and, most frightening, fire trucks, and plenty of cover for the prostitutes, dope peddlers, petty thieves, and more serious criminals any careless resort town attracts.

Yet new hotels continued to rise. And remarkably, with all its faults, Waikiki could still have become an exceptional urban resort. Although the possibility of recalling the quiet, low, quasi-colonial, quasi-Polynesian character that the kamaainas nostalgically remembered had long since been lost, Waikiki still had a unique character. For one thing, earlier landmarks continued to hold precarious leases on a mortgaged life; for awhile yet there remained the Moana, Halekulani, and Royal Hawaiian Hotels—the earliest, original three—a stretch of pleasant, low-rise shops along Kalakaua Avenue, the main street, the building still called Gumps, designed for that San Francisco merchant in the 1920s by island architect Hart Wood, and others. They continued to contrast with the new modern structures in a naive, quite charming manner that could not be counted on to remain much longer without some conscious effort at assistance.

More important to Waikiki's urban character were the physical characteristics: qualities that could be used or ignored but could never be eliminated or basically changed. There was the sea on one side and the mountains on another, of course, but in addition Waikiki has the great advantage of being physically bounded and contained. On its mauka border and its Ewa edge facing downtown, the Ala Wai Canal separates it from the rest of the city; on the Diamond Head side there are the great open spaces of Kapiolani Park; and makai lies the ocean. This meant that Waikiki could not dribble off in ragged outlines as many tourist places do.

Along Waikiki's borders, actually, some attractive edge areas have developed. One of the most pleasant is an excellent, unexpected bit of design detail at the Diamond Head end, where Kapiolani Park begins. A broad plaza and wide steps lead down to the sand, shaded by tall palm trees and several hau tree terraces. Buildings, beach, and people meld there in a way that few oceanside resort towns have succeeded in achieving. Buses stop at that point and there are open showers on the beach, used by young locals as well as middle-aged tourists. The hotels opposite spew pink-skinned American and camera-snapping Japanese visitors onto the plaza and altogether there is a happy compound of colors and countenances in a setting that mingles ocean shore and city strand.

Other parts of Waikiki are not so pleasant and some are downright dangerous. The state, some time ago, appropriated funds for physical improvements which the city administration for a long while refused to spend. It said there was no development plan to guide the work (its own planning job, undone). The state proposed that *it* spend its own money and go ahead with the essential work. Robert Way called a press conference to declare that suggestion "irresponsible."[18] And the years went by with nothing being accomplished save the granting of more permits for more hotel construction. It would have been possible at any point, granted cooperative action, to make a choice among the many Waikiki plans that had already been prepared. A final urban solution could have been designed to govern the physical improvements that were so badly needed, but the city council, the decision-making body, seemed satisfied to play its own game of searching for planning substitutes.

In 1975 the council's members came to their own resolution of the riddle of Waikiki—by passing a bill declaring the area a "special design district." This was another substitute, not only for planning but for urban design as well, with broader implications than any of the others being considered. It was distortion of another concept that had been used well in several mainland jurisdictions as an attempt to improve on conventional zoning in districts where unusual design considerations prevailed—around university or hospital complexes, near specially designed cultural centers, and so on. Honolulu's council, however, saw it as a means of removing zoning restrictions and placing land use decisions in its own hands wherever problems of planning and design were unresolved. Waikiki seemed one such area. Kakaako was an obvious candidate. Thomas Square, it was suggested, might be another, the slopes of Mt. Tantalus a third. Now that the council had taken over the function of general planning, why should it not also assume the rights and responsibilites that went with urban design?[19]

The pageant continued, however. The council adopted a resolution calling for a statement of urban design principles and controls to be incorporated in each of the development plans which would follow its general plan—still without defining the term urban design. In 1977, with the advice of a large citizen advisory group, the council mounted a program to teach the *public* what the words meant. Experts from the mainland were invited as lecturers. Few seemed to find ironical the fact that one of them, Rai Okamoto, San Francisco's planning director, had been a member of the RUDAT team whose urban design concept for Kakaako had been ignored.

If urban design problems seemed particularly acute on Oahu, where the great majority of Hawaii's population had gathered, they were certainly not restricted to that island. During the later 1960s, an ambitious attempt was made to demonstrate the broad need for urban design and illustrate its potential value for all the islands. A five-part research and study project on the subject was initiated in 1968 by the State Foundation on Culture and the Arts, financed largely by the National Foundation on the Arts.[20] The meaning of urban design was widened, in these studies, to include the design problems faced anywhere, even in open country, where urban expansion impends, and the term "environmental design" was added to enlarge the definition.

Conflicts seem inevitable between the forces of conservation and those of development. Can they be resolved by careful planning? The physical arrangements of nature and those imposed by urban man seem irreconcilable. Can they be conformed through thoughtful urban design? Will social disagreements and political arrangements permit careful planning and thoughtful design to be accomplished? And if they are completed, will they have any effect on the ways resources are used? These are basic questions that face the lands of Hawaii from now on, after the many uses and misuses they have suffered. The fate of the five projects sponsored by the state foundation in 1968 and 1969 may suggest answers to them.

chapter 13

To Preserve and Enhance

THE State Foundation on Culture and the Arts secured
funds in 1968 which allowed it to commission five studies in
the urban, environmental stage of land planning in Hawaii.
There were three broadly stated purposes of the project (officially called Environmental and Urban Design Proposals and
abridged to EUDP).[1] One objective was to discover ways to
"preserve and enhance" Hawaii's natural qualities as urban
growth continued; another was to see whether carefully
researched planning and design could "reconcile conflicting
influences" on the environment (primarily the pressure for
development vis-à-vis the urgency of conservation); and a
third was to seek ways to "correlate effectively" the man-
made environment and nature's own. In short, the five
consultants were asked to demonstrate, through the planning
and design process, how urban development might continue
in Hawaii without destroying the islands' natural qualities.

The firms who received the commissions consisted of two
considered primarily land planners (Walter K. Collins &
Associates and Donald Wolbrink & Associates), one primarily
architectural (John Carl Warnecke & Associates), another engaged mostly in landscape architecture (the office of George
S. Walters), and, for the fifth, the technical staff of the

Oahu Development Conference, consisting of a planner (Aaron Levine) and an architect (William A. Grant). Whatever their individual backgrounds, the principals who worked on the EUDP assignments for these firms were well based in all the planning and design disciplines. The director and coordinator of the entire project was architect Alfred Preis, executive director of the state foundation, who had conceived the idea for the studies, arranged for the financing, developed the procedures and proposed a coordinating method for the work, and organized and correlated the commissions as they proceeded. In addition to funding from the National Foundation on the Arts, financial help was secured from the four counties, several state agencies, and the Oahu Development Conference. Several "special consultants" were appointed, three drawn from the mainland (architect Robert L. Geddes, landscape architect and educator Garrett Eckbo, and historian-critic Alan Temko) and others (including this writer) chosen locally. Their task was to help guide the projects as they progressed and judge them analytically, even critically, when they were completed.

Few exercises in urban design have ever had more generous goals, broader sponsorship, or better-qualified participants. Care was taken that there be no professional conflict between the consultants and the county planning departments; advice was sought from the islands' planning directors throughout the progress of the work; and high hope was held that the results of the studies would be directly useful in the urban design programs of the individual counties. Beyond that feeling of local responsibility, EUDP set itself a mission to discover "key design issues," as the project's program phrased it, that might arise in any place where nature is being disturbed by human activity. One intent of the project (particularly as it had the backing of a national foundation) was to let others, in different locations, profit from the findings and conclusions. The consultants and their critics had in mind, then, that the issues they uncovered and the solutions they proposed could have wider than Hawaiian significance.

Fifty Miles of Design

An adviser to the project, Robert Geddes, noted that the assignments illustrated an extreme "diversity of scales."[2] One of the studies with tremendous scale in physical magnitude and potential impact was the task given to the Collins office: to analyze the environmental effects of a highway the state proposed to build along the Kona coast of the Big Island and design the best corridor for it.[3] The road to be studied would go from Kawaihae, an ancient settlement located on a deep-water harbor near the northern tip of the island, to Hookena, another historic spot, now a sleepy village on a quiet beach cove below a cliff pocked with old burial caves. The road would be part of a belt highway encircling the island, but this fifty to sixty-miles stretch needed special design care—precisely because of the "conflicting interests" that EUDP hoped to reconcile.

One interest clearly lay in preserving scenic beauty. The coast is uniquely picturesque. Along its northern half it rises fairly gradually from a shoreline dotted with secluded white beaches toward the lower slopes of one of the island's two great mountains, Mauna Kea (the white mountain, its tips covered with snow in some months). Here the road would cross many miles of lava, in some places bare from recent flows, in others old enough to be covered with sufficient earth to support low vegetation, but not populated anywhere. Further inland along this part of the coast, the land is used for ranching (the great Parker Ranch is located here) and there are several small towns.

For its southern half, the highway would have to find a corridor along steeper cliffs below Mauna Loa (the long mountain, encompassing in its span a number of still-active volcanic craters). Some of the richly vegetated slopes bear crops of coffee and macadamia nuts and support a number of small settlements (mauka agricultural communities, Collins' report called them), peopled mainly by a mixed Hawaiian and Japanese stock. Obviously, then, the road would have the opportunity to demonstrate dramatic scenery to its travelers and the responsibility to respect, not scar, the landscape.

The historic background of the area was another factor that both provided design restraints and promised travel advantage. Kamehameha the Great was born on the northern part of this coast and his first great military success was at Mokuohai, further south along the route being studied. Captain Cook had been welcomed and then killed at Kealakekua Bay, along the same stretch of shore. During the later Polynesian period, the Kona coast was the most heavily populated part of the islands. A tremendous inventory of artifacts remains, some restored and accessible, most concealed by modern undergrowth, scattered along the shoreline and dug into the cliffs. Heiaus, petroglyphs, trails, burial caves, and salt ponds abound. Any road carved through the area would have to respect this display of stone-age history yard by yard and make possible reconstructions and exhibits where they could be seen and appreciated.

Past history, then, would have to be preserved, as well as present beauty respected. And, in addition, the road corridor must be designed to serve a reasonable future. Those who held Kona lands were anxious by now to profit from them, and the list of owners, headed by the Bishop Estate and the Parker Ranch, was a roster of Big Five companies and kamaaina trusts. Governor Burns had said repeatedly that he envisioned the area's future as a "Gold Coast" of resort expansion and retirement home development. Collins and his associates realized fully that the highway they were to locate and design could either act as servant to this growth, merely providing access to developments as they occurred, or as master of a consciously conceived plan to "preserve and enhance" those qualities the coast possessed.

Unfortunately, there was no plan for the Kona coast to serve as basis for a road's design; there was, in fact, no policy on which a plan could be based. In its foreword Collins' report said: "It is urgent that a firm policy for the future of

West Hawaii be established. Public decisions must be made in the near future if the present quality of the environment is to be preserved and enhanced."⁴ Lacking a policy to guide their assignment, the planner-designers developed their own program (as Honolulu's RUDAT team had had to do), intended hopefully to be "directed toward assisting public officials and others in making these decisions."

The strongest policy recommendation the report made was that urban development along the coast—whether in the form of resorts or residential communities—should be limited in amount, focused in location, and controlled in design. The consultants took the position that "the concept of urbanization of all West Hawaii is not warranted."⁵ They argued for preservation of agriculture and ranching in many areas. For others they pointed to the practical difficulties of lava-covered land not suitable for development, climate along parts of the shore too hot and dry to please tourists and retired mainlanders, and an inadequate water supply for extensive population growth.

Critic Alan Temko had a somewhat different reaction to the likelihood of intensive development along the coast. Although he agreed that the ecology of the study area was "deeply unfavorable" for unreserved urbanization, he believed that fate to be inevitable—in time large-scale investment would be made in a water supply system and the highway itself would open up previously inaccessible lands for speculative development. "It will be California and Arizona all over again," he predicted, "water and the freeway leading to almost incredible increases in land values."⁶

Temko urged Collins to propose a means of public benefit from this "unearned increment of private landowners through public investment" in the road. The legislature in Hawaii had often toyed with the possibility of taxing in some way the "unearned increment" when agricultural or conservation land was zoned for urban uses and became suddenly worth thousands instead of tens of dollars an acre. But this

would be a different kind of private benefit: enhancement of
private lands by public works. Hence Temko felt it called for
a new, even "revolutionary," kind of compensation,[7] one
which might, on the Kona coast, provide low-cost housing or
pay for building a university campus or a much-needed hospital. The report, however, recommended that development
on this coast should be strictly limited and carefully located,
rather than thankfully accepted for its tax returns.

The selection and design of a highway corridor was, after
all, the basic assignment given the consultants, important as
analysis of its impact was, and Temko agreed with the other
consultants that the design itself was "attacked with sensitivi-
ty and responsibility." The great environmental differences
between the northern and the southern halves, and the
several purposes the highway would serve along its route,
made necessary different design approaches in different sections of the corridor. The report stressed the differences. The
"vast, strong, raw, almost scaleless" quality of the northern
part would call on the highway to make a "bold statement."
The steeply sylvan character of the southern portion, "more
intimate in scale," suggested that the highway respect the
woodland and "blend into the landscape."

In addition to passing through different kinds of environments, the road was planned to serve several different functions along its length. In the Kawaihae area and again in its
center portion, at the older town of Kailua and at a newer
development on Keauhou Bay, it would provide access to
resort districts. In between, across the rugged lava fields and
along the often rocky coast, it would be a multipurpose
facility: capturing sweeping views of the shoreline, reaching
some developed locations, and allowing efficient, comfortable passage. South of Kailua, edging the cliffs and then
looping down to the waterfront, it would be primarily a
scenic route, opening access to places of visual beauty and
historic significance. Each kind of road required a different
design. The planners carefully specified grades, widths, sorts
of access, rights of way, intended speeds, and relations of

lanes to one another and to the land they lay on. All these factors would help determine the best general location—the broad corridor—within which the highway would be built.

Realizing that they themselves, in this study, could not attack all the specific urban design problems for particular places along the route (even if there had been policies on which such design might be based), the consultants over and over pointed to the additional work that was necessary. "Waimea needs a plan for its future growth and urbanization," the report said. It urged the state to prepare "a definitive recreation plan" for the area of Kiholo. It reminded the county that "an updated and expanded plan for Kailua-Keauhou needs to be prepared." A "specific plan should be prepared for conservation" of the Kealakekua historic area, it pointed out, and it proposed that "an effort should be made toward further planning of the small communities" shelved on the hills south of Kailua.

Some important accomplishments were achieved by this careful study, even though many of its recommendations were ignored. The state's highway engineers took advantage of the Collins analysis of alignment for part of the road's corridor when actual design was started a few years later. But when it came to nuances and details of the road's design, the careful specifications of the Collins study were disregarded. The route that was opened in March 1975 as the Queen Kaahumanu Highway turned out to be another standardized, straightaway turnpike stretched between Kailua and Kawaihae. The county's Planning Department recognized some of the report's suggestions for concentration of resort areas in its general planning, and Collins' emphasis on the need for retaining the shoreline's scenic and historic qualities influenced later planning. Urban design studies were begun for a number of the larger towns. The historic-scenic area around Kealakekua and Honaunau Bays, with its proposed loop to the coast (planned in considerable detail in a commission given later to this writer and landscape architect George Walters),[8] stirred the opposition of some local landowners.[9]

It went forward, in the following years, only to the extent of state acquisition of a few historic sites.

The county's general plan, in its generalized policy statements, undoubtedly drew some benefit from the Collins study, as its designers had hoped. Two planning and design assignments that followed the EUDP project were given to the office of Donald Wolbrink & Associates in 1975: a "Kona community" development plan, intended to apply the broad policies of the county's general plan to this coastal area, and an urban design study for Kailua village.[10] Wolbrink was familiar with Collins' work (the EUDP consultants met in joint session regularly) and shared the desire to keep farming and ranching alive on the Kona coast (while recognizing that "the immediate potential for particular crops is uncertain"). He too proposed a planned concentration of resort development rather than willful dispersal. For Kailua, where random construction and haphazard design had spoiled the town's pleasant qualities, he presented an urban design that, if it were followed, could make further growth more orderly.

Even with this additional planning and design work, the future of the Kona coast is still uncertain. Influences continue to conflict. When the overall economy faltered in the mid-1970s, the pressures for additional development in the north slackened (although, as tourism resumed its growth, and other industries to replace the Kohala sugar plantation seemed hard to find, servicing visitors became an ever more attractive option to the local people). The residents of Kailua argued the merits of urban design versus its restraints to individual business. On the old belt road to the south, Captain Cook, Kealakekua, and other towns remain sleepy communities dependent on crops with limited marketability.

There was no question in anyone's mind that in time the new highway, hopefully designed to guide growth, would generate growth. Wolbrink in 1975, like Collins, Temko, and others in 1968, recognized that inevitably "the resort and visitor industry will play a more and more dominant role in the future of Kona"—but with what speed and in what direction remained undetermined. Some critics feel today that the Collins office should have concentrated more sharply on details of road design and less on land use impact. But the planner-designers who worked on the EUDP study still insist, even more strongly than they did in their 1968 report, that no details of urban design for the Kona coast, whether for highways or hamlets, can have much meaning until the state and county together decide what overall design the future of the great shoreline should have.

The Reshaping of Honolulu

Another assignment of sizable scale was given to the Oahu Development Conference professionals: an urban design study of the central Honolulu waterfront.[11] It was a project which raised interesting questions about urban design as a pragmatic process, because the report that was produced inclined toward the practical, the possible, in the hope that it might have some real, immediate influence on decisions about to be made. The design that was proposed (beautifully presented) would unquestionably have improved existing conditions on the waterfront greatly. It shied away from the ideal, even the innovative, to avoid being considered unrealistic. And yet a decade after the study was made few of its recommendations have been adopted. One wonders: Would more radical proposals have had greater impact? Was the report too "bland," as one of the critics suggested, to stir popular imagination and stimulate political action?

The shoreline to be studied measured seven miles in length, extending from the airport that lies about three miles east of the city's central business district to Diamond Head, rising from the shoreline some four miles west of downtown. Because of its lineal extent, Levine and Grant divided their study area into five sections. After a review of current development intentions and a search for public policies that might affect design proposals, alternative plans were indicated for

each of the five sections. Some of the alternatives shown
were developed by the consultants themselves; more were
drawn from proposals that had already been made by others.
Finally an overall design plan was constructed, representing
"the preferences of the consultant staff in the fall of 1968"
from among the alternative choices.

The first section of the study went from the airport to the
western part of the harbor. The principal proposals were for
a new road from the air terminal toward Waikiki, bypassing
downtown by tunneling under the harbor; development of a
flat, sandy-fringed, unused island lying in the harbor's
mouth (prosaically known as Sand Island) as an industrial
park related to air and sea port activities; and provision of
a maritime museum and a basin for historic ships at the
harbor entrance.

To some critics of the study, sinking under the harbor a
part of the road from the airport to downtown (which is just
as ugly in Honolulu as in any other American city) did not
seem to be enough betterment of its design. As Garrett
Eckbo commented, the eager tourist's inevitable reaction
must be: "Is this the tropical paradise I dreamed of?"[12] The
use of Sand Island became a controversial issue soon after
the report was issued—residents in nearby Kalihi and Palama
(localities short of recreational facilities, among other depri-
vations) demanded that it be made a peoples' park rather
than an industrial park ("a euphemism for a row of factories
with landscaped front yards," said Eckbo of that term).[13]
Ultimately, some years after the EUDP study, a compromise
was reached: beach park, industrial buildings, and a
municipal sewage disposal plant now share the land. Plans
for the highway under the harbor, which had long been considered, were dropped when fixed-rail rapid transit was
seriously deliberated.

For the next section of the design, the downtown area and
the stretch of harbor bordering it, three alternative plans
were drawn. One showed high-rise apartments on the water
below Chinatown, as several developers were planning; the

others would keep buildings along the waterfront low. Several downtown urban configurations (building "envelopes") were suggested. The strongest feature proposed, all critics agreed, was a tree-lined waterfront promenade that would relate facilities along the harbor and link them to downtown pedestrian malls by footbridges across the waterfront highway. This proposal continued to surface from time to time and was part of the Downtown Improvement Association's 1975 urban design. But, along with the rest of downtown's potential, it remains a design only on paper.

The third section that was studied, past the harbor, was the Kakaako–Ala Moana area, including the 1,200 acres which the AIA's RUDAT team analyzed some six years later. Three alternative design plans were drawn for this part of the waterfront also. None would change its existing primary use as a center for small industries ("occupied by activities that traditionally seek inexpensive land," as the report noted) but simply suggested that the automobile circulation pattern and the district's general appearance be enhanced by "street improvement and tree planting." For the Fort Armstrong shoreline area where the RUDAT study later proposed a new in-town waterfront park, the EUDP report suggested only that the edges be developed as park-promenade.

Several alternatives were shown for improvement of the present Ala Moana Park: a popular place, overcrowded on holidays and weekends, focus of many of the "conflicting influences" that EUDP hoped to reconcile. There had once been ambitious plans to enlarge the park at both ends, in crescent form, and add an islet in its embrace—the whole to be known as Magic Island. The Dillingham Corporation had wanted at one time to create additional land there for hotel sites, and together with the Bishop and Victoria Ward Estates at another time made plans for an apartment-resort complex on adjacent lands facing the park. The Oahu Development Conference's EUDP study illustrated all these design possibilities and favored, in its final plan, expansion of the park at its Waikiki end onto one arc of the Magic Island crescent

that had already been built. Another design suggestion the
report made for this stretch of the waterfront was widening
Ala Moana Boulevard itself to make it a landscaped freeway
at grade (rather than an elevated highway, a possibility which
had previously been considered).

To some of the critic-commentators, retaining the auto-
oriented character of the neighborhood, with a freeway and
an improved secondary-street system, was a disappointing
proposal. Historian-critic Temko regretted that no more had
been suggested for the shorefront than an extension of the
beach park at one end. Concepts of recreation have changed,
he pointed out, and such places as Copenhagen's Tivoli Gardens make passive parks seem "inadequate and obsolete."[14]

For Waikiki's problems, the study did suggest more "bold
and imaginative" designs, the critics felt, although the design
concentrated on improvement of the beach and amelioration
of traffic problems. For the beach, the consultants recommended widening of the sandy area, providing a continuous
waterfront promenade past the proliferating hotels, and
maintaining the few low-density and open-space spots that
remained along the shore. To lessen traffic tangles and de-
congest central Waikiki it was proposed that Kuhio Avenue,
the central longitudinal street, be converted to a mall and
widened in some places to form "vest-pocket" parks. And
then, to care for the traffic flow, it was suggested that a new
boulevard be built on the mauka side of the Ala Wai canal,
parallel with the one on the makai Waikiki side. In addition
to these physical changes, several public policies were recommended, from institution of a one-way street system to some
form of architectural and landscape design control.

At the eastern end of their study area the consultants proposed a grand climax for this part of Oahu's coast. They
urged that there be no hesitation about making the waterfront at Diamond Head public property conserved for park
use. Their design showed it as a continuation of Kapiolani
Park along the shore, respecting the "craggy character" of
the great cone and providing additional beachfront recrea-

tional space. From the critics there was nothing but applause for this recommendation, which has also appealed to the general public. Prodded by community insistence, the city council has declared Diamond Head a special scenic-cultural-historic district and has taken steps to limit further construction along the shore,[15] although acquisition of land to make the area of a public park has lagged, hampered by costs and hindered by landowners' opposition.

All in all, ODC's part of the EUDP project was "neat and concise," as one of the consultants put it. The report was handsomely illustrated, well organized, and highly readable; in fact, Eckbo said, it was a primer for the accepted urban design process. It began with a description of the "three available devices" by which development can be governed—land use control, architectural control, and a public works program geared to the design's objectives—and an assurance that "when these three devices are combined and applied properly they can achieve any reasonable design objective" (a belief that critic Temko found "not convincing"). Certainly the absence of action since the report was issued has not given comfort to the argument; few of the twenty-two specific proposals in the report have been carried out. Extension of Ala Moana Park, improvement at one end of the Waikiki beach, institution of a one-way street system in Waikiki, and moves to protect the Diamond Head shore can be counted as accomplishments, offset by such decrements as loss of shoreline open space to the Waikiki Sheraton Hotel and continued deterioration of the harbor shore. The record is particularly disappointing since, as one commentator said, the study seemed modestly to say "this is what may happen," rather than "this is what could happen" or even "this is what should happen."[16]

It must be granted that the three devices ODC considered essential have not been used: land use controls have not been applied to further any agreed-upon design; architectural controls have not existed; the city's public works program, especially in Waikiki, has become a political instrument rather than a design tool. But in addition another essential factor has been missing: community objectives have never been determined. Levine and Grant noted the lack of clear-cut policy goals along the Honolulu waterfront, as Collins had on the Kona coast, but they felt that they recognized "informal" development policies, expressed in capital budget programs and the city's zoning code, which would only need additions and modifications to encompass their design proposals and make them work. This never happened.

"To Direct Hilo's Growth . . . "

The EUDP study with the most creative vision of Hawaii in the years ahead, inevitably urbanized but developed in a manner that suited its tropical setting, came from the office of George Walters, landscape architect.[17] He was assigned the task of creating an overall urban design for the city of Hilo, on the island of Hawaii, a study area stretching about three miles along the Hilo Bay shoreline between two peninsular terminals at either end of the city. The project's stated objective was "to direct Hilo's growth . . . in a manner harmonious with the city's natural environment and with its economic and cultural objectives." Walters too had to face the fact that there *were* no clear-cut objectives—economic, cultural, social, or physical—to design for. He had to assume them or interpret them as best he could from scarce, sketchy data. The task required great imagination: this second largest city in the Hawaiian Islands has a proud, lingering past but no clear future at all.

A substantial native settlement before the white man's arrival, the scene of an important battle in Kamehameha I's rise to power on his home island, chosen early as a mission station when the churchmen came, Hilo developed rapidly in the nineteenth century as a commercial center. During the whaling period its protected harbor welcomed ships putting in for supplies, and when coffee and then sugarcane plantations were established nearby, it became a busy shipping port. It was a stable community through the intervening years,

Walters' report noted, until its airport was enlarged in 1967, allowing it to receive trans-Pacific planes from the mainland. Then the town caught tourist fever and began expanding rapidly. Hotels were built in quick succession, most of them along the Waiakea peninsula that marks the southeastern end of Hilo Bay.

At the time of the EUDP study, Hilo still depended largely on sugar as its economic base (Hilo Sugar Company, a subsidiary of Big Five member C. Brewer & Co., was operating a sugar mill in the city and processing some thirty thousand tons a year), but it was looking more and more to tourism for its stake in Hawaii's future. The only trouble was that no city in the state had less to offer the tourists who were taken there as part of package tour itineraries. There was nothing to do in Hilo, and very little to see, visitors discovered, and they seldom stayed more than one night on their way to some more interesting and attractive place.

The city's climate typically ranges from cloudy to rainy; showers fall on the average of three hundred days a year. Physically, Hilo is unattractive. It rests on a flat plane tilting five hundred feet from the lower slopes of Mauna Loa to the bay, crossed by several rivers flowing from the mountains but with few distinguishing surface landmarks. As the report noted expressively, it is "under constant threat of destruction from the very environmental forces that created it—the mountains and the sea." Both tsunamis (seismic tidal waves) and lava flows from volcanic eruptions have battered the area numerous times, and as late as 1960 swells triggered by an earthquake in Chile wiped out some parts of the town and seriously damaged others. The downtown area, already quite shabby, decayed further in discouragement after that, and a great swath of desolated land south of the business district was cleared and left unused. Further back from the water the city's streets, largely lined with shops, form what Walters called a "loosely woven urban fabric." On beyond that, subdivisions (some divided but never developed) meander toward the foothills to form a ragged urban edge.

With no policy guidelines from state or county and no

design objectives from the city itself, the EUDP study set its
own program. It was a landscape architect's vision: to
change Hilo into a tropical botanic paradise, to make its
climate an advantage rather than a handicap, to turn its need
for new commercial activities to account, to utilize its great
expanse of wasted urban land—by making of Hilo a City of
Flowers. Whereas Honolulu had grown past the point where
any dream of tropical garden-city planning could be realized,
Hilo, Hawaii's next sizable city, arced around the islands'
second busiest harbor, still had that opportunity. Hilo
already had a flourishing business activity in raising and selling tropical plants. Walters proposed to expand it, organize
it, display it, and utilize it to give the city the character it
had always lacked.

Because of the underlying City of Flowers theme, the Hilo
study, more than any other EUDP report, was able to unify
individual parts of its design in an integrated concept—an
image that was based on a sensitive visual perception of the
area being studied. The "surround" elements, as Walters
called them, were examined first: the cloud cover, so constant that "there are no strong contrasts of light and shadow
. . . edges of objects are less distinct and perceptions of
depth become limited"; the gray "vertical backdrop" of the
two great mountains; even the shape of the city itself, "low
in texture and irregular in pattern."

Specific design proposals were made in six key areas within
this surround and then synthesized in urban patterns of
movement and form (circulation, lighting, building masses)
within the flowered-city theme. There were some doubts expressed about this design process by the project's advisory
consultants. It was the approach of an artist, an architect as
sculptor, a landscaper as painter. The toughest critic, Alan
Temko, was not convinced that visual, floriate distinction
was enough for an urban design concept. Perhaps "the whole
cultural development of the area" would be a better objective
to reach for.

Walters knew, however, that it would have been presump-

tuous and somewhat ridiculous for an urban designer to try
to map the cultural future of Hilo's mixed population: about
15 percent haole, somewhat less than that with Hawaiian
blood, and more than half of Japanese descent, one generation removed from plantation life. What he did instead
seemed to him and to others of his critics to be a potentially
more productive process: he suggested a design that would
give visual structure to a town that was socially and physically confused, as a frame on which could be constructed any
ultimately desirable future.

Walters' detailed design proposals covered a wide range of
issues, from better location of the airport to improvement of
appearance and use of the hotel strip. The City of Flowers
theme would reach its apogee in the part of Hilo that had
been most ravaged by the 1960 tsunami: a hundred acres of
land mostly lying well-nigh bare, some used as parkland and
some loosely occupied by random commercial-industrial
structures.

Much of this land was state-owned. Some had been acquired by the city for redevelopment, and the Bishop Estate
and C. Brewer held sizable pieces. Through the flat terrain
flowed two rivers and a drainage canal, joining at the bay as
a narrow harbor for sampans, small commercial fishing
craft. On the inland side of this extensive open space a
federally supported redevelopment activity, known as the
Kaiko'o project, had built a ten-foot bank (as protection
against future tidal waves) and created an earth-fill platform
on which state and county office buildings had been built
and a hotel and shopping center were planned.

For the lower open spaces Walters planned a coordinated
series of active, usably scaled parks and a system of continuous paths that could connect the resorts on the Waiakea
peninsula with the downtown area. Private landowners' plans
for resort development along the rivers would be related to
the parkway system, and a hostel and convention center were
proposed as a focus for visitor activities.

On the level above this park-resort-promenade development, Walters urged careful architectural and landscape control for the redevelopment activities that were planned. (The proposed hotel, for instance, should be low in silhouette, he said, set in gardens, blended with the parklands below it.) Toward downtown on this terrace, a great tropical plant display space was proposed—a Kaikoʻo Floral Center— retained above the park below by a lava-rock wall.

The concept of a "city existing on two horizontal planes" was extended to the old downtown area, where the lower level would be a prolongation of the bayfront parks. Parking areas would be depressed and planted out of view, and the upper terrace would be a continuance of more structured urban spaces. Here, above the threat of new tsunamis, protected by an undulating lava-rock wall that could drip with flowering plants, parts of the old government center would be preserved and new buildings would be planned on a modest scale.

The ways in which all these individual design areas would be merged in the City of Flowers theme were described in detail. Tree lines, tree masses, shrubbery, and ground cover were to be used as design tools. Tree-lined boulevards would "define the urban center and establish the character of the city from all approaches." Intensity of planting and kinds of plant material were to vary as purposes and functions changed. Nonflowering trees would be massed in open parts of the city and along the waterfront to act as a visual foil to the blossoming trees.

How did this creative design for Hilo's future—"orderly, convincing, comprehensive, sensitive and imaginative," as Garrett Eckbo described it;[18] "based on consistent methodology,"[19] Temko felt—fare in the years that followed? In 1968 Hilo seemed to have the opportunity and the reason to grasp at such a concept. The redevelopment agency was completing the Kaikoʻo development and anticipated federal support for a downtown renewal project; the county planning department was completing its general plan study, conscious of urban design needs; the tourist industry was seriously worried about

Hilo's lack of visual attraction. Yet ten years later Hilo was the same city Walters had described so well. Some new studies were being made, this time by Collins' planning firm, and many of Walters' ideas were being proposed anew (with full friendly credit)—but none had been implemented. A few improvements had been carried out along the bay. Small gestures had been made toward better use of the beach. Some suggestions for simplifying waterfront traffic were being restudied, and a well-designed, low-profiled, but not too successful resort had been built on C. Brewer's land (hiding itself with its own lush landscaping from the broad wasteland that still lay around it). Walters himself had been retained by the state to make further park plans for that unused land, but none had been carried out. On the Kaiko'o terrace above, a tall, broad, ugly hotel had stubbornly been constructed with redevelopment agency blessing.

The basic design ideas in the report—the City of Flowers concept, with its great floral display, and the idea for a city on two levels to step the sloped plane visually and supply protection from tsunamis functionally—"never caught on," as George Walters ruefully admitted some years later. The city still could not make up its mind about its future.

Design Problems on Maui

Three separate design problems on the island of Maui, posing three quite different problems in Hawaii's development, were assigned to the architectural and planning firm of John Carl Warnecke & Associates.[20] They involved the towns of Lahaina, Wailuku, and Makena—all scenes of ancient Polynesian settlements, each of which had played a role in Hawaii's nineteenth-century social and economic changes. In territorial times and since then, however, the three locales had fared very differently and now faced dissimilar futures.

The island of Maui is divided into two parts by a narrow neck which starts between Lahaina and Makena on one side and reaches Wailuku on the other. One of the assignments

was to design the future of a four-mile coastal strip on east
Maui from Makena Bay, around which clustered the houses
remaining from what had been one of Maui's busiest port
towns, to La Perouse Bay, named for the French explorer
who, searching for the elusive Northwest Passage, took on
provisions there in 1786. The Hawaiian settlements that had
once surrounded the two bays and stretched between them
were gone without replacement; cattle and produce from the
slopes of Haleakala were no longer shipped from Makena
but now went through Wailuku. (Even to call Makena a village anymore, as the Warnecke report said, "is to exaggerate
its size.") Back from the coast, grazing lands of the Ulupalakua Ranch covered the volcano's foothills. The shore itself
was a forest of tangled *kiawe* growth interrupted by wastes
of lava and separated strands of black and white beach.
This was easily the least urbanized site of any of the EUDP
projects.

The Warnecke report called it a wilderness coast, but it
evinced an odd sort of wildness, dotted with remnants from
many ages. Flows from Haleakala's many eruptions covered
much of the land, some grown over and some still bare,
forming a desolate protuberance into the sea at one point
and shaped into cinder cones at other places. House platforms and oddments from Polynesian times remain in abun-
dance, close by ruins of a military radio-range station and
not far from an open dump of discarded washing machines,
stoves, and oil drums. An abandoned quarry dates one
period of coastal activity, a fishing-boat ramp another, and a
few shanties and shacks remain from a different time. Access
to this almost deserted shore is by a road best traveled on
foot or by four-wheel drive.

Two landowners in the area (Ulupalakua Ranch and the
Matson Company) anticipate extensive development. The
state's own plans for the region have included from time to
time a park at Makena, a scenic road along the coast, and a
small boat harbor at La Perouse Bay.

The Warnecke designer-planners suggested instead that the

four-miles strip be kept as a "genuine wilderness area." Impossible as this would have been (people had already intruded too many times), the hyperbole was useful, because many natural forms and colors and textures remained that were worth preserving. Specifically the report proposed that Makena town grow as a low-density, marine-oriented, residential-resort community, that the cinder cones and a fine stretch of white-sand beach be declared beach-reserve conservation areas, that a rustic park be built, a simple camping ground be planned at La Perouse Bay, and a trail lead on to campsites in the hills beyond.

The Warnecke planners advised, in sum, that "the most important commitment that can be taken with regard to this area is to leave it alone." They cautioned that "even planners must sometimes learn not to 'improve' on nature." The dictum thus laid down is accepted by many conservationists and environmental planners, but not by all. Its contrary—a belief that raw nature can often, by human standards, be enhanced—was in fact the guiding principle in most of the EUDP designs. In any event, none of the careful work the Warnecke study proposed, intended to touch the wilderness lightly, has been accomplished, and at least the Makena end of the study area seems about to receive a heavy development hand. A thousand-acre development of luxury residential and resort facilities is proposed by Seiku Fudusan Co. of Japan, which, because it promises to provide jobs, includes among its advocates a number of Makena residents and the ILWU.

The second point of the triangle of studies on Maui was in the town of Wailuku—aimed specifically at the county's civic center, which is located there. The Wailuku area had developed as the center of commercial activity on Maui after the decline of the whaling industry and the increase in plantation agriculture. The adjacent community of Kahului, originally a settlement on the breakwater of Wailuku's harbor, had outstripped its sister town in the later years of the nineteenth century, controlling as it did the seaport (and, in time, the airport). Wailuku thus was a rather quiet county seat

and adjunct to a growing business community at the time the
EUDP studies were made. It was, moreover, repository of
several historic structures and residence of some seven thousand people, in itself facing growth as the public service
center of an expanding island economy.

For some decades Maui had lost population as agriculture
became mechanized. In the 1960s and 1970s, however, the
increase in tourist activities brought people and prosperity
back to the island. Government's duties (and payroll) began
to increase. The first public building in Wailuku had been a
courthouse built in the early years of this century (still standing), and others had been added through the years until seven
government structures were spread out along the town's central High Street. Now a new county office building was being
planned—with no urban design in mind.

High Street is the Wailuku end of the road that crosses the
island's neck from the other coast. In the town, all the public
structures are on the north side of the street. On its south
side are several well-preserved older buildings: a coral-block
church built in 1835 and named for Kaahumanu, two early
mission houses, and a large plantation manager's home put
up before the end of the century. Past this cluster of landmarks High Street stops and one must choose to go to the
right, toward Kahului, or to the left, toward the spectacular
needle peak of Iao ("cloud supreme") where a park now
provides a flowery viewpoint for the green-covered punctua-
tion at the rise of the mountains.

The design that the Warnecke planners proposed had two
main objectives. One was to give a sense of cohesiveness to
the community as a whole—integrating government, commercial, and residential areas while keeping for each a sense of
identity and specifically improving circulation through the
town so that island traffic would not have to split the community core in two. The other aim was simply to suggest a
better grouping for the civic center buildings. A design was
proposed, then, bringing together the disparate landmarks
around a series of plazas, some green, some paved, planned
for their visual as well as their functional impact. High Street

was to be closed for vehicular traffic at the town center and planted for pedestrian movement. Traffic would be bypassed around an enlarged civic-cultural nucleus.

Details of the design are not important now. None of it was ever adopted. Neither the town's residents nor their officials were interested in the least with planning principles or nuances of design. The county building went ahead as originally intended. The "special committee of interested citizens" the report suggested be formed to oversee future development was never organized. Wailuku's people were satisfied to let things happen as they would outside their own homes, screened from each other and the rest of the community by Hawaii's lush verdure.

The third attempt of the Warnecke planners to suggest preservation and enhancement of a Maui environment was in the town of Lahaina. Favorite residence of Kamehameha I, early missionary settlement, capital of the kingdom from 1820 to 1845, popular port for shore-hungry crews of whaling ships, later lying outside the path of new development, Lahaina remained far into the twentieth century a quiet, unspoiled shelter for native traditions. Then in the 1960s Amfac, Inc., descendant of the Big Five firm of American Factors, Ltd., began development just north of the town at Kaanapali Beach, a magnificent broad span of white sand sloping gently into clear azure waters.

As Amfac's modest early plans expanded to a long strip of large hotels at Kaanapali and as other beaches farther on began to be built up, the fate of Lahaina was sealed. Inevitably its streets were overrun with boutiques and restaurants. The broad-verandaed Pioneer Inn on the harbor, built in 1912, was "improved" by an imitative addition; plans were drawn for a new twelve-story hotel on the waterfront close by; a large shopping center laid down its asphalt parking spaces as condominiums began to appear on the fringes of town and subdivisions sprouted on the hills behind.

There was no lack of effort to restore and preserve the many structures of earlier periods—churches, schools and homes of the missions, a fort, a printing press, a courthouse,

numerous plantation buildings. A historic district was set
aside, piecemeal restoration of a number of places was
begun, and the county made use of a federal grant to study
future development. Yet rapid expansion and modern
"progress" were inevitable. As the EUDP report pointed
out, property values were rising in close ratio to the volume
of new nearby construction and landowners were itching to
realize the gains that more intensive development in the town
itself would bring.

The Warnecke firm made no attempt to *design* Lahaina, as
George Walters had tried to design Hilo. Its aims were more
modest: simply to study what made the old community tick,
to analyze its characteristics and qualities so as to provide a
design guide for future growth. It was concerned with "preservation and evolution of traditional elements peculiar to
Lahaina" (roofs, facades, verandas, balconies, door and
window types). Thus another of Hawaii's perennial problems
was added to the many being considered in the EUDP
studies: whether respected traditions of the past could be
preserved as values changed in the present.

It may be unfair to say that this study had no long-range
benefits. Perhaps some of the shop-owners along Front
Street, modernizing their old false-gable roofs, battened
facades, and overhanging balconies, gained design inspiration
from the Warnecke researchers. None of the proposals for
circulation through the town or for terraces, parks, and
plazas have been used, however. Lahaina is still fighting
growth's manifestations in greater population and taller
buildings, each year with a bit less success. The lesson seems
to be that conservation of a culture and its physical tokens, if
it is at all possible in the face of change, must come from
values still deeply held, not through imposed details of
design.

Invitations to Design Kauai

The planning firm of Donald Wolbrink & Associates was
given the assignment to make design studies of two different

environments on the island of Kauai, quite separate in character although closely related in distance.[21] One was the town
of Koloa, where Ladd & Company had started Hawaii's
earliest sugarcane plantation, located several miles inland
from the other part of the study, Poipu Beach, where two
miles of sandy shore stretch along the coast. Koloa is still a
plantation town. Occupied mostly by descendants of the
workers who were located there in the nineteenth century, it
struggles to keep its identity in the face of declining economic
support from the cane fields. Poipu Beach is a popular
tourist attraction. Reached through Koloa, it tries to maintain its attractiveness in the face of diffusive development.
Each was bound to interact on the other and any design plan
for the area would have to include both.

Koloa had reached its low point about 1960, after Grove
Farm Company, the present owner-operator of the plantation, made clear its decision to plan for development of its
lands. Younger people were leaving, jobs were in jeopardy,
local stores were losing business to more distant but more
modern shopping centers, the movie house was closed from
lack of patronage—and the discouraged residents watched
increasing numbers of strangers drive past to Poipu Beach
hotels. But the fruits of tourism soon spread, and some of
Poipu's new prosperity reached Koloa. Home building
perked up. Townspeople got jobs in the new waterfront
resorts. A bank and a new grocery store opened. It was an
ambiguous future, though, that Koloa was facing at the time
the Wolbrink firm undertook to study its design potentials.
Just two things seemed certain: the growing of sugarcane
in the area would decrease and the construction of hotels
would accelerate: all three of the large local landowners had
prepared plans making that future obvious. What would
happen to the old town of Koloa and its people was not at
all clear in any of those plans, however.

Poipu, as a town, is a small settlement; only its beach
gives it importance. A small stream coming down from the
slopes of the island's largest peak, Waialeale, empties into
the sea there, and during early plantation days its estuary

provided the only "harbor" along this coast. A boat landing, long ago cut into the rocks at the stream's mouth, is used today only by pleasure craft. For rest and recreation the beach is perfect: it has an almost ideal climate, protected from the trade winds, with little rainfall; it enjoys a romantic, scenic mountain backdrop. Until a few years before the EUDP studies the only buildings in Poipu were a few old homes from earlier times and some scattered beach houses belonging to Koloa people.

During the 1960s, however, tourism discovered Poipu's charms. Several small hotels were placed along the rocky coast to the west of the stream and a very pleasant cottage-type resort was built on Poipu Beach itself. Then one after another new hotels of various sizes and differing quality began to appear. The Sheraton chain put up a rambling complex (later sold to Japanese interests) and the boom was on. By 1968, when Wolbrink began his study, there were about five hundred hotel rooms in or around Poipu. At least that many more were planned.

The Koloa-Poipu district, including the two target areas, offered many invitations for design. The Wolbrink firm thoroughly inventoried the region and listed seventy-two items that called for design attention—ranging from a careless county dump to unattended Polynesian artifacts, including cinder cones, sand dunes, the bay and its beaches, not too well tended, as well as a pleasant stream almost unnoticed in Koloa, the mill, a white church, and two brightly hued temples. Some situations needed correction, some resources required protection, some assets wanted improvement.

How to turn this inventory into a unified design? Other plans, public and private, had been inclined to ignore older values that remained and had concentrated on future potential. The state's general plan encouraged further hotel development in the Koloa-Poipu area generally; its land use plan classified the pahoehoe lava stretch between Koloa and Poipu as urban land, ready to be built upon. On the other hand, the county's general plan showed considerable public park space along the shore and suggested a policy of slowed growth for the entire region. The plans that had been prepared by private landowners (Grove Farm Company, McBride Sugar Company, the Knudson Trust Estate) had no relation to one another but in combination would pretty well develop the whole Koloa-Poipu region.

Three designs were drawn by the Wolbrink firm, in broad general form but with careful heed paid to all seventy-two of the inventoried items. One, an overall plan for the region, concentrated first on access to the area and circulation through it, proposing to make the main road a truly scenic corridor from which the landmarks, improved where necessary, would be visible and accessible to the traveler. Between Koloa and Poipu the road would pass through open lands, developed only for outdoor recreation, so that both town and beach might retain the qualities that distinguish them.

A design plan for Poipu aimed to provide for both local people and visitors "a pleasant, comfortable, and intimate environment in scale with its small beaches and gentle topographic change." Its character was recognized to be that of a seaside resort, but it would be carefully designed as a linear community that would include hotels, apartments, and individual homes.

Koloa, in the center of the study area, would remain "surrounded by green . . . the visual and functional core for the people who call the region 'home'," the third plan indicated. The character of the town would be kept rural by retaining its broadly open central space, preserving the church and temples, finding green patches along the shores of the stream, and surrounding all this with well-defined, carefully limited residential neighborhoods.

The EUDP critic-commentators rather liked this project and had high hopes for its success. It was unquestionably the most conscientiously detailed of all the studies. Temko commented on the fact that the "many relatively small-scaled problems" were "seen always within a larger context,"[22] although Eckbo worried that the solutions for so many issues "might not add up to a cohesive design."[23] Temko wondered, as he had with regard to other reports, whether sociocultural problems had been sufficiently considered. He asked: "Who are the people in these communities . . . in what ways are they and their communities changing . . . what are now (and what will be in the future) their cultural relations to one another and to visitors from the mainland?"[24] The question he raised was essentially whether a "rural" or a "Hawaiian" way of life can continue to exist within a tourist destination area.

Both critics were particularly impressed with the concluding sections of the report, which tabulated and characterized the "key design issues" the study had uncovered and then went on to discuss possible resolutions of these problems. Like most of the other reports, this one insisted that any design, to be successfully implemented, "must begin with a basic understanding and agreement on the program objectives."[25] Knowing seventy-two specific problems, the planners admitted, is not enough.

In Koloa-Poipu, as in the other areas studied, very little of the proposed design was carried out. Additional hotels have been built haphazardly along the shore (the county planning commission recommended reducing the height of one proposed waterfront hotel but voiced no opinion on the wisdom of building at *any* height on that site), public parks and public beach access are still missing, and most of the landmarks remain inaccessible and unseen. Grove Farm is "out of the sugar business," as an economic report put it, and Koloa has passed from despondency to depression. The landowners are slowly beginning to implement their own unrelated development plans.

The Lesson of EUDP

The EUDP program accomplished two important things. First, it showed skillfully that it was *possible* in Hawaii in

1968, on all the islands, at various scales, to design well a fusion of man-made and natural environments, to preserve and enhance, to reconcile, to correlate. But then it showed that under existing conditions it was not *probable* that such designs could be realized. From these two conclusions it seems as though a third judgment should result: how the *possible* designs could have become *probable*. The successes of EUDP should be helpful as a means of understanding its failures so as to increase its value.

Wolbrink's tabulation of the key issues in his report served a useful purpose by indicating the cardinal questions for which public policies were needed. In his study and the others, three basic design issues had arisen continually: they were questions of best land uses (design of *purpose*), questions of best urban arrangement (design of *form*), and questions about the relationship and the junction of natural and man-made elements (design of *contact*). At building-design scale these are familiar problems to an architect: best use of site qualities, best ordering of building functions, best union of place and purpose, site and structure. In the course of their studies it had become clear to the EUDP designers that at urban-design scale these issues can be met only when firm public policies are supported by effective legislation. Hence they tended to conclude, perhaps too quickly, that more "controls" were needed.

Wolbrink, for one, listed a number of kinds of legislated control that seemed necessary, and his tabulation was not greatly different from those of the others who undertook similar reviews. It ranged from stricter land use designations to the governance of building heights, devlepment densities, land coverage, and landscaping to setbacks on sites and even to signs on structures. But asking simply for legal sanctions to support a proposed design is not enough, as these designers knew. Hawaii's state and county governments already have legislation giving them considerable control over the way land is used. If more decrees were the only need, they could easily enough be attained; handbooks of rules and regulations clutter the desks of government administrators. Regulatory policies—statutes which place under the aegis of a government agency decisions that would otherwise be made by individual citizens—are effective only when they result from broad popular demand or, at the least, find wide public concurrence. Even then, legislated controls may be ineffective—and are always revocable.

At any rate, the basic design problems these designers were trying to solve—problems of land use, development design, circulation through and connections between the varying environments—were made difficult by two characteristics of Hawaii's lands which no additional controls were likely to change. One of these conditions was individuality of land ownership; the other was fluctuation of land use. The decision made way back in the 1840s that anyone could own, sell, and buy land in Hawaii had so splintered the guardianship of land and so disunited decisions about its best uses that coordinated planning and design faced tremendous odds. And then the 1964 Land Use Law had clearly not succeeded in stabilizing broad land uses according to suitability, as it had intended. Whether the design problem was that of a road, a city, or a wilderness beach, the designer knew that farmland might unpredictably become a suburb or a resort and a conservation reserve might arbitrarily be turned to some active urban purpose. Under these circumstances, land use planning is uncertain and environmental design is vain.

If this were a how-to-do-it essay rather than a how-it-was-done critique, it might prescribe a procedure for successful urban design by drawing lessons from the difficulties that EUDP encountered. The first admonition to future designers would probably be to help persuade the general populace to concern itself about planning and design, for its own good, for the public benefit, as policy guide to its political leaders. For architects and planners this would mean involvement in community activities to a greater degree than many of them want—to an extent that might seem to distract them from their true professional functions. For the public, it would mean new attention to problems usually ignored or considered only subjectively.

The second counsel might also be unpalatable to design-centered architects and plan-oriented planners: it would be to help public administrators look beyond the wishes of those supporters with the greatest financial and political clout, help them find out their total constituency's desires about land uses, and then help them form these desires into public policies. Repellent as many planners and designers find such political activism, some have tackled it willingly and at times effectively. Disinclined as most politicians are to set policies in the public interest, some of them, these days, are finding the task intriguing and rewarding.

A third suggestion would be that both professional advice and public care should be given to the drafting of those controls—rules and regulations resulting from such policies as might be adopted—which designers consider so essential. If poorly drawn, they can be more detrimental than helpful. A further bit of advice in this regard might be: Never count on controls to produce good design. Like zoning ordinances, design controls are at best negatively useful; they explain what must *not* be done and leave it up to designer and client to suggest what *should* be done.

The final lesson from EUDP, then, is that effective urban design is produced by effective urban designers. If effectiveness includes participation in public affairs and involvement in political action, it also calls for technical competence and informed judgment. For the professional, there is a large how-to literature on urban design; for the public and those it elects to office, there is a growing body of information and advice on the subject.

In a professional sense, production of a satisfactory comprehensive design for Honolulu's ragged waterfront or Hilo's random urban form requires special skills—wider in scope than the design of a building, but more particularized than the general planning of a city. Some of the EUDP projects suffered from too broad a vision (Collins' study of the Kona

coast, perhaps) while others lost their full value by too close
attention to details (Wolbrink, possibly, with Poipu-Koloa's
seventy-two pinpointed design issues).

Scale is an ever-present problem in urban design. A concerned citizen, whether a designer-planner or a layman in
that field, must decide at what scale of activity involvement
is likely to have some success. Does a city's design improve
when small advances are made (human-scale achievements,
some call them)—like the construction of a public building or
the setting aside of some well-arranged public space? Or
must one wait for the larger advance—the improvement of a
whole waterfront, the design of an entire town, even the
finding of better form and function in a downtown, a Kakaako, a Waikiki—before one can be sure that something
worthwhile has been accomplished?

The EUDP project seems to give us conflicting testimony
in this respect. It can be argued that it was better to try for
the big benefit, as Walters did in urging that Hilo become a
flowered city, but it can also be claimed that dividing Honolulu's waterfront into five shorter, almost unrelated parts
with many minor problems made some smaller achievements
more possible. The larger aims were seldom realized, but
then neither were many of the less ambitious objectives
reached. Probably the most useful advice is to be happy with
small profits when they can be made but to relate them always to a larger context—perhaps a lot of them can be added
up to greater gains. Maybe, in that way, the system of unrelated, inconsistent land use decisions can be cheated for a
time while the public and its designers wait for firm public
policies. If a decent design for a building in Honolulu's civic
center, an extension of Ala Moana Park, a lower-rise hotel
on the Poipu shore, a preserved landmark at Lahaina can be
achieved, these benefits should not be declined. Because no
one, just now, even with national, state, and county sponsorship, seems to be able to improve the overall design of
Honolulu or Hilo or Wailuku or Makena. The achievement
of satisfactory environmental and urban designs, as well as

success in drawing and following satisfactory environmental and urban plans, will require radical revisions, once again, in our attitudes toward the land. What those revisions might involve is the subject of the next chapter.

chapter 14

Closing the Options

AT the conclusion of this investigation into the treatment of the lands of Hawaii, some supposition about their future seems called for. Hawaii has not lacked forecasts of what might come—from devotees of conservation and from advocates of growth. Most of it has been extravagant guesswork, in the interest of one prejudice or another, because few techniques have been developed for visualizing far-distant goals and laying plans to reach them. If there is confusion about methods of short-range planning, there is complete confoundment about long-long-range future planning.

Nonetheless, prognostications into the future became fashionable in the 1960s and 1970s, as scholars in many fields started to study the implications of two directions humankind was taking: the frightening prospects of continued exponential growth, on the one hand, and the enticing possibilities of greater mastery of technology, on the other. As the literature of futurism mounted, as study of the future rose in stature to the rank of a recognized discipline, as conferences and commissions on The Year 2000 met in many places from Washington to Oslo to Tokyo, Hawaii was caught up in the movement. In 1969 funds were appropriated for a governor's conference on The Year 2000 in Honolulu also. After a great deal of preliminary work and talk, the conference was held the following year, attended by several hundred people willing to spend three days discussing alternative possibilities for the future of the islands—alternatives, not absolutes, because positing alternative futures is the only method that has so far been devised for planning thirty years or so ahead.[1]

In fact, very little "planning" of future destinies has been attempted in the field of futuristics; most of the work has been prognostication of several separate fates that may lie before us, assuming that one or another is likely. The two techniques that most futurist studies employ are assumption of *alternative futures* and construction of *scenarios*. Their use has seemed necessary because of the evident difficulty in fixing positive goals and objectives for any point in time more than fifteen or twenty years forward. (Some students of the subject think ten or twelve years is the limit.) Human values have changed from age to age in the past, in somewhat unpredictable ways. Now values, and therefore social goals, are changing at ever-increasing rates, in ever-shortening time spans—no longer in eras or centuries, but by generations. Scientific knowledge, inventions and discoveries of major significance, even the application of innovative technologies, also come faster and faster.

Alternative futures are guesses at objectives that may be valid later in time, as distinguished from the targets that a short-range planner sets up with some certainty. They may be informed guesses with differing degrees of information, and they may be creative guesses with varying amounts of imagination, but they are never sure—they are not plans. Scenarios are hypothetical stories about the sequence of events that may lead to those alternative futures. It is a fascinating game that the futurists play. And it has important potentials. It could help us prepare for change by having some foreknowledge of what the future may hold, and it should help us control the process of change to our advantage. However, the game is usually played as a test of skill in forecasting.

One early work in the field, Herman Kahn and Anthony J.

Weiner's *The Year 2000*, prided itself in developing "surprise-free" projections (with certain "canonical variations" as escape valves) from a study of the way things have been going for a long time—what they called "long-term multifold trends." Interest in their methodology waned some years later when it was realized they had overlooked depletion of resources—energy sources as well as arable land—in their calculation of long-term trends. Other futurists of that period speculated on the speed of change rather than its nature. Literature in the field was replete with charts and graphs showing upward-swooping elliptical curves, and Alvin Toffler wrote of impending social impacts in his best-selling *Future Shock*.

Later prognosticators began paying more attention to the possibility of *choice* among future alternatives. Socioeconomist Robert Theobold wrote and taught a hortatory thesis that a revolutionary "alternative future for America" could be "the new society we must create."[2] John McHale, who spoke in Hawaii on several occasions, was articulate in his *Future of the Future* about "the potential capacity of human beings to determine their own futures."[3] Yehezkel Dror, political scientist, wrote about the "tension and even contradiction" between prophecy and planning, but he offered little in the way of solutions.[4] Rene Dubos, research biologist, spoke of "willed futures"; yet willing a future is not charting a way to reach it.

Difficult as the process of long-long-range planning is, different as it may be from conventional planning methods, it need not be an impossible technique. The first step, clearly, is to make a tentative selection among the alternative goals that have been imagined. Moves can then be made toward the chosen objective until changing values or other unpredictable events (perhaps diminishing resources) require a change in direction. Then new alternatives can be considered and a new course set. Some futurists compare the process to climbing to a plateau, resting, assessing where one is and where one is heading, and then starting on again, perhaps toward a changed objective.[5] It is a precarious process, to be sure, one requiring flexibility of mind and of movement and great care not to block, by present action, a future direction that might become desirable.

Some of these problems were explained to the attendants at the conference in Honolulu, who were indoctrinated in the ongoing techniques of futuristics by local doctrinaires and a battery of invited speakers. But in the end prophecy was more appealing than planning. Alternative isolated futures dreamed for Hawaii and scenarios imagined to reach them were by and large the content of the meetings. The editors of a book titled *Hawaii 2000,* based on the proceedings of the conference, recognized that what had emerged was a "fragmented picture of Hawaii's future" lacking any "precisely planned forward-action programs."[6]

The conference was by no means fruitless, however. A continuing state commission on futures was established as a sort of watchdog for long-range implications in current events. Several excellent papers were prepared by task forces during the preconference and final meetings. (Some ignored the mandate to seek "alternative holistic scenarios,"[7] as John McHale put it in a triple-barreled cliché, enjoying instead some old-fashioned exhortation.)

The future of Hawaii's lands was discussed in a number of the sessions, including those on the economy, housing and transportation, and science and technology, but most importantly by the task force assigned the subject of the natural environment. Headed by planner Walter Collins, the group speculated on alternative ways the land surface of the islands might be treated in the far future.[8] There was agreement on the newly learned truths of futurism: that values were changing rapidly, that future options should not be blocked by present actions, that imagination must be given full play in dreaming of futures. (It was fancied, for instance, that existing urban concentrations, even Honolulu, might be relocated away from the shores to "selected valleys, where self-contained communities in compact vertical structures would line the sides" and "the valley floors would remain as great natural parks.")[9]

It was the scenario game, played with zeal by task force members who included land estate trustees, developers, and other businessmen as well as architects and planners. No commitments needed to be made; these were prognoses, not plans. But quite surprisingly, out of the task force meetings came a reasoned bit of futures planning to which all seemed to subscribe. It was a farsighted scheme for public control and management of the physical environment: "pooling of private and public lands, together with offshore waters and air rights, into custody of a central trust."[10] The pragmatic members of the task force still felt safe, even as they gave birth to this creative idea; they were writing a scenario, composing fiction. Since even preparation of a long-range statewide land use plan was unlikely, they could be confident that schemes for ways to make it work were but pleasant fantasies. Yet somehow there was a real ring to the words describing this possible alternative, which one senses today in reading them.

Disappointed that the task forces at the conference had tended toward single-aimed recommendations rather than alternative-goaled speculations, the editors of *Hawaii 2000*— George Chaplin, editor of the *Honolulu Advertiser* and chairman of the conference, and Glenn Paige, political science professor—included some alternative-futures dreams of their own in the book: a restored Hawaii based on principles and precepts of the early Hawaiian people; a "coconut republic" where all could bask in the tropical sun; an "ecological commonwealth" centered around "experimental environmental symbiosis"; an Ideal American State where all the traditional dreams come true, from liberty to lavish living; a battlefield for struggle of the oppressed against the entrenched, with the scenario describing final victory for an enlightened "collective leadership"; an experimental society where all kinds of innovative, even revolutionary, social, political, technical ideas would be "nurtured and tested."[11]

Many fancied futures have been suggested for Hawaii since that time. John McHale, in a later talk added his story line: a "Pacific Geneva" which would be a research and communication center attracting "a new kind of tourism."[12] John Young, a management consultant, saw along with Fred Smith that Hawaii could become "the locus of the Pacific" in commerce, finance, and communication.[13] Yet half a dozen years after Governor Burns' conference, the several study groups appointed by his successor, Governor Ariyoshi, had a more mundane vision of a future Hawaii: it would remain a haven for land developers, these pragmatists predicted, bolstered by outside capital, with tourism of the traditional type its top industry.

Several lessons had been learned, though, from the professional futurists who had guided the 1969 conference—primarily the idea of developing alternatives in planning or even in *looking* ahead. From that time on, scarcely any kind of report called for by the state or the counties or, for that matter, by private organizations dared appear without describing alternative choices. Stewart Udall's open-space plan began by hypothesizing two possible Year 2000 futures for Hawaii's lands: Hawaii I, which would result from continuation of long-term trends, and Hawaii II, which would come about if an open-space plan were adopted. The state's general-plan revision program included four growth alternatives to choose from. The Honolulu City and County general-plan revision program produced several alternative development plans for Oahu. At about the same time the Oahu Development Conference analyzed four alternative urban growth "strategies."[14] The Honolulu Chamber of Commerce and the state cosponsored a study of alternative economic futures. The state's Department of Planning and Economic Development studied the comparative environmental and economic effects of three alternative development patterns for the central agricultural plains of Oahu, and the Hawaii Environmental Simulation Laboratory at the state university analyzed the long-term effects of three alternative futures for the Kaneohe Bay area on Oahu's windward coast.[15]

The list could go on and on. A mass of comparative data was thus collected which could have guided administrative heads and legislators at state and county levels in their decision making. It did not. The game of constructing scenarios into the future ended when a printed document was submitted. The idea of analyzing alternatives was not at all new to the planning profession: every planner knows that even to achieve short-term objectives it is wise to examine different ways to reach them—but every planner also knows that choices must be made among the possible routes and some incremental forward movement begun. Now, however, there was an avid wish in the community to see alternatives but an unwillingness to choose among them.

One reason for inaction could have been another lesson learned from futurism: that distant goals may not remain the same and that care must be taken not to block future choices of other options. This stricture is easy to twist into a reason to protect the status quo, to let current trends continue until an inevitable change in values corrects things. No present move will block future options if no move is made. And with no effort on our part, everyone has been told by the futurists, change is sure to be soon and sharp.

The game of alternative futures gives another excuse for inaction. One alternative offered in all the many reports called for in Hawaii in the 1960s and 1970s was to let present practices continue. Udall called his Hawaii I scenario "continuation of present trends." Shelley Mark, in the *Growth Policies Plan* he prepared for the state, described his Plan I as "continuation of existing policies." Intended as a kind of control factor, from which other options differ in some manner, this in itself becomes an alternative future—invariably the one which those who dread change will choose. And when no other choice is formally made, when inaction continues in the community as all the alternatives are studied without any apparent selection, a decision is in fact being

made: the alternative to "continue existing policies" has
ineluctably been chosen.

As successive sessions of the state legislature passed time in
the new capitol building in the 1970s without any conclusive
action being taken to mend flaws in the Land Use Law, to
curb the arbitrary reclassifications of the Land Use Commission, to give teeth to the environmental protection policies
that had been adopted, to set up an effective planning process, it became clear that this was a conscious choice among
alternatives. Hawaii's indecision makers were not stupid.
They knew perfectly well which future for Hawaii's lands
they were selecting: the one that present trends would produce.

An Ecosystem under Pressure

It seems, then, that two questions have to be posed about the
future of Hawaii's lands. One would ask: what will be their
probable fate? The answer would be in the nature of prediction or prognostication, based largely on extrapolation of
past and present trends into the times ahead. Since there is
no indication that any alternative future except continuation
of present trends will be chosen (by the elected officials who
form government's administration, by the legislature or
county councils where policies are formed and laws enacted,
or by a large enough proportion of the electorate which
places these political figures in office and since those trends,
as the reading of any daily newspaper attests, are a prolongation of the building on open land which brought about the
Land Use Law in 1964 and continued after the law was
passed (immediately with Mililani Town on Oahu, later with
Kaanapali Beach on Maui, a few years ago at Princeville on
Kauai's Hanalei Bay, day after tomorrow at some sunny spot
on the Big Island's south Kohala coast), the prediction seems
obvious. It is for more of the same.

Yet there are many people living in the islands who are not
ready to accept that apparent inevitability. It is not, to them,

a reasonable lot for the lands of Hawaii, which they love for qualities far greater, they think, than sales and rental value. They continue to look for answers to the second question: what *could* be the destiny of Hawaii's lands? What they want is not a prediction, but something more in the nature of a prescription. To prescribe is to advise, and advice in land matters is not welcome. Prescriptions offered by respectable professionals like medical doctors are generally followed, but very few persons in the newer professional field of land management are that highly regarded. Certainly the injunctions of those experts who have traveled to Hawaii to advise its people and their political leaders have not been observed. And yet, having reviewed the story of the lands of Hawaii from Polynesian times until now, having seen how their ownership has changed hands, having examined the various ways those lands have been used and the several ways they have been valued, having considered the occasional attempts, usually unsuccessful, to set policies, draw plans, and devise designs for their handling, one should have learned something. One should be able to offer advice. Perhaps the question should not be what *could* happen (that still seems to call for alternatives, with all their indecision) but what *should* happen. Better to ask for a definite remedy.

More than one medication may be needed to cure a malady, however. In this case, first, there is a quantitative question: in what *degree*, to what *extent,* should Hawaii's land surface be subjected to human encroachment? The matter of how heavily Hawaii's lands should be loaded is being studied with deliberation, and without much public or political attention, as a result of the environmental policy act passed by the state legislature in 1974. Obviously, each different microenvironment has its own "carrying capacity," which it is possible but not easy to determine. Certainly the investigations under way by state agencies, the work of the university's Environmental Simulation Laboratory, and continuance by a number of people of the efforts to quantify costs and benefits of urbanization (begun in the state's Central Oahu Planning Study and discussed in a larger context in the university's conference on Public Costs of Private Development) must be taken seriously, encouraged, directed firmly, and pursued with vigor.

Environmental overloads in a human society are caused by one major factor: uncontrolled population. The state of Hawaii—through its people, in its politics, with its policies—will have to stop pussyfooting on this issue. No prognostication can foresee and no scenario can invent a future where land is handled with respect if the number of people who must use it is not limited. Limited, not slowed. To slow population growth is merely to moderate its continuing increase. To limit it, on the other hand, is to set bounds to its final measure. Hawaii's land surface is limited in a degree which can be determined; the population that the state can care for, then, must have a limit which can also be computed.

These statements can be qualified, of course. Calculations of the extent of the islands' lands include valleys and mountains; arable stretches and arid; sandy beaches and rocky coasts; green swards and black crusts. Thus there can be endless arguments over the limits to *usable* land for its many uses. Further, an environment's point of overload can arbitrarily be placed high or low by changing certain factors in the equation. For instance, the current disputes among behavioral scientists about desirable urban densities[16] have made it fashionable to point to Hong Kong (the example used to be the city of New York) as an environment which carries a weight of human habitation far in excess of Hawaii's likelihood for many years. The fact that Hong Kong, a *continental* island quite close to a large land mass, is quite different in character from Hawaii's *mid-ocean* islands is conveniently forgotten.

Too often, unfortunately, these qualifications are quibbles. They are evasions of important issues, cavils over essential truths, of the kind that are common whenever hard decisions have to be made. The most bothersome of these purposeful equivocations should be, really, the easiest to overcome. It is the one that pokes fun at the idea of "ecological damage" occurring as population increases. This is supposed to be an argument by long-haired naturalists and of no real concern to practical businessmen. The jibes are weaker, however, as ecology becomes a better-understood word in quite common parlance. Recently the study of particular problems within *island* ecologies has come to be an important field in itself, and a special concern is now being manifested for *Pacific* island ecosystems. That this aspect of the future of the Hawaiian island group has been overlooked locally, except by a few scholars, that it has not been an integral part of commission studies and legislative discussions about problems of the land of Hawaii (and the sea and the air), is quite incredible.

It may be (one can charitably assume) that commissioners and legislators, by and large, do not understand the impact of *any* ecosystem. Perhaps they do not realize that it means the interactions of all individual things within an environment, living and not living, and that it should, therefore, be our most important consideration.[17] Perhaps they do not much care that there are stable ecosystems, firm and steady, and unstable ones, likely to deteriorate—with the unstable instances (increasing, these days) being "at the root of most of the economic loss, political disturbance, and social unrest in the world," as one scholar has put it. They should worry, however, at the disturbing fact that in island economies like Hawaii's, ecosystems are more easily upset than they are on the major continents. The reasons are not difficult to understand.

The ecosystems of the various Pacific islands—quite different from one another in many ways (as are the high-mountain, low-atoll, and reef-lagoon islands themselves in physical character)—are alike in that they have a reasonably common history of major disturbances to their stability through intrusions from outside the Pacific regions. These interferences have been harmful in several ways. For one, until very recently most of the contacts have been between native ecosystems depending on elementary technologies and imported systems based on sophisticated technologies: "societies that only yesterday were in the Stone Age precipitously catapulted into the Nuclear Age."[18] Certain islands seem to have adapted to this violent change more easily than others; to some it has been disastrous. The reasons for the violence of the impacts are apparently many. At times the major factor has been importation of flora and fauna: cattle trampling indigenous herbs and shrubs, for instance. At other times people have been the force of drastic physical change, destroying forests and letting shorelands erode.[19] And then there were the violent human contacts between natives and newcomers— interactions within the ecosystems at the highest level of living things—resulting in the kinds of shock that decimated the Hawaiian people. Some scientists explain this as importation of a continental economy and ecology familiar with worldwide horizons to a small group of midocean lands with insular horizons. Island ecologies are "circumscribed and circular," as one says;[20] and the importers, in many cases still based back home, are apt to be "far removed from the consequences" of their imports.[21] The fact that this characterization applies so aptly to the invasion of the billion-dollar tourist industry to Hawaii and, less eagerly so far, to other Pacific island groups has not escaped the attention of experts at environmental protection.

Beyond the historic results of rapid change, however, the present effects on island ecologies of current development and the foreseeable impact of likely future trends are worrisome to serious scholars of the subject. Islands are microscopic land globs, different from continents in many respects—some of their qualities, such as equable climate, very easy to take, as any tourist knows. The major physical characteristics, of course, are separation from other land areas and limitation in size. These qualities affect the diversity of elements within the ecosystem, resulting in fewer species and less rivalry among them—until conditions are disturbed and exotics introduced—and limit the availability of natural resources—land, primarily, but also those resources on it and below it.

Most important, however, and most seldom recognized, is the tendency of an island ecology to become unstable when its accustomed isolation is destroyed.[22] Along with that characteristic there is a tendency to react to change more quickly, more violently, than is the case with a continental ecosystem. Limitation in dimension, quantity of resource, and specie stock apparently results in an island experiencing major reactions from even minor changes. "The buffering effects of great size and diversity are lacking," explains one authority.[23] Hence islands' microecological relationships must be guarded with particular care and the loads they are asked to carry must be strictly restricted. "Only so many people can find support on a given island," says anthropologist Roland Force, drawing a conclusion which would seem obvious if it were not so generally ignored.[24] In recent conferences this point has received especial attention, with Hawaii's Oahu held as the unwholesome example. It is, of course, the primary reason why densities which places like Hong Kong or New York City allow themselves could be totally destructive to the Bahamas or Tahiti or Hawaii. Yet on many ocean islands today the ecosystems are no longer stabilized but are in a process of continued growth—a growth in no way related to availability of resources. It is not difficult to arrive at the manifest answer to this part of the question. As a federal government demographer says: "No elaborate theoretical formulations are required to document the statement that rates of growth such as those that are now occurring cannot long continue in the finite worlds of island ecosystems."[25]

Necessarily, then, any responsible prescription for a healthy continuing life for the lands of Hawaii has to include the bitter pill that the state must set specific, strict limits to its population by every effective means, including control of inmigration. If it is unconstitutional, now, to prevent free movement of free people, then the Constitution will have to be changed. As there were once kapus forbidding certain personal associations among the Polynesian Hawaiians, there were social taboos and constitutional prohibitions preventing full civil rights for the later Americans. In law, at least, they have been removed. A short time ago it seemed impossible to attain completely equal rights for women in America; now no one is so sure. Social changes and shifts in values come on quite quickly these days, as the futurists warn. "The trend of modern court decisions shows a continuing enlargement of the scope of public purposes to meet the needs of a growing nation," writes a land law expert.[26] Those public purposes, one Supreme Court decision affirmed, include the making of a community "beautiful as well as healthy, spacious as well as clean, well-balanced as well as carefully patrolled."[27] When it is working toward a planned objective, a local society can fix bounds for its physical expansion, the courts have ruled. Governor Ariyoshi's argument for population control in his State of the State message—that newcomers are taking jobs from locals and adding to the relief rolls—is one that the courts are not likely to support in today's antidiscrimination mood (that, in fact, they have rejected in other instances). On the other hand, setting limits to population growth under a planned, nondiscriminatory program is no longer an inconceivable accomplishment.[28] Rather, in today's temper, misuse and possible destruction of natural resources is the unforgivable sin. What is inconceivable now is that the Supreme Court of the United States of America will rule, when the issue is properly raised, that its country's Pacific-archipelago state must commit ecological suicide.

There is also a qualitative aspect to the question: what should be the destiny of Hawaii's lands? It asks how this finite, ecologically fragile resource should be governed (managed, planned, designed) so that the islands will not form a dangerously unstable eco/economo/sociosystem. Assume that overload has been prevented. In what ways, then, can the people of Hawaii arrange for the use (or nonuse) of their lands to their (the people's and the lands') best advantage? This part of the question has been pretty well answered, at least by implication, in the preceding chapters.

First of all, it is essential to have, and utilize, an environmental plan—by definition, a plan for managing those conditions, circumstances, and physical surrounds that affect the members of Hawaii's ecosystem. Hawaii must stop playing political games with the planning process. No longer must planning be used as a means of granting favors, exerting power, and enjoying jobbery. Other states are guilty of this mischief, too, but somehow the island state, entering the union late, was quicker at adapting the tricks of political patronage (which many of the other states have outgrown) than learning the lessons of democratic leadership (which many of the other states are freshly undertaking).

As part of its move to develop a plan for guarding its environment, Hawaii should again take an advance position on land use planning. Instead of pretending confusion about the essential steps in what is known as general planning—that is, setting goals and determining ways to reach them in a defined jurisdiction—in order to avoid making a plan which might restrict profitable maneuvers, as the state legislature is doing, or in order to gain political power by controlling the making of plans, as Honolulu's city council has done, lawmakers must state clearly what has to be done, in sequence, and then do it. That would be a bold move only because it would be so easy. The bill that could have but never did become an act would only have to be retrieved from the capitol's trash baskets.[29] It says simply that the state will determine policies which its people want, the counties will develop plans which apply those policies to themselves, and then the state will bring the county plans together in a comprehensive plan for the entire state.

The physician making this prescription would have to assume, of course, that the patient had the common sense to care for his general health. The state would have to have an office of planning within the office of the governor; professional contact between state and county planning offices would have to be established; the state's Land Use Commission would have to be restricted to the function the law originally intended—a review of land classifications every five years, with the interim applications for self-serving changes eliminated.

Environmental planning embraces much more than physical arrangement. Important as it would be to have a land use plan emerge from the simplified planning process, an economic plan would also be essential. A *plan* for Hawaii's socioeconomic future would be quite different from the *assumptions* which have so far been made. It has been assumed that although the military and at least the remnants of a plantation agriculture would continue as important producers of revenues and jobs, tourism would grow until it became the main support for life on the islands. Beyond these easy assumptions, several tantalizing *hopes* have been held out from time to time for additional activities which might provide energy, locally, for a stable island ecosystem: oceanography, volcanology, forestry, and the raising of exportable plants among them. If carrying capacities are to be respected, however, the assumptions must be reexamined and the hopes must be made into plans.

Hawaii has, indeed, remarkable opportunities to advance the science and develop the practical potentials of oceanography: physical opportunities, obviously, through its location, and financial as well, with the federal government avid to excel internationally in this new field. It has a great chance to advance development as well as research in new energy sources. It has the best likelihood of any place to lead in the advancement of tropical agriculture. And there is always the possiblity of making the state a mid-Pacific communications center, as so many very intelligent people have suggested.

These occasions come to Hawaii precisely because of its ocean-island ecological characteristics. The sea, with so much to be drawn from it, surrounds the islands' sharp reefs deeply; the mountains still hold vital volcanic heat and power; the very qualities of weather have their practical uses. Nutrients and minerals from the ocean, energy from deep-water and thermal tapping, from movement of the constant winds, and from the perpetual sun, foods from the rich soil to guide others toward tropical growths which, some say, may be the salvation of a hungry world—many people in still-developing countries would consider these potentials alone a great boon, a god-given base on which to build a stable society. They would react in amazement to Hawaii's bland acceptance of easy answers—such as the state's ever greater dependence on the most recent foreign intrusion on its fragile ecology, the demonstrably destructive international tourist industry.

The *way* to handle the *what* of environmental load on the lands of Hawaii, then, is to make careful plans. Nothing very revolutionary about that, surely. No amendments to a national constitution are needed, simply changes in local political attitudes.

The Matter of Ownership

There would still be no assurance, however, that the new program would work well. Even with a limit set to the number of people who might make use of the islands' environments, in ways that were planned, there would remain the problem of making sure that the plans were carried out. The power lying in ownership of land, we have seen, can render the best-intentioned administrative controls useless. There must be, then, a human aspect to the remedy as well as the impersonal quantitative and qualitative components. It seems as though ways to manage land in the future must include proposals for change in land tenure. Hawaii has seen land ownership pass from king to monarchy, from Hawaiians to haoles, from government to individuals, from many to few. It has seen power over land's uses pass from single masters to many owners, to buyers and leasers, to statesmen and politicians, to speculators and developers. Which system has been best? Is there a better one?

The clear alternative to private ownership would seem to be public ownership. Through the largest part of human history land has not been a private commodity (not until Britain's Tenures Abolition Act of 1660, insofar as the western world is concerned),[30] but has been held by a group, family, tribe, or ruling authority. In the modern era, however, fee-simple private tenure has become so firmly entrenched in western mores, so completely accepted as part of capitalist values, even so thoroughly rooted in democratic principles (man, his property, his homely castle), that its rightfulness dare not be questioned. For centuries any alternative has been considered unrealistic, even radical.

So impressed were the early lawmakers in America with the sanctity of private ownership that they followed the lead of England's Magna Charta and in 1789 wrote its guarantee into the United States Constitution as the Fifth Amendment.[31] Since then, what has become known as the "taking clause" ("nor shall private property be taken for public use, without just compensation") has frightened most public policy planners away not only from any consideration of actual seizure but, until recently, even from public control of land-property's uses, in the fear that that too might be considered a kind of taking.[32] England some time ago resolved the issue of controls, at least, by legislation which set clear guidelines for determining when regulation becomes confiscation requiring payment. In the United States the solving of the taking issue has waited, rather, for the courts of law to face up to the economic, social, and, of course, legal problems involved in interpretation of the constitutional clause.

Liberalization of provisions for public acquisition of private land when a public need was indicated began as early as the passage in 1868 of the Fourteenth Amendment to the Constitution. This amendment reiterated the prohibition against the government's taking anyone's property "without due process of law," but it made no mention of compensation. The Supreme Court corrected that omission in a subsequent decision, however, and the issue lay quiet until the

middle of the twentieth century. During the 1950s two kinds
of government land acquisition, under new legislative programs, raised the question sharply and required the courts to
define more clearly the term "public use." First, expanded
public works activity (including, importantly, the federal
highway program) required a tremendous amount of urban,
suburban, and rural land for its implementation. Then the
federal urban renewal program, incepted in the Housing Act
of 1949, was based on public acquisition for redevelopment,
of degraded urban land.

The courts' decisions have been increasingly liberal in
tolerance of the public use justification of such taking. In
1952, Florida's Supreme Court said that it was "inconceivable that anyone would seriously contend that the acquisition
of real estate," for uses set forth in a redevelopment plan,
was for a "public use or purpose."[33] But in 1969 a Puerto
Rico court (upheld later by the U.S. Supreme Court) ruled
that private property could be taken—even for future,
unidentified public uses—if the acquisition was part of a
long-range planned program.[34] Obviously the change in attitudes that had taken place in that time was opening up even
further possibilities for public control over land's uses.

The most far-reaching expansion of the public-taking,
public-planning, public-use principle up to this time has been
a program known as land banking. A land bank, in these
terms, is a reserve of land acquired and held by a public
entity for future public use. (It was protest over such an acquisition that led to the 1969 Puerto Rico court decision.)
The purposes of land banking as it has been used are several.
Often the land has been held for a later public works program, when its price might have greatly increased. In many
cases land has been banked to check speculation and unreasonable increases in the cost of a community's urban real
estate. Increasingly, land banking is being used to control the
direction, rapidity, and quality of urban growth. If zoning
and subdivision regulation have failed to halt sprawl, public
securement of lands lying in the path of anticipated develop-

ment—with their gradual re-release into private hands conditioned on observance of a communitywide land use plan—is a drastic alternative which has often proved successful.

The ingredients of a successful land-banking program, then, have been preparation of a plan with sufficient validity to foresee directions of growth (so that the right land can be banked), consistent implementation of the plan (so that the banked land can be released for development at the right times, in the right places), and mandated observance of the plan (so that the land, when it is released, will be developed in the public interest).

The idea of banking land to assure its best future use goes back to the early years of the century, in some western countries, and at least to the 1940s in the United States.[35] The Netherlands started land banking in 1901, and now almost all its communities have land-bank programs of some sort. Israel has had a land-bank program for many years. Sweden and Denmark are no strangers to the concept; the eighteen fine towns surrounding Stockholm were planned and built on publicly banked land. England's new towns that ring London could not have been carried through without a long-time public holding of the essential lands.

In the United States there have been a number of minor instances of land banking: in Philadelphia for an industrial development program, in California for a long-range highway construction plan, in many cities, by now, for urban renewal purposes. So far there has been only one instance in American territory of a major banking program for the control of overall community development. In Puerto Rico, in 1961, a study made to analyze urban growth problems resulted in the establishment of the Puerto Rico Land Administration and the inception of a land acquisition, banking, and development program which has been operating with considerable success since.[36] At the least, a wild inflation in land costs has been drastically curbed and fervent urban sprawl which was filtering into San Juan's fringes has been led on more orderly courses. Its most ardent advocates regard Puerto Rico's experiment as a major breakthrough in land management techniques.[37]

It has taken a while for the idea of land banking to lose the somewhat startling aspect it had to Americans when their West Indian commonwealth, Puerto Rico, adopted it as policy, but now the concept has become quite respectable. The National Commission on Urban Problems in 1968 recommended that states acquire land in advance of development, with federal assistance, "to control the timing, location, type and scale of development."[38] The American Institute of Architects in 1972 issued a report urging the federal government to acquire immediately a million acres of land for future community development.[39] The Urban Land Growth and New Community Development Act of 1970, had it come to a vote and passed Congress, would have authorized a major government program of prior public land purchase.

There is nothing really radical about the way land banking is now conceived and has been used. It constitutes guardianship rather than confiscation; in time, under certain conditions, the land returns to private ownership. Almost always its ultimate use is for development; it is a means of *directing* growth, not preventing it. Legally, constitutionally, it is a sound practice; the criterion of public use is observed and just compensation is paid. "Within the traditions of property law," says one writer on land laws, "there is nothing particularly radical in visualizing land being owned by the sovereign and being channeled out to persons who would hold it only as long as they performed the requisite duties that went with the lands."[40] In feudal times, he points out, these duties were allegiance to the lord; in early Hawaii, he might have noted, they were support of the king; in modern America, they could perfectly well be observance of a community development plan.

Should the banking of at least parts of Hawaii's lands, to assure their best use in the public interest, become part of the prescription for their optimum future? Certainly the idea ought to be carefully considered. This is one of the most innovative directions that has yet developed for statewide land management. Hawaii, in its present predicament, would be very foolish to turn its back on land banking as a solution to the problems of preserving its islands' ecosystems. But Hawaii has special opportunities, which no other state has, to achieve a special kind of "public" control over its lands' treatment—at a greater scale of usage than even Stockholm achieved, for broader purposes than even Puerto Rico found. The policy that Hawaii might pursue, which has already seemed to a number of its people a worthy proposal, has been called land *pooling* rather than banking.

The procedure for pooling land in the public interest (and for the private benefit of most landowners) would begin with the formation of a public trust. This foundation would be governed by an elected board of trustees (quite separate from the government) nominated "from a cross section of the community . . . reflecting a broad range of skills," as some supporters of the concept have suggested.[41] If it was successful, the end result would the assemblage of all Hawaii's lands once again under singular control—to be used in the ways and for the purposes to which they are best suited. The moves to accomplish this end and the structure of its administration could take any one of many forms. To begin with, the one suggested in 1968 by the task force on the environment during the Governor's Conference on the Year 2000 might be reexamined. A good deal of careful thought was given to its composition, and it is a provocative scenario which could still be rewritten in a number of ways.

What was proposed by Walter Collins and his task force associates was that all land in the islands be consolidated into a publicly controlled foundation by various means, "with shares held proportionally by the contributing members, similar in manner to a mutual fund investment or a condominium." The land that had been pooled could be leased back to its original owners (or, presumably, to others, if prior owners did not wish to reassume it) for varying periods, with the leases requiring adherence to a state land-use plan. Income from the leases would form an investment pool which would provide dividends to the shareholders.

There will be enough arguments brought forward to show why this simple, direct idea would never work, so let us consider its advantages and the reasons why it could be *made* to work. First, as the task force pointed out, the very fact that land ownership is concentrated in Hawaii would be an advantage. The government-owned land and that held by the handful of principal landowners, including the trusts and estates (over 90 percent of the total) could be brought into the pool first—hopefully on a voluntary basis—immediately, if the will was there. Smaller holdings and the individual fee-simple parcels could be added later, when the scheme was working smoothly, by the process of eminent domain when that was necessary.

The big trusts would no longer have to worry about ways to get the most out of their holdings, as they do now (even foolishly putting good agricultural land into urban uses or searching for sometimes marginal production): the dividends produced for them by their former lands could continue to fulfill their commitments to beneficiaries. Land which the foundation determined should best be left undeveloped could remain that way. No one owner would suffer the financial consequences. Leasehold, with which Hawaii has long been familiar, not always happily, would become the only method to secure private land use. The leasing of land, however, would not work just to the advantage of the large landowners but would become an instrument for the use of land in the public interest. No longer would the thrust be toward "breaking up" the large estates, as it is now and has long been. It would be toward their further consolidation for the public good.

The land trust idea did not make much of a splash at the Year 2000 conference; speculative generalities were more comfortable to contemplate than a specific possible plan. One lengthy review of the book which the conference produced praised most of the other panel reports but did not mention that of the task force on the environment. Five years later, however, Senator John J. Hulten (land economist by profession) introduced a bill in the legislature which would have authorized the first step toward the first plateau: it called for a study of the economic potentials of land pooling under government administration.[42] Other legislators were not interested, but a tinge of reality had been added to the future-planners' dreams. Reading of Hulten's bill, Walter Collins dropped a note to this writer from a South Pacific island which had asked his land planning advice (counsel of the kind his home island so badly needed and did not request). The note simply said "Aha!"

Other land management experts have revived the scheme from time to time. Fred Smith, the Rockefeller adviser, suggested in a talk in Honolulu in 1974 that "a public-benefit corporation" might be formed in Honolulu to buy up private lands and lease them out for development according to an islandwide land use plan. Smith was not thinking in such broad terms as the Year 2000 group had been; he spoke only of large landowners with adjacent holdings pooling their land (in a way "similar to New York's Urban Development Corporation")[43] and of their "working with" the city and state governments, not of their forming a common trust. The reason he gave for thinking a land pool essential was his reiterated belief that a rapidly growing population would require much additional housing in new communities, not that he considered it a means of refining land management procedures for a stabilized population. Nevertheless, the general idea was there. Smith had to be added to those whose scenarios for the future were some form of "taking" for the public good.

Walter Collins had estimated that it would require seventy-five years to gather all the lands of Hawaii into a public trust. That length of time might indeed be needed for the modern industrial society that Hawaii has become to relinquish its dependence on the doctrine of private land ownership, for the private trusts to discover the advantages of public trusteeship, and for the people of the state to convince themselves that they should assume control of their common heritage.

Of the inheritors of the land, the native Hawaiians might benefit most from placing their heirdom under control of a public of which they form, now, only a part. It may even be that they could soon move to make the idea possible. Their native rights claim now includes a demand for the return of 2½ million acres to descendants of the aborigines. No indication has yet been given of any intended use of this land, beyond gaining the most profit from it for the greatest number of those with Hawaiian blood. If the grant, assuming that it will be awarded under those conditions, is to have any lasting benefits to the Hawaiians, it will have to avoid the probable fate that has been sketched as answer to question number one—continuation of present development trends. That land will have to be handled as well as the remaining million and a half acres, and if the best method for handling it is to pool it under a public trust, then the native Hawaiians should welcome the proposal. Even if monetary return from their lands remains a dominant concern, that need could be satisfied by the dividends from the major investment they would have made in Hawaii's future.

The Ultimate Variable: Time

There is the prescription, then: set limits to the population, allow this populace to plan the best ways to use its lands, then give it the power to carry out its plan through its own trust. It is a perfectly feasible program. It could be adopted at any time by those who govern public policies. Will it ever be undertaken, though? It would be opposed, by every means possible, by those who have the power to make political decisions or the power to influence them. All the straw-man arguments would be used against it: that "no growth" is economically impossible, that land planning is socially inflexible, that government control is constitutionally confiscatory, that public power is politically dangerous.

Nevertheless, to someone who has examined a number of other alternative futures, it seems the most likely of them all to come about in time—if by then there will be enough time left to allow it to come about. It seems the most plausible answer to today's problems that can be devised today, since private control of land is so generally found to work against the public interest and government control is so easily subverted for private aims. Its acceptance, in time, will be historically phenomenal: Hawaii, moving from a land system tightly controlled in the public interest (life would have been intolerable otherwise), will have moved back to a land system tightly controlled in the public interest (life will, again, have become intolerable otherwise). The control, however, will have changed from one absolute kingly hand to many, commonly joined. Time would have stood fast in Hawaii, in that one respect, even as times had changed.

Time, in truth, has become the ultimate variable in any futures plan for Hawaii, the key character in any forward-looking scenario. As alternatives are being debated, time is running out. Soon the choices will no longer lie within the subtle grays of enhancement or preservation of the environment, of improving the quality or changing the direction of expansion—they will be between the blacks and whites of growth or stabilization, of agriculture or subdivisions, of saving or losing green valleys and white beaches. Now the press of time supports the leveling of the land, because that is how our time is being spent—and later will be too late for change.

The early Hawaiians had a remarkable perception of time, its periods and its passage, the cycle of the seasons and of life itself, which the modern people of Hawaii have lost. The sense of time has been supplanted with a sense of hurry. The pleasure of doing things has been replaced by a need to get things done. The fusion of the present with the past, as precursor, and with the future, as successor, in a continuous flux where time just now is formed by times earlier as it molds time to come—this is a concept little understood in modern Hawaii. There is only a sketchy knowledge of the islands' past in the present state. History, for most, is a pleasant fiction written by nostalgic kamaaina haole ladies and popularized by James Michener. There is no care, even, to pronounce the mellifluous place names properly, and little curiosity about their origins.

If there is no interest in a real past, neither is there much concern about an actual future. For many, today, Hawaii is only a temporary business stop anyway. Money from other places, along with the people who manage it, comes and goes quickly. Time in Hawaii, for them, is the moment of building, developing, selling.

Even to the kamaainas and long-time residents time seems unimportant in Hawaii. The days are successively pleasant. Vistas still stretch across vast open spaces. Plantations continue to cover much of the low country and huge ranches still roll across the foothills. Until now, one can walk long lengths of empty beach and hike far distances into the mountains. What is there to worry about? In time, solutions will be found for all the problems of growth and expansion. Changes will come, of course, but change is an inevitable, even welcome, partner of the passage of time. All of that might be true if time would only move leisurely—but time in Hawaii moves more rapidly than time in most other places. There, a mere two hundred years have spanned the full story of lands' significance to man.

It is not what the land looks like today or any other day that will matter in the long run; what we see just now is a scratch of time in a sequence that stretches far back and will extend far forward. Today is quickly gone, but there is still time, barely, to make present performance respect past tradition and leave open future choices. But the options are closing, rapidly.

Epilogue: Scenario for the Future

THIS book began by telling about the past of Makaha Valley on Oahu's leeward side. It is going to close by wondering about the future of the Waiahole and Waikane valleys directly across that island on its windward side. No place in the Hawaiian islands could provide a more representative setting or cast of characters for playing out the next scene in the drama of those islands' lands. Here the capsule chronicle of land and people which Hawaii tells is even further condensed. Here the future alternatives of differing scenarios are most clearly seen.

The depth of background the setting provides is evident from the names these valleys carry. Waters *(kai)* dedicated to Kane, dominant male in the Hawaiian pantheon, lay at the foot of one, and so it was known earlier as Wai-a-Kane. Waters where the magic *ahole* fish lived (foe to evil spirits and protector of lovers) lay below the other, which was called Wai-ahole. The valleys lie between ridges leading down from the peaks of the Koolau range—rugged with rifts from Pleistocene eruptions, smoothed as dikes were filled with lava and covered with ash, finally carpeted with sufficient soil to make their floors softly green and richly fertile. They support a self-sufficient population of mixed ethnic heritage with a large, proud share of Hawaiian blood.

The principal characters in the current stage of the story of those lands symbolize several periods in Hawaii's modern history. One is Elizabeth Loy Marks, daughter of Lincoln L. McCandless, one of three brothers who arrived in Honolulu in the 1880s to start a long and profitable career of drilling artesian wells. Brother John was active in the political movements which led to the overthrow of the monarchy; Lincoln, for a term, was the territory's delegate to Congress. No small part of the profits from their essential business was the acquisition of land in various places in the islands, so that the McCandless heirs inherited some 36,000 acres of desirable Hawaiian soil. Lincoln's daughter Elizabeth, principal heir to the landholdings, married attorney Lester Marks and became a respected horticulturist, collector of Hawaiiana, member of protectionist societies, and generally, for many years, a good and kindly konohiki to the native tenants of her lands. The principal properties owned by the McCandless heirs (Elizabeth Marks et al., as they are recorded on tax maps) were an extensive ranching acreage on the Big Island and on Oahu the western tip and the Waiahole-Waikane valleys, where income to the estate came primarily from leases to small farmers.

Another character in the story, who represented a different phase in Hawaii's history, was Joe Pao, born a "poor boy" in Kauai, as he liked to say, who went to work after grade school as apprentice blacksmith for the Inter-Island Steamship and Navigation Company and in 1946 began selling real estate. Soon he was buying raw land himself and before long he was developing it into residential subdivisions. Pao was an optimist about the future, from his point of view. He predicted that within twenty-five or thirty years there will be no pineapple or sugarcane growing on Oahu. "There shouldn't be," he said. "We haven't even scratched the surface of home building."[1] Through his career Pao (whose name means, in Hawaiian, to scoop out) was careless about per-

missions and regulations; among the many complaints and
sometimes suits brought against him were two cases of disturbed boulders falling on houses he had built, one of sand
pumped from the mouth of a public stream in Kailua to
use on a project of his called Enchanted Lakes (an action
defended by city officials who soon owned homes there),
and another of cutting an illegal slice from a Manoa Valley
hillside which remained visibly raw for a long time and
became known as Pao's Cut.

In December 1974, representing Elizabeth Marks et al.,
Joe Pao requested the State Land Use Commission to reclassify from agricultural to urban use a thousand acres of
McCandless land in the Waiahole and Waikane valleys. He
was refused. Yet in June 1975, Pao bought some of the land
from Mrs. Marks (who had shifted it to her sole ownership
through internal negotiations with the other heirs) and op-
tioned more. He announced publicly that he was making
plans to build 7,000 homes there, over a ten-year period, for
22,000 people.[2] In the meantime, he and Mrs. Marks told the
people in the valleys that they must move from their farms
and their homes or be evicted, even though they were using
the land in the way the law specified. (Pao died of leukemia
two years later, leaving his role in the final scenes of the
story to a hui he had formed, called Windward Partners.)

The script now brings in a group of characters who represent a stiffening of attitudes toward indiscriminate development: they oppose the Pao-McCandless schemes. Some are
visibly and audibly on stage, like the governor ("The State is
not going to compromise . . . I am very angry and upset")
and the mayor ("I oppose any development in that area").[3]
Others, such as the State Land Use Commission, which
would have to change its mind about rezoning if the development were to go ahead, and the State Department of Health,
which would have to approve changes in stream flows and
provisions for sewerage treatment, the Department of Land
and Natural Resources, the State Agricultural Department,
the State Transportation Department, the Office of Environ-

mental Quality Control, and a number of city agencies, all involved in one way or another, are offstage voices often heard repeating the words of the governor and the mayor.

Then finally there are the people who live in the valleys. They have formed into several huis, some broadly composed of residents, some representing farmers and lessees of the land, some organized from Hawaiian families who have been there since the Great Mahele. They claim that land titles, at least in the ahupuaa of Waikane, are not clear. A voice occasionally breaks from the chorus claiming a kuleana for itself; the overall harmony is an insistence that they will not move from their homes and their farms—except through the use of force.[4]

It seemed as though there could be no ending to this scenario for many, many years. Joe Pao and his partners, along with Mrs. Marks, appeared willing to bide their time (and while Pao lived, at least, to compromise in the end, as he had done before). None of the other actors were moving from their positions. Then unexpectedly, in early 1977, things seemed to reach a climax. Elizabeth Marks secured a court order allowing her to evict some eighty tenants in Waiahole valley, and served the necessary papers. The plot drew tense as many of the residents publicly burned their notices.[5] At the common request of the adversaries, the governor searched for a way to prevent a nasty confrontation.

Three days before the deadline for eviction Governor Ariyoshi announced his solution to the impasse—a shocker, as the headlines said.[6] The state would buy from Mrs. Marks 600 acres of Waiahole land, for $6 million. The land, which housed most of those threatened with eviction, would be leased back to the resident farmers—and to others—whose holdings would be reformed in village clusters.

Was this a finale for the drama, or just a pause between scenes? Was it only a compromise adopted under pressure? Or would it prove to be a step toward public ownership and control of land to be leased out for planned uses? Certainly many problems remained unsolved. There was no assurance that homestead farming would work any better than it had through Hawaii's modern history. Piece-meal land acquisition by the state, as particular issues arose, could not answer the broad need for using all the islands' lands in the public good. These acres would now be under the jurisdiction of state agencies with no great record of land planning and land management. In fact, although the State Land Use Commission, shortly after the governor's move, rejected again a request from Pao's partners for reclassification of lands in Waikane Valley to urban uses, there was no long-term assurance that any of the local residents except those living on the 600 acres acquired by the state would be any better off than before the purchase.

Quite clearly the end of the story of the valleys of Waiahole and Waikane has not yet been told. The conclusion will depend on the course Hawaii's people adopt. If they are willing to accept the *probable* future of the islands' lands then the farms in the valleys will some day be replaced by subdivisions. There may be some suspenseful moments as the story unfolds further, when codes and regulations—and public purchases—prove effective in some instances, but in the end these restraints and respites will not stop development. They never have. But if the people of Hawaii should opt for the *possible* course, should elect to limit developmental growth and lay plans for public trusteeship of their lands, then the mountain shoresides like Waikane and Waiahole could be preserved for the uses they deserve.

Notes

Authors referred to in these notes will be found in alphabetical order in the bibliography along with titles of their works consulted. If that listing shows more than one work by an author, its title is given here in abbreviated form; otherwise only the author's name is given. Two frequently quoted sources are further abbreviated: *HA* for *Honolulu Advertiser* and *HSB* for *Honolulu Star-Bulletin*.

PREFACE

1. Spelling, pronunciation, and basic meanings are drawn from Pukui and Elbert, *Hawaiian-English Dictionary*.

2. Spelling, pronunciation, and probable meanings are drawn from Pukui et al., *Place Names of Hawaii*.

PROLOGUE

1. Makaha several hundred years ago is described in Ii, p. 97.

2. Present ethnic and occupational characteristics of Makaha area are drawn from University of Hawaii, *Atlas*, pp. 104 ff. and 145 ff.

3. Chinn Ho's architect for Makaha Inn and surrounds was William Pereira & Associates of Los Angeles.

4. For ages of the islands in the Hawaiian archipelago see Stearns, pp. 74–78.

5. Poems (meles) about Kauai and Hanalei are quoted in *Ancient Hawaiian Civilization,* chap. 17 by E. R. Plews, pp. 188, 190.

6. Population figures are from Schmitt. Missionaries made unofficial census counts from 1831 on; first government census was in 1850. Earlier statistics are reviewed and somewhat altered in State of Hawaii, *Data Book,* 1975, table 1.

7. *Ancient Hawaiian Civilization,* chap. 25 by E. H. Bryan, Jr., p. 274.

8. Hawaiians' cultivation of land is noted in Cook and King, Ledyard, and Vancouver (who is quoted), among others.

9. Villages are described by Ledyard, pp. 128, 129; those formed by kinship are discussed by Handy and Pukui, *Polynesian Family,* chap. 1, p. 3 ff., in relation to extended family; for those near chiefs' courts, see Malo, pp. 63, 64.

10. For ancient land divisions and tenure system, see W. D. Alexander, *Brief History;* Chinen, *Original Land; Ancient Hawaiian Civilization,* chap. 7 by J. H. Wise, with comments by M. Kelly, p. 321. The land system was well described in Principles of the Land Commission of 1845 (given in Thurston, *Fundamental Laws,* p. 137 ff.).

11. Hobbs, "The Land Title," says that nowhere in Polynesia was there a system "quite like" the Hawaiian; W. D. Alexander, *Brief History,* notes that the Hawaiian system differed from the tribal system (as in New Zealand) and the communal system (as in Samoa).

12. The trail at Halawa is described in Ii, p. 95.

13. For story of the stadium curse, see *HA* (24 November 1973 and 27 November 1973) and *HSB* (3 December 1973).

CHAPTER 1

1. Mumford, *Myth,* contains a discussion of our early, compatible relation to the earth and its products, especially on pp. 99–135. For a more thorough treatment of the subject, see Oparin, generally.

2. McHarg, particularly on p. 156 ff., discusses disastrous results of ignoring ecological balances. See also Commoner, especially chap. 7.

3. For speculation on future dangers of worsening man-nature relationship, see McHale, pp. 66 ff. and 208 ff., and Hardin, overall.

4. Stearns, McDonald, and Kyselka, and Carlquist all tell of the geological origins and formation of the Hawaiian archipelago. See especially Stearns, chap. 4.

5. See Fornander for early speculations on Polynesian movements and origins of Hawaiian peoples. For brief, more contemporary discussion, see P. H. Buck, chap. 2 in *Ancient Hawaiian Civilization,* with comments by Emory, p. 319. Studies and formulation of new theories continue even today.

6. For further knowledge of the general history of each of the five

periods defined here, without consulting original sources, much readable secondary material is available. For the first period see especially Kamakau, Ii, and Malo. For the second period add Kuykendall, vol. 1 (for his account of the land reform movement see chap. 15), and for the third period include Kuykendall, vols. 2 and 3. Daws, *Shoal,* provides additional researched material and fresh insights for all these periods and continues on into the fourth, territorial period, which Fuchs also documents, exhaustively. The fifth, post–Pearl Harbor period awaits its historian.

7. On postwar Americanization see Daws, *Shoal,* chap. 9; Coffman, p. 8 ff.; Lind, *Hawaii's People,* chap. 5; Simpich, especially chap. 5.

8. Cook's death and events leading to it are described in numerous personal journals of the time. For secondhand account by a Hawaiian, see Kamakau, pp. 102, 103. For a haole's personal story, not too favorable to Cook, see Ledyard, pp. 146, 147.

9. Kamehameha's campaigns and conquests were described in detail, early, by Kamakau; later, from hearsay, by Fornander; and still later, through research, by Kuykendall, vol. 1, pp. 29–51, and Daws, *Shoal,* pp. 29–44.

10. Haole supply of firearms and ships is noted by Kamakau, particularly on pp. 147–153. Kuykendall, vol. 1, pp. 40, 42, 46–48, cites additional instances.

11. Lind, *Hawaii's People,* p. 19.

12. Campbell, pp. 126–128.

13. Kamakau, pp. 146, 147; also Ii, pp. 69, 70.

14. See Brennan for story of Parker Ranch.

15. The Robert Kilday story: Kingdom of Hawaii, Land Commission, *Foreign Register Testimony,* vol. 1, no. 2.

16. For discussion of ecological effects of early importations, see E. H. Bryan, Jr., in *Ancient Hawaiian Civilization,* chap. 25; also R. A. Rappaport, p. 155 ff., in Fosberg (ed.), *Man's Place.*

17. Ii, pp. 94, 120.

18. Stokes, "New Speculative Phases."

19. Ii, pp. 55, 56.

20. Chinen, *Original Land,* notes that early land transactions were considered binding "excepting only such claims as the government of the Sandwich Islands may make on the land." All land ownership documents taken before the Land Commission, recorded in *Foreign Register Testimony* volumes, contained similar provisos.

21. For brief accounts of the careers of individual missionaries see Hawaii Mission Children's Society, *Missionary Album.*

22. The cession of Hawaii to Great Britain is described in Kamakau, pp. 350–355. The king's speech (which Kuykendall, vol. 1, p. 216 n., says "gave great offense to the British officers present") is reported by Kama-

kau, p. 364. Much of the Kamakau volume was drawn from his articles published in the Hawaiian-language paper *Ke Au ʻOkoʻa,* of which the issues carrying his story of the return of sovereignty by Admiral Thomas are missing. Kuykendall, vol. 1, chap. 13, and Daws, *Shoal,* pp. 114–119, document the episode from other researched sources.

23. Continuation of Charlton's land claim is reflected in Kingdom of Hawaii, *Privy Council Records,* through 1845 and 1846 and in Land Commission *Foreign Register Testimony.*

24. *Foreign Register Testimony,* vol. 1, no. 75.

25. Ibid., no. 4.

26. Proclamation of 1841 was reported in *Polynesian,* 10 June 1841.

27. Kingdom of Hawaii, *Privy Council Records,* 15 June 1846.

28. Ibid., 25 July 1846.

29. Much of the evidence presented in testimony recorded in Land Commission hearings is supported by bills of sale or evidence of inheritance.

30. Robinson sale to Ridley to Pelly: op. cit., vol. 1, no. 3. Blanchard claim, ibid., no. 17.

31. Hobbs, *Hawaii: A Pageant,* contains much documentary material tending to show missionaries' innocence of land speculation intent.

32. A. C. Alexander, *Koloa Plantation,* recounts events in Ladd & Company story. Joesting, p. 98 ff., adds interesting material. Kingdom of Hawaii, *Privy Council Records,* 11 November 1846 and succeeding weeks, cover phases of the negotiations and suit from the government's point of view. Ii's remark—"that might deceive . . . "— is from meeting of 6 January 1847.

33. For economics of early farming ventures, see Morgan, pp. 96–98.

34. Ellis, p. 18.

35. American capital in Hawaiian land: Hobbs, *Hawaii: A Pageant,* quotes J. R. Belsher's *Around the World in 1840.* Daws, "Honolulu, First Century," p. 216, uses similar figures.

36. Kamehameha III's sympathy with his people in this regard is indicated in comments in Kingdom of Hawaii, *Privy Council Records,* 15 June 1846 and 8 January 1847.

37. Petition and reply were translated in *Friend,* 12 June 1845 and 1 August 1845.

38. Translated in *Hawaiian Spectator,* July 1839, pp. 347–348.

39. Thurston, *Fundamental Laws,* p. 1 ff.

40. Ibid., under heading "Principles Adopted," p. 137 ff.

41. The *Mahele Book* is in Archives of Hawaii. Chinen, *Great Mahele,* describes the division process and reproduces sample mahele pages as well as royal patents and land awards.

42. See Kingdom of Hawaii, *Registers* of testimony and *Index* of awards, in Archives of Hawaii.

43. Kingdom of Hawaii, *Laws* of 1850, pp. 146, 147.

44. S. B. Dillingham, "Evolution of Hawaiian Land Tenures."

45. Kingdom of Hawaii, *Laws* of 1850, p. 202.

46. For description of Honolulu in 1820 see Ellis, p. 11 ff.; Kamakau, pp. 272 and 277; and numerous comments in Judd and in Bingham.

47. For Honolulu in the early 1840s, see *Polynesian,* 1840 through 1842, particularly issue of 17 October 1840 (from which come quotes herein).

48. *Polynesian,* 17 October 1840.

49. Kingdom of Hawaii, *Laws* of 1842, chap. 8, given in Thurston, *Fundamental Laws,* p. 43.

50. *Polynesian,* 5 September 1840.

51. Hawaiians' difficulties with city life are discussed in Daws, "First Century," pp. 495-519. Hobbs, *Hawaii: A Pageant,* and Lind, *Hawaii's People,* also comment on this phenomenon. Kuykendall, vol. 1, p. 272 n., writes of the "floating population." *Polynesian,* 6 March 1841, had editorial on economic problems involved, which were also discussed some years later in Privy Council (Kingdom of Hawaii, *Privy Council Records,* 8 June 1847).

52. Castle & Cooke cash book for 1866, in Hawaiian Mission Children's Society Library: *Cooke Papers* (hereafter called simply *Papers*).

53. *Friend,* 1 August 1845.

CHAPTER 2

1. For study of continually increasing influence of Americans in Hawaii, see Tate.

2. General histories commonly comment on this characteristic. Mark Twain wrote of Lunalilo that he had "an intellect that shines radiantly through floods of whisky." *Paradise of the Pacific,* January 1910. Stevenson, p. 93, in letter to Charles Baxter, described Kalakaua as "a very fine fellow, but . . . what a crop for the drink!"

3. Haole consolidation of controls was achieved partly through reciprocity among themselves. The Castle & Cooke firm helped the C. Brewer Company get started. They bought shares in one anothers' ventures "to see them prosper" (or to secure their business; e.g., "to sell them lumber"). All cooperated when Dillingham started a railroad to Ewa. See various Cooke and Castle *Papers,* particularly CMC to GHC (11 January 1890) and to JAH (11 December 1889).

4. Charles Montague Cooke wrote to Paul Isenberg (Cooke *Papers,* 27 March 1893): "It would be an advantage to have a Republican form of government if the natives did not outnumber the white vote . . . and will not Japan step in and demand the franchise for her 20,000 subjects . . . ?"

5. Tate writes: "the underlying cause of the *coup d'etat* was the deter-

mination of the propertied class . . . to direct and control government policy."

6. On the revolution, from different points of view, see Blount; Thurston, *Memoirs;* Liliuokalani. Kuykendall, vol. 3, chap. 21, provides a carefully researched, dispassionate account.

7. For social history of plantation-worker groups, see Fuchs, pt. 1.

8. Records of owners and factors indicate that the discipline maintained on plantations made normal Hawaiian life-styles impossible. Castle *Papers* contain letter from E. Bond, former missionary, later manager at Koloa, to S. N. Castle, 3 July 1874, reporting "scenes" when dancing was one time permitted: "men and women excited with liquor, dancing late into the night and exhibiting the lowest, vilest brutality and beastliness."

9. One manager complained (ibid., letter PBC to STA, 17 April 1890) that a shipload of Chinese "are to have $15.00 [a month] and not $13.00 as was reported." The low wage scale bothered the consciences of some, but a manager at Lihue wrote his superiors (Cooke *Papers,* PEB to CMC, 25 June 1891) urging that "all interested should join to find cheaper and more laborers" and also that "all should join in procuring cheaper food for the laborers."

10. For Spreckels' biography, see Adler.

11. For agriculture in second half of nineteenth century, much material is in *Hawaiian Annual, Pacific Commercial Advertiser, Polynesian,* and other periodicals of that period. Kuykendall summarizes all this in vol. 2, chap. 5. See also Morgan, pp. 159–173. Regarding crops other than sugarcane, Cooke *Papers* contain references to investments in tea, coffee, fruit, cotton—even an ostrich farm. *Polynesian,* 29 August 1840, reported a silk farm of 100,000 trees on Kauai, promising to be "one of the most important branches of domestic industry."

12. For reviews of nineteenth-century architecture, see Neil (pp. 7–15; Fairfax, pp. 7–9; Historic Buildings Task Force, *Old Honolulu,* for photographs); article by Hawaii Chapter, AIA, in *Hawaiian Annual,* 1968, pp. 161–182. Neil has bibliography of material on this subject.

13. Transportation: for general discussion, see Kuykendall, vol. 3, pp. 95–97; for tramways: *Pacific Commercial Advertiser,* 15 January 1889; for railroads: Hungerford.

14. For review of early utility construction, see Kuykendall, vol. 3, p. 94 ff. Developing use of artesian water is documented in McCandless. Cooke *Papers,* journal entry of 16 July 1889, notes an early order for telephone poles.

15. See *Hawaiian Annual,* 1915, pp. 103–109, article by J. M. Lydgate entitled "The Vanishing Kuleanas." For comments on this and other data, see Levy, pp. 851, 866, 867.

16. Editorial was in *Maile Quarterly,* September 1865; response, in March 1866 issue.

17. Lydgate, op. cit.

18. Levy, p. 86.

19. History of the Makalupu Hui is covered in A. C. Alexander, *Koloa Plantation*. Cooke, *Papers,* PCB to WHR, 6 March 1888, notes instruction to plantation manager to "buy up as many shares of Makalupu Hui as he can from the natives," believing that "he can secure enough shares to give [Koloa Sugar Company] almost the majority."

20. Land as the king's personal property: Kuykendall, vol. 1, p. 288 n., comments that "the king could (and did) own other land as a private individual, but the crown lands had a different status."

21. For historical review of crown lands, see Spaulding. As for their disposition, Horwitz et al. (p. 110 and table 14) calculate that 750,000 acres of crown and government lands were under lease by 1890.

22. Spaulding estimates that Liliuokalani lost $50,000 annual income from crown-land leases when she was overthrown. Thurston, *Memoirs,* suggests between $50,000 and $100,000. The ex-queen sued the government, unsuccessfully, over this presumed loss.

23. On transfer of crown lands after the revolution, the Constitution of the Republic, Article 99 (Thurston, *Fundamental Laws,* p. 198), provided: "That portion of the public domain heretofore known as Crown Land is hereby declared to have been heretofore and now to be the property of the Hawaiian government." The Treaty of Annexation (ibid., p. 243) with the United States provided that "the Republic of Hawaii also cedes and hereby transfers to the United States of America the absolute fee and ownership of all public government or crown lands." The Organic Act (ibid., p. 257) contained a similar provision.

24. Horwitz et al., app. 1, p. 186 ff., list sales from 1846 to 1893, with average prices per acre by years.

25. Ibid., table 24.

26. Hawaiian commoners' difficulties in adjusting are noted in Lind, *Hawaii's People,* pp. 102, 103. Pockets of Hawaiian life (specifically Kau) are described in Handy and Pukui, *Polynesian Family,* and more generally in Lind, *Island Community.* Fuchs, p. 71, comments on the phenomenon.

27. For thorough documentation of social-political developments in first half of twentieth century, see Fuchs.

28. Lind, *Hawaii's People,* table 8, p. 28. Schmitt and also Gardner and Nordyke use similar data, with slight divergences.

29. Fuchs, p. 259, gives instances of income returns of 40 to 60 percent in territorial period, drawn from Honolulu Stock Exchange data. Cooke and Castle *Papers* indicate huge dividend rates even before turn of century: Haiku Plantation stock paid 53 percent in 1890, C. Brewer & Co. showed return on capital of 40 percent in 1897, Hawaiian Argicultural Co. paid dividends of 35 percent in 1899.

30. A year after passage of Act 44 of 1903, a 913-acre reserve was

established at Kaipapau on Oahu, followed by an 18,940-acre reserve at the Hamakua Pali on Big Island. Today such reserves amount to more than a million acres (State of Hawaii, *Data Book,* 1976, table 87).

31. Land owned and controlled by principal landowners is tabulated in Woodrum, tables 28 and 29. For informed and entertaining account of landed trusts and estates, see Simpich, p. 128 ff.

32. For formation of Bishop Estate, see Bishop, *Journal.* For researched contemporary account, not friendly to trustees, see four articles by B. Sullam in *Hawaii Observer,* September and October 1975.

33. Lands set aside for U.S. defense agencies are listed in Horwitz et al., pp. 61–107, in text, figures, and tables.

34. For excellent collection of photographs of Honolulu at various stages in its development, see Scott.

35. Urban growth, architecture, and building construction in first half of twentieth century are documented in many articles listed in Neil's bibliography. His introductory text, Fairfax, and the Historic Building Task Force's *Old Honolulu* give additional data. *Hawaiian Annual* has useful source material, especially in editions for 1899, 1901, and 1925.

36. That Alexander Young Building was considered large at the time of its construction is indicated by comment in Cooke *Papers* (letter to FJC, 16 March 1901): "The glass for the Young Building is a big proposition, as of course we knew it would be."

CHAPTER 3

1. For a short, readable account of the World War II years in Hawaii, see Joesting, chap. 16. For more detailed reviews, see Allen and Anthony.

2. Lind, *Japanese,* written during the war years, tells of the condition and reactions of AJAs and the attitudes of other residents.

3. Fuchs, chap. 16, documents postwar business changes.

4. For a breezy but informed account of postwar politics, see Coffman, especially first five chapters.

5. Governor Burns appointed his brother Edward state tax director in 1962, and they announced a new policy for real-estate assessment, reflecting the highest and best use of land "to aid small businesses" and "force development of idle land." See *HA,* 17 December 1962.

6. Hawaii's housing deficiency in 1960 was shown in U.S. Census Bureau statistics and a survey by Federal Housing Administration, reported in *HA,* 2 December 1961 and 28 December 1961.

7. *HSB,* 27 February 1961.

8. In his address to the 1961 session of the legislature, Governor Quinn said, "agriculture is, and must remain, an important element of the economy of Hawaii" (*Journal,* First Legislature of the State of Hawaii, pp. 19, 20). In that year direct income and revenues to the state from

agriculture were much greater than those from tourism although considerably less than those from the military. See State of Hawaii, *Data Book,* 1976, table 166.

9. Horwitz et al., p. 54, quoting state interdepartmental memos, describe Quinn's land policy as including (1) widespread ownership of land and (2) conservation of land resources.

10. Horowitz and Meller, p. 2. Land and politics in Hawaii are discussed for periods before 1960 in Fuchs, especially chaps. 14 and 15; for the 1960s, in Horowitz and Meller.

11. See Horowitz and Meller, pp. 49, 50. *HSB,* 13 February 1961, gave full page to Democrat and Republican party positions during 1961 legislative session, indicating minor variances on basic issues.

12. *HSB,* 23 July 1959. Policy is analyzed in Horwitz et al., p. 53. Horbwitz and Meller, p. 6, explain use of phrase "Great Hoax" during 1961 session.

13. Democrat's land policy: *HA,* 18 February 1959 and 6 May 1959; *HSB,* 27 February 1961.

14. Horowitz and Meller, from privileged observation granted them, fluently tell of party policies in 1961 legislature.

15. State of Hawaii, *Data Book,* 1975, table 92, shows "major private owners" holding 1,917,560 acres in 1968, while "other owners" had only 270,219 acres.

16. Governor's message to the 1961 state legislature; State of Hawaii, *Journal* of legislature, 1961, pp. 19, 20.

17. *HA,* 2 January 1961.

18. Bartholomew & Associates, *An Index.*

19. Legislation on land planning in 1957: Act 35, Land Study Bureau; Act 234, Water Reserves; Act 150, Territorial Planning Office and General Plan. See State of Hawaii, *Revised Statutes.*

20. Act 187 of 1961, Land Use Law, has been amended a number of times: e.g., Act 205 of 1963 added *rural* district and clarified authorities of state and counties; Act 32 of 1965 modified the process of boundary changes "to alleviate any hardship imposed on the petitioners"; Act 182 of 1969 defined "open space" and called for an open-space plan; Act 136 of 1970 ordered the commission to establish shoreline setbacks for development. See ibid.

21. In the press, only *HSB,* 12 July 1961, immediately reported the law's passage, in a small second-page story quoting Governor Quinn as saying *he* had proposed "the essential features of the Act." Horowitz and Meller noted that H.B. 1279, enacted as Act 187, only as "a measure designed to raise taxes on undeveloped land," did not refer to its land-zoning provisions.

22. Term "greenbelt" was a misnomer, as many recognized. It intended to imply that some land would be kept green, not that defined *belts* of

green land would separate distinct urban communities, which is common meaning.

23. *HA,* 8 April 1962.

24. Bartholomew & Associates, *Land Use Districts.*

25. Eckbo et al., *Land Use Districts,* p. 8. Effect on conversions is factually documented ibid. and in Marshall Kaplan et al., *Second Five Year,* is reviewed in Overview Corporation, p. 33 ff., and evaluated in Bosselman and Callies, *Quiet Revolution,* p. 28 ff., and League of Women Voters, *Land Use Law,* p. 5 ff.

26. Act 187 contains generalized statements in its Declaration of Purpose but no further assertion of objectives. Godwin and Shepard, p. 23, say "the commission was given no guidance in law on the relative emphasis to place on such major controversies as tourist-related development versus preservation of natural and scenic attractions, or agricultural land conservation versus the supply of land for reasonably priced living accommodations."

27. Eckbo et al., in 1969; Marshall Kaplan et al., in 1974.

28. A number of examples are given in this book: Salt Lake, Mt. Olomana, Waipio, Kahuku, Kaluakoi. Overview Corporation, p. 165, advised that assessment of State Land Use Commission should not be by numbers of applications approved or acres rezoned but by "the overall impact on Hawaii's environment." Overview concluded that "experience has demonstrated" that the Land Use Law "does not contain sufficient safeguards to insure fulfillment" of environmental protection.

29. *HSB,* 10 April 1964.

30. See *HSB,* 1 January 1964, for application and ibid., 9 April 1964, for approval.

31. Conflicts of interest found by Attorney General Kanbara are described in *HA,* 12 October 1970. Same paper, same date, had story saying Kanbara "pulled no punches."

32. *HSB,* 29 April 1967.

33. Tangen accused of conflicts of interest: *HA,* 6 January 1973; court says charges unfounded, ibid., 9 December 1973.

34. H.B. 808 in 1973 session.

35. Council of State Governments, *Land,* p. 3.

36. Act 187 Preamble: State of Hawaii, *Revised Statutes.*

37. Term "quiet revolution" is title of Bosselman study.

38. In 1962 legislature, bill was introduced to "postpone" action by the commission (*HA,* 8 April 1962); Commissioner Myron T. Thompson witnessed "fierce pressures" to repeal the law (*HSB,* 29 July 1965); "strong attempts" for repeal in 1964 and 1965 were reported in the press (*HSB,* 12 December 1964).

39. Population growth figures are rounded from State of Hawaii, *Data*

Book, 1976, table 1. Ethnic population percentages are drawn from Gardner and Nordyke, table 9.

40. For illustration of Oahu's urban configuration in the 1960s, see City and County of Honolulu, *General Plan, 1964.* Growth of individual suburban areas is described in *HA,* 3 December 1975 (article by Bob Krauss), for Kahala; in Neil, p. 61, for Hawaii Kai; in University of Hawaii, *Kaneohe Alternatives,* for Kaneohe.

41. Number of visitors: State of Hawaii, *Data Book,* 1976, table 99; hotel rooms: ibid., table 297.

42. Contretemps between Luka Nalui and David McClung took place during an angrily heated hearing on H3 reported in *HSB,* 17 April 1974.

CHAPTER 4

1. From talk by Alice Spalding Bowen in series on Design for Living in Hawaii, at Honolulu Academy of Arts, January and February 1972, transcribed but not published.

2. For Ellis' trip around Hawaii, see his *Journal.* For 1974 reenactment, see series of articles by Krauss in *HA,* 18 July 1973 through 18 August 1973.

3. Early neglect of heiaus: Ellis, pp. 56, 73. Neglect of Kukaniloko birth stones: Samy Amalu's column, *HA,* 15 June 1975.

4. *HA,* 11 August 1973.

5. Example of tourisms historic restorations: King Kamehameha Hotel in Kailua, Kona, island of Hawaii, was built on beach at Kamakahonu, residence area of Kamehameha I, neglecting remnants of monarch's personal heiau. When hotel was rebuilt in 1976, *HA* and *HSB,* 25 April 1976, reported "authentic" restoration of the heiau and other structures of the original compound, to serve as "backdrop for commercial luaus and dinner time torchlight ceremonies."

6. *HA,* 9 November 1975.

7. Of eighty-five historic buildings on Oahu listed by Historic Buildings Task Force *(Old Honolulu),* only twelve are more than one hundred years old.

8. Fairfax, p. 53.

9. At meeting attended by writer, held 1 May 1972, reported (without this comment) in *HSB,* 2 May 1973.

10. Protests against highway construction at Kahaluu, Waiahole, and Waikane were reported in the press periodically, e.g., in *HA,* 8 June 1972 and 12 April 1976; against development at Niumau, *Hawaii Observer,* 16 April 1974; at Kalama Valley, *HSB,* 17 August 1972.

11. See Lind, *Island Community,* pp. 309–313. A good summary was made by Nancy Bannick in her talk for the Design for Living series.

12. Honolulu Redevelopment Agency in Chinatown: *HA*, 2 March 1973. Washington HUD official said redevelopment would "insure Chinatown's viability," *HA*, 27 March 1973.

13. Indigenous and endemic species in Hawaii: see Carlquist. For brief informative reviews, see *Ancient Hawaiian Civilization*, chap. 26 by A. F. Judd and chap. 27 by H. S. Palmer. In 1977, the U.S. Interior Department noted that more than half of America's endangered plant species are located in Hawaii. *HA*, 18 June 1977.

14. Introduction of exotic species: birds, *HSB*, 6 July 1973; deer, *HA*, 9 July 1973; goats and sheep, *HA*, 25 March 1976.

15. Defacement above Manoa Valley residential area became known as Pao's Cut, was finally replanted by university students (*HA*, 5 July 1973); another cut on Mount Olomana, also made by Pao, while grading without a permit (*HA*, 18 December 1970), remained visible for years.

16. Damage caused by runoffs from construction (algae death, smothered coral, etc.) was documented in numerous studies by university groups and well reported in press: e.g., *HSB*, 29 August 1973; *HA*, 12 February 1974. Floods resulting from development: *Hawaii Observer*, 12 June 1973.

17. *HSB*, 20 March 1973 and 21 March 1973.

18. Office of Environmental Quality Control was established in 1970; Environmental Quality Commission was appointed in 1974.

19. State of Hawaii, Department of Health, *Air Pollution Implementation Plan*, mimeographed, 1973.

20. Babbie, *Maximillion Report*, was published and promoted by a civic group called Citizens for Hawaii.

21. *HSB*, 6 December 1972.

22. Comment was by Dr. Rudolph Rummel, professor of political science, at East-West Center symposium, reported by *HA*, 23 June 1972. Comments by other participants included one by Dr. James Dator that the report "leaves out everything that's important, as far as I am concerned."

23. Essay by Dator was stimulated, he wrote, by a column written by this writer (*HA-HSB*, 7 May 1972), who "for some reason saw fit to refer to me as a 'techno-optimist'."

24. *HSB*, 15 November 1973.

25. See Heller and Heller, for reasons, volume, impact.

26. State of Hawaii, *Data Book*, 1975, table 308 (drawn from Heller and Heller), shows that in 1961 just 12 island businesses were owned by Japanese interests; by 1972 number had grown to 94. For discussion of Japanese investments in Hawaii, see *Fortune* magazine, September 1975, p. 42 ff.; see also article in *Hawaii Observer*, 11 June 1974. Investment in Hawaii's hotels by 1974, reported by U.S. Commerce Department, was $350 million (*HSB*, 4 May 1976), with Kenji Osano owner of most. Angry reaction to his purchase of Royal Hawaiian: *HSB*, 30 July 1974 and 10 October 1974.

27. John G. Simpson, president, Hawaii Visitors Bureau, quoted in *HSB*, 20 April 1973.

28. *HSB*, 29 August 1973.

29. *HA*, 30 August 1974.

30. Excitement subsided: Japanese government's advice, *HSB*, 25 June 1973; Chinn Ho, *HSB*, 29 August 1973; Kanahele, *HA*, 21 April 1973 and 1 September 1973.

31. Duran's display of developers' plans was shown, among other places, at Design for Living series.

32. State of Hawaii, *Central Oahu Planning Study*.

33. State of Hawaii, *Hawaii Tourism Impact Plan*, vol. 1, tables 3.5, 3.6, 3.7, indicate plans for resort-residential projects on 96,643 acres.

34. Story was researched by Esterman from files of Land Use Commission.

35. Land sales to out-of-state investors have been regularly reported in the press, too often to make reference listings feasible.

36. Overview Corporation, chap. 3.

37. Figures are rounded from State of Hawaii, *Data Book*, 1975, table 1, and Gardner and Nordyke, table 1. Comparative growth rates are given in State of Hawaii, *Growth Policies Plan*, p. 16.

38. Densities on Oahu: University of Hawaii, *Atlas*, p. 100. Densities in U.S. Urban Land Institute, *Density*, p. 38 ff.

39. Population projections for state; State of Hawaii, *Data Book*, 1976, table 9. For Oahu: City and County of Honolulu, *Planning for Oahu: An Evaluation*, pp. 10, 11.

40. State of Hawaii, *Data Book*, 1976, table 166.

41. Oahu Development Conference, *Report 44*, January 1974.

42. Visitor arrivals, average number, expenditures: State of Hawaii, *Data Book*, 1975, table 98.

43. State of Hawaii, *Report of Governor's Economic Advisory Task Force*, pp. 10, 11. For summary of *Report of Tourism Advisory Committee to Governor*, see statement by its chairman, Thomas H. Hamilton, *HSB*, 13 November 1975.

44. Other growth trends are largely taken from State of Hawaii, *Data Book*, 1975: personal income, table 163; bank deposits, table 185; construction, table 264.

45. Craven's prediction of hordes of refugees was in 1970 talk to Hawaii chapter, American Institute of Architects. For description and drawings of arcologies, see Soleri. Craven described his concept of artificial islands in *HSB*: 15, 16, 17 December 1971.

46. Fred Smith's predictions of great growth were made in talk to Honolulu Chamber of Commerce, published in part as article, *HSB*, 22 June 1973.

47. *Hawaii Observer*, 28 May 1974, interview.

48. *Hawaii Business,* April 1974, interview.

49. Television commercials were used during 1972 by Honolulu realtor Jerry Assam.

CHAPTER 5

1. Conflict of development and conservation is described in Rockefeller Brothers Fund's admittedly "hopeful" report, *The Use of Land,* especially in chaps. 3, 7, 8.

2. *HA,* 3 April 1976.

3. State of Hawaii, Department of Land and Natural Resources, *Regulation 4.*

4. Administration of conservation lands and establishment of zones and subzones, ibid., as well as other DLNR regulations.

5. State of Hawaii, State Land Use Commission, *Regulations,* say: "Land with topography, soils, climate or other related factors that may not be normally adapted to or *presently needed* for urban, rural or agricultural uses shall be included in this District" (emphasis added).

6. *HA,* 13 December 1975.

7. *HSB,* 22 April 1972.

8. League of Women Voters, *Conservation,* p. 11, says: "the uses, value, ownership, resource-capacities, etc., of state-owned and Conservation District lands is not available."

9. Malo, pp. 16, 17.

10. University of Hawaii, Land Study Bureau, *Detailed Land Classification;* U.S. Department of Agriculture, Soil Conservation Service, *Soil Surveys;* same agency, *Soil Survey Interpretations;* all of these in volumes for each island. University of Hawaii, *Atlas,* p. 39, discusses use of new classification system in Hawaii.

11. Council of State Governments, *Data Needs,* p. 2: "The collection and storage of data represents both an essential activity and a source of major problems in land use planning."

12. H. B. Emerson, *Friend,* 50, 1892, pp. 55–60, discusses discontinuance of games. Malo, pp. 214–234, describes many Polynesian Hawaiian games and sports in detail and notes gambling, especially p. 225. Ellis wrote of this "malignant practice," as did many early chroniclers.

13. See Malo, p. 141 ff. Beckwith, in *Kumulipo,* p. 18, and *Hawaiian Mythology,* pp. 33–37, relates makahiki to legends of Lono (for whom Cook was taken, Kamakau, p. 93).

14. *Paradise of the Pacific,* January 1888, p. 4.

15. Ibid., July 1899, p. 1, and October 1903, pp. 17, 18.

16. Appel explains Hawaiian trail systems.

17. Development of Moanalua Gardens, *Hawaiian Annual,* 1914, pp.

75–84. "Cannibalization" is term used by Neil, p. 9. Liliuokalani Gardens are illustrated in *Paradise of the Pacific*, August 1916, pp. 8, 9; Ala Moana Park is pictured, ibid., May 1934. Present-day appeal for preservation of Moanalua Valley: see Moanalua Gardens Foundation.

18. State of Hawaii, Department of Planning and Economic Development, *State Comprehensive Outdoor Recreation Plan*.

19. Park totals: State of Hawaii, *Data Book*, 1975, tables 108, 109, 110.

20. Ibid., table 112.

21. *HSB*, 1 October 1975; *HA*, 14 October 1975.

22. On Oahu, Planning Commission approved ordinance on 15 December 1971; council adopted it on 31 January 1972, as reported in *HA* on following days.

23. Pele legend: see under *Alia-pa'akai* in Pukui et al., *Place Names*, p. 11.

24. Coffman, p. 84.

25. *HA*, 13 September 1957.

26. Ibid., 1 November 1957.

27. Planning Commission approval, *HSB*, 12 August 1966; Tangen's testimony, *HA*, 15 July 1966; staff recommendation, *HSB*, 26 August 1966; approval by Land Board, *HSB*, 9 September 1966.

28. *HSB*, 14 March 1974.

29. Article by Tuck Newport in *Hawaii Observer*, 28 October 1975, which reviews Salt Lake's history.

30. Request for rezoning, *HSB*, 2 June 1972; local residents' division, ibid.

31. Tom Coffman, *HSB*, 3 June 1972, wrote that Fasi "told this reporter and others" of Ching's contribution.

32. *HSB*, 2 June 1972.

33. Kamm and Etherington.

34. City and County of Honolulu, Department of General Planning, *An Evaluation*, p. 157, notes deficiency in parklands, commenting that in central Honolulu land is so costly that meeting standards "is not feasible" and satisfying future needs "is simply not possible."

CHAPTER 6

1. See Meadows et al., pp. 137–141; also, for Hawaii, Chaplin and Paige, pp. 285–287.

2. Malo, p. 206.

3. Handy and Pukui, *Polynesian Family*, p. 3.

4. Beckwith, *Hawaiian Mythology*, pt. 1, especially chap. 9.

5. Early Hawaiian farming methods: Malo, pp. 201–208; Kamakau, p. 237; *Ancient Hawaiian Civilization*, chap. 10 by J. R. Wichman; Handy

and Pukui, *Polynesian Family,* p. 176; and Pukui and Elbert, *Native Planters,* throughout.

6. Malo, p. 206, says some improvident farmers "planted all at once," while others would "plant a little at a time during months suitable for planting." Morgan, p. 51, says, however, there was "an astonishing lack of provision against future wants."

7. Malo, p. 42 ff.

8. Malo, p. 44.

9. Growth of general agriculture in first half of nineteenth century: Kuykendall, vol. 1, chap. 9; Morgan, pp. 96–98.

10. Missionaries' appeal for agricultural help was in a "memorial" prepared in 1836 and sent to American Board of Commissioners for Foreign Missions. An early missionary group included a farmer (Daniel Chamberlain), supposed to teach natives "agricultural and mechanical arts," who returned home soon, discouraged. See Hawaii Mission Children's Society, *Missionary Album.*

11. Edward Bailey merged his early sugar cultivation with Wailuku Plantation and helped form Haiku Sugar Co. Elias Bond started Kohala Plantation (turning dividends for some time over to church). William Harrison retired from mission to manage Lihue Plantation. Ibid.

12. R. C. Wyllie wrote in *Friend,* 2, 1844, p. 61, that islands' "prosperity [depends] mainly on the whale ships."

13. Wolbrink, *Kona,* pp. 81, 82, notes that as late as 1960 Kona had twelve coffee mills, but only two by 1970.

14. Kingdom of Hawaii, *Laws* of 1842, chap. 14, in Thurston, *Fundamental Laws.*

15. Kuykendall, vol. 1, pp. 317–319; State of Hawaii, *Data Book,* 1975, table 249.

16. *Polynesian,* 20 June 1857; *Hawaiian Annual,* 1877, pp. 45–49; Kuykendall, vol. 2, p. 157.

17. Early sugarcane planting is mentioned by Malo, p. 205. For later periods, see Morgan, pp. 173–195; Kuykendall, vol. 1, pp. 314–317, for 1840–1848; ibid., pp. 323–333, for 1849–1854; vol. 2, pp. 140–149, for 1855–1874; vol. 3 for 1875–1893; Fuchs, especially chap. 9, for 1900–1960. For current statistics, see State of Hawaii, *Data Book,* 1975, tables 246, 247, 248.

18. For pineapple production in various periods see Kuykendall, vol. 3; Fuchs; Morgan; *Data Book,* 1975, tables 246, 247.

19. Fuchs, p. 249.

20. State of Hawaii, *Data Book,* 1976, table 87.

21. University of Hawaii, *Atlas,* p. 146; *Data Book,* 1975, table 252.

22. Agricultural export items are summarized in Woodrum, p. 347, from U.S. Department of Agriculture data.

23. *HA,* 21 May 1976.

24. *HA,* 23 May 1976: "Ariyoshi backs farming . . . residents want tourist push."

25. *HA,* 26 October 1975.

26. *HSB,* 14 August 1975.

27. *HA,* 8 February 1976, 24 April 1976, 4 May 1976; *HSB,* 28 April 1976.

28. *HA,* 6 June 1975, 24 April 1976.

29. *HA,* 14 April 1975.

30. *HSB,* 18 May 1976.

31. *HSB,* 24 July 1974.

CHAPTER 7

1. Ledyard, pp. 103, 129.

2. Beckwith, *Hawaiian Mythology,* p. 327, notes that legends of Menehune people have them living in caves and in various places describes the cave homes of the gods.

3. House construction is described in Kamakau, pp. 237, 238; Malo, p. 118 ff.; *Ancient Hawaiian Civilization,* chap. 6 by E. S. C. Handy; Handy and Pukui, *Polynesian Family,* pp. 7, 12–15; Ellis, p. 224. Malo, pp. 119, 120, gives diagrams of typical framing methods.

4. *Ancient Hawaiian Civilization,* pp. 70, 71; Handy and Pukui, *Polynesian Family,* p. 8.

5. Ellis, p. 147.

6. See Prologue, n. 9, for references on village groupings.

7. Bingham thought that native houses were "adapted to the taste of a dark, rude tribe living on roots, fish and fruit."

8. Vancouver's visit to a royal home is discussed by Thomas Many, *Honolulu Mercury,* July and August 1929. Kotzebue told of Namahana's "pretty little house."

9. See Peterson for imported construction materials. Cooke *Papers,* in early journals of Castle & Cooke, show increasing quantity of such items being handled.

10. See Scott for reproductions of early drawings of Honolulu houses.

11. Neil, p. 10.

12. Fuchs, pp. 47, 48.

13. *Hawaiian Annual,* 1898, p. 12 ff., article by Sanford Dole, "Hawaiian Land Policy."

14. Horwitz et al., p. 37.

15. Ibid., p. 24.

16. Ibid., p. 37. See also Vause and see Humphries, throughout. Failure is explained in some detail in Territory of Hawaii, Land Law Revision Commission, *Report of December 31, 1946.*

17. Fuchs, pp. 172, 173.

18. Hawaiian Homes Commission Act of 1920, as it is often called, is officially an act of 9 July 1921, chap. 42, 42 Stat. 108.

19. Vause, p. 131. Horwitz et al., p. 39, write of "the political-economic agreement."

20. Horwitz et al., p. 39: homestead plots "consisted largely of marginal land, the bulk of which was not suitable for agricultural homesteads." Fuchs, pp. 173, 174, quotes a kamaaina remembering it as "rotten" land and a director of the Hawaiian Homes Commission reporting that most was in remote areas or forest reserve sections.

21. Humphries, p. 98; Fuchs, p. 73.

22. Territory of Hawaii, Commissioners of Public Lands, *Report, 1926,* p. v.

23. *HSB,* 13 December 1975, story by H. Ashton.

24. *HSB,* 22 February 1976, in a series of twelve articles on "Land, Hawaii's Green Gold," by Bob Krauss.

25. Ibid., particularly articles on 25 and 27 February 1976.

26. Ibid., 27 February 1976, quoting Bob Hill, volunteer for Kalihi-Palama Community Association.

27. Acts 184 and 185 of 1975.

28. Estates' successive reactions: *HA,* 14, 19, and 29 May 1976, and 31 December 1976.

29. State of Hawaii, Office of the Lieutenant Governor, *Hawaii's Crisis.*

30. Marshall Kaplan, *Housing in Hawaii.*

31. For a brief, informed look at this problem, see *Saturday Review,* 12 February 1972, article by J. P. Fried, "Any Hope for Housing?" Fried lists difficulties of construction costs, land costs, costs of financing, property taxes and zoning, and he analyzes limited help of government subsidies.

32. Average sales price: *HA,* 13 June 1976. Median income: State of Hawaii, *Data Book,* 1976, table 172.

33. State of Hawaii, Department of Planning and Economic Development, *Housing for Hawaii's People.*

34. Overview Corporation, p.

CHAPTER 8

1. Kaiser's meeting with trustees was witnessed by this writer. The 1965 plan for Hawaii Kai was prepared by John Carl Warnecke & Associates.

2. The city's general plan change accommodating Kaiser's plan was approved by the City Planning Commission on 11 Feburary 1966.

3. See Rockefeller Brothers Fund, particularly chap. 6 for economic arguments ("incentives and opportunities") supporting open-space protection.

4. See Livingston & Blayney.

5. See State of Hawaii, Department of Planning and Economic Development, *Central Oahu.*

6. University of Hawaii, Center for Engineering Research, *Public Costs.*

7. For methods of quantifying environmental and social costs, ibid., especially contributions by Schwind, p. 16, and Holstrom, p. 62.

8. Rose, p. 38.

9. Ibid. "Retention of land . . . ," p. 42. "Risk bearing . . . ," p. 41.

10. *HA,* 11 March 1972, responding to column by this writer, *HA,* 21 February 1972.

11. Memo to Department of Land and Natural Resources from Dr. R. M. Kamins, 21 April 1975, pointed to a "considerable area" where government in Hawaii had not reserved mineral rights. Reservations were applied during Kamehameha III's reign, the memo notes, but later the reservation clause was "seemingly dropped," then was recently reestablished.

12. As on the American mainland. Clawson, p. 72, notes that by 1776 "the concept of fee-simple ownership of land was firmly established" in the colonies. Council of State Governments, *Land,* p. 3, adds that "as population grew, . . . the traditional concepts of land as a commodity . . . were not questioned or tested." Rockefeller Brothers Fund, p. 22, speaks of America's "traditional assumption that urbanization rights arise from the land itself."

13. Kamakau, p. 175, describes Kamehameha I's traditional redistribution of land after conquests.

14. Horwitz et al., p. 3, pp. 108–159.

15. Simpich, p. 198.

16. Chinn Ho's Ilikai story: *Hawaii Business,* April 1974.

17. Land sales at $2,000 an acre (to Tokyu Corp.) and $3,600 an acre (to Kobayashi Development Corp.): *Hawaii Observer,* 25 June 1974.

18. Or lease the land, as the Sheraton Corp. did with Bishop Estate land on which Sheraton Waikiki was built, then sold to Kenji Osana.

19. Advertising ran for several months in 1975.

20. State of Hawaii, *Data Book,* 1976, table 87, indicates 74,429 acres of "undeveloped subdivision" on island of Hawaii.

21. Senator D. G. Anderson, quoted in *HSB,* 30 July 1974.

22. Princess' will provided somewhat equivocally that "my said trustees shall not sell any real estate . . . unless in their opinion a sale may be necessary . . . for the best interest of my estate."

23. *HSB,* 21 July 1973, quotes Rev. Abraham Akaka: "The selling of our land for pennies a square foot is shocking to our people."

24. *HA,* 21 June 1973.

25. *HSB,* 25 July 1973.

26. *HSB,* 25 October 1973.

27. Such as Amfac, on Kauai; Campbell Estate, on Oahu; C. Brewer, several places, "to balance off sales"; *HA-HSB,* 9 July 1974; *HA,* 10 April 1974 and 5 May 1974; and many other reported instances.

28. Kamakau, pp. 130, 177, 231, 232; Malo, pp. 53, 145.

29. Kingdom of Hawaii, *Law* of 27 December 1826.

30. *Polynesian,* 4 March 1841.

31. *Polynesian,* 12 July 1851.

32. Kingdom of Hawaii, *Civil Code and Session Laws* of 1858–1859.

33. From ½ percent for wholesaling to 4 percent for retail services and businesses.

34. *HSB,* several 1974 articles by Jerry Tune.

35. *HA,* 13 September 1967.

36. For critical discussion of this rezoning, see Meckler.

37. Fuchs, pp. 226–241.

38. Kahuku theme park application was by F. R. Schuh, was questioned by this writer and F. Sullam on Planning Commission, *HSB,* 25 November 1971. This writer received Tangen's call.

39. Application approved by Planning Commission, *HA,* 12 January 1972; by Land Use Commission, *HA,* 4 February 1972.

40. H.B. 1225 of 1971.

41. Rose, p. 46.

42. State of Hawaii, Department of Planning and Economic Development, *The Visitor Industry* (by Mathematica) and *Hawaii Tourism* (by staff). See also annual research reports and monthly bulletins of Hawaii Visitors Bureau.

43. Hawaii Visitors Bureau expenditures were $2.5 million in 1974, with 75 percent of income from the state. State of Hawaii, *Data Book,* 1975, table 103.

44. Ibid., table 149.

45. See Merrill for treatise on this entire subject.

46. See State of Hawaii, *Data Book,* 1975, table 98; Temporary Visitor Industry Council, *Report,* p. 6; Hitch, pp. 1–45.

47. Preliminary paper by M. A. Ghali, of the University of Hawaii's Economic Research Center, 1973, reported in State of Hawaii, Temporary Visitor Industry Council, p. 19.

48. For analysis of potential effects of tourist tax, see Temporary Visitor Industry Council, *Report,* app. G. Through 1976, the legislature avoided imposing such a tax, although newspaper polls indicated voter approval.

49. State of Hawaii, Department of Planning and Economic Development, *The Visitor Industry,* p. 4.

50. *HA,* 13 June 1967, article by E. Tanji.

51. Ibid., quoting T. Ishikawa.

52. Kaanapali Beach master plan was prepared in 1965 for Amfac by John Carl Warnecke & Associates, with advice from several hotel-specialist architects.

53. State of Hawaii, Temporary Visitor Industry Council, *Report,* p. 13.

54. Legislators' tour was reported by both *HA* and *HSB* during June 1975 (editors of both made the trip), using mainly anonymous quotations. Newspaper editorial was by George Chaplin, *Advertiser* editor: *HA-HSB,* 6 July 1975. A similar trip was made to south Pacific resorts in 1976, eliciting similar comments.

CHAPTER 9

1. For discussion of relationship of power and land in early Hawaii, see Hobbs, "The Land Title."

2. Horwitz et al., pt. 2.

3. Marshall Kaplan et al., *Technical Report 1,* notes: "The absence of an overall state land use plan or policy has . . . shifted power over land uses to the counties. . . . The influence of private developers is also enhanced by the absence of a state strategy."

4. Malo, p. 58. For laws in ancient Hawaii, see Malo, chap. 38. Kamakau, p. 175, describes laws "made" by Kamehameha, proscribing evil actions such as murder, theft, and the taking of property.

5. Kuykendall, vol. 1, p. 9.

6. Kamakau, p. 32.

7. Ibid., p. 175.

8. Ibid., p. 229.

9. Letter from William Richards to Charles Wilkes, 15 March 1841, cited in Kuykendall, vol. 1, p. 274.

10. Ibid., p. 73, referenced from *Missionary Herald,* 17, 1821.

11. Hobbs, *Hawaii: A Pageant,* especially chap. 4, and app. B. Kuykendall, vol. 1, p. 340, cites sources making same point.

12. Gerrit P. Judd's work and finances are reviewed in Joesting, pp. 149–151, and Daws, *Shoal,* pp. 128–131. For formal biography, see Judd, *Dr. Judd.*

13. Kamehameha V's constitution: Thurston, *Fundamental Laws,* p. 181 ff. Kalakaua's constitution: ibid., p. 181 ff.

14. Ibid., p. 195 ff.

15. Blount, p. 120, quoting Queen Liliuokalani's protest handed to Dole at time of takeover.

16. Blount, pp. 126, 140 ff.

17. See note 4 in chapter 2 regarding Cooke *Papers,* letter from C. M. Cooke to Paul Isenberg, 27 March 1893 on this subject.

18. Representative H. R. Gibson: "Manifest destiny says, 'Take them in'." *Congressional Record,* 3 June 1898.

19. Judd, *Informal History,* p. 121.

20. Constitution of the Republic of Hawaii, Thurston, *Fundamental Laws,* p. 198.

21. Republic of Hawaii, *Civil Laws* of 1897. For analysis, see Horwitz et al., pp. 5–15.

22. *Civil Laws* of 1897, sect. 169. Emphasis is added.

23. Horwitz et al., fig. 1, p. 63.

24. Newlands Resolution (Joint Resolution of 7 July 1898) provided that "Congress . . . shall enact special legislation" for "management and disposition" of Hawaii's lands and directed the president to appoint a commission to administer the arrangement (Thurston, *Fundamental Laws,* p. 243). Organic Act (An Act to Provide a Government for the Territory of Hawaii; act of 30 April 1900) had similar provisions (ibid., p. 247).

25. Act of 18 March 1959.

26. Organic Act said: "no corporation, domestic or foreign, shall acquire and hold real estate in Hawaii in excess of 1,000 acres." Thurston, *Fundamental Laws,* p. 251.

27. Report, made by a Colonel Compton, is in U.S. Archives, Washington, D.C.

28. Horwitz et al., p. 20 and notes 33 and 34. These writers found the procedure marked by "informality" and difficult to research. Other lands acquired by the federal government during this period are described, ibid., pp. 61–105 and listed in tables 8–13.

29. Construction of military installations is reviewed in Judd, *Informal History,* pp. 125–128.

30. Horwitz et al., p. 20.

31. Fuchs, p. 184, points out that Wilson delayed appointing a governor for the territory, being occupied with "more important affairs on the mainland" and, p. 195, that FDR, visiting the islands in 1934, "ate and drank his way through a series of receptions given by the Army and Navy and Harvard graduates." See also Fuchs, chap. 7, on *No New Deal for Hawaii.*

32. Fuchs, especially chap. 10; Daws, *Shoal,* chap. 8; Judd, *Informal History,* chap. 14.

33. Fuchs, pp. 249, 250; Daws, *Shoal,* p. 313.

34. In 1900 there were 37,000 Hawaiians and part-Hawaiians to 29,000 Caucasians (including Portuguese and Puerto Ricans); in 1940 there were 50,000 part and full Hawaiians to 112,000 Caucasians. Gardner and Nordyke, table 9.

35. *HA,* 4 December 1975, article by Douglas Woo; *HA,* 14 December 1975, column by this writer.

36. Fuchs, p. 214 ff.

37. Most thorough study of unionism in Hawaii, to 1960, is Fuchs, pp. 214 ff. and 354 ff.

38. *Hawaii Business,* July 1973, pp. 31–40.

39. This writer was consultant in planning to the university during much of the early thrust toward a central Oahu campus.

40. Eckbo et al., *West Oahu College.*

41. Eckbo et al., *Land Use Districts,* p. 51.

42. State of Hawaii, Department of Planning and Economic Development, *Central Oahu Planning Study.*

43. Policy memoranda were written in preparation of Department of Planning and Economic Development's *Growth Policies Plan.*

44. Heald, Hobson Associates.

45. *HA,* 28 January 1976, story was headlined "U.H. May Attempt Bypass of LUC Rezoning Refusal."

46. Planning consultant was this writer.

47. Coffman, chap. 3.

48. Architect introduced to governor and mayor was this writer.

49. Godwin and Shepard, pp. 14–20.

50. Ibid., p. 16.

51. *HA,* 6 February 1975.

52. *HA,* 1 July 1970.

53. *HA,* 2 May 1972.

54. Original board was entirely haole. John Clarke, appointed in 1924, was first part-Hawaiian. Today two part-Hawaiians are trustees: Richard Lyman, Jr., and Myron Thompson. Strong appeals were made for Hawaiian appointee in 1971 when vacancy occurred, but AJA Matsuo Takabuki was named. Successful demands were raised in 1974, resulting in Thompson's selection.

55. For analyses of Hawaiian Native Claims Settlement Act (H.B. 15666 of 1974), see Jones (prepared for Congressional Research Service) and Levy, p. 881 ff.

56. *HSB,* 15 February 1976 and 11 April 1976.

57. *HA,* 21 November 1975.

58. *HSB,* 11 February 1975.

59. *HSB,* 9 March 1976.

60. Liliuokalani, pp. 273–275.

61. Stokes, who contends that the ancestor from whom Princesses Ruth Keelikolani and Bernice Pauahi were descended, Kaoleioku, was not a son of Kamehameha I, as he is listed in later genealogies, but of Kalaniopuu, king of Hawaii before Kamehameha's accession, as he is recorded in genealogies before 1843, according to Stokes' sources.

62. *HSB-HA,* 15 February 1976, quoting Donald Wright, former president of Alaska Federation of Natives.

PART 3 INTRODUCTION

1. For summaries of state land-control measures adopted in 1960s and 1970s, see Bosselman and Callies, *Quiet Revolution;* Tager, for American Institute of Architects; Council of State Governments, *Land Use Puzzle* and *Land;* Rockefeller Brothers Fund, especially pp. 55–72. More thorough studies of legislation in Oregon, Vermont, Florida, and Hawaii are in Conservation Foundation series.

2. Godwin and Shepard, p. 23.

3. Ibid., p. 25, notes "language that either implies that all objectives can be simultaneously achieved or that fails to establish priorities."

CHAPTER 10

1. Mumford, *Culture of Cities,* p. 146, writes of "the suppressed land hunger of the Europeans" with its outlet in "opening up of the New World."

2. For land policies in nineteenth-century Europe, particularly England, see Haar; in America of that time, see Johnson and Barlowe.

3. Mumford, *Culture of Cities,* chap. 3.

4. Ibid., especially chap. 6; Giedion, pp. 609–680.

5. When Dr. Judd took office in 1842, he noted this fact as well as that the national debt was $60,000 and that the government had no accounting or auditing system—in correspondence annotated by Kuykendall vol. 1, p. 233, and noted by Judd, *Informal History,* p. 71.

6. Chinen, *Just Compensation.*

7. *Islander,* 26 May 1875.

8. Morgan, p. 182.

9. Horwitz et al., pp. 45, 46.

10. Council of State Governments, *A Legislative Guide,* p. 4, notes that under President Theodore Roosevelt a White House council was held in 1906 to consider need for conservation of "the fundamental sources of wealth of this great nation," inspiring most states to set up conservation agencies.

11. Territory of Hawaii, Land Law Revision Commission, *Report,* 31 December 1946, p. 55.

12. State of Hawaii, Act 187 of 1961, Declaration of Purpose.

13. Federal Housing Act of 1961 authorized funds for grants to states for open-space planning, an action which resulted in many plans of varying quality. See Scott, p. 569.

14. In Act 182 of 1969.

15. For description of McHarg's methodology, see Conservation Foundation, *Three Approaches;* for case studies using the method, see McHarg, throughout.

16. Overview Corporation, p. 7.

17. Several times a number of interested persons (including this writer) were called together for nonsubstantive briefings, primarily on methodology. In talks to citizens groups Udall was even more closemouthed about the trend of his studies.

18. Overview Corporation, pp. 167–172, gives an excellent summary of common land-conservation methods. For more full discussion, see Whyte, chaps. 3–7.

19. State of Hawaii, Temporary Commission on Statewide Environmental Planning, *A Plan*, p. 13.

20. Ibid., p. 8 ff.

21. Ibid., pp. 35–42.

22. Environmental Policy Act: Act 247 of 1974. Environmental Impact Statement Act: Act 246 of 1974.

23. State of Hawaii, Temporary Visitor Industry Council, *Report*, pp. i, 24, 77.

24. Economic plateau was predicted by W. H. Hillendahl, vice-president, Bank of Hawaii, *HA*, 7 July 1976.

25. *HA*, 16 January 1976.

26. *HA*, 13 October 1976.

27. City and County of Honolulu, Department of General Planning, *An Evaluation*, p. 7.

28. State of Hawaii, Department of Planning and Economic Development, *Growth Policies*, p. 28 ff.

29. Ibid., pp. 57, 58.

CHAPTER 11

1. Altshuler, p. 209, defines planning as "the effort to infuse activity with constancy and consistent purpose."

2. Cook and King, quoted in *Ancient Hawaiian Civilization*, p. 79.

3. Ledyard, p. 128.

4. Neil, p. 10.

5. Scott, p. 335 ff.

6. *Hawaiian Annual*, 1907, pp. 97–105, urged "beautifying" of Hawaii. *Pencil Points*, December 1916, contained "Plea for a More Tropical Honolulu." Planner Charles Mulford Robinson was called to Honolulu in 1906 by Board of Supervisors to prepare beautification plan. Mainland architects Ralph Adams Cram and Bertram Grosvenor Goodhue, among others, did work in Honolulu, searching for a "Hawaiian style" in the 1920s. See Neil, pp. 18 ff. and 53 ff.

7. *Pencil Points*, January 1945, illustrated competition for Honolulu's civic center.

8. See *Hawaii Observer*, 21 August 1973, article by B. Baker on early official planning efforts in Honolulu.

9. Mumford, *Whither Hawaii?*

10. Ibid.

11. See *Pencil Points,* June, July, September 1944; January, July, December 1945.

12. For purposes and definitions of city planning, see Altshuler and also Schnore and Fagin; for history of city planning in America, see Scott.

13. For philosophical concept of general plan see Kent, pp. 12 ff. For history of general planning in America, see Scott, pp. 493, 494 ff.

14. Supreme Court of Hawaii, Dalton et al. vs. City and County of Honolulu et al., 51 Hawaii, 1969.

15. A. Black, "The Comprehensive Plan."

16. State of Hawaii, Department of Planning and Economic Development, *Growth Policies,* p. 2.

17. Ibid., p. 3.

18. Letter from Dr. Mark to this writer, 20 May 1974.

19. Act 189 of 1975 called for new state plan.

20. City and County of Honolulu, Department of General Planning, *An Evaluation,* p. 1.

21. Charter Commission's general-plan position was bolstered by study of national trends made by staff aide Phyllis Turnbull. See City and County of Honolulu, Charter Commission, *Urban Planning and Policy,* 1972.

22. City and County of Honolulu, Department of General Planning, *Proposed Objectives* and *An Evaluation.*

23. Same source, *The Planning Process,* 1972.

24. *An Evaluation,* p. 3.

25. Ibid., p. 144 ff.

26. See, for example, *HA,* 4 January 1975, and *HSB,* 8 February 1974, 4 June 1974, and 25 October 1974.

27. State of Hawaii, Department of Planning and Economic Development, *State Planning,* pt. 2, summary, first two pages (unnumbered).

28. Ibid.

29. State of Hawaii, Land Use Commission, *Five Year Review,* by Eckbo et al., p. 118.

30. State of Hawaii, *Hawaii Revised Statutes,* chap. 201, sect. 23: "the Department of Planning and Economic Development shall prepare a general plan in sections, one for each county."

31. H.B. 2381, 1975.

32. *Star-Bulletin* editor called for Way's removal. This writer, in *HSB-HA* column of 29 June 1975, called for consultant services.

33. *HA,* 7 June 1975, quoting corporation counsel: "We express grave uncertainty as to whether this phase of the revised general plan will survive judicial scrutiny."

34. *HA,* 13 May 1976.

35. City and County of Honolulu, City Council, *New General Plan.*

36. *HA,* 12 August 1976.

37. See, for example, *HSB:* 11 October 1974, 23 October 1974, 28 December 1974.

38. H.B. 808, 1973.

39. When this writer mentioned financial hurts caused by commission's arbitrary decisions (*HSB-HA,* 5 January 1975), a number of developers called and wrote to agree. Most notable unexpected refusal was of Bishop Estate's request for reclassification of Waiawa Ridge in Oahu.

40. Act 193 of 1975.

41. For the study, see Catanese. Letter explaining methodology: Catanese to this writer, 20 June 1972.

42. AIA study group financed by Ford Foundation reported to sponsor on *Some Observations.*

43. Later AIA study group made findings known in *Honolulu Rudat,* "Issues and Findings" section (pages not numbered).

44. Pacific Urban Studies and Planning Program, conceived, achieved, and headed by Professor Tom Dinell.

45. Oahu Transportation Study was undertaken in 1963 after federal funds were requested (Senate Resolution 48, 1961) and granted and City and County of Honolulu expressed intention to participate (Council Resolution 69, 1962). Study was undertaken in 1963 and completed (issued in three volumes) in 1967.

46. Daniel, Mann, Johnson & Mendenhall, *Preliminary Engineering Evaluation Program.*

47. Potential effect of H3 on windward communities was studied by Eckbo et al., *Socio-Economic Study.*

48. Court challenges to EISs are almost always on procedural rather than substantive matters.

49. Alternative routes would invariably cause damage to existing communities.

50. See Hawaii Revised Statutes, sect. 37–62.

51. State of Hawaii, Department of Planning and Economic Development, *State Planning,* pt. 3.

52. See analysis of effects in League of Women Voters, *State Planning,* p. 16.

53. Early zoning in the United States is discussed in Scott, p. 75.

54. Urban Land Institute, *Density,* pp. 26–32.

55. Potomac Institute, *Urban Growth.*

56. *HA,* 26 July 1974.

57. See article by Jerry Tune in *HSB,* 16 October 1975.

58. Costonis, "Development Rights."

59. Costonis, "The Chicago Plan."

60. McElroy.

61. *HA,* 4 January 1975.

62. Act 176 of 1975.

63. F. P. Bosselman wrote *Quiet Revolution* for Council on Environmental Quality in 1971; P. Myers wrote *Slow Start in Paradise* for Conservation Foundation in 1974.

64. *HSB-HA,* 29 June 1975.

CHAPTER 12

1. Act 119 of 1973.

2. Story by Douglas Carlson in *HSB-HA,* 8 December 1974.

3. *Hawaii Architect,* September 1973, throughout.

4. Spreiregen.

5. This writer chided Planning Department for ignoring urban design in a column in *HSB-HA* in April 1974. Response was by Donald Clegg, deputy planning officer, in letter to editor of *Advertiser.*

6. Lynch, especially pp. 1–14.

7. Wolbrink & Associates, *Kailua Village.*

8. AIA, *Rudat.*

9. Clegg, in letter cited in note 5 above, called it a "quickie, shallow job."

10. *HA,* 30 April 1970.

11. City and County of Honolulu, Department of General Planning, *Proposed Objectives,* p. 90.

12. *HA,* 16 November 1975.

13. State of Hawaii, Department of Planning and Economic Development, *Kakaako.*

14. *HA,* 10 April 1974.

15. Leo S. Wou.

16. See Gruen & Associates, *Planning for Downtown.*

17. Downtown Improvement Association, *Space Design,* credited to staff member Harold Senter.

18. *HSB,* 14 June 1974, and *HA,* 15 June 1974.

19. See article by Tune in *HSB,* 16 October 1975. Waikiki legislation was Bill 144.

20. For State Foundation on Culture and the Arts, *Environmental and Urban Design Projects,* see references to Belt, Collins & Associates; Oahu Development Conference; Walters; Warnecke & Associates; and Wolbrink & Associates in following chapter.

CHAPTER 13

1. State of Hawaii, State Foundation on Culture and the Arts, *Revised General Application to National Foundation on the Arts,* 17 April 1967,

p. 6. Applications and correspondence referenced hereafter are in Office of Director of State Foundation.

   2. Memorandum to Alfred Preis, 13 August 1968. (Henceforth all quotes from critics are noted Memo, of certain date, written by person quoted to Preis.)

   3. Belt, Collins & Associates, *EUDP*.

   4. Ibid., p. 4.

   5. Ibid., p. 32.

   6. Memo, 17 July 1968, p. 1.

   7. Memo, 28 August 1968, p. 2.

   8. Creighton and Walters.

   9. *HA,* 25 June 1976.

  10. Wolbrink & Associates, *Kona Community* and *Kailua Village*.

  11. Oahu Development Conference, *EUDP*.

  12. Memo, 1968, undated, p. 19.

  13. Ibid., p. 20.

  14. Memo, 17 July 1968, p. 4.

  15. *HA,* 9 October 1975.

  16. Memo, 1968, undated, p. 18.

  17. Walters, *EUDP*.

  18. Memo, 1968, undated, p. 8b.

  19. Memo, 5 July 1968, p. 1.

  20. Warnecke & Associates, *EUDP*.

  21. Wolbrink & Associates, *EUDP*.

  22. Memo, 11 October 1968, p. 2.

  23. Memo, 17 July 1968, p. 4.

  24. Memo, 18 July 1968, p. 2.

  25. Wolbrink & Associates, *EUDP,* p. 230.

CHAPTER 14

   1. See Chaplin and Paige, throughout.

   2. Theobold, p. 26.

   3. McHale, p. 8.

   4. Chaplin and Paige, p. 123.

   5. Sometimes because of new developments. Dator, *Neither Here nor There,* writes: "frequently when we reach the limits of one mode, a transformation occurs which pushes the old limits aside and places new ones far beyond our reach—for a time."

   6. Chaplin and Paige, p. 457.

   7. Ibid., p. 412.

   8. Ibid., pp. 176–197.

   9. Ibid., p. 195.

10. Ibid., p. 191 ff.

11. Ibid., pp. 465–472.

12. *HA*, 25 March 1973.

13. *HA*, 25 September 1975.

14. Oahu Development Conference, *Alternative Urban Growth Strategies.*

15. University of Hawaii, Hawaii Environmental Simulation Laboratory, *Kaneohe Alternatives.*

16. State of Hawaii, Temporary Commission on Statewide Environmental Planning, *A Plan,* p. 13.

17. Term "ecosystem," defined as interaction of all things in an environment, living and nonliving, is attributed to A. G. Tansley, in *Ecology* 16, 1935, pp. 286–307.

18. R. W. Force, in Force and Bishop (eds.), *The Impact,* p. 354.

19. Mangenot.

20. Cowan.

21. Ibid., p. 340.

22. Force, in *The Impact,* p. 351: "any stimulus imposed upon their relatively precarious natural balance is likely to have far more serious effects than if it were imposed upon a continental milieu."

23. Fosberg, in *Man's Place,* pp. 5, 6.

24. Force, in *The Impact,* p. 360. Fosberg, in *Man's Place,* p. 4, makes similar statement.

25. Taueber.

26. Bosselman, *Alternatives,* p. 49.

27. Berman vs. Parker, 348 U.S. 26 (1945).

28. Potomac Institute, p. 3.

29. H.B. 2381, 1975.

30. Roberts, p. 26 n., writes: "The Act made owners of land holders, in the same way that holders of personal property were owners."

31. England's Magna Charta is generally considered the first limitation on the rights of eminent domain, that is, the right of a government to take private property for public purpose. See Bosselman, *Alternatives,* p. 42.

32. Impact of "taking clause" is analyzed in Bosselman et al., *The Taking Issue.* See also Council of State Governments, *Land,* p. 7, and Rockefeller Brothers Fund, p. 24.

33. Supreme Court of Florida, 60 So. 2d 663 (1952).

34. 393 U.S. 14 (1968) upheld Ross case decision.

35. European land banking, U.S. Department of Housing and Urban Development, *Selected Aspects;* American land banking, Flechner.

36. Puerto Rico Laws, Ann. tit. 23 311f(j), 1964.

37. Fishman and Gross, pp. 916–924. See also Bosselman and Callies, *Quiet Revolution,* and Tager, *Innovations.*

38. U.S. National Commission on Urban Problems, pp. 252, 253.
39. AIA report is *America at the Growing Edge*.
40. Roberts, p. 43.
41. Collins, in Chaplin and Paige, p. 193.
42. *HSB*, 25 September 1971. See also column by this writer, *HSB-HA*, 11 January 1976, and response by H. L. Miller, *HA*, 31 January 1976.
43. *HA*, 22 June 1973.

EPILOGUE
1. D. Pellegrin, in *HA*, 23 July 1975.
2. *HA*, 18 July 1975.
3. Governor, *HA*, 23 July 1975; mayor, *HA*, 18 July 1975.
4. *HA*, 22 April 1976.
5. *HSB*, 3 January 1977.
6. *HSB-HA*, 27 February 1977.

Bibliography

Adler, J. *Claus Spreckels: The Sugar King in Hawaii.* Honolulu: University of Hawaii Press, 1966.

Alexander, Arthur C. *The Koloa Plantation: 1835–1935.* Honolulu: Star-Bulletin Press, 1937.

Alexander, William D. *A Brief Account of the Hawaiian Government Survey.* Honolulu: Bulletin Steam Print, 1889.

_____. *A Brief History of Land Titles in the Hawaiian Kingdom.* Honolulu: Advertiser Steam Plant, 1882.

Allen, Gwenfread E. *Hawaii's War Years.* Honolulu: University of Hawaii Press, 1950.

Altshuler, Alan. *The City Planning Process.* Ithaca: Cornell University Press, 1965.

American Institute of Architects. *Some Observations on the Current Land-Use Development in the State of Hawaii.* Committee Report to Ford Foundation. Mimeographed. Washington, 1973.

_____. *Honolulu Rudat.* Privately printed. Honolulu, 1974.

_____. *America at the Growing Edge: A Strategy for Building a Better America.* Privately printed. Washington, 1973.

Ancient Hawaiian Civilization: A Series of Lectures Delivered at the Kamehameha Schools. 2d rev. ed. Rutland, Vt.: Charles E. Tuttle, 1965.

Anthony, J. Garner. *Hawaii under Army Rule.* Honolulu: The University Press of Hawaii, 1975.

Apple, Russel A. *Trails: From Steppingstones to Kerbstones.* Honolulu: Bishop Museum Press, 1965.

Babbie, Earl E. *The Maximillion Report.* Privately printed. Honolulu, 1972.

Bartholomew, Harland H. & Associates. *An Index of Available Information on Land Use in Hawaii.* Prepared for Territory of Hawaii, Planning Office, Honolulu, 1957.

———. *Land Use Districts for the State of Hawaii.* Prepared for State of Hawaii, Land Use Commission. Honolulu, 1963.

Beckwith, Martha W. *The Kumulipo: A Hawaiian Creation Chant.* Reprinted ed. Honolulu: University Press of Hawaii, 1972.

———. *Hawaiian Mythology.* Honolulu: University Press of Hawaii, 1977.

Belt, Collins & Associates. *West Hawaii Highway Corridor Study.* Environmental and Urban Design Proposals for the State of Hawaii, State Foundation on Culture and the Arts. Privately printed. Honolulu, 1968.

Bingham, Hiram. *Residence of Twenty-one Years in the Sandwich Islands.* Hartford: H. Huntington, 1847.

Bishop, Charles. Journal. Ms., Archives of British Columbia.

Black, Alan. "The Comprehensive Plan." In *Principles and Practice of Urban Planning,* edited by William Goodman and Eric Freund. Washington: International City Managers' Association, 1968.

Blount, James H. *Report to U.S. Congress: Hawaiian Islands.* Executive Document no. 47, 53d Cong. 2d sess. Washington, 1893.

Bosselman, Fred P. *Alternatives to Urban Sprawl.* Prepared for National Council on Urban Problems. Washington: U.S. Government Printing Office, 1968.

Bosselman, Fred P. and Callies, David. *The Quiet Revolution in Land Use Control.* Prepared for Council on Environmental Quality. Washington: U.S. Government Printing Office, 1971.

Bosselman, Fred P.; Callies, David; and Banta, John. *The Taking Issue.* Prepared for Council on Environmental Quality. Washington: U.S. Government Printing Office, 1973.

Brennan, Joseph. *The Parker Ranch of Hawaii.* New York: John Day, 1974.

Campbell, Archibald. *Voyage Around the World: 1806–1812.* Edinburgh: A. Constable, 1816.

Candeub, Isadore I. "New Techniques in Making the General Plan." In *Urban Planning in Transition,* edited by Ernest Erber. New York: Grossman, 1970.

Carlquist, Sherwin J. *Hawaii: A Natural History.* Garden City: Natural History Press, 1970.

Catanese, Anthony J. *Testing an Emerging Model of State Planning: A Report Card.* Atlanta: Georgia Institute of Technology, 1973.

Chaplin, George, and Paige, Glenn D. (eds.). *Hawaii 2000*. Honolulu: University Press of Hawaii, 1973.

Chinen, Jon D. *The Great Mahele*. Honolulu: University of Hawaii Press, 1958.

_____. Just Compensation in Eminent Domain Proceedings. Privately printed. Honolulu, 1962.

_____. *Original Land Titles in Hawaii*. Privately printed. Honolulu, 1971.

Clawson, Marion. "Historical Overview of Land Use Planning in the United States." In *Environment: A New Focus for Land Use Planning*, edited by Donald M. McCallister. Washington: National Science Foundation, 1973.

Coffman, Tom. *Catch a Wave: A Case Study of Hawaii's New Politics*. Honolulu: University Press of Hawaii, 1973.

Commoner, Barry. *The Closing Circle*. New York: Alfred A. Knopf, 1971.

Conservation Foundation. *The New Oregon Trail, So Goes Vermont, Slow Start in Paradise, Zoning Hawaii*. Privately printed. Washington, 1970–1976.

_____. *Three Approaches to Environmental Resource Analysis*. Privately printed. Washington, 1969.

Cook, James, and King, James. *Voyage to the Pacific Ocean*. 3 vols. London: W. and A. Strahan, 1784.

Costonis, John J. "Development Rights Transfer: An Explanatory Essay." *Yale Law Journal* 83 (1973).

_____. "The Chicago Plan." *Harvard Law Review* 85 (1972).

Council of State Governments. *Data Needs and Resources for State Land Use Planning*. Privately printed. Lexington, 1974.

_____. *Land: State Alternatives for Planning and Management*. Privately printed. Lexington, 1975.

_____. *Land Use Puzzle*. Privately printed. Lexington, 1974.

_____. *A Legislative Guide to State Land Use Planning*. Privately printed. Lexington, 1975.

Cowan, Ian M. "Micro-ecosystems in Sharper Focus." In *The Impact of Urban Centers in the Pacific*. Honolulu: Pacific Science Association. 1975.

Creighton, Thomas H., and Walters, George S. *The South Kona Coast Historic and Recreation Area Plan*. Prepared for State of Hawaii, Department of Land and Natural Resources. Privately printed. Honolulu, 1969.

Daniel, Mann, Johnson & Mendenhall. *Preliminary Engineering Evaluation Program*. Prepared for City and County of Honolulu, Mass Transit Division, Department of Traffic. Honolulu, 1972.

Dator, James A. "Neither There nor Then: A Eutopian Alternative to the

Development Model of Future Society." In *Futures, Special Publication* (1973):87–141.

———. *The Limits to the Limits of Growth*. Privately duplicated. Honolulu, 1972.

Daws, Gavan. "Government and Land in Hawaii." *Hawaiian Historical Review,* vol. 2, no. C, (1967).

———. "Honolulu, the First Century: Influences in the Development of the Town to 1876." Ph.D. dissertation no. 100, University of Hawaii, undated.

———. *Shoal of Time*. Honolulu: The University Press of Hawaii, 1975.

Dillingham, Sanford B. "Evolution of Hawaiian Land Tenures." *Papers of the Hawaiian Historical Society,* no. 3, 1892.

Dinell, Tom. *Filling the Calabash: How Much Is Too Much?* University of Hawaii, Pacific Urban Studies Program. Privately printed. Honolulu, 1974.

Downtown Improvement Association of Honolulu. *Space Design Concept for Downtown Honolulu*. Privately printed. Honolulu, 1975.

Eckbo, Dean, Austin & Williams. *General Plan for the Island of Kauai*. Joint venture with Muroda, Tanaka & Itigawa. Prepared for Department of Planning, Kauai. Honolulu, 1970.

———. *Hawaii Land Use Districts and Regulations Review*. Prepared for State of Hawaii, Land Use Commission. Honolulu, 1969.

———. *Socio-Economic Study: The Effects of Change on a Windward Oahu Community*. Prepared for State of Hawaii, Department of Transportation. Honolulu, 1973.

———. *West Oahu College Preliminary Site Selection Evaluation*. Prepared for University of Hawaii. Honolulu, 1972.

Ellis, William. *Journal of William Ellis*. London, 1827. Reprint. Honolulu: Advertiser Publishing Company, 1963.

Estermann, Philip I. *Kaluakoi*. Mimeographed. Honolulu, 1973.

Fairfax, Geoffrey W. *Architecture of Honolulu*. Sydney: Island Heritage, 1972.

Fishman, Richard P., and Gross, Robert D. "Public Land Banking." *Case Western Law Review* 921(1972):899–975.

Flechner, Hervey L. *Land Banking and the Control of Urban Development*. New York: Praeger, 1974.

Force, Roland W., and Bishop, Brenda (eds.). *The Impact of Urban Centers in the Pacific*. Honolulu: Science Foundation, 1975.

Fornander, Abraham. *An Account of the Polynesian Race*. 3 vols. London, 1878–1885. Reprinted. Honolulu: Charles E. Tuttle, 1969.

Fosberg, Francis R. (ed.). *Man's Place in the Island Ecosystem*. Tenth Pacific Science Congress. Honolulu: Bishop Museum Press, 1963.

Friend. Journal, Honolulu.

Fuchs, Lawrence H. *Hawaii Pono: A Social History.* New York: Harcourt, Brace & World, 1961.

Gardner, Robert W., and Nordyke, Eleanor C. *The Demographic Situation in Hawaii.* Papers of the East-West Center Population Institute, no. 3. Honolulu, 1974.

Giedion, Siegfried. *Space, Time and Architecture.* 3d ed., enlarged. Cambridge: Harvard University Press, 1959.

Godwin, R. Kenneth, and Shepard, W. Bruce. *State Land Use Policies: Winners and Losers.* Privately duplicated. Corvallis: Oregon State University, 1974.

Gruen, Victor & Associates. *Planning for Downtown Honolulu.* Prepared for City and County of Honolulu, Departments of Planning and Public Works. Honolulu, 1968.

Haar, Charles M. (ed.). *Land and Law: Anglo-American Planning Practice.* Cambridge: Harvard University Press, 1964.

Handy, E. S. Craighill, and Pukui, Mary Kawena. *The Polynesian Family System in Ka-'u, Hawaii.* Rutland, Vt.: Charles E. Tuttle, 1972.

Hardin, Garrett J. *Exploring New Ethics for Survival.* New York: Viking, 1972.

Hawaii Architect. Journal of American Institute of Architects, Hawaii chapter.

Hawaii Business. Magazine, Honolulu.

Hawaii, Kingdom of. *Laws.* By years. Archives of Hawaii.

_____. *Privy Council Records.* Archives of Hawaii.

_____. Board of Commissioners to Quiet Land Titles (Land Board). *Foreign Register, Testimony, Awards.* Archives of Hawaii.

Hawaii Mission Children's Society. *Missionary Album.* 3d enlarged ed. Honolulu, 1969.

Hawaii Observer. Weekly newspaper, Honolulu.

Hawaii, State of. Department of Health, Air Sanitation Branch. *Air Pollution Implementation Plan.* Mimeographed. Honolulu, 1973.

_____. Department of Transportation and Department of Planning and Economic Development. *Oahu Transportation Study.* 3 vols. Honolulu, 1967.

_____. Department of Planning and Economic Development. *Central Oahu Planning Study.* Honolulu, 1973.

_____. _____. *Data Book.* Annual.

_____. _____. *General Plan Revision Program.* 6 vols. Honolulu, 1967.

_____. _____. *General Plan Revision Program: Growth Policies Plan.* Honolulu, 1974.

_____. _____. *Hawaii Tourism Impact Plan.* Honolulu, 1972.

————. ————. *Housing for Hawaii's People.* Honolulu, 1977.

————. ————. *Kakaako: An Urban Design Demonstration Study.* Honolulu, 1975.

————. ————. *State Comprehensive Outdoor Recreation Plan.* Honolulu, 1971.

————. ————. *State Planning in Hawaii: Legislative Inventory and Analysis.* Mimeographed. Honolulu, 1972.

————. ————. *The Visitor Industry and Hawaii's Economy: A Cost Analysis.* Honolulu, 1970.

————. Department of Land and Natural Resources. *Accountants' Report (Peal, Marwick, Mitchell).* Honolulu, 1971.

————. ————. *Regulation 4, Providing for Land-Use Regulations within the Conservation Districts.* Regulations of State Land Board. Honolulu, undated.

————. Environmental Quality Commission. *Environmental Impact Statements: Regulations.* Honolulu, 1975.

————. Governor's Economic Advisory Task Force. *Report.* Honolulu, 1976.

————. House of Representatives. *Journal of the First Legislature, 1962.* Honolulu, 1962.

————. Office of the Lieutenant Governor. *Hawaii's Crisis in Housing.* Honolulu, 1970.

————. *Hawaii Revised Statutes.* Honolulu.

————. Legislative Reference Bureau. *Digest of Dalton, et al. vs. City and County of Honolulu, et al.* Honolulu, 1969.

————. State Foundation on Culture and the Arts. *Environmental and Urban Design Projects.* 5 report vols. Honolulu, 1968.

————. Temporary Commission on Statewide Environmental Planning. *A Plan for Hawaii's Environment.* Honolulu, 1973.

————. Temporary Visitor Industry Council. *Report.* Honolulu, 1973.

Hawaii, Territory of. Commissioners of Public Land. *Reports.* Archives of Hawaii.

————. Land Law Revision Committee. *Reports.* Archives of Hawaii.

Hawaiian Annual. Periodical. Honolulu.

Hawaiian Spectator. Periodical. Honolulu.

Heald, Hobson & Associates. *A Plan for Meeting the Future Growth of the University of Hawaii.* Privately duplicated. New York, 1967.

Heller, H. Robert, and Heller, Emily E. *Economic and Social Impacts of Foreign Investment in Hawaii.* Prepared for Economic Research Center, University of Hawaii. Honolulu, 1973.

Historic Buildings Task Force. *Old Honolulu: A Guide to Oahu's Historic Buildings.* Privately printed. Honolulu, 1969.

Hitch, Thomas K. *The Impact of Major Exports on the Hawaiian Economy.* Privately printed. Honolulu, 1972.

Hobbs, Jean. *Hawaii: A Pageant of the Soil.* Stanford: Stanford University Press, 1935.

_____. "The Land Title in Hawaii." *Hawaiian Historical Society Report.* 1931.

Honolulu Advertiser. Newspaper.

Honolulu, City and County of. Charter Commission. *Urban Planning and Policy: A Political Symbiosis.* Research Report no. 5. Mimeographed. Honolulu, 1972.

_____. City Council. *New General Plan: Statement of Objectives and Policies.* Honolulu, 1976.

_____. Department of General Planning. *Planning for Oahu: An Evaluation of Alternative Residential Policies.* Honolulu, 1974.

_____. _____. *Planning for Oahu: Proposed Objectives and Policies for the Revised General Plan.* Honolulu, 1974.

_____. Planning Department. *General Plan, Oahu.* Council Ordinance no. 2443. Honolulu, 1964.

_____. _____. *The Planning Process in Evolution: A Working Paper.* Honolulu, 1972.

Honolulu, Hawaiian Mission Children's Society Library. *Elias Bond papers.*

_____. *Charles Montague Cooke papers.*

_____. *Samuel N. Castle papers.*

Honolulu Magazine. Monthly magazine.

Honolulu Mercury. Journal.

Honolulu Star-Bulletin. Newspaper.

Horowitz Robert H., and Meller, Norman. *Land and Politics in Hawaii.* East Lansing: Michigan State University Press, 1966.

Horwitz, Robert H., and others. *Public Land Policy in Hawaii: An Historical Analysis.* Prepared for Legislative Reference Bureau, University of Hawaii. Honolulu, 1969.

Hulten, John J. *Report to the Mayor and Board of Supervisors of the City and County of Honolulu.* Privately printed. Honolulu, 1958.

Humphries, Grace. "Hawaiian Homesteading: A Chapter in the Economic Development of Hawaii." Master's thesis, University of Hawaii, 1937.

Hungerford, John B. *Hawaiian Railroads.* Reseda, Calif. Hungerford Press, 1963.

Ii, John Papa. *Fragments of Hawaiian History.* Reprinted. Honolulu: Bishop Museum Press, 1963.

Islander. Journal, Honolulu.

Joesting, Edward. *Hawaii: An Uncommon History.* New York: W. W. Norton, 1972.

Johnson, Vernon W., and Barlowe, Raleigh. *Land Problems and Politics.* New York: McGraw-Hill Books, 1954.

Jones Richard S. *Comparison of Alaska Native Claims Settlement with Property Rights of Native Hawaiians.* Prepared for Congressional Research Service. Library of Congress. Washington: U.S. Government Printing Office, 1973.

Judd, Gerrit P., IV. *Dr. Judd, Hawaii's Friend.* Honolulu: University of Hawaii Press, 1960.

———. *Hawaii: An Informal History.* New York: Crowell-Collier, 1961.

Judd, Laura Fish. *Honolulu: Sketches of the Life, Social, Political and Religious, in the Hawaiian Islands from 1828 to 1861.* New York: Anson D. G. Randolph, 1880.

Kahn, Herman, and Wiener, Anthony J. *The Year 2000.* New York: Macmillan, 1967.

Kamakau, Samuel M. *Ruling Chiefs of Hawaii.* Reprinted. Honolulu: Bishop Museum Press, 1961.

Kamm, Gregory, and Etherington, Bruce. *Recreative Space as a Measure of Horizon Population.* Privately duplicated. Honolulu, 1974.

Kelly, Marion A. "Changes in Land Tenure in Hawaii: 1778–1850." Master's thesis, University of Hawaii, 1956.

Kent T. J., Jr. *The Urban General Plan.* San Francisco: Chandler, 1964.

Kotzebue, Otto von. *A New Voyage around the World.* London, 1830. Reprinted. New York: Da Capo Press, 1967.

Kuykendall, Ralph S. *The Hawaiian Kingdom.* 3 vols. Honolulu: University of Hawaii Press, 1938–1967.

League of Women Voters of Hawaii. *Conservation and Hawaii's Conservation Districts.* Bulletin. Mimeographed. Honolulu, 1972.

———. *Facts and Issues: Hawaii's Land Use Law.* Bulletin. Mimeographed. Honolulu, 1972.

———. *State Planning in Hawaii: A Primer.* Bulletin. Mimeographed. Honolulu, 1972.

Ledyard, John. *A Journal of Captian Cook's Last Voyage to the Pacific Ocean.* Hartford, 1783. Reprinted. Corvallis: Oregon State University Press, 1963.

Levy, Neil M. "Native Hawaiian Land Rights." *California Law Review* 63 (1974).

Liliuokalani, Queen of Hawaii. *Hawaii's Story by Hawaii's Queen.* Boston: Lothrop, Lee and Shepard, 1898.

Lind, Andrew W. *An Island Community: Ecological Succession in Hawaii.* Chicago: University of Chicago Press, 1938.

———. *Hawaii's People.* 3d ed. Honolulu: University Press of Hawaii, 1974.

_____. *Japanese in Hawaii Under War Conditions*. New York: Institute of Pacific Relations, 1942.

Livingston & Blayney. *Foothills Environmental Design Study*. Prepared for City of Palo Alto, California. Privately printed. Palo Alto, 1971.

Lydgate, John M. "The Vanishing Kuleana." In *Hawaiian Annual,* 1915.

Lynch, Kevin. *The Image of the City*. Cambridge: Technology Press and Harvard University Press, 1960.

MacDonald, Gordon A., and Kyselka, Will. *Anatomy of an Island: A Geological History of Oahu*. Honolulu: Bishop Museum Press, 1967.

Maile Quarterly. Journal. Honolulu.

Malo, David. *Hawaiian Antiquities*. Reprinted. Honolulu: Bishop Museum Press, 1971.

Mangenot, G. "The Effect of Man on the Plant World." In *Man's Place in the Island Ecosystem*. Honolulu: Bishop Museum Press, 1963.

Marshall Kaplan Gans Kahn & Yamamoto. *Housing in Hawaii: Problems, Needs and Plans*. Prepared for State of Hawaii, Department of Planning and Economic Development. Honolulu, 1972.

_____. *Second Five Year District Boundaries and Regulations Review*. Prepared for State of Hawaii, Land Use Commission. Honolulu, 1974.

McCandless, James Sutton. *A Brief History of the McCandless Brothers*. Honolulu: Advertiser Publishing Company, 1936.

McElroy, Michael M. M. "A Preservation Plan for Honolulu's Financial District Landmarks." Master's thesis, University of Hawaii, 1974.

McHale, John. *The Future of the Future*. New York: George Braziller, 1969.

McHarg, Ian L. *Design with Nature*. Garden City: Natural History Press, 1969.

Meadows, Donella H.; Meadows, Dennis L.; Randers, Jørgen; and Behrens, William W., III. *The Limits to Growth*. For The Club of Rome. New York: Universe Books, 1972.

Meckler, David H. "Hawaii's Land Use Law and Its Land Use Commission, Past Present and . . . " Independent study program for State University of New York, Syracuse, School of Landscape Architecture. Privately printed. Honolulu, 1973.

Merrill, William D. "Hotel Employment and the Community in Hawaii: A Case Study in Development Planning." Ph.D. dissertation, Department of Urban Design, University of Edinburgh, 1974.

Moanalua Gardens Foundation. *Moanalua*. Privately printed. Honolulu, 1971.

Morgan, Theodore. *Hawaii: A Century of Economic Change, 1778–1876*. Cambridge: Harvard University Press, 1948.

Mumford, Lewis. *The Culture of Cities.* New York: Harcourt, Brace, 1938.

———. *Myth of the Machine.* New York: Harcourt, Brace, 1966.

———. *Whither Hawaii?* Report to the City and County of Honolulu Park Board. Honolulu, 1938.

Myers, Phyllis. *Zoning Hawaii.* Conservation Foundation, Special Report. Privately printed. Washington, 1972.

———. *Slow Start in Paradise.* Conservation Foundation. Washington, 1974.

Neil, J. Meredith. *Paradise Improved: Environmental Design in Hawaii.* American Association of Architectural Bibliographers. Papers. Vol. 8. Charlottesville: University Press of Virginia, 1972.

Oahu Development Conference. *Summary: Alternative Urban Growth Strategies.* Prepared for U.S. Department of Transportation. Privately printed. Honolulu, 1973.

———. *The Military—A Growth Industry for Hawaii.* Report no. 44. Privately printed. Honolulu, 1974.

———. *Urban Design Study of the Honolulu Waterfront.* Prepared by Aaron Levine and William A. Grant for Environmental and Urban Design Studies for State of Hawaii, State Foundation on Culture and the Arts. Privately printed. Honolulu, 1968.

Oparin, Aleksandr I. *The Origin of Life on Earth.* Reprinted. Translated by Ann Synge. New York: Academic Press, 1957.

Overview Corporation. *From the Mountains to the Sea: State of Hawaii Open Space Plan.* Prepared for State of Hawaii, Department of Planning and Economic Development. Privately printed. Honolulu, 1972.

Pacific Commercial Advertiser. Periodical. Honolulu.

Paradise of the Pacific. Magazine. Honolulu.

Pencil Points. Magazine. New York.

Peterson, Charles E. "Pioneer Prefabs in Hawaii." In *Hawaii Journal of History* 5 (1971).

Polynesian. Newspaper. Honolulu.

Potomac Institute. *Controlling Urban Growth—But for Whom?* Privately printed. Washington, 1973.

Pukui, Mary Kawena, and Elbert, Samuel. *Native Planters in Old Hawaii.* Honolulu: Bishop Museum Press, 1972.

———. *Hawaiian Dictionary.* Honolulu: University of Hawaii Press, 1971.

Pukui, Mary Kawena; Elbert, Samuel H.; and Mookini, Esther T. *Place Names of Hawaii.* Rev. and enlarged ed. Honolulu: University Press of Hawaii, 1975.

Pukui, Mary Kawena, and Korn, Alfons L. *The Echo of Our Song.* Honolulu: University Press of Hawaii, 1973.

Roberts, E. F. "The Demise of Property Law." *Cornell Law Review* 1(1971):36–50.

Rockefeller Brothers Fund. *The Use of Land: A Citizens' Policy Guide to Urban Growth.* Edited by William K. Reilly. New York: Thomas Y. Crowell, 1973.

Rose, Louis A. *Taxation of Land Value Increments Attributable to Rezoning.* Prepared for University of Hawaii, Economic Research Center. Privately printed. Honolulu, 1971.

Schmitt, Robert C. *Demographic Statistics of Hawaii: 1778–1965.* Honolulu: University of Hawaii Press, 1968.

Schnore, Leo F., and Fagin, Henry (eds.). *Urban Research and Policy Planning.* Beverly Hills: Sage Publications, 1967.

Scott, Edward B. *The Saga of the Sandwich Islands.* Lake Tahoe: Sierra Tahoe Press, 1968.

Simpich, Frederick, Jr. *Anatomy of Hawaii.* Reprint. New York: Avon, 1973.

Soleri, Paolo. *Arcology.* Cambridge: M.I.T. Press, 1969.

Spaulding, Thomas M. *Crown Lands of Hawaii.* University of Hawaii, Occasional Papers no. 1. Honolulu, 1923.

Spreiregen, Paul D. *Urban Design: The Architecture of Towns and Cities.* New York: McGraw-Hill Books, 1965.

Stearns, Harold T. *Geology of the State of Hawaii.* Palo Alto: Pacific Books, 1966.

Stevenson, Robert Louis. *Travels in Hawaii.* Edited by A. Grove Day. Honolulu: University Press of Hawaii, 1973.

Stokes, John F. G. "Kaoleioku: Paternity and Biographical Sketch." In *Hawaiian Historical Society, Report.* 1934.

_____. "Some New Speculative Phases of Hawaiian History." In *Hawaiian Historical Society, Report 92.* 1934.

Tager, Richard N. *Innovations in State Legislation: Land-Use Management.* Prepared for American Institute of Architects. Privately printed. Washington, 1974.

Tate, Merze. *The United States and the Hawaiian Kingdom.* New Haven: Yale University Press, 1965.

Taueber, Irene B. "Demographic Instabilities in Island Ecologies." In *Man's Place in the Island Ecosystem.* Honolulu: Bishop Museum Press, 1963.

Theobold, Robert. *An Alternative Future for America.* Chicago: Swallow Press, 1968.

Thurston, Lorrin A. *Memoirs of the Hawaiian Revolution.* Honolulu: Advertiser Publishing Co., 1936.

_____. (ed.). *The Fundamental Laws of Hawaii.* Honolulu: Hawaiian Gazette Co.. 1904.

Toffler, Alvin. *Future Shock*. New York: Random House, 1970.

Tregaskis, Richard. *The Warrior King: Hawaii's Kamehameha the Great*. New York: Macmillan, 1973.

University of Hawaii. Center for Engineering Research. *Summary Proceedings of a Conference on the Public Costs of Private Development*. Privately printed. Honolulu, 1973.

———. Department of Geography. *Atlas of Hawaii*. Edited by R. Warwick Armstrong. Honolulu: University Press of Hawaii, 1973.

———. Hawaii Environmental Simulation Laboratory. *Kaneohe Alternatives: An Application of Impact Methodology*. Prepared for State of Hawaii, Office of Environmental Quality Control. Privately printed. Honolulu, 1974.

———. Land Study Bureau. *Detailed Land Classification*. Bulletins for each island. Privately printed. Honolulu, 1965–1968.

———. Pacific Urban Studies Program. *Toward a Population Policy for Hawaii*. Privately printed. Honolulu, 1970.

Urban Land Institute. *Density: Five Perspectives*. Special Report. Privately printed. Washington, 1972.

U.S. Department of Agriculture, Soil Conservation Service, and State of Hawaii, Department of Land and Natural Resources. *Soil Survey Interpretations*. 5 vols. Privately printed. Honolulu, 1972.

U.S. Department of Housing and Urban Development. *Urban Land Policy: Selected Aspects of European Experiences*. Washington: U.S. Government Printing Office, 1969.

U.S. National Commission on Urban Problems. *Building the American City*. Washington: U.S. Government Printing Office, 1968.

Vancouver, George. *Voyage of Discovery to the North Pacific Ocean*. 3 vols. London, 1798. Reprinted. New York: Da Capo Press, 1967.

Vause, Marylyn M. "The Hawaiian Homes Commission Act, 1920: History and Analysis." In master's thesis, University of Hawaii, 1962.

Walters, George S. *The City of Hilo: East Hawaii Project*. Environmental and Urban Design Proposals for State of Hawaii, State Foundation on Culture and the Arts. Privately printed. Honolulu, 1968.

Warnecke, John Carl & Associates. *Environmental Design Study of the Makena–La Perouse, Wailuku and Lahaina Areas*. Environmental and Urban Design Proposals for State of Hawaii, State Foundation on Culture and the Arts. Privately printed. Honolulu, 1968.

———. *Hawaii State Capitol Civic Center Master Plan*. Prepared for State of Hawaii, Civic Center Policy Committee. Privately printed. Honolulu, 1968.

Whyte, William H. *The Last Landscape*. Garden City: Doubleday, 1968.

Wolbrink, Donald H. & Associates. *Environmental Design Study of the Koloa-Poipu Area*. Environmental and Urban Design Proposals for

State of Hawaii, State Foundation on Culture and the Arts. Privately printed. Honolulu, 1968.

_____. *Kailua Village Urban Design Study*. Prepared for the County of Hawaii, Department of Planning. Honolulu, 1975.

_____. *Kona Community Development Plan*. Prepared for the County of Hawaii, Department of Planning. Honolulu, 1975.

Woodrum, Don. *This is Hawaii*. Honolulu: Book Publishers Hawaii, 1974.

Index

⼈ Production Notes

The text of this book has been designed by Roger J. Eggers and typeset on the Unified Composing System by the design and production staff of The University Press of Hawaii.

The text and display typeface is English Times.

Offset presswork and binding is the work of Vail-Ballou Press. Text paper is Glatfelter P & S Offset, basis 55.